Calvino and the Age of Neorealism

CORPO VOLONTARIO DELLA LIBERTÀ
ADERENTE AL C. L. N.
IMPER A

2ª DIVISIONE D'ASSALTO "GARIBALDI,, FELICE CASCIONE

Cognome e nome Caldini Diolo

Grado Garibaldino

Brigata V   Battagl. I   Distacc. II   Squadra III

II COMMISSARIO   IL COMANDANTE

Lucia Re

C·A·L·V·I·N·O

and the

Age of Neorealism:

Fables of Estrangement

STANFORD UNIVERSITY PRESS

STANFORD, CALIFORNIA

Stanford University Press
Stanford, California
© 1990 by the Board of Trustees of the
Leland Stanford Junior University
Printed in the United States of America

CIP data appear at the end of the book

Frontispiece: Calvino's partisan card

This book is lovingly dedicated to the memory of

my father, Ettore Re (1917–89)

Acknowledgments

This book was originally conceived and drafted during my tenure of a Fellowship from the National Endowment for the Humanities. Research for the book and the preparation of the manuscript were also supported by several UCLA Academic Senate Grants.

I would like to thank Rebecca West and Gregory Lucente for their perceptive and helpful readings of the manuscript. Marga Cottino-Jones, Peter Haidu, and Vincent Pecora contributed valued insights and advice. Amy Morris, Peggy Kidney, and Pasquale Verdicchio provided essential and much appreciated assistance as bibliographers and typists. I am grateful to Caroline McManus for her fine copyediting and to Helen Tartar of Stanford University Press for her extraordinary promptness and patience. My thanks as well to Kathy Komar, Ross Shideler, Arnold Band, Larry Barth, Francesca Santovetti, Pier Maria Pasinetti, and Paul Vangelisti for their interest in my work, their support, and their friendship. Finally, to Jon Snyder, my best and most critical reader over the last few years, I owe unlimited gratitude for his unconditional love and his dedication in following the making of the book every step of the way.

L.R.

Contents

Calvino and the Age of Neorealism

Introduction

A mode of writing is an act of historical solidarity. . . . It is the relationship
between creation and society, the literary language transformed by its social
finality, form considered as a human intention and thus linked to the great
crises of History.   —Roland Barthes, *Writing Degree Zero*

Today Italo Calvino's reputation as one of the great writers
of our century rests chiefly on his allegorical fables, fantastic
tales, and "postmodern" novels, whose ingenious formal design, subtle and ironic intelligence, and sheer delight in storytelling have made his name famous throughout the contemporary world. Often compared to writers such as Jorge Luis
Borges, Raymond Queneau, and Thomas Pynchon, Calvino has
attracted the admiration of readers and literary critics not only
because of his narrative craft, but also because his work engages
in a creative dialogue with contemporary aesthetic, philosophical, and even scientific thought. One critic, for example, has recently pointed out that the protagonist of Calvino's last novel,
Mr. Palomar (1983), embodies Calvino's thoughts on the newest
theories of phenomenology, description, narration, and herme-
neutics.[1] Another critic notes that Calvino's tireless testing of the
codes of contemporary discourse makes his work "so far the
most successful attempt to integrate Marxism, structuralism,
and existential phenomenology."[2] Calvino's path through the
labyrinth of twentieth-century thought (which has been called
his "repeated conquest of contemporaneity")[3] has inspired a wide
variety of critical responses to his work. These range from traditional thematic and New Critical readings to structuralist dis-

sections, sociological interpretations, semiotic reader-response analyses, deconstructions, and studies in a phenomenological, existentialist, or—more rarely—in a psychoanalytic key. In the English-speaking world, readers and critics of Calvino on the whole think of him as a writer of metafiction, thanks in part to John Barth's influential 1980 essay "The Literature of Replenishment: Postmodernist Fiction," which discusses Calvino at length in this light.[4] The large body of critical work that has grown up around Calvino's fiction in recent years has generally concentrated on the renowned works of the 1960's through the 1980's, such as *The Cosmicomics* (1965), *The Castle of Crossed Destinies* (1969–73), *Invisible Cities* (1972), *If on a Winter's Night a Traveler* (1979), and *Mr. Palomar* (1983). Calvino's untimely death in 1985 has not noticeably altered this trend. At most, if critics think at all of the early Calvino—for he was born in 1923 and worked as a writer for virtually all of his adult life—it is in terms of the allegorical trilogy of the 1950's, entitled *Our Ancestors* (*The Cloven Viscount*, 1952; *The Baron in the Trees*, 1957; and *The Nonexistent Knight*, 1959), which some still believe to be his finest work.

Yet there is another Calvino, one who is still largely unknown today and who has much to tell us about the more famous postmodern author of the same name. Calvino's early years as a writer in Italy are deeply marked by the vibrant atmosphere of the postwar Reconstruction and the neorealist movement in the arts that accompanied it. The sense of political commitment found in his work of this period is inseparable from his experience as a partisan in the anti-Fascist Resistance during World War II and as a militant member of the Italian Communist Party (PCI). One historian has defined the young writer of the 1940's and early 1950's as "Calvino the revolutionary."[5] In his short stories, essays, newspaper reportage, and—above all—in his first novel, *Il sentiero dei nidi di ragno* (*The Path to the Nest of Spiders*, 1947), Calvino participates in the controversies of postwar European culture over a "littérature engagée," realism, modernism, and the nature of a new culture opposed to all forms of totalitarianism. Although he eventually broke with the PCI and turned away from organized politics, Calvino never abandoned his belief in the necessity of the writer's engagement in the contemporary world or in the value of a "committed" practice of narrative fiction. Calvino's ethics of writing, although it informs all of his work from the 1940's on, has by and large been overlooked by his critics. Most studies of the development of Calvino's work as a whole point to a discontinuity between the "neorealist" Calvino and the master of the fantastic and the metafictional who emerges with the allegorical trilogy; only with "the great leap forward" of the trilogy does Calvino attain the status of a true world writer. Indeed, most studies of Calvino's work—particularly in the English-speaking world—begin with the trilogy and devote scant attention to the "other" Calvino.[6] In his essays, though, Calvino himself repeatedly argues for the importance of his early work in directing his subsequent development as a writer: "My story . . . now seems to me all contained in that beginning. . . . Your first book already defines you . . . and this definition is something you may then carry with you for the rest of your life, trying to confirm it or extend or correct or deny it; but you can never eliminate it."[7] Calvino's novel offers us an invaluable point of entrance into the corpus of his fiction: the importance of *The Path* is comparable in more ways than one to the importance of *Armance* for understanding the work of Stendhal (whose *Charterhouse of Parma* was Calvino's own favorite novel).

This is a book about that "other" Calvino, but its purpose is not only to show that he is already very much the writer that the world would come to know in the decades following the decline and disappearance of neorealism in Italy. In Calvino's first novel, the major themes, controversies, and aesthetic premises of neorealism are reflected and refracted as if in a kaleidoscope. While *The Path* in some ways typifies neorealist fiction, it also provides us with unexpected insights into the nature of neorealism because it persistently seeks to force its way to the very limits of what can be said within a "neorealist" approach to fiction writing. Some of the misunderstandings that surround Calvino's early work are caused by misunderstandings about Italian neorealism itself—particularly neorealist fiction—as a strictly documentary practice of representation that seeks only to denote the real. Neorealist works of art are, paradoxically, often dismissed as "failures" on the basis of the fact that they fail to fulfill their own documentary intent as a kind of "reconstituted reportage,"[8] as if that were the sole basis of neorealist aesthetics. The first part of this study is therefore devoted to a reassessment of Italian neorealism in terms of twentieth-century theories of realism and of the political function of art. The issues at stake in the European debate on realism and modernism, involving figures as diverse as Roman Jakobson, M. M. Bakhtin, Georg Lukács, Ernst Bloch, Bertolt Brecht, Jean-Paul Sartre, Theodor Adorno, and Roland Barthes, are essentially the same ones with which neorealist writers and filmmakers in Italy are concerned. A more balanced grasp of the European context of Italian neorealism is necessary, moreover, if we are to understand the full complexity of the single most significant achievement of neorealist narrative, namely Calvino's *The Path to the Nest of Spiders*.

"A novel," Calvino writes, "is a narrative that signifies and is interpretable on a multiplicity of intersecting levels."[9] This is indeed the case with *The Path*, a novel whose reading demands not so much the rigor of a single interpretive methodology as a criticism that can shift dimensions and move through its discursive space of "a multiplicity of intersecting levels." The intimate dialogue that Calvino's early work establishes with postwar European culture, for instance, requires its readers to approach it with some understanding of the history of that culture and that period (and this has often puzzled and put off recent readers of the work). At the same time, though, there is no denying that the historical horizon of the work is revealed to us only from within our own critical and historical position in the post-modern world. "We can never forget," Calvino comments, "that what books communicate often remains unknown even to the author himself, that books often say something different from what they set out to say."[10] We are today bound to discover in *The Path*, and in Calvino's other early works, something different from what he set out to say, or even what he says—in his 1964 preface—that he set out to say. Understanding a literary text can never lead to a reassuring familiarity with it; on the contrary, the understanding generated by our encounter with a literary text is always definable as a kind of defamiliarization or estrangement of understanding, which constantly leads us further and further from the point of origin. The classic concept of defamiliarization or estrangement (*ostranenie*) is that of the early-twentieth-century Russian formalists, particularly Victor Shklovsky. *Ostranenie* defines an effect of defamiliarization that can operate at various levels: as the "making strange" of what we think of as "the real" by a work of art which defies representational conventions; as the defamiliarization of artistic form itself produced by a work that transgresses and redefines the boundaries of a genre or aesthetic code; as the "internal" defamiliarization of a text which ironically displays its own fictionality; and, finally, as the critic's defamiliarization of a given work's interpretive tradition through a reading that allows for a new and different perception of the work itself. Calvino's novel, with its "multiplicity of intersecting levels," not only deploys all of these formal strategies of estrangement but also explores the notion of estrangement itself—as one of the foundations of cognition and understanding—in a number of different ways, and compels the reader to modulate with him from one level to the next, for estrangement in *The Path* may at a given point be seen in historical, social, psychic, or political terms. In particular, the Marxian notion of estrangement as alienation (*Entfremdung*) and the psychoanalytic/Hegelian concept of the estrangement of the self in the formation of the subject play central roles in the work, and to concentrate exclusively on either one or the other would reduce the complexity and the power of Calvino's discourse. Calvino himself, in a lecture delivered at the New York Institute of the Humanities in March 1983, points out the following about the notion of estrangement and its importance to literature: "An important international trend in the culture of our century, what we might call the phenomenological approach in philosophy, the estrangement effect in literature, urges us to break through the screen of words and concepts and see the world as if it appeared for the first time to our sight." [11] In an earlier essay, Calvino refers to an "estraniazione del senso" ("estrangement of meaning") as something performed by the literary text when it brings together and interrogates the most diverse contemporary disciplines; this is, he adds, the principal practice of literature today. [12] In yet another essay, he calls for literature to engage in an "agonistic dialogue" with the discourses of science and philosophy, even as it "calls its own linguistic conventions into question." [13] While his own practice of literary estrangement has been readily detected in his metafictional works,[14] critics have failed to recognize its presence in *The Path* or in the other early fiction.

Calvino and the Age of Neorealism, in an effort to follow in the path of Calvino's narrative practice of shifting levels, combines a series of close readings with discussions of the broad speculative and theoretical issues that transversally intersect with this story of the war and the Resistance. Chapters 1 and 2 analyze the theory and practice of neorealism as a whole and situate them in relation to the Resistance and the Reconstruction in Italy. Chapter 3 begins with an analysis of Calvino's partisan stories of 1945–46 and continues with a narratological study of the structural devices, narrative strategies, and modes of emplotment that are employed in *The Path* in order to defamiliarize or "make bare" the conventions of Italian neorealism and its narrative representation of the Resistance. Chapter 4 offers a contextual and thematic analysis of the novel, setting it in the specific historical and political situation of 1943–47 in Italy and showing how Calvino represents the historical reality of the partisan struggle in a way that challenges both the then-prevalent image of the Resistance and the politics of the Italian Communist Party. Chapter 5 investigates Calvino's innovative use of the generic conventions of the *Bildungsroman* in *The Path* and its relation to the question of the subject's formation. This chapter offers a reading of some of the novel's key passages in which a metaphoric displacement of a literal meaning and of the metonymic sequence of the plot occurs. This reading foregrounds the presence of psychoanalytic themes and problems in *The Path*; rather than seek to psychoanalyze the author or the characters, though, it is directed toward the way in which the questions of desire and the subject are incorporated into the work's structure. Chapter 6, finally, looks at *The Path* as a self-estranging text, one that—in an agonistic dialogue with its own narrative codes and the philosophical and political ideas that inform them—raises the question of the limits of narrative totalization and its relation to the ethical imperatives of modern mass politics.

1 • Realism and Italian Neorealism

Encoding the Real

The goal of realist art, Roman Jakobson argues in a 1921 essay entitled "On Realism in Art," is to achieve the highest possible degree of verisimilitude in the reproduction of reality: we call "realistic" works that seem to us to mirror objectively our experience of the real.[1] Jakobson, however, also points out that there is a constitutive ambiguity in any definition of realism, for intentionality and subjective perception play a crucial role in both the production and the reception of realist art. The intentionality is that of the artist, and the subjective perception is that of the audience (readers, critics, viewers, spectators, etc.), both of whom have a particular notion of what is real and what appears realistic. Classical and Romantic artists have at various times asserted that their aesthetic program was based on the principles of verisimilitude and objectivity, or, in other words, realism. In the nineteenth century, a canonical definition of realism first emerged and gradually became, Jakobson argues, dominant in aesthetic discourse; ever since, critics have measured realism against the standards of verisimilitude set by nineteenth-century realism. Erich Auerbach's definition of realism in his classic work *Mimesis* (1946) is a case in point: "In so far as the serious realism of modern times cannot represent man otherwise than as embedded in a total reality, political, social, and economic, which is concrete and constantly evolving—as is the case in any novel or film—Stendhal is its founder."[2] For Auerbach, Balzac and Stendhal are the prototypes of modern realism because they conceive of the "present as history" (*Mimesis*, p. 480). From their work, Auerbach derives a twofold "rule" for all realist literature: "The serious treatment of everyday reality, the rise of more extensive and socially inferior human groups to the position of subject matter for problematic-existential representation, on the one hand; on the other, the embedding of random persons and events in the general course of contemporary history, the fluid historical background" (*Mimesis*, p. 491). Jakobson contends, however, that any such prescriptive definition of realism ignores the fact that verisimilitude in art is entirely a matter of aesthetic convention. Although the figurative arts may generate the illusion of an absolute and objective representation of the real, he observes, the notion of "natural" verisimilitude in verbal expression or in a description in a work of fiction has no philosophical validity. Even in the figurative arts (and, we may add, in film), the depiction of the object is entirely based on a conventional code of representation. Only if we are familiar with the code's conventions can we read the text or see the painting as realistic, just as we are unable to understand a sentence unless we know the language in which it is uttered.[3] The automatization of the code allows the text or image to become a kind of ideogram linked to the represented object by an association of contiguity. We may recognize the represented object immediately, Jakobson continues, but we no longer "see" the painting or text, for we have "forgotten" the conventional nature of the code that sustains it. In order for the ideogram to become visible again, it must then be deformed and a new mode of interpretation formulated for it. The aesthetic innovator discovers in the object a reality which was previously invisible and seeks to impose upon the code a different kind of perception of it. A violation of the previously-canonized compositional form leads to a renewed understanding of the aesthetic system itself and of the world that it represents.

Deformation (or defamiliarization) is what allows us to "see" the represented object anew;[4] since it is more visible, it is also more "real." Jakobson points out that the literal level of aesthetic expression has nothing to do with this renewal of perception. On the contrary, tropes and figures are more likely to throw an object into relief and to "help us see it" by "doing violence" to the code to which we have grown accustomed as expressing the norm and which leads us to take the object for granted ("On Realism in Art," p. 40). In literature, words that are normally used to describe or narrate may progressively lose their evocative "literary" power; they no longer tell us anything because they are no longer surprising. Realism renews itself by breaking through sedimented layers of narrative language, portraying the object with traits previously considered unnecessary, irrelevant, or nonliterary. Characterization through "unessential" traits becomes more realistic, paradoxically, than that of the literary tradition. The "condensation" of narrative through the description of details or the narration of episodes seemingly unnecessary to the plot, while present in nineteenth-century "high" realism, is, Jakobson maintains, a characteristic feature of modern, "revolutionary" realism ("On Realism in Art," pp. 41, 43). The accumulation of "superfluous," "useless" descriptive details becomes, in fact, a key strategy for the signification of the real in modern literature from Flaubert on, as Roland Barthes notes in his essay "The Reality Effect."[5] While the constraints of *le beau style* and the structural imperatives of the story are, according to Barthes, "a safeguard against a downward spiral into endless detail" ("The Reality Effect," p. 13), Flaubert's practice constitutes a break with the classical tradition of the *vraisemblable*. Aristotelian verisimilitude functionalizes every detail in terms of the internal coherence of the plot and allows for no notation "which is justified only by its conformity to 'reality'" ("The Reality Effect," p. 15). Flaubert's *vraisemblance*, on the other hand, is modelled on the paradigm of historical discourse as *historia rerum gestarum*. The inclusion of details and notations that are inessential to the structural coherence and motivation of the narrative is justified by their reference to "concrete reality" and to what "actually took place." In principle, however, there is no limit to the amount of detail that may then be accumulated by the writer, for when discourse is no longer guided by structural constraints, "there is nothing to tell the writer why he should stop . . . at one point rather than another: . . . there would always be some corner, some detail, some nuance of location or color to add" ("The Reality Effect,"

p. 14). The most realistic narrative imaginable, Barthes points out in an apparent paradox, "unfolds in an unrealistic manner"; the "external" verisimilitude of Flaubert's realism is in fact a "referential illusion," or rather, a reality effect. Random detail, which is simply "there," creates the impression of a "direct collusion" between the referent and the signifier, functioning as a sign from whose tripartite structure the signified has seemingly been expelled. But although such a sign, Barthes adds, claims to denote reality directly, it can in fact only signify it: "It is the category of the 'real,' and not its various contents, which is being signified; in other words, the very absence of the signified, to the advantage of the referent, standing alone, becomes the true signifier of realism" ("The Reality Effect," p. 16). Flaubert's "external" verisimilitude, then, breaks with previous codes of verisimilitude and is in turn vigorously contested in both the nineteenth and twentieth centuries; thus the concrete meaning of realism is a wholly relative one.[6] It is no doubt for this reason, as Jakobson observes, that every new mode of realism thinks of itself as a neorealism ("On Realism in Art," p. 43).

Nowhere in the history of twentieth-century European literature is this relative meaning of realism any clearer than in Italy in the decades of the 1940's and 1950's. Moreover, perhaps at few other moments in the history of modern European culture is the political value of realism so crucial an issue for artists and critics alike. How can art at once revise our understanding of the real through formal strategies, and also possess a progressive political purpose? The non-coincidence, often even the opposition, between political vision and formal innovation constitutes the conflict at the very heart of Italian neorealism and makes neorealism itself a testing-ground for the modern European debate on literature's engagement with the real. The question of the formal qualities of realism and its political-ideological purpose, as it emerges in the European critical arena from the rise of the *Neue Sachlichkeit* in Weimar Germany (shortly after Jakobson wrote his essay on realism) to the Bloch-Lukács debate on modernism and the studies of Bakhtin, Brecht, Adorno, Sartre, and Barthes, is fundamental for both neorealist art and its critics, who seek new ways to represent the real that are at once aesthetically *and* po-

litically progressive or even revolutionary. Their work stands today as eloquent testimony to the arduous nature of this search
for a passage from aesthetics to politics.

•

"'Neorealism' was not a school," Calvino writes in his 1964
preface to *The Path to the Nest of Spiders*, but rather "a collection
of voices" (p. vii; 9). The variety of stylistic approaches, thematic
choices, narrative registers, generic forms, and ideological connotations discernible in the vast body of nonfiction, fiction, and
film associated with Italian neorealism makes the latter a phenomenon in postwar Italian culture whose contours are difficult
to define with precision.[7] Neorealism was not a "school" because it had no real "leaders"; no set of principles to govern its
discourse was ever agreed upon by those involved. Neorealism
was, furthermore, never an organized movement. Unlike Italian
Futurism, for example, there were never any neorealist mani-
festos and no specific programs; neorealism did not center on
one city or one region, nor did its proponents belong to the
same generation or the same social group. In many ways, neorealism was as decentered, as scattered and dispersed, as the
cultural life of Italy itself in those years when the nation was
struggling to rise up out of the ashes of Fascism. What then, if
anything, do films as diverse as Luchino Visconti's *Ossessione*
(*Obsession*, 1942) and *La terra trema* (*The Earth Trembles*, 1947),
Roberto Rossellini's *Roma città aperta* (*Rome Open City*, 1945) and
Paisà (*Paisan*, 1946), Vittorio De Sica's *Sciuscià* (*Shoeshine*, 1946)
and *Ladri di biciclette* (*Bicycle Thieves*, 1948)—to mention only a
few of the "classics" of Italian neorealist cinema—have in common with each other and with works more or less directly associated with neorealist literature, such as Cesare Pavese's *Paesi
tuoi* (*The Harvesters*, 1941) and *Il compagno* (*The Comrade*, 1947),
Vasco Pratolini's *Cronache di poveri amanti* (*A Tale of Poor Lovers*,
1947), Elio Vittorini's *Uomini e no* (*Men and Not Men*, 1945), and
Renata Viganò's *L'Agnese va a morire* (*Agnese Goes to Her Death*,
1949)? Is there a general narrative poetics which subsumes this
heterogeneous plurality of textual "voices" and allows us to

understand the multiple points of contact between them as defining neorealism itself?

In his invaluable 1964 preface to *The Path*, Calvino describes the general atmosphere of the period in which the "explosion" of neorealism took place in Italy, namely the years immediately following the end of World War II. The "explosion" of neorealism, Calvino explains, was "less an artistic event than a physiological, existential, collective event" (p. v; 7), directly linked to the experience of the war, the fall of the Fascist regime, the ensuing civil war, and the liberation of the country from Nazi occupation. While in fact a number of texts that treat typically neorealist themes or adopt a quasi-neorealist style appeared in Italy before the end of the war, the phenomenon that Calvino calls the "explosion" of neorealist narrative took place essentially in the immediate postwar period. Alberto Moravia's novel *Gli indifferenti* (*Time of Indifference*, 1929) and Carlo Bernari's *Tre operai* (*Three Workers*, 1934) are often considered to be the precursors of literary neorealism, while films of the Fascist period such as Alessandro Blasetti's *La tavola dei poveri* (*The Table of the Poor*, 1932) and Raffaello Matarazzo's *Treno popolare* (*The People's Train*, 1933) contain elements which anticipate neorealist cinema.[8] Two works fundamental for the future direction of the development of neorealism in Italy were completed between 1941 and 1942: Cesare Pavese's *Paesi tuoi* and Luchino Visconti's *Ossessione* (which was not, however, released to the public until well after the end of the war). The term *neorealismo* first began circulating widely in Italy in this period; the Marxist critic Giuseppe Alicata uses it in his 1941 review of Pavese's novel, and Eugenio Montale also employs it in his review of Vasco Pratolini's 1942 "slice-of-life" novel, *Via de' Magazzini*.[9] In both of these works, however, a sense of political commitment and a passionate adherence to the social issues of the present—which are among the most prominent features of neorealism and help to motivate its particular stylistic practices—are either negligible or absent altogether. It is the collective experience of the war itself, the civil war, and the Resistance which triggers the explosion of a "committed" narrative practice in both Italian literature and film, as well as an intense debate over the political and ideological function of art, and a search for a new realism and new modes of expression.

The debate that took place in the most important Italian newspapers and journals in the postwar period concerning the questions of realism, the function of art, and art's contribution to the cultural and political regeneration of the nation not only accompanies the development of neorealism, but is in fact an integral part of it. Never before in the history of modern Italian culture had fiction making (including narrative cinema) and its concerns been so important a part of the whole "social text." Neorealism is not simply a body of literary and critical work; it also involves a folk tradition of narrative, in the sense of texts written by nonprofessional authors who came from lower social strata and subaltern groups. The sudden proliferation of "paraliterary" genres and subgenres is indeed one of the most distinctive traits of neorealism: memoirs, diaries, sketches, short docufiction, and chronicles. This "other" literature, motivated by the desire to bear witness to history and to contribute to the narrative reconstruction of the recent past, as well as to the reconstruction of Italian life after the Liberation, significantly influenced the direction of neorealism, not only in terms of themes but also in terms of language. Neorealists—including those who, like Vittorini, Moravia, Pratolini, and Rossellini, had expressed themselves in an entirely "literary" language before the war—incorporated into their work a range of regional variants of the Italian language, as well as dialects, with the aim of reinstating the communicative and referential functions of narrative language. Neorealism also brought with it an unprecedented contamination not only of different voices—of "low" and "high" stylistic levels, particularly in the mimetic representation of speech—but also of genres and modes of discourse as well. Vittorini's 1945 novel about the Resistance, *Uomini e no*, typifies this tendency. It is part historical novel, part autobiography, and part docufiction, with episodes which appear to have been lifted directly out of the partisan broadsheets and interpolated with lyrical interludes, along with pamphletlike passages of a political and ideological nature, and metalinguistic passages which reflect on the very act of writing the text. *Uomini e no* is a highly composite and heteroclite text, a mosaic of many voices and styles, and Vittorini himself later thought of it as a failure, because he was unable to "orchestrate" the different voices and stylistic levels in order to achieve what Bakhtin called a "dia-logical tension" among them. Nevertheless, *Uomini e no* remains one of the most powerful—if not altogether exemplary—texts of the neorealist corpus.

Two main phases may be distinguished in the history of Ital-ian neorealism. The first phase, 1943 to 1948, coincides with the period from the beginning of the *Resistenza armata* to the collapse of the anti-Fascist coalition and the emergence of the Christian Democrats as the majority party. The second phase begins in the "Counter Reformation" atmosphere of the Cold War, with the increasing Stalinization of the Communist Party's cultural pol-icy, and ends in the mid-1950's, with the exit en masse from the Communist Party by leftist intellectuals after the Soviet invasion of Hungary (1956) and the advent of new forms of consumer capitalism in Italy. The collapse of the Soviet myth and the power of de-Stalinization coincide, not surprisingly, with the end of the myth of *il popolo* ("the people") for the Italian intelli-gentsia. The mass movement of the Italian rural populace into the cities in the 1950's happened just as the industrial working class started to become more depoliticized, deserting the labor union of the leftist parties (CGIL) to join the *sindacati aziendali* (a clear sign, writes the historian Giampiero Carocci, that "the Re-sistance and its ideals were only a distant memory, while the 'economic miracle' was around the corner").[10] Born in an atmo-sphere of national solidarity and fed by the fervor of the postwar Reconstruction, neorealism is in its first phase an experimental and at times revolutionary (in both a political and formal sense) artistic movement. The debate between authors and critics— including the official PCI critics—is characterized in this period by an unusual openness and flexibility. In the second phase, however, the retrenchment of the PCI into a defensive position in Italian politics largely contributes to transforming this dialogue into a confrontation that at times verges on a state of cultural warfare. Francesco De Sanctis's, Antonio Gramsci's, and Georg Lukács's works are used increasingly by PCI "militant" critics to prescribe paradigms for literary realism; a new form of Party cen-sorship emerges both explicitly (in the form of reviews and criti-cal assessments) and implicitly (in the form of self-censorship by "committed" neorealists). This second phase may be called, to extend our historical analogy, the "Mannerist" phase of neorealism, in which its original innovations are transformed into conventions. Many neorealists end up conforming to these conventions; others, like Calvino, go on to estrange radically neorealism itself through different practices of writing.

In order to understand neorealism not only in its Italian context, but in its European one as well, however, the principal issues at stake in the European debate on realism and politically committed art need to be examined in detail. This debate is vital to grasping the full import, and the full complexity, of the first "neorealist" novel that Calvino—that most European of all the Italian writers of his age—published. Let us take a closer look, then, at the theoretical terms of this debate as it develops in Europe, starting with the period between the two world wars and going up to the height of the Cold War era, which runs roughly parallel to the development and decline of neorealism in Italy.

The Politics of Realism

In Italy the word *neorealismo* and its variant *neo-realismo* first appeared in the 1920's as a (rather imprecise) rendering of the German *Neue Sachlichkeit* ("Neo-objectivism"), a term referring to an avant-garde artistic movement which represented a recoil from the "subjectivism" and the nonmimetic tendencies of Expressionism by advocating an art rooted in history and engaged in the objective depiction of the harsh social reality and the political and economic conflicts of post–World War I Germany.[11] The painters Georges Grosz and Otto Dix were among the leaders of this movement; their highly polemical and controversial works (soon to be censored as "degenerate art" by the Nazi regime) depict the horrors of the war, as well as the suffering and the difficult living conditions of the lower classes, while denouncing the greed of the ruling class. In German literature, this movement produced or influenced a wide variety of narrative and theatrical works whose themes range from the vicissitudes of the war itself (as in Arnold Zweig's 1927 novel *Der Streit um den Sergeanten Grischa; The Case of Sergeant Grischa*) to the impact of the postwar economic crisis on everyday life in the cities (as in Hans Fallada's 1932 *Kleiner Mann—Was Nun?; Little Man, What Now?*) to a satire of bourgeois hypocrisy (as in Erich Kästner's 1931 *Fabian*). The common ideological denominator of these works is a propensity for social criticism (the movement left its mark on the political theater of Bertolt Brecht and Erwin Piscator as well). While the *Neue Sachlichkeit* did not directly influence Italian neorealism, there is a clear thematic and stylistic affinity between the two, for both attempt to focus directly and objectively on the socioeconomic reality of a specific moment in modern history.[12] Both represent reactions, triggered by the trauma of a world war and of its consequences, against previous "subjectivist" art forms. Hermeticism and lyrical symbolism, which were dominant modes in Italian literature in the 1920's and 1930's, were opposed by the neorealists as modes of escapist and elitist art. Both Neo-objectivism and neorealism make recourse to "popular" modes of aesthetic discourse, that is, representational and low-mimetic forms, including sequential plots and story lines that are highly motivated, causally and sequentially structured, and verisimilar both internally and externally (in terms of real time and space). Furthermore, both de-emphasize aesthetic ambiguity and self-referentiality in favor of a more directly message-oriented use of language. It is not by chance that a novel like *Kleiner Mann—Was Nun?*, the moving story of a young married couple struggling with unemployment and inflation, became world-famous in the 1930's and was twice adapted for the screen.

While the derivation of the term "neorealism" from the German *Neue Sachlichkeit* is punctually noted in most discussions of neorealism,[13] the similarity between the two movements has gone mostly unnoticed. There is, moreover, yet a further link between German Neo-objectivism and Italian neorealism. The attack on Expressionism revived and grew into a debate over realism itself and the political role of art among left-wing European émigré intellectuals in the 1930's and 1940's. This debate—at the center of which stood the Hungarian communist critic Georg Lukács—closely resembles the debate that tore apart the Italian cultural Left about ten years later. Although a number of his essays were published in Italy in the 1940's,[14] there is no solid evidence that Lukács's views influenced Italian art and thought in any significant way before the translation of his most important critical works into Italian between 1950 and 1953.[15] However, Palmiro Togliatti—the head of the PCI, as well as the most severe and influential critic of "decadent" art in postwar Italy—was a member of the Comintern executive committee and resided in Moscow almost continuously between 1934 and 1943, in the very years when Lukács was the most prestigious voice of Marxist literary criticism in Europe and a resident of Moscow himself. Togliatti's ideas on art and the cultural policy of the PCI in the 1940's do indeed bear the traces of some of the most intransigent of Lukács's opinions. Conversely, the views of some of Togliatti's opponents, who defended the autonomy of art as well as the revolutionary political value of modernism and its avant-gardes—most notably Elio Vittorini and Franco Fortini—are not far at all from the views of Lukács's chief opponents in the 1930's, Ernst Bloch and Bertolt Brecht. The European debate about realism, particularly in the ideas of Lukács, Brecht, Bloch, Adorno, and Sartre, is therefore valuable for the broader understanding of the philosophical and political implications of Italian neorealism that it provides.

The anti-Expressionism of the new objectivists, who had often—like Dix and Grosz—once been Expressionists themselves, was revived by Georg Lukács's scathing 1936 indictment of Expressionism published in the German journal *Internationale Literatur*, and then in 1937–38 by a series of articles by Lukács and others which appeared in the émigré journal of the German anti-Fascist Popular Front, *Das Wort* (published in Moscow). Expressionism as an avant-garde movement had ceased to exist in the early 1920's, but as the first German manifestation of modernist art, it became the symbolic pawn in the heated debate between Lukács, Ernst Bloch, and Brecht on the historical meaning of modernism in general. Bloch refutes Lukács's critique of Expressionism on the ground that it fails to come to terms with the work of specific artists and poets (such as Klee, Kandinsky, Trakl, and Heym) and above all with the revolutionary character of modernist and avant-garde movements. In his 1936 article,

Lukács argues that while the Expressionists claim to penetrate the essence of reality, their tendency to stylize and formalize their art excessively makes it subjective and solipsistic, an abstract reflection of "the forlorn perplexity of the petty-bourgeois caught up in the wheels of capitalism." [16] Bloch objects to Lukács's critique as a classic example of a schematic sociological analysis of art, and he goes on to expose the flaws inherent in Lukács's prescriptive notion of "true" art as an art that objectively reflects the real in its organic totality, representing in synthetic form the entire network of relations which make up society as an integrated whole and highlighting the perspective for positive revolutionary change inherent in the socioeconomic structure. Lukács's argument that the Expressionists subjectively and arbitrarily associate heterogeneous, unrelated pieces of reality torn from their context is, writes Bloch, the expression of a regressive, nostalgic, and obsolete view—derived from nineteenth-century bourgeois culture and literature—of the real as a coherent totality. Furthermore, he intimates, Lukács's notion of the political function of art closely resembles the naive efforts of the *Neue Sachlichkeit* artists and thinkers to address specific contemporary social issues in their work, thus hoping to contribute to the reformation of a society which was in fact increasingly and immediately torn apart by the conflicts which led to the rise of Nazism in Germany. [17]

By breaking with traditional bourgeois art, which projects a mystified image of the real as an integrated totality, the disruptive strategies of Expressionism on the one hand constitute—according to Bloch—a more authentic and accurate reflection of the disintegration of bourgeois society and the alienation of the subject in the age of capitalism's involution into totalitarianism, and on the other hand help to expose the lacerating contradictions and repressed elements of human experience which bourgeois ideology constantly attempts to cover up in its effort to maintain its cultural hegemony. For Bloch the "negativity" of Expressionist art, its critique of traditional forms and its unveiling of the subject's loss of a stable identity and worldview all have positive political implications—for they contain a hidden kernel of hope that discloses the prospect of a different world beyond the disintegration of the present one. Reacting to similar attacks on the "decadence" of modernist art by Marxist critics in the 1940's in Italy, Franco Fortini takes a position parallel to Bloch's, defending (as we shall see in Chapter 2) the political value of modernism and its art of "negativity."

In his long rejoinder to Bloch, entitled "Realism in the Balance," Lukács summarizes the views on art that he held more or less continuously from the early 1920's to the end of his life. He argues, first of all, that no true art can put aside the objective vision of the real as an integrated totality:

Does the "closed integration," the totality of the capitalist system, of bourgeois society, with its unity of economics and ideology, really form an objective whole, independent of consciousness? . . . There should be no dispute on this point. Marx says: "The relations of production of every society form a whole." . . . If literature is a particular form by means of which objective reality is reflected, then it becomes of crucial importance for it to grasp that reality as it truly is, and not merely to confine itself to reproducing whatever manifests itself immediately and on the surface. If a writer strives to represent reality as it truly is, i.e. if he is an authentic realist, then the question of totality plays a decisive role.[18]

Totality for Lukács is the essence itself of the real, which is to be understood and represented not in its deceptively discontinuous and fragmented surface appearance but in its profound organic wholeness: "What matters is that the slice of life shaped and depicted by the artist and re-experienced by the reader should reveal the relations between appearance and essence without the need for any external commentary" ("Realism in the Balance," p. 34). Lukács entirely dismisses avant-garde modernism (his chief straw man is Joyce) on the grounds that it represents a shallow and subjective mimesis of experience and reality and merely mimics the chaotic appearance of the real, rather than trying to master it. It is the isolated state of mind of a specific class of bourgeois intellectuals, with its "home-made" vision of the contemporary world, that generates the aberrant dissolution of traditional (Aristotelian) narrative forms: "For writers who adopt this kind of stance towards reality there obviously cannot be any action, structure, content or composition in the 'traditional sense.' . . . The decision to abandon any attempt to mirror objective reality . . . permits no creative composition, no rise and fall, no growth from within to emerge from the true nature of the subject-matter" ("Realism in the Balance," pp. 42–44). While Bloch's argument begins with an assessment of Expressionist painting and poetry, Lukács shifts the focus of his discourse entirely to narrative fiction. Extended narrative fiction is indeed the privileged mode of aesthetic expression for Lukács because it permits the global, synthetic representation of an entire world in all its multifaceted and multilayered complexity.

Although he adopts the Aristotelian notion of mimesis as the cardinal principle of aesthetic composition, Lukács (as well as most other advocates of the theory of reflection) short-circuits the crucial distinction that Aristotle makes between the discourse of poetry and the discourse of history. For the Greek philosopher, in fact, the organicity of mimesis is true precisely because it constructs an artificial and fully motivated narrative order, one that is the opposite of the haphazard chain of historical events that must be faithfully registered in the writing of historians. The truth of poetic mimesis consists in its grasping-together of the events that make up the plot, according to two "universal" human categories of understanding, probability and necessity.[19] Aristotle defines poetry and historiography antithetically; the former is unified, intelligible, and organically constructed to fulfill the human desire for narrative order, while the latter is open-ended, difficult to grasp, and disjointed in its juxtaposition of a succession of heterogeneous and contradictory events reported paratactically in order to fulfill the need for a complete and objective record. Lukács, by contrast, collapses poetry and historiography together; for him, the truth of art is one and the same with the truth of history. The narrative order of great realist literature corresponds to the inner structure of reality itself, for the irreducible heterogeneity of the events which fill historical time for Aristotle is nothing but a surface effect, according to Lukács; it is the optical illusion of an individual observer lacking objective understanding and the necessary overall grasp of historical totality. Mimesis, for Lukács, is not exclusively a matter of the internal coherence of the work of art (as it is for Aristotle), but of the duplication of the order inherent in historical reality. Thus Expressionism and other forms of modernist avant-garde art lack the truth of great art, either because they duplicate the chaotic surface appearance of the real or because they are purely "formalist" and have nothing to do with the real order of history. Most neorealist narrators approach the representation of historical reality in a way similar to that which Lukács endorses. In general they presuppose that this reality possesses an intrinsically narratable order which may be synthesized by the narrator without either distortion or transfiguration. Thus they also share for the most part Lukács's prejudice against all modern "formalisms"—even though some of the best among them (such as Visconti and Calvino) appear to us today to have been skilled formalists in their own right.

The idea that history is a coherent totality and that the development of history follows a necessary narrative pattern is, as Bloch points out, directly derived from the tradition of German idealism and neo-idealism. Lukács's model of history as the organic unfolding of a unified action through time is Hegelian;[20] the agents, vicissitudes, contents, goals, and nature of the principles of probability and necessity that give the action its specific shape are for Lukács derived, on the other hand, from Marx's great metanarrative of history as the history of class conflicts. For Lukács, the only "progressive trend" in modern literature is provided by the "major realists" of the nineteenth century, that is, those writers who—like Balzac—had such a powerful grasp of the objective reality of their time that their works faithfully reflected it, thus transcending the author's own subjective (and often reactionary) political views. Among the true realists Lukács includes both the chief exponent of socialist realism, Maxim Gorky, and one of the major Neo-objectivist writers, Arnold Zweig. Like Balzac, Lukács argues, Gorky had such a lucid grasp of the real relations emerging over the course of history that he was able to anticipate current developments in the Soviet Union through a series of "typical" prophetic figures ("Realism in the Balance," p. 47). In *Sergeant Grischa*, on the other hand, Zweig correctly anticipated the reality of the forthcoming second world war by showing how war represented the continuation and intensification of "normal" capitalist barbarity. This prophetic discernment of the direction of history and of the objective but not immediately obvious tendencies of society "and indeed of mankind as a whole" makes the true realist writers an "authentic ideological avant-garde" ("Realism in the Balance," p. 47). True realism is never a photographic reproduction of the original reality, Lukács notes, or a straightforward account of how things really happened. This is a crucial point for Lukács, and it allows him to differentiate his notion of realism from "false" realism, such as tendentious socialist realism or documentary realism. Documentary realism, like its nineteenth-century antecedent, naturalism, never rises above the level of immediacy; in its one-dimensionality, it fails to grasp the dialectic of part and whole, appearance and essence. Documentary and naturalist works are static and devoid of tension because of their focus on surface detail, in the same way that the "history of particulars" makes historiography's truth inferior to the universal truth of literature for Aristotle.

Conversely, realism cannot be propagandistic art either, because the latter is always bad (that is, false) art, inasmuch as it is the illustration of an abstract concept rather than a reflection of the real. This last point is, however, the major stumbling block of Lukács's entire system. What is at stake in his theory is precisely the possibility of creating a politically progressive literature that is neither utopian fantasy nor party dogma. But is the positive tendency towards the transcendence of reification, commodity fetishism, and alienation really discernible in the historical reality of late-capitalist societies, or even Soviet society? Or is this socialist perspective simply another ideological abstraction? In *Realism in Our Time* (first published in West Germany in 1958), Lukács concedes that while the socialist perspective theoretically enables the writer to give a more comprehensive and profound account of man as a social being, in practice socialist realism has generated no true art comparable to what Lukács sees as the achievement of non-socialist "critical realism." The possibility of a reconciliation of the two appears indeed as Lukács's own utopian desire: "Both work with the same material but they apply themselves in different ways to the exploration of social reality. The deeper they probe, the closer will social reality approximate to the desired socialist society, and the closer will grow the ties between critical realism and socialist realism. In the process, the negative perspective of critical realism will gradually be transformed into a positive, socialist perspective."²¹ Lukács's longing for the nonalienated integration of the individual into the life of a socialist society, where the private will no longer be sealed off from the public, where the desire of individuals will no longer conflict with the needs of the collectivity, and where the history of the individual's development will be harmoniously reconciled with the history of society, is a motivating force behind his valorization of traditional, large-scale narrative realism. The great modern critical realists are, for Lukács, visionary writers; it is precisely because they expose the contradictions and reveal the forces of change in history in all their complex ramifications that the "underlying essence" of history itself "shines through" in their works ("Realism in the Balance," p. 39). This "essence" is none other than the totality of the universal history of humanity. Thus Lukács poses as a model of realism a practice of writing in which a nonreified and nonalienated relationship between the individual and the world is still represented as at least an immanent possibility and where history itself still appears as a positive and meaningful process.

Among his contemporaries, Lukács finds this philosophy of history to be embodied in the *Bildungsroman* structure of novels such as *Buddenbrooks* and *Tonio Kröger* by Thomas Mann or *Jean Cristophe* by Romain Rolland, and discerns in them the same integration of individual and collective history that he had praised as the great achievement of Balzac and of nineteenth-century historical novels by Walter Scott, Tolstoy, and Alessandro Manzoni. The kind of *Bildungsroman* favored by Lukács is the one most oriented toward a historical realism, the same kind that Bakhtin—in an essay written about the same time as the Lukács-Bloch exchange in *Das Wort*—calls "the most significant" because in it "man's emergence is accomplished in real historical time, with all of its necessity, its fullness, its future," rather than "against the immobile background of the world." In the realistic *Bildungsroman*, Bakhtin says, man "emerges *along with the world* and he reflects the historical emergence of the world itself. . . . The organizing force held by the future is therefore extremely great here—and this is not, of course, the private biographical future, but the historical future."[22] The similarity between Lukács's notion of the "typical" as a character that embodies the complexity of a historical moment and Bakhtin's "emerging individual" is evident. Yet Lukács's conception of how the history and perspective of an individual acquires historical significance is, in the last analysis, rather more reductive than Bakhtin's. Individualism itself for Lukács is a category of bourgeois decadence, part of the "crisis of modernity," and his aversion to autobiographical and psychological modes of narration, as well as to all modernist experiments with the representation of the inner life of the subject and of the human mind, is as strong as his dislike—in sharp contrast to Bakhtin—for Dostoyevsky, whose *Notes from the Underground* is, according to Lukács, "one of the first descriptions of the decadent individual."[23]

The same aversion to "modernist" individualism and psychological analysis is characteristic of neorealism; neorealist fiction, for example, generally attempts to represent individual experience as historically "typical" through the mode of the *Bildungsroman* or through an epic-scale realism modeled on the nineteenth-century prototypes of Manzoni and Verga (to mention only two). However, the neorealists' efforts to disclose the meaningfulness of history in socialist or Marxist terms all too often lapse into the very sort of didactic socialist realism criticized by Lukács, or into mere party propaganda. Renata Viganò's *L'Agnese va a morire* is a prime instance of this tendency in neorealist fiction. Aldo Vergano's 1946 film, *Il sole sorge ancora* (*The Sun Rises Again*), exemplifies this same tendency in neorealist film. By contrast, Calvino demonstrates a far more flexible and "dialogical" approach to the *Bildungsroman* and develops an altogether original notion of the "modern epic" as a mode of historical representation in *The Path to the Nest of Spiders*.

Lukács's rejoinder to Bloch was written in the historical context of the Popular Front, a fact which should be borne in mind in order to understand fully the political poignancy of his position and of his critique of the subjective individualism of the avant-garde. An essentially similar stand against the "decadent" aesthetics of modernism and of the avant-garde is later taken (at least implicitly) by many Italian neorealist writers and film-makers and, more explicitly, by Italian Marxist critics in the years that stretch from the beginning of the *Resistenza armata* through the end of the first decade after the Liberation. (A revival of the once-fertile tradition of the avant-garde in Italy takes place only in the mid-1960's with the radical experimentalism of the "Gruppo '63" and of the so-called *neoavanguardia*, which in many ways revives the disruptive strategies of Expressionism.) The neorealists, like Lukács, sought to link the mass (or, in Gramsci's terms, "national-popular") appeal of "genuine" realism to the political imperatives of the historical moment. Genuine realism, Lukács argues, "can appeal to readers drawn from a broad cross-section of the people."[24] In contrast to this, "the broad mass of the people can learn nothing from avant-garde literature." Lukács continues: "Precisely because the latter is devoid of reality and life, it foists onto its readers a narrow and subjectivist attitude to life (analogous to a sectarian point of view in political terms). . . . The taxing struggle to understand the art of the 'avant-garde' . . . yields such subjectivist distortions and travesties that ordinary people who try to translate these atmospheric echoes of reality back into the language of their own experience find the task quite beyond them" ("Realism in the Balance," p. 57). Lukács is, quite clearly, conscious of the ambiguity inherent in the notion of "popular" or mass literature, which is usually thought by most bourgeois critics to be synonymous with so-called "bad" literature. The decadence of the cultural aspirations and the taste of the masses in the capitalist era has contributed to the entrenchment of mediocre art, but "retrograde traditionalisms, such as regional art (*Heimatkunst*), and bad modern works, such as thrillers, have achieved mass circulation without being popular in any true sense of the word" ("Realism in the Balance," p. 53).

Notwithstanding their attempt to speak the language of the masses, neorealist works—including neorealist films—were generally not at all popular in postwar Italy. It is often forgotten today that neorealist films constituted only a small portion of the films produced in Italy at the height of what is usually thought of as the "neorealist era" of Italian cinema.[25] Costume dramas of the kind produced during Fascism, light comedies, and melodramas continued to be the most popular postwar forms of cinema for the masses and were infinitely more successful at the box office than neorealist films, with the sole exception of Rossellini's *Rome Open City*, which brought in more money than any other Italian film in 1945.[26] Interestingly, however, commercial adaptations of nineteenth-century novels—including Stendhal, Pushkin, and Victor Hugo—were also among the most successful mass-market films produced between 1945 and 1955, a fact which seems at least in part to confirm Lukács's views on "traditional" realism's appeal to the masses.[27]

Bertolt Brecht (whose work became increasingly well known in Italy in the 1940's, chiefly through the efforts of *Il Politecnico*) sought to create a political theater for the masses, but he never really obtained the kind of audience support and interest for which he had hoped.[28] In a series of commentaries on Lukács's ideas which were supposed to appear in *Das Wort* in 1938, but were only published in 1967 (it is not known whether they were rejected by the editors or whether Brecht thought it more prudent not to publish them, given the dramatic conditions of institutionalized terror in the Soviet Union),[29] he argues for a realistic but "mass" art, while vehemently attacking Lukács's idea of realism as obsolete. The socioeconomic reality of capitalism, Brecht points out, has undergone such radical modifications in the twentieth century that to adopt the narrative paradigm of nineteenth-century realism means to be resolutely unrealistic. The configuration of the human subject, the way it is shaped by history, and its way of relating to the social context and to history itself all require different modes of cognition and representation.[30]

Brecht's "epic" theater, his alienation devices (*Verfremdungseffekten*) for the defamiliarization of what is thought to be "natural" in human beings and history, and his recourse to a variety of styles, modes of representation, and generic forms reflect a notion of realism (similar to Calvino's own dialogical intertwining of codes and modes of discourse) that is much more flexible than Lukács's: "Reality changes; in order to represent it, modes of representation must also change" ("Remarks," p. 82). Yet his commitment to political and mass art often makes for the kind of populism that Adorno so vehemently stigmatizes in his 1962 essay "Commitment."[31] For Brecht, much as for the Italian neorealists, realistic art for the people is a form of commitment dictated by historical circumstances: "The demand for a realistic style . . . has acquired a certain inevitability. The ruling classes use lies oftener than before—and bigger ones. To tell the truth is clearly an ever more urgent task. Suffering has increased and with it the number of sufferers. . . . There is only one ally against growing barbarism—the people, who suffer so greatly from it. It is only from them that one can expect anything. Therefore it is obvious that one must turn to the people, and now more necessary than ever to speak their language" ("Remarks," p. 80). Notwithstanding the generosity of these intentions, the failure of Brecht's theater actually to develop a mass audience and the schematic nature of some of his work raise the question of the very possibility of a successful political art. This is a question that all the neorealists attempt to answer in widely different ways in their work.

Although Brecht does not say so, Lukács's notion of realism is rooted in a politically motivated nostalgia for the classical epic as the sole genuine narrative paradigm. His valorization of narrative as Aristotelian mimesis—the dynamic representation of the organic unfolding of the whole of an action—is in itself a reflection of his own dialectical philosophy of human history. Narration is the privileged mode of representation of human history as a dialectic of events and as human action which produces meaningful change. In his early Hegelian study, *The Theory of the Novel* (1914–15)—a work which is his most profound and fundamental contribution to literary theory—Lukács establishes the epic as the model against which all other forms of literary discourse are to be measured. In what is an essentially mythic but heuristically invaluable interpretation of the Greek civilization of antiquity which produced the first epics in the West, Lukács describes Greek society as a nonalienated one in which daily life and historical meaning, individual and collective existence, subject and object, life and essence are not yet separate from each other. The Greek world represents, in other words, an integrated totality which is fully and directly represented in the Greek epic. When tragedy replaces epic as the dominant mode of representation, this fact reflects the beginning of a process of dissolution and alienation. The modern novel constitutes, at least in Lukács's eyes, an attempt to recover the organic totality of the epic, an attempt which must rely on the ruses of the artistic imagination, since the objective historical conditions which made possible the epic are no longer present. The modern novel becomes the narrative of a symbolic search signifying mankind's longing for a utopian reconciliation of subject and object, individual and collectivity, private life and history.[32] Lukács bases a whole descriptive typology of the novel on these premises, emphasizing the ironic character of the novel as a genre conscious of its own problematicity and of the illusory, utopian nature of its search (which does not detract, however, from the positive ethical and intellectual value of the search itself). In this early text, such a utopian reconciliation is more a matter of a formal harmony within the textual space of the novel than of its thematics, or, even less so, of the objective reflection of the real (making it similar to Adorno's notion of the novel), but after his "conversion" to Marxism, Lukács instead interprets novelistic irony (and Romantic irony) as the incapacity of the bourgeois writer to come to terms with the totality of history itself. Henceforth Lukács's analysis of realism focuses on the idea that the novelist must provide an objective reflection of the real through a paradigmatic story line which conveys the only true sense of history, that is, its being an integrated totality of past, present, and future, as well as the process of its production through human labor and human action. Paradoxically, what was earlier the mythical wholeness of the epic world turns into the actual objective integrity of the modern world, whose unveiling becomes the task of the writer. All the traits which become increasingly dominant in modern and modernist narrative, from Flaubert on, constitute for Lukács a betrayal of true realism: the loss or disruption of plot, the increasing inconsequentiality of human action, and the static and alienated time of the subject, eventless in itself and cut off from historical events.

Lukács's vision of the novel as the "modern epic" retains a political and ethical value that clearly cannot be dismissed. Yet while Lukács admires most of all the great realists' ability to fuse together the story of an individual life with the collective history of a society at a moment in which the two meaningfully and dramatically intersect, in the reality of the modern experience of time and of the subject such moments, as Fredric Jameson points out, "have become relatively rare":

And there are others in which nothing real ever seems to happen, in which life is felt as waiting without end, perpetual frustration of the ideal (Flaubert); in which the only reality of human existence seems to be blind routine and the drudgery of daily work, forever the same day after day (Zola); in which, finally, the very possibility of events seems to have disappeared, and the writer seems relatively reconciled to a framework in which the truth of the single day can stand as the microcosm of life itself (Joyce). In these historical situations, even when the literary work itself seems violent and agitated, such explosions will turn out on closer inspection to be mere imitations of events, pseudoevents, imposed from above by the novelist, who despairs of evolving any genuine events from the colorless stream of experience itself. . . . And where modernism resolutely assumes its situation, it abandons plot entirely, renounces narration in the older sense, and seeks to make a strength of its basic weakness. (*Marxism and Form*, pp. 200–201)

The return to traditional forms of emplotment in neorealism is inextricably linked to the specific historical and cultural "eventfulness" of the war and the Resistance. While most neorealists seek to orient their fiction in the direction of Lukács's later theory of objective "reflection," however, Calvino's strategy in *The Path* is much closer to the argument of Lukács's early *Theory of the Novel*. Calvino incorporates Romantic irony and self-reflexivity into his fiction, and Lukács identifies these in his early work as characteristic devices of the modern epic; yet, at the same time, Calvino still maintains the inseparability of plot (*mythos*) and action (*praxis*) in both aesthetic and political terms, even though he is an heir to the modernist sense of "suspicion" in regard to plot.[33] It is this that distinguishes him most clearly from other neorealist writers of the same period and that points to his notion of the need for narrative totalization in both contemporary aesthetics and politics.

•

The resolute modernist assumption of the historical situation of the subject in an age of alienation and reification may indeed be found in the Italian tradition in the novels of Italo Svevo, *Una vita* (*A Life*, 1892), *Senilità* (*As a Man Grows Older*, 1898), and above all *La coscienza di Zeno* (*Confessions of Zeno*, 1923), as well as in Luigi Pirandello's theater and in his novels, such as *Il fu Mattia Pascal* (*The Late Mattia Pascal*, 1904) and *Quaderni di Serafino Gubbio operatore* (*The Notebooks of Serafino Gubbio, Cinematograph Operator*, 1915). This tradition was either ignored or consciously opposed by the neorealists in what may be called a radically Lukácsian rejection of modernism and a return to traditional plot and narration, often with the very same epic resonance (as in the case of Visconti's and Rossellini's respective masterpieces, *La terra trema* and *Rome Open City*) that Lukács had indicated as the true spirit of realism. The crisis of the subject which constitutes the central problematic of the great Italian modernist writers is, with few exceptions, absent from neorealist literature and film. The Italian neorealists were not, for the most part, ready or willing to take up the problem of the subject after the end of the war. In Italian neorealism the notion of the individual remains relatively unproblematic, and even if it is rarely like Lukács's world-historical individual, it is generally as stable, familiar, and historically integrated an entity as it is in Lukács's humanist perspective. The Italian neorealists adopt on the whole—with some notable exceptions in the works of Vittorini, Visconti, and above all Calvino—a Lukácsian view of the subject which, in Adorno's words, reflects "a state of mind that has been completely purged of every vestige of psychoanalysis."[34]

For Adorno, political art is indeed no less of an illusion than Lukács's notion of mimesis as the reflection of the real and the prophetic blueprint of the future: "Since the work of art never focuses directly on reality, it never makes the sort of statement found elsewhere in the realm of knowledge to the effect that this or that is the case. . . . Its logic, then, is not that of subject and predicate, but of internal harmony. Only by means of the latter, by means of the relationship it creates between its component parts, does it adopt a stance."[35] Given the fundamental autonomy of the work of art, Adorno argues, the notion of "commitment" in art may be dismissed as a mystification. Even existentialist commitment, in Adorno's assessment of Sartre's 1946 *What Is Literature?* (a text which was very influential in postwar Italy and in the development of a neorealist sense of engagement), is but an empty illusion. For Sartre, committed literature—unlike propaganda or other forms of political paraliterature—awakens in the reader the sense of his freedom to choose, a freedom which alone makes authentic existence possible.[36] But according to Adorno, "within a predetermined reality," a reality wholly saturated with alienation and the reification of human relations, "freedom becomes an empty claim" ("Reconciliation Under Duress," p. 180). "It is not the office of art to spotlight alternatives," Adorno continues, "but *to resist by its form alone* the course of the world, which permanently puts a pistol to men's heads" ("Reconciliation Under Duress," p. 180; my italics). Adorno's apocalyptic vision of modernity is such that he can find Lukács's "beliefs in the ultimate rationality, meaningfulness of the world and man's ability to penetrate its secrets" ("Reconciliation Under Duress," p. 172) irremediably naive. Yet it is this very same belief that Calvino (who constantly upholds—unlike Adorno—the positive value of Enlightenment rationality) never relinquishes in his works, even though he shares Adorno's views on the substantial autonomy of aesthetic discourse and on the formal structuring of literature as an act of resistance.

For Adorno, as for Bloch, Lukács's aversion to Joyce, Kafka, Beckett, and the entire tradition of avant-garde modernism, as well as his preference for traditional narrative realism, are evidence of his constitutive blindness to the alienated historical reality of modernity—a reality, ironically, which Lukács himself had first helped to define with his 1922 study *History and Class Consciousness*: "The supreme criterion of his aesthetics, the postulate of a reality which must be depicted as an unbroken continuum joining subject and object, a reality which, to employ the term Lukács stubbornly adheres to, must be 'reflected'—all this rests on the assumption that the reconciliation has been accomplished, that all is well with society, that the individual has come into his own and feels at home in his world" ("Reconciliation Under Duress," p. 176). Yet it is in the work of the great modernists, on the contrary, that the only authentically objective representation of modernity can be found, according to Adorno. In modernity, aesthetic discourse holds such a highly mediated relation with the real that it can never be the direct "reflection" of the latter, nor, for that matter, can political commitment in art be a matter of authorial intention or overt thematics that the masses can readily understand. Political commitment thus understood places art in a false position, for the very need to speak plainly in the language of politics forces it to relinquish all claims to true aesthetic signification, which is always difficult, ambiguous, and self-reflexive.

Revolutionary political messages in art are bound to be conveyed in aesthetically reactionary forms, so that political art is always to some extent "bad" art. But the reverse, Adorno claims, is not true: aesthetically revolutionary forms do not convey reactionary messages. On the contrary, it is the radical explosion of traditional bourgeois aesthetic forms such as mimetic realism that makes modernist and avant-garde art politically revolutionary as well. As autonomous works of art, "they firmly negate empirical reality, destroy the destroyer" ("Reconciliation Under Duress," p. 190). This negation is the only possible response to the negativity of society and the nightmare of universal reification; modernist art is a negation of a negation, and this is the source of its positivity. Authentic art in the modern era never directly refers to what merely exists but becomes its "essence and image," that is, an aesthetic form of epistemological appropriation of the real: "Even the suggestion that the world is unknowable, which Lukács so indefatigably castigates in writers like Eliot or Joyce, can become a moment of knowledge. This can happen where a gulf opens up between the overwhelming and unassimilable world of things, on the one hand, and a human experience impotently striving to gain a firm hold on it, on the other" ("Reconciliation Under Duress," p. 163). In an age of inauthenticity, authentic art both reveals this inauthenticity and indirectly denies it through the aesthetic harmony of its form, providing the reconciliation of subject and object which is the privilege of any fully empowered aesthetic discourse: "The contradiction between the object reconciled in the subject, i.e., spontaneously absorbed into the subject, and the actual unreconciled object of the outside world, confers to the work of art a vantage-point from which it can criticize actuality. Art is the negative knowledge of the actual world. . . . Only by virtue of this [aesthetic] distance, and not by denying its existence, can the work of art become both work of art and valid consciousness" ("Reconciliation Under Duress," p. 160).

Adorno's own argument, despite its persuasive critique of Lukács, is predicated on two questionable assumptions. The first concerns the nature of historical experience and the second the political nature of aesthetic discourse. Adorno's vision of history is essentially a tragic one, and while, as he puts it, after Auschwitz such a vision may be essentially more accurate than Lukács's Marxist narrative paradigm with its future-oriented optimism, it is also a vision that forecloses (as becomes particularly clear in his objections to Sartre's notion of "choice") any hope for a positive political praxis. The epistemic positivity of authentic art, on the other hand, which Adorno discerns in art's ability to "break free" of the immediacy of historical existence and to realize an inner formal harmony (which is the symbolic analogue of a nonalienated and nonreified world), ends up placing *all* formally accomplished works on the same level without differentiating among them. Although Adorno states at one point, quoting Sartre, that it is objectively impossible for an anti-Semitic novel to be a "good" novel, his own framework—unlike Sartre's—provides no justification for this assertion.

One of the targets of Adorno's essay on commitment is indeed Sartre's notion that literature may also be an instrument of intersubjective communication whereby language is not foregrounded in itself but rather is used to "disclose" a certain aspect of the world and to produce a certain response in the reader. Adorno concedes that, as Sartre says, "the writer deals with meanings"; he adds, however, "Of course, but not only with them. If no word which enters a literary work ever wholly frees itself from its meaning in ordinary speech, so no literary work, not even the traditional novel, leaves these meanings unaltered, as they were outside it" ("Reconciliation Under Duress," p. 178). Yet this objection hardly seems to address the issue. Sartre's point is not that the language of prose fiction is not or should not be different from ordinary language ("style makes the value of prose"), but that its discourse is "interesting" rather than disinterested, that is, conceptually engaged and bound up with the historical world. This is what Sartre means by "prose" as opposed to "poetry." In a literature that is entirely "poetic" and/or disengaged from the real, "the world and things become inessential, become a pretext for the act which becomes its own end" (*What Is Literature?*, p. 35). Thus the disengagement that for Adorno signifies a symbolic freedom from the alienation of the modern historical world constitutes for Sartre a doubling of that alienation.

The "valorization" of alienation which Sartre denounces as the prevailing attitude of contemporary "disinterested" literature "is not," he adds, "a matter of arbitrarily introducing defeat and ruin into the course of the world, but of having no eyes for anything but that. . . . If it is true that the word is a betrayal and that communication is impossible, then each word itself recovers its individuality and becomes an instrument of our defeat" (p. 36). Inasmuch as literature—even in its most abstract non-representational form—discloses an image of the world, communicates a meaning, and projects an attitude (the image of a way of being in the world), literature assumes a specific position within the context of the sociopolitical discourse of its time. This positioning of literature makes it, in Sartre's view, a politically symbolic act. It is from this perspective that it becomes possible for him to denounce the regressive "message" of all literature that does not engage its reader in a quest for freedom.

Behind Sartre's argument in *What Is Literature?* and his sweeping argument against the withdrawal of twentieth-century literature into more or less disruptive forms of experimentalism and intertextuality which turn it away from communicative and referential functions, is the historical situation of 1946. In this situation, European intellectuals once again found themselves face to face with history itself, a history made dramatically and inescapably present by the events of World War II and the Resistance. The perspective from which Sartre speaks is thus radically different from that of Adorno's essay, written fifteen years later, on the occasion of the publication of Sartre's book in German translation. When Adorno wrote both his scathing attack on Lukács and his essay on commitment, he was the Director of the Institute for Social Research in Frankfurt. His essay on Lukács was published in *Der Monat*, a journal created by the U.S. Army in West Germany and financed by the Central Intelligence Agency.[37] Lukács was at that time silenced in his own country, Hungary, where his department at the University of Budapest had been closed down and his works censored after he had given his support to the Hungarian revolt of 1956. The Cold War context from which Adorno writes undeniably differs from the context of renewed political optimism and commitment to the construction of a new society which forms the background to Sartre's 1946 text. The explosive growth and decline of neorealism in Italy takes place in the course of about a decade, between the conclusion of World War II and the tragic suppression of the Hungarian revolt at the height of the Cold War (which is the historical context of Adorno's two essays). For many Italian writers and intellectuals, including Calvino himself, the year 1956, with Kruschev's attack on Stalin at the Twentieth Congress of the Soviet Communist Party, followed by the events in Hungary, led to the difficult decision to quit the Italian Communist Party, which had backed the Soviet action. The Lukácsian, Brechtian, and Sartrean notions of a politically committed realism then appeared once again as an empty illusion to most, and Adorno's pessimistic vision of art as essentially autonomous and disengaged was more widely accepted throughout Western Europe.

In 1960, Pier Paolo Pasolini published a brilliant poem entitled "In morte del realismo" ("Upon the Death of Realism") in the form of a parody of Antony's funeral oration of Caesar in Shakespeare's tragedy. The poem is a passionate eulogy and elegy of (neo)realism, of its "mixed, harsh, vulgar style" born in the "light of the Resistance" from the hope generated by the defeat of Fascism. Its "ideological body" treacherously slain by the forces of reaction, its passion for the real dismissed by the new Brutuses (the "honorable" advocates of "purist" writing), realism nevertheless leaves as its inheritance *"settantacinque lire"* ["seventy-five *lire"*] worth of a "renewed sense of history": "It is little, nothing / compared to the millions of metahistory / and capital: but it is something." Realism also leaves in its testament, Pasolini notes, the works of a few writers that cannot be forgotten: Gadda, Moravia, Levi, Bassani, Morante, and, above all, Calvino: "E vi lascia Calvino. La sua prosa / piuttosto francese che toscana, il suo estro più volterriano che / strapaesano: la sua semplicità / non grigia, la sua misura non tediosa, / la sua chiarezza non presuntuosa. / Il suo splendido amore per il mondo / lievitato e contorto della favola" ³⁸ ("And it leaves Calvino. His prose / more French than Tuscan, his fancy more Voltairean than / provincial: his simplicity / (never grey), his sense of proportion (never tedious) / his clarity (never presumptuous). / His splendid love for the world, / leavened and contorted, of the fairy tale"). Even after its official "death," neorealism was indeed to leave its indelible mark, the traces of its "passion for the real," on Calvino more than on any other Italian writer of the postwar era.

The Neorealist Chronotope and the Art of Storytelling

The experience of the war and the pervasive sense that with the end of Fascism everyone in the country could once again speak freely, expressing his or her opinions without fear of censorship or repression, generated an unprecedented, if transient, phenomenon in modern Italian culture: the development of an oral mode of narration. Calvino writes in his preface to *The Path* that

with our renewed freedom of speech, all at first felt a rage to narrate: in the trains that were beginning to run again, crammed with people and sacks of flour and drums of olive oil, every passenger told his vicissitudes to strangers, and so did every customer at the tables of the cheap restaurants, every woman waiting in line outside a shop. The grayness

of daily life seemed to belong to other periods; we moved in a varicolored universe of stories. So anyone who started writing then found
himself handling the same material as the nameless oral narrator. The
stories we had personally enacted or had witnessed mingled with those
we had already heard as tales, with a voice, an accent, a mimed expression. . . . Some of my stories, some pages of this novel originated in
that new-born oral tradition, in those events, in that language. (p. vi;
7–8)

This sudden flourishing in Italy of a mass practice of storytelling
constitutes one of the chief preconditions for neorealism. Notwithstanding the heterogeneity of its individual works, neorealism in general appropriated and developed two essential
traits of the oral tradition described above by Calvino: it told
stories about ordinary people, and it told them in a language accessible to all. In film, nonfiction, literary fiction, and even poetry, neorealism is essentially a *narrative* art. It corresponds to
that "smania di narrare," the urge to narrate one's story and listen to the stories of others, which was so widespread in Italy at
the end of the war. In the immediate postwar period, newspapers—including those which, like *L'Unità*, had been clandestine broadsheets during the war years in northern Italy—
and new periodicals, which had sprung up all over the country
(often with the most rudimentary of resources), helped to contribute to the "rebirth" of Italian cultural life. These were often
literally flooded with manuscripts from their readers.[39] They
were real-life stories, chronicles, personal accounts and reminis-
cences, pages of diaries, anecdotes, short stories, and poems,
mostly written by nonprofessional or first-time writers. What
made these stories worth telling and listening to, and what led
to the desire to write them down, to transcribe them, to publish
them, and to read them? What generated this unprecedented
"opening up" of the channels of communication in a country
where the literacy rate was still astonishingly low and where
access to the media had been so severely curtailed for so long?
One of the determining factors was, Calvino suggests, the existence of a common frame of reference understood by all, which
was none other than the collective experience of the war. The
war had, after all, profoundly affected daily life in the North and

the South, in the cities and the countryside alike, in a way that few historical events on the peninsula ever had done before. "Having emerged from an experience, a war and civil war *that had spared no one*, made communication between the writer and his audience immediate," writes Calvino (p. v; 7: my italics). "We were face to face," he continues, "equals, filled with stories to tell; each had his own; each had lived an irregular, dramatic, adventurous life; we snatched the words from each other's mouths." The momentous events of the war and of the struggle for national liberation, which had brought havoc and devastation to Italy, marked the overall development of a history in which—for the first time in living memory—everyone had participated in some way. This history appeared in itself as a master narrative or universal plot under which all these individual or microstories could be subsumed. The Liberation constituted the predetermined point of narrative closure, where all stories symbolically came together in a unified and positive resolution. It provided the necessary "sense of an ending," serving as the place from which it was possible to look back in retrospect in order to start retelling what had happened and in order to make sense of it.

After the landing of the Allied forces in Sicily in July 1943, Victor Emmanuel III, the King of Italy, ordered Mussolini's dismissal and arrest, appointing Marshal Pietro Badoglio as prime minister on July 25, 1943. Mussolini's ouster was greeted with spontaneous outbursts of public enthusiasm all over Italy. The regime had clearly lost the war that it had been fighting for three years (but had never been prepared to fight), and it was generally expected that the new government would immediately sign an armistice with the Allies. But in fact July 25 marked the beginning of one of the most chaotic phases of the conflict, with the advent of the joint government of the King and the army for the so-called "forty-five days." Demonstrations and strikes were immediately and violently suppressed by the police, and Badoglio announced the continuation of the war on the side of the Germans, hoping to "gain time" in order to present Italy as a prospective partner of the Allied forces, rather than having to undergo the humiliation of an unconditional surrender. A few of the Fascist organizations were immediately liquidated through "decree-laws," some political prisoners were freed, and anti-Semitic laws were no longer enforced. However, Badoglio and the King both resolutely opposed the proposal by the anti-Fascist committees of the clandestine forces in Rome and Milan to grant complete freedom to the press and to form a new government composed of representatives of all the anti-Fascist political parties. The Ministry of Popular Culture (known to all Italians as the notorious "Minculpop") continued to censor the press until after the armistice, and the government decided that elections of a new Chamber of Deputies would be held only after the end of the war—until then, political parties would remain illegal.

Immediately after Mussolini's arrest, the Germans began to prepare for the armed occupation of Italy, and they accelerated the movement of their troops onto the peninsula, clearly expecting the imminent defection of the Italian government. While the Anglo-American forces heavily bombarded cities and industrial centers all over Italy and the Germans kept massing troops on the mainland, Badoglio's government started to negotiate an armistice with the Allies. Its confused, contradictory, and unrealistic demands led to a series of misunderstandings and delays. Badoglio kept postponing the official declaration of surrender, hoping to ensure the safeguard of Rome (which, however, was already practically surrounded by German troops), of the government, and of the royal family. When Eisenhower refused to delay the armistice one more time and issued the official proclamation on September 8, Badoglio was finally forced to broadcast the order to cease hostilities. Once more, however, his incompetence and lack of principle simply made a bad situation worse, for the precise nature of his orders was deliberately left unclear. Badoglio called for the Italian armed forces to repel attacks from *any* quarter and thus left the military in a situation of total anarchy, where all had to fend for themselves as best they could; perhaps tens of thousands of men—many of them far from Italy—died as a consequence. Panicked by the sudden turn of events, the royal family and Badoglio then fled from Rome in secret, leaving the capital in the hands of the Germans, and finally ended up

in Brindisi in southern Italy, safely behind Allied lines. This bla-
tant display of cowardice and cynicism deeply shocked even the
most apolitical Italians and permanently tarnished the reputation
of the royal family; the day of the armistice agreement marked the
beginning of the armed Resistance in Italy. The disintegration of
the army, the void left by the government's collapse and the
King's flight from Rome, the landing of the Allies at Salerno, the
news of Mussolini's rescue by German glider troops, and the subsequent formation of a neo-Fascist "Social Republic" in German-
occupied Italy led thousands of Italians to join the partisan ranks.

From 1943 to 1945, the Italian Resistance was a mass movement only partially linked to the underground resistance that
had been carried out for two decades by a handful of dedicated
anti-Fascists in Italy and abroad.[40] The number of partisans in
the armed bands grew from about nine thousand in the fall of
1943 to more than two hundred thousand in the spring of 1945.[41]
Thirty thousand partisans were killed, and tens of thousands
were imprisoned and tortured. Men and women belonging to all
social strata, including many previously pro-Fascist Italians, ex-
Fascist militiamen, draft evaders, army deserters, factory workers, farmers, businessmen, lawyers, students, and intellectuals
joined in the struggle. Like Calvino himself, 80 percent of the
partisans belonged to the younger generation, which had never
known a non-Fascist Italy. The stubborn resistance of the German army against the Allied offensive in the South made the
contribution of the partisans and their civilian supporters in
Nazi-occupied northern Italy significant, if certainly not decisive, for the final Allied victory. While southern Italy lived
through the Allies' agonizingly slow advance, with daily air
raids on the cities, central and northern Italy became the stage
for bloody partisan warfare, often in the mountainous areas behind the enemy lines, as well as in the cities where—as in Florence—full-scale insurrections were organized. A series of industrial strikes and uprisings in the major northern cities after
April 19, 1945 climaxed in a general insurrection in the remaining occupied parts of the country on April 25, the "day of Liberation." Mussolini was captured and summarily executed by
the partisans, and his bullet-riddled body was displayed in
downtown Milan.

The new government was formed with representatives from all anti-Fascist parties belonging to the Committee for National Liberation (CLN), which had acted as a provisional government after the liberation of Rome in June 1944 and had supplied the political and military leadership of the Resistance in the North. Although the cities and countryside of Italy were devastated by the war, the economy was in shambles, and the nation was faced with both the enormous task of the Reconstruction and an uncertain political future, most Italians seemed to think during the first few months of post-Liberation euphoria that they had at last come to the happy ending of a long and dramatic story.

Italy, then, had been divided in half for almost two years, and in that time the Italian people had lived in circumstances that were radically different from those of the preceding twenty years. Even though only a relatively small minority had actually gone off to fight with the partisans, everyone's life had in some way or another been changed by the war and the civil war. Families were torn apart, and many individuals were thrown into unfamiliar ways of life, whether as refugees, partisans, or civilians trying to survive; few escaped completely the violence of those years, as the war scourged the peninsula from one end to the other. Afterwards, as people travelled all over Italy to return to their old homes and jobs or to find new ones, there was a general sense that all had been part of a collective historical narrative that no one had seen in its entirety, but whose plot now had to be recounted and reconstructed. To that collective history everyone had a contribution to give, some episode to add; life itself seemed, as Calvino remarks in the preface, a "varicolored universe of stories." July 25, September 8, and April 25—the crucial dates of Mussolini's arrest, of the armistice agreement, and of the Liberation—marked the beginning, the middle, and the final denouement of the epic tale that the nation had just lived through.

As the French contemporary historian Pierre Nora points out in regard to the "metamorphosis" of historical events in contemporary history, the participation of the masses in global conflicts such as World War II and the parallel development of the mass media have helped produce both a "democratization of history" and a new notion of the present itself as history.[42] Historical events are no longer things which pertain only to "the past" and are no longer confined to a time that no longer "is," a self-enclosed sequence capable of being objectively analyzed, scrutinized, and carefully reconstructed by professional historians in its entirety. On the contrary, historical events happen "now," or at least this is a widespread perception that has been generated by the direct involvement of the masses in the destinies of their countries, on the one hand, and by the impact of the mass media on collective behavior, on the other hand. In the context of the war in Italy, the radio—above all else—serves to sanction the importance of an event, to "build it up," and to assure its immediate dissemination among the masses, producing discussion, interpretation, and action. Eisenhower's radio broadcast announcing the armistice at 6:30 P.M. on September 8, 1943, for example, forced Badoglio to follow immediately afterward with his own tragically ambiguous broadcast at 7:45 P.M. on the same day. The whole *imbroglio* of the King's flight from Rome, the astonishment and dismay of the populace, and the series of reactions which led up to the abolition of the monarchy in the 1946 referendum may be traced back to that historical "radio-drama," or "radio-triggered" historical drama. The contemporary historical event is, as Nora notes, a kind of "monster" from traditional historiography's point of view. In traditional historiography, the "event" was the monopoly of the historians' discourse; the historian gave it its place, function, and value, and "nothing entered history without his consent" (p. 145). But now the event comes to the historian from the outside with all the weight of a "historical given," before time has "done its work," and prior to any possible explanation of it. An ever-increasing number of circumstances and "trivial" facts—*faits divers*—from the present have been instantly promoted to the status of historical events as a consequence of the power of the mass media in the modern world. The nature of historical events in modern times thus undergoes a "democratic" metamorphosis which threatens the traditional notion of "event" as a category of historical discourse.

The narrative explosion in postwar Italy, then, was not simply an anachronistic recurrence of the oral tradition of storytelling which had flourished in the predominantly peasant and artisanal culture of preindustrial Italy as an expression of communal life and its values. The circumstances of the war and the Resistance—their "eventfulness"—had indeed provided both the adventurous "raw material" of human life (a *realtà romanzesca*) and a communal atmosphere that revived the oral tradition of storytelling which had been absent in much of Italy since the nineteenth century. The gathering and transcribing of proverbs, sayings, folktales, fairytales, and *novelle* flourished in Italy, thanks to scholars and amateurs alike, who attempted to preserve the tone, diction, and spontaneity of the oral narrators even when the original material had been subject to a literary reworking.[43] The masters of literary *verismo*—the Italian counterpart of French naturalism—often took their inspiration directly from the oral tradition, removing as far as possible the traces of the mediating presence of the writer and of all literary "interference" and striving to recreate the voice of the original anonymous storyteller. In his famous letter to Salvatore Farina written as an introduction to the story entitled "L'amante di Gramigna" ("Gramigna's Mistress"), Giovanni Verga purports to retell to his friend the original story as he first had heard it and presents his voice as simply one more in the chain of narrators through which the story has passed from mouth to mouth. "I shall repeat it to you, just as I picked it up along the paths in the countryside, with nearly the same simple and picturesque words that characterize popular narration."[44] Furthermore, the story is, Verga claims, a historical account of an actual event, a simple "human fact" taken from real life. The storytelling practices that Verga and Capuana seek to reproduce in their fiction were already dying out in the final decades of the nineteenth century. Yet, in a different form, and with different social and ideological connotations, this concern for the oral tradition reemerges in Italy in the fiction produced in the 1940's. It is certainly not by chance that Verga's work serves as one of the major models for both neorealist filmmakers and writers, for Verga and the *veristi* provide an example of how the oral tradition may be successfully incorporated and refracted within the structure of aesthetic (rather than merely documentary) texts.

Visconti's first wartime film project was an adaptation of Verga's "L'amante di Gramigna." He was, however, unable to carry it out, because of the opposition of Fascist censors. "L'amante di Gramigna" is the story of an "illicit" erotic passion that undermines the traditional moral codes of woman's role as wife and mother (marriage plus family), and it is therefore thematically and ideologically very close to Visconti's *Ossessione* (although the latter is an adaptation of James M. Cain's *The Postman Always Rings Twice*). However, the censors' real objections were to the story's focus on the figure of a *bandito* or *brigante*, Gramigna. Although he wreaks havoc on rural life, disrupting with his sudden raids the usual routine of harvests and markets, he becomes a heroic figure of epic dimensions in Verga's story. The tales told of his ability to defy the law by eluding an ever-growing number of police and soldiers sent out to capture him travel from mouth to mouth across the countryside. Alone, hiding out in the *macchia*, Gramigna is able not only to resist the forces of the law but also to kill with his primitive musket a vast number of his heavily armed opponents during a series of *imboscate*. Thanks to these stories of his legendary feats, Peppa falls in love with him and deserts her family on the eve of her own wedding to another. *Banditismo*—the phenomenon of *briganti* living *alla macchia*—was an ancient tradition in Italy, and, after the Unification in 1870, the *briganti* in the South carried out a guerrilla war against the new state and its coercive policies of taxation, military conscription, and general exploitation of the already-impoverished peasants. Over the course of the twentieth century, *brigantismo* and *banditismo* gradually were transformed into such criminal associations as the *casanove*, *'ndrangheta*, and the *mafia*, which Fascism was unable to eradicate and which still persist today.

The Resistance revives the age-old tradition of *banditismo* as a form of rebellion against oppression and restores its link to the folk tradition of storytelling thematized in Verga's story. The oral accounts of partisan *gesta* which went from mouth to mouth and were then transcribed and published in the form of very short stories in the partisan papers and broadsheets constitute, according to Maria Corti (developing one of Calvino's own insights), a fundamental matrix for the topology and narrative style of neorealism.[45] The partisans were customarily referred to by the Nazis and the Fascists as *banditi*. Signs bearing the words *Achtung! Banditen!* were posted during the occupation wherever the presence of partisan bands was likely or suspected. *Achtung! Banditen!* is the title of Carlo Lizzani's first film (1951), a full-scale epic about the Resistance; in the sixth episode of Rossellini's *Paisà* (*Paisan*, 1946), as the corpse of an executed partisan drifts down the Po river, an onlooking German soldier remarks, "Partizanen, Banditen!" The title of the first history of the Resistance to be published after the war, *Un popolo alla macchia* (1947) by Luigi Longo, also alludes to the tradition of *banditismo*, as does one of the most powerful documentary narratives about the Resistance, Pietro Chiodi's *Banditi* (1945). If Visconti's *Ossessione* is the first neorealist "text" (according to the filmmaker, the word *neorealismo* was first used by his editor, Mario Serandrei, to describe the style of the film),[46] Verga's story can be said to belong to the prehistory of neorealism and the Resistance itself.

The essential difference between these two respective nineteenth- and twentieth-century practices of storytelling, and their various literary reworkings, lies in the way that each articulates and represents time and space. In other words, the difference lies in what we may call—following Bakhtin—their chronotopic organization. The elements of time and space that we find in a story like "L'amante di Gramigna," more specifically, bear the traces of what Bakhtin calls the "folkloric chronotope." The "folkloric" articulation of time and space corresponds to an agricultural and artisanal stage in the development of society where time and space are instinctively conceived of as essentially unified, cyclical, and "natural."[47] Everyday life, and the life-sequence of the individual, are perceived and represented as integral parts of the life-sequence of the family, the community, and its labor, with its familiar cyclical rhythms directly linked to the rhythms of nature and the endless collective struggle for survival. This unity of time and space, individual and community, and nature and history, Bakhtin argues, is totally unselfconscious for those who live in such a world. It becomes apparent only retrospectively, "in the light of later perceptions of time in literature (and in ideology in general), when the time of personal, everyday family occasions has already been individualized and separated out from the time of the collective historical life of the social whole, at a time when there emerged one scale for measuring the events of *personal* life and another for measuring the events of *history*" ("Forms of Time," p. 208). This "bifurcation of time" and the increasing separation of the plot of history from the plot of personal existence correspond to the era of industrial capitalism and to the increasing separation of "private" events from "public" ones. "Only against the background of this later bifurcation of time and plotting can we see the measuring of the immanent unity of folkloric time. Individual life-sequences have not yet been made distinct, the private sphere does not exist, there are no private lives. Life is one, and it is all thoroughly 'historicized' (to use a later category)" ("Forms of Time," p. 209).

It is precisely from the perspective of this incumbent bifurcation of time that Verga looks back to the folkloric chronotope and nostalgically attempts to reinscribe it into his texts, most notably his great novel *I Malavoglia* (*The House by the Medlar Tree*, 1881). *I Malavoglia* tells the story of a family of fishermen who live in a small coastal village called Aci Trezza in eastern Sicily. The family's life together, and the very fabric of the community to which they belong, are shown to disintegrate progressively under the pressure of the new modes of capitalist production and of the increasing alienation of individuals from the product of their labor, from each other, and from the community. The overall theme of the novel is the collapse of the folkloric chronotope itself and the subsequent emergence of the isolation of the alienated individual on the one hand—with his private life-story and destiny—and of impersonal *événementiel* history on the other hand, with its abstract economic and political mechanisms. *Mastro don Gesualdo* (1889), the second novel of Verga's unfinished cycle *I vinti* (*The Doomed*), in which the author intended to show the effects of "progress" on the entire Italian class structure, is no longer the story of a family whose lives are reciprocally interwoven and integrated into the age-old collective time and space of a secluded fishing community, but the story of an individual who climbs the social ladder from simple workman to member of an aristocratic family at the cost of end-

less humiliation and alienation from his own family. History itself is only a backdrop to the protagonist's story in Verga's novel,
even though that story is carefully and realistically reconstructed and set in its sociopolitical context.

In all its forms, but particularly in the historical novel, nineteenth-century narrative deals with the bifurcation of time and
the increasing compartmentalization of social life, which splits
the private from the public, the psychological from the social, the
individual from the historical. The folkloric chronotope that to a
large degree still informs the "choral" narrative of *I Malavoglia*
allows for a representation of individuals as the community sees
them and talks about them, for in it "the interior time of individual life does not yet exist," writes Bakhtin, "the *individuum* lives
completely on the surface, within a collective whole" ("Forms of
Time," p. 207). The same "exteriority" of individuals, who lack
any story apart from that of the community, also typifies the
characters of the classical epic, according to Bakhtin: "Individual
life-sequences are present in the epic as mere bas-reliefs on the
all-embracing, powerful foundations of collective life. *Indi-
viduums* are representations of the social whole, events of their
lives coincide with the events of the life of the social whole, and
the significance of such events (on the individual as well as on
the social plane) is identical. Internal form fuses with external:
man is all on the surface" ("Forms of Time," p. 218). In the era
of industrial capitalism, the *Bildungsroman* and the novel of
"high" realism do away with the kind of idyllic nostalgia for the
folkloric chronotope whose traces can still be discerned in
Verga's *I Malavoglia*, but not *Mastro don Gesualdo*. Bakhtin points
out that the only attempts to provide a symbolic reconciliation of
the individual life-story with "History" in the nineteenth-
century realist historical novel all rotate, perhaps paradoxically,
around the theme of war: "This fundamentally historical theme,
which has other motifs attached to it, such as conquest, political
crimes, and the deposing of pretenders, dynastic revolutions,
courts, executions and so forth—is interwoven with personal-
life narratives . . . but the two themes do not fuse. The major
task of the modern historical novel has been to overcome this
duality: attempts have been made to find a historical aspect of
private life, and also to represent history in its 'domestic light'"

("Forms of Time," p. 217). This is indeed the case with both Alessandro Manzoni's *The Betrothed* and the majority of Walter Scott's novels, for example. And indeed, the theme of the war in Italy, derived directly from the actual "historical experiences" of individuals as they themselves retold them, provides the specific chronotopic organization of Italian neorealist narrative in its first phase, reintegrating the narratives of individual life-sequences— perceived and represented as inherently historical—into the larger time-sequences of History itself. The plot of History—the sequence of events through which the life of nations, and of the world, is channelled and represented—is not parallel, external, or superior to the story of the individual; rather, the two are perceived and represented as parts of the same chronotope.

Although neorealism reproduces in many ways the conditions of the folkloric chronotope, the community of discursive and narrative exchange that it represents is no longer the precapitalist rural or artisanal community still to be found in nineteenth-century folk narrative and in the narratives of the *veristi*. It is, rather, a community made up of urban and semirural masses whose identity is defined by the experience of the war and of the struggle for liberation. The notion of *il popolo*—"the people"—is central to all neorealist narrative fiction, film, and criticism. The term *il popolo* refers, for the neorealists, to all those who had come out into the historical arena and had become visible and audible as historical protagonists through the events of the war. Its connotations are thus sharply opposed to the Fascist use of the term *il popolo italiano*, which indicated a hierarchically organized structure, based on rigid social stratification and the institutionalization of class differences, and wholly subordinate to the superior and abstract "reality" of the totalitarian state.[48] The neorealist notion of *il popolo* often excludes all class distinctions and in this sense has both distinctly archaic as well as utopian and even religious overtones. The term evokes, for the Italian neorealists, both the world of the folkloric chronotope and that of Marx's postcapitalist utopia, as well as Alessandro-Manzoni's religious vision of *gli umili* ("the humble") as historical subjects in *The Betrothed*. Granted, the *popolo* of neorealist narrative was—in retrospect—a myth, an imaginary construct, and neorealist populism has been and continues to be stigmatized as the chief ideological fallacy of neorealism.[49] Yet this myth was so pervasive and productive that it controlled and shaped the narrative work of Marxist and non-Marxist narrators alike in the 1940's and early 1950's in Italy. Vittorio De Sica wrote in 1948 that his film *Ladri di biciclette* was devoted to "the suffering of the humble," for, in the history of such individuals, "the loss of a bicycle is an important event, tragic and catastrophic."[50] Like De Sica, many other neorealists use the terms *il popolo* and *gli umili* to refer generically to the lower strata of Italian society, which serve at once as their subject and their audience, but rarely emphasize the more specific Marxist notion of the proletariat or "working class." There is indeed a general (although by no means universal) tendency in neorealist narrative to shun any use of overtly class-oriented discourse in favor of a somewhat vague humanism (thus the Hungarian Communist Party, fearing that the film's political message was not clear enough, added an epilogue to *Ladri di biciclette* when it was released there, pointing out that, since it was a true workers' state, such problems as unemployment and crime no longer existed in Hungary). Humanism is often found at the political roots of neorealism; it reflects a "united-front" politics which urges cooperation rather than confrontation, calling for a collective effort to build a truly human, and humane, society. From today's vantage-point, the postwar "boom" years of neorealism—1945 to 1948—do indeed appear as a period of cultural and political illusions for the Italian intelligentsia. Yet, on the other hand, in no other period of modern Italian culture has there been a more pervasive politicization of narrative discourse; the indiscriminate, often unqualified condemnation of neorealist literature by many recent critics, who attack it as a kind of writing "contaminated" by extraliterary political concerns, and/or by *velleitarismo*, is more a reflection of the renewed compartmentalization of cultural life in contemporary Italy than an objective assessment of neorealism itself.

•

In his 1936 essay "The Storyteller: Reflections on the Works of Nikolai Leskov," Walter Benjamin writes that "experience which is passed from mouth to mouth is the source from which all storytellers have drawn. And among those who have written down the tales, it is the great ones whose written version differs least from the speech of the many nameless storytellers." Leskov's work, which is still close to the living immediacy of the oral tradition of storytelling, makes us realize "that the art of storytelling is coming to an end" in the modern age.[51] "More and more often," Benjamin writes, "there is embarrassment all around when the wish to hear a story is expressed. It is as if something that seemed inalienable to us, the securest among our possessions, were taken from us: the ability to exchange experiences" ("The Storyteller," p. 83). In his essay, Benjamin relates the loss of the storytelling tradition directly to the changes in the texture of social experience brought about by new capitalist modes of production, and he refers to World War I as the event which first brought an awareness of these changes to the surface:

With the [First] World War a process began to become apparent which has not halted since then. Was it not noticeable at the end of the war that men returned from the battlefield silent—not richer, but poorer in communicable experience? What ten years later was poured out in the flood of war books was anything but experience that goes from mouth to mouth. . . . A generation that had gone to school on a horse-drawn streetcar now stood under the open sky in a countryside in which nothing remained unchanged but the clouds, and beneath these clouds, in a field of force, of destructive torrents and explosions, was the tiny, fragile human body. ("The Storyteller," p. 84)

Benjamin's penetrating observations about postwar Germany are equally applicable to postwar Italy. After World War I in Italy there was nothing comparable to the narrative explosion which followed World War II; the most powerful literary expression of the loss of the ability to "exchange experiences," almost of the very ability to speak, is found in the war poetry of Giuseppe Ungaretti. In a highly rarified, laconic, almost mutilated language, Ungaretti depicts the agonizing solitude of the individual subject torn from all that was once familiar and faced with both the horror of trench warfare and the fragility of the body itself.

Lyric poetry becomes the privileged mode of literary expression in Italy after World War I, and prose itself takes a resolutely antinarrative turn; the genres of the poetic "fragment" and of the prose-poem predominate in fiction, as opposed to the novel or even the novella. The modern Italian tradition of "hermetic" lyric poetry, of which Ungaretti is an early figure and Eugenio Montale the greatest exponent, appears as the most authentic mode of literary expression between the two wars, for it captures the increasing isolation in Italy of the individual from the framework of a community, with the subsequent loss of reciprocity of narratable experience. All links with history seem to be severed in this poetry, sealed off in an endless dialogue between the self and both its private phantasms and poetic fathers. After 1922, the new Fascist state only adds to the sense that the self-enclosed space of hermetic literary discourse was the only "safe" one for the individual seeking to preserve some degree of freedom, beyond the pressures of public life and history itself: "Non domandarci la formula che mondi possa aprirti"—reads the last stanza of a famous poem by Montale—"sì qualche storta sillaba e secca come un ramo. / Codesto solo oggi possiamo dirti, / ciò che *non* siamo, ciò che *non* vogliamo" ("Don't ask for a formula that might / open worlds to you; just a few maimed syllables / dry as a twig. All we can say today / is what we are *not*, what we *do not* want").[52] Even in the fictions of a genuinely gifted narrator such as Federigo Tozzi, the theme of solipsism is the principal springboard for storytelling. In his novel *Il podere* (*The Farm*, 1918), the peasant world that for Verga still embodied the folkloric chronotope is ripped apart by the fetishization of wealth, which reifies human beings and prevents any intersubjective contact other than in the form of reciprocal acts of violence and cruelty. In Tozzi's narratives there is no dynamism; his plots are static, made up of "frozen" sequences of time, and time itself is incomprehensible and fundamentally oppressive, wholly alienated from the human subject.[53]

Contrary to World War I, World War II was not fought in Italy in trenches on the borders of the country. World War II was such a universal experience that there was no need for those returning from combat to tell the others what it was like (an impossible task in the modern era, as Benjamin points out). Every story was understandable to all (or at least it seemed so) because every story was inscribed within the same chronotope. In Italy, World War II did not reduce the survivors to silence, as had happened earlier in the century. Neorealism reverses the lyrical hermeticism and narrative aphasia, the focus on the private sphere and on the solitude of the alienated self, the withdrawal from political commitment and the separation of private from collective history that had characterized literary discourse in Italy between the two wars. The characters and voices of neorealist narrative, even when they speak in the first person, tend to be seen from the outside; like the characters of folktales, fairy tales, and the classical epic, neorealist characters exist "on the surface." Their "outside"— what they do and say in the stories through which they move— is what they are, and their stories are always told as belonging to a motivated and sequential historical time, charged with meaning for the subject and for the *socius* itself. Neorealism, above all, aims at a kind of communication involving what Jakobson has called the referential, conative, and emotive functions of language, which diverge from the poetic and metalinguistic functions that dominate the more strictly "literary" discourse prevalent in Italy between the two wars.[54] Neorealist narrative is oriented towards context, for it aims to refer to a reality beyond itself and to convey concrete, objective information about it. The political design of this referential narrative, furthermore, orients it toward its readers or audience, inasmuch as it asks the reader/ viewer to consider the narrated material in a particular optic, and it presents itself as a story told with the purpose of teaching the addressee something, and sometimes even to *do* something, as a result. Neorealism is deeply concerned with the pragmatics of its art, that is, the relationship between signs and interpreters; it is a rhetoric, in other words, of the real.

Neorealism, Commitment, and Communication

Italian neorealism, as a movement, takes up with a renewed sense of urgency the question of the aims and conditions of a historically and politically engaged aesthetic practice; its development and its disappearance coincide, historically and ideologically, with the distance that separates Sartre's 1946 *What Is*

Literature? from Adorno's essays at the end of the 1950's. The influence of Sartre's theater and fiction on Italian writers of the neorealist era is not as powerful and visible as that of his philosophy of engagement and its notion of the historical necessity of communicative prose.[55] Sartre's ideas were debated in *Il Politecnico*, the most important journal of the Italian postwar cultural rebirth, whose editor was Elio Vittorini from 1945 to 1947. Along with neorealist docufiction, as well as articles, essays, and reports on the most important cultural, political, and economic questions of the time, *Il Politecnico* published translations of texts by Lukács, Brecht, and Sartre himself, including Sartre's first editorial for *Les Temps modernes*, which in turn published a translation of Vittorini's first editorial, which called for the creation of a new European culture. All the crucial issues touched on by Sartre in *What Is Literature?*, which was originally published in serialized form in *Les Temps modernes* in 1946, resonate in the works of Italian neorealists and in the Italian debate on realism and the politics of art; indeed, the ambiguities of Sartre's theory are often the very same ambiguities and contradictions that haunt neorealism.

Sartre's notion of commitment reinstates the full circuit of communication to the language of literature; writer and reader are dialectically interdependent components of the literary act for Sartre. It is the reader who allows the work of literature to come into existence in the world, inasmuch as the work is an instrument of mediation between two minds and can never be mere self-analysis or self-reflection. Since literature is, at the same time, steeped in the lived (*le vécu*) and the concrete, writing and reading are both deeply historical acts. This emphasis of Sartre's on the referential and denotative functions of language implies a radical de-emphasis of form. Hence his opposition to "poetry" (a code word for formalistic art) and to the solipsism of bourgeois art forms. The disgust that nineteenth-century bourgeois writers such as Flaubert feel for the mediocrity of their own class, Sartre argues, leads them into an increasingly difficult double bind. While the masses were increasingly becoming a force for progressive change, they had no culture or leisure; bourgeois writers therefore could not choose them as their audience without abandoning "advanced" forms of writing—inaccessible to such readers—and betraying and alienating their art. Thus, Sartre argues, while still effectively maintaining a link with the bourgeois order and public, the writer withdraws into solitude, "and rather than assume responsibility for the public which he had slyly chosen, he concocted the notion that one write for himself alone or for God. He made of writing a metaphysical occupation, a prayer, an examination of conscience, everything but a communication" (*What Is Literature?*, p. 23). The writer tries to raise himself above his class by abandoning "the government of men and goods" to the bourgeoisie and by making his profession a spiritually superior kind of priesthood; it is at this point that literature begins to talk exclusively about and to other literature. "From 'art for art's sake' to symbolism, including realism and the Parnassians, all schools agreed that art . . . taught nothing, it reflected no ideology, and above all it refrained from moralizing" (*What Is Literature?*, p. 128). By contrast, Sartre advocates the primacy of prose as a twentieth-century mode of writing fully compromised with the reality of history, one that awakens its audience to its own freedom and to the potential for social change that can be found in the present and in the future. The writer must use language as an instrument of communication, appealing to the freedom of the reader to become involved in the real issues of the day; the medium of prose is, in short, a transparent pane of glass that "reveals" the world.

Upon the publication of *What Is Literature?*, Sartre was accused by a variety of sources of seeking to murder literature, of defending the validity of socialist realism and other socially oriented "bad" art, of calling for a new populism, and of denying the only true form of commitment for the writer: active involvement in a revolutionary political party. These are the very same charges that were levelled against neorealism, at different times during its history, by its detractors. In his 1960 poem about the death of realism, Pasolini attacks the "purist" Italian novelist Carlo Cassola as representative of this assault on the principles of realism; Cassola is, for Pasolini, an "honorable man" who speaks for the forces of reaction, for whom realist art's political aims are disquieting and must be discredited. In his 1958 critique of neorealism, "Ideologia o poesia?" ("Ideology or Poetry?"), Cassola indeed directly associates Italian neorealism with Sartre's work, arguing that both are marred by ideological prejudices and that in both "there was not one crumb of poetry."[56] On the contrary, in his preface to the 1950–51 survey on neorealism, in which all the most important voices of neorealism and its critics participated (and which constitutes a key document in the history of neorealism), Carlo Bo cites Sartre as an example of the successful integration of philosophical ideas into literary representation. The equilibrium of Sartre's work is similar to that of the "best" realists, Bo contends, namely those who are neither didactic nor naively mimetic.[57]

The committed and realistic prose (in the Sartrean sense) which emerged in Italy with the war was in effect deeply marked by the intrinsic ambiguities in the very notions of commitment, realism, and prose. Commitment in fiction often took the form of a mediocre and melodramatic socialist realism, as in Renata Viganò's *L'Agnese va a morire*, a novel about the Resistance celebrating the heroism and the "spontaneous" Communism of a "woman of the people." The belief that literature could avail itself directly of the language of everyday life in order to provide immediate access to things "as they really are" generated—particularly in the second, "Mannerist" phase of neorealism—a long series of mostly dreadful "real-life" novels and docufiction, exemplified by a number of works in the series *I Gettoni*, published by Einaudi under Elio Vittorini's direction between 1951 and 1958.[58] The axiom that writing ought to be for the people and about the people led a writer as talented and as steeped in the tenets of modernism as Cesare Pavese, in his 1946 novel *Il compagno* (*The Comrade*), to disguise his own literary tastes and to reduce his narrative style to a colloquial, paratactic, and flat "low mimetic" one. The novel tells the story of an apolitical, egoistic lower-class man from Turin who becomes involved in the Resistance and progressively acquires a class consciousness, finally joining the Italian Communist Party. But, apart from *Il compagno*, Pavese also gave neorealism two of its finest works of fiction, the novels *La casa in collina* (*The House on the Hill*, 1948) and *La luna e i falò* (*The Moon and the Bonfires*, 1950). Neither of these novels is usually associated with neorealism, and Pavese himself never accepted the definition of "neorealist" for his work, because soon after the war this label became synonymous with "bad" realist writing; Pavese, like Pasolini, preferred to speak simply of realism.[59] Neorealist film also often resorted to melodrama and to populism, celebrating the working class as a new breed of heroes on whose broad shoulders all hope for the impending regeneration of Italian society rested.

This opposition to "poetry" in the Sartrean sense,[60] and specifically to "exquisite" and formally refined lyrical *ermetismo* and poetic prose which had been dominant in Italy between the two wars, had two negative consequences for Italian neorealism.[61] First of all, it led many to believe that it was possible to write without reference to the preexisting literary tradition and to bracket completely the "literariness" of literature, which had formerly cut it off from historical reality and political responsibility. Secondly, the rejection of the solipsistic self-analysis and self-reflectiveness of lyrical poetry and prose, in order to make literature once again an act of interpersonal communication, resulted in many cases in the suppression of the problematic of the subject and the individual psyche. This aversion to all questions of psychic life is visible, for instance, in Pavese's *Il compagno*. The first half of the novel, despite its consistent rigorous naturalistic restriction of focalization to the protagonist's "low" point of view, is narrated in the first person, and even though there is no attempt to "psychoanalyze" or to disclose the depth of his inner life, the text captures through its syncopated rhythm and the naked reporting of events by the narrator the painful and contradictory dialectic of the protagonist's desire. The first section of the novel is the story of what Calvino would call a "difficult love," an Ariostesque search for an object of desire—in this case, a woman—whose own desire constantly eludes and deludes the protagonist, drawing him into a spiral of deception and self-deception. When, in the second section, the protagonist nears the end of his search, this same object of desire becomes the symbol of all that is vacuous and corrupt in petit bourgeois Fascism. Yet when the communist cause finally gives the protagonist his true identity, the novel becomes schematic and inverisimilar, for it represents a transparent attempt on Pavese's part to fulfill his own desire for a "stable" political identity that would enable him to resolve the contradictions of his existence. It is only when he unequivocally exposes the gap between private and public, between the subject's desire and the alienating coerciveness of the social and historical order, as he does in *La casa in collina*, that Pavese's voice becomes compelling and poetic. *La casa in collina* is a novel about the *Resistenza armata* as seen through the eyes of an (autobiographical) protagonist who, while recognizing the objective historical need for commitment and action, is incapable of either and remains an outsider on the margins of "history," a history which he cannot help but see as a horrifyingly permanent civil war.

The alienated situation of Pavese's protagonist in *La casa in collina* is conveyed in a forceful and dramatic language which makes this work a more authentic example of Sartrean commitment and realism than *Il compagno*. While the argument of Sartre's *What Is Literature?* about the role and function of literature may at first glance appear prescriptive and reductive, a more attentive reading reveals that in fact this is not so. Sartre's book, while undeniably liable to misinterpretation because of the paradoxical terminology that it adopts, provides an invaluable description of how literature can become committed without jeopardizing its literariness and its freedom. Sartre is very careful to emphasize that committed literature can in no way be "party-line" literature or propaganda. As an appeal to the reader's freedom, a work of art cannot dictate or make demands: it must "present," Sartre says, a situation as a kind of gift to the reader's consciousness and allow for critical reflection (*What Is Literature?*, p. 49). But his most crucial contribution regards the issues of realism and totality, to which Sartre attributes a political and ideological function similar to Lukács's, but from an essentially new perspective which allows him to overcome the rigidity of the latter's ideas: "It makes little difference whether the aesthetic object is the product of 'realistic' art (or supposedly such) or 'formal' art. . . . The creative act aims at a total renewal of the world. Each painting, each book is a recovery of the totality of being. Each of them presents this totality to the freedom of the spectator. For this is quite the final goal of art: *to recover this world by giving it to be seen as it is, but as if it had its source in human freedom"* (*What Is Literature?*, pp. 56–57, my italics). From the perspective of Sartre's phenomenological ontology, totality is not a reality that exists and can be "reflected" in art. The dichotomy between realistic reference (giving the world to be seen as it is) and fictional reconstruction (but as if it had its source in human freedom) displaces the totalizing possibility of synthesis into the future. Realism is never a contemplation of the whole, as Lukács claims, and is never objective, since perception itself is always partial and naming itself a modification of the object (*What Is Literature?*, p. 61). Thus the world that art discloses is a specific historical situation. The author "engages" himself by presenting this world in its negativity as well as in its potential for positive change through creative action (*What Is Literature?*, p. 236). The (deferred) totality of art, whereby the "antinomy of lyrical subjectivity and objective testimony would be left behind" (*What Is Literature?*, p. 152), coincides with the totality of a classless society. In such a society, free of all forms of coercion and alienation, literature would realize its full essence, namely the totality of the individual.[62]

This Marxian utopian horizon, with its emphasis on the need to communicate the positive potential for historical change, in no way implies Sartre's submission to the politics of the French Communist Party. He is quite outspoken in this regard, and his outspokenness is doubtless the reason why his work was so severely condemned by communists not only in France, but in Italy as well. Alberto Moravia's famous 1946 essay, "L'uomo come fine" ("Man as an End"), a text deeply influenced by Sartre's ideas, was published only in 1954.[63] Although Moravia was never a member of the PCI, he actively and openly supported it, and his decision not to publish the essay for eight years reflects the unwillingness of Italian left-wing intellectuals to undermine what was at the time a relative unity of the Left. The PCI's assessment of existentialism in general coincided with the orthodox European Marxist point of view, which held that it was an ideological product of the decaying bourgeoisie. But Sartre was particularly disliked by Italian communists because he persisted in exposing the contradictions of European communist parties after the war, such as their often blind allegiance to Stalin and his policies, their political compromises with reactionary forces in power, their authoritarian discipline within the party itself, and their willing manipulation of their own working-class constituency.[64] Sartre points out, in particular, the paradox of the reappropriation of bourgeois ideological constructs by the European communist parties. To make themselves acceptable to the bourgeoisie, communist parties "talk its language: the language of family, country, religion, morality." This in turn places bourgeois intellectuals who have joined the communist cause in an unbearable position: "They have fled the ideology of their class or origin only to find it again in the class they have chosen. Work, family, country [the motto of Vichy France]—no more laughing at it, they've got to sing it" (*What Is Literature?*, p. 263). Gramsci's own theories, which were extremely influential in Italy after the war, are deeply conservative in this respect, arguing for coercion and strict regimentation in matters of sexuality, the family, morality, and education ("justified" by the strategic political needs of the working class), as well as for a "national-popular" literature. Yet, from Sartre's perspective, such ideas are fully inscribed in the same system from which Gramsci sought to free himself and his fellow communists.

A writer, Sartre concludes, cannot be a member of the communist party and still be a writer: "The politics of Stalinist Communism is incompatible . . . with the honest practice of the literary craft." A perpetual Kafkaesque trial, he adds, is the fate that awaits the communist writer, in which everything he writes can be held against him; he is "presumed guilty in advance" (*What Is Literature?*, p. 260). Creating positive working-class heroes or putting communists in novels will not help, for "if they have faults, they run the risk of displeasing; if too perfect, they bore" (*What Is Literature?*, p. 261). Pavese's *The Comrade* did in fact universally displease PCI intellectuals; so did Visconti's adaptation of Verga in *La terra trema*. Pavese, Vittorini, Moravia, and Pratolini were among those under constant attack in party newspapers and journals, particularly after the period of relative cultural tolerance between 1945 and 1947 had ended. The history of neorealism is also the history of a cultural-ideological "war" between leftist writers and the PCI, which explains to a large degree the apparent schizophrenia of many well-intentioned neorealists. Pavese's suicide in 1950 was perhaps the most tragic result of this situation; the closing of *Il Politecnico* after 1947, and Vittorini's withdrawal from the Italian literary scene, were other equally revealing symptoms of the Kafkaesque atmosphere described by Sartre.

For Sartre, political engagement means that the work of art is, like the human being itself, an absolute end. Thus while art must engage itself and its reader in a critical reflection on the real and on the prospect of change through the historical action of *homo faber*, it can in no way compromise itself with a Machiavellian political practice. However, neither can the artist ignore the historical reality of class conflict or pretend to transcend it by elevating himself to a "parasitic aristocracy" of the spirit. The task of the writer is to expose the contradictions of bourgeois society and its fundamental negativity, while simultaneously disclosing the possibility of revolutionary change. This possibility, which is the writer's hope, Sartre says, lies with the working class. The artist and the worker share a task that is both destructive and constructive: "At the time that we are discovering in the art of writing freedom in its two aspects of negativity and creative surpassing, he is trying to free himself and, by the same token, to free all men from oppression forever" (*What Is Literature?*, p. 252). Sartre's view of the working class is, however, characteristically skeptical: "I do not believe in the 'mission' of the proletariat, nor that it is endowed with a state of grace; it is made up of men, just and unjust, who can make mistakes and who are often mystified. . . . The majority of the proletariat, straightjacketed by a simple party, encircled by a propaganda which isolates it, forms a closed society without doors or windows" (*What Is Literature?*, p. 253). The task of communication that Sartre sees as crucial for engaged art is therefore a problematic one. Since "there can be no question of popularizing" (*What Is Literature?*, p. 268), because art would immediately turn into deception, the working class remains a *virtual* public for the modern writer:

"They will not hear a word that we shall say to them" (*What Is Literature?*, p. 253). Only the mass media can to a certain extent provide access to the masses of workers, and learning how to use these media is one of the principal tasks of the modern artist, Sartre observes: "There is no need to popularize. The film, by its very nature, speaks to crowds. It speaks to them about crowds and about their destiny" (*What Is Literature?*, p. 268).

Visconti's *La terra trema* may be seen as the most persuasive of all neorealist attempts to realize the Sartrean ideal in this sense. Visconti was by far the most intellectual and sophisticated "formalist" among the neorealist directors and the one who made the fewest concessions to popularization in his work. He was well acquainted with Sartre's work and directed several of his plays, including *Huis clos* (*No Exit*). Visconti's brief 1943 essay, "Cinema antropomorfico" ("Anthropomorphic Cinema"), has a distinctly Sartrean ring to it and anticipates some of Sartre's own ideas in *What Is Literature?*:

What has led me to a creative activity in film? (Creative activity: labor of a living man among living men. With this term—it must be clear—I do not intend to refer to something pertaining exclusively to the realm of art. Every worker, living, creates something: as long, that is, as he is able to *live*). . . . I think that only through a genuinely felt experience, nourished daily by an objective and sympathetic scrutiny of human existence, can one arrive at artistic "specialization."

But to arrive at it does not mean to shut yourself off in it, breaking all concrete links with society—as often happens—to the point that specialization turns into a pretext for evading the real or, in cruder terms, into a cowardly abstention. . . .

I have been attracted to film-making above all by the commitment to tell stories of living men: of men alive in things, not of things in and of themselves.

The cinema I am interested in is anthropomorphic cinema. . . .

Any different solution . . . will always appear to me a mystification of reality as it unfolds before our eyes: made by men and constantly changed by them.[65]

Visconti's *La terra trema* was, however, a commercial failure in Italy, a fact which would seem to confirm Sartre's skeptical hypothesis about the purely virtual nature of the masses as an audience for engaged art. Only in a classless society (the society in which, according to Marx, everyone would be free to be "also" an artist) could engaged art be anthropomorphic in Visconti's sense or, in Sartre's words, "anthropological": "Involved in the same adventure as his readers and situated like them in a society without cleavages, the writer, in speaking about them, would be speaking about himself, and in speaking about himself would be speaking about them. As no aristocratic pride would any longer force him to deny that he is in a situation, he would no longer seek to soar above his time and bear witness to it before eternity, but as his situation would be universal, he would thereby express himself completely. . . . Literature would really be anthropological, in the full sense of the term" (*What Is Literature?*, p. 157).

Although he refers to it only in passing, Sartre's utopian vision is one of art as a collective phenomenon where the opposition between writer and reader, subject and object, and individual and community is no longer a conflictual one, and the text is capable of synthesizing a universal truth. This in turn implicitly relies on classical art—and specifically, as in Lukács's aesthetics, the epic—as a model, for the epic is "of collective origin" (*What Is Literature?*, p. 138), and the universal truth of which Aristotle speaks is possible in ancient poetry (and remains possible to some degree prior to the nineteenth century) because the poet is "in harmony with society as a whole" (*What Is Literature?*, p. 35). Artist and audience once shared the same myths and spoke the same language; poetry had a communicative power, a concrete meaningfulness and a confidence that was lost with the advent of the nineteenth century. In order to overcome this radical break in the circuit of communication and in the very nature of historical experience, the artist must learn to speak plainly, in prose, almost as if the very contractual agreement on which language is based had to be renegotiated once again.

This project for a modern prose is at the basis of literary neorealism. But while Sartre—unlike Lukács and Brecht—had few illusions about the proletariat either as an ideal audience or as possessing a privileged mode of consciousness, many Italian neorealists clung to such beliefs well into the 1950's. These artists and writers were unable to come to terms with their own distance—as bourgeois intellectuals—from the masses and often compensated (adhering to Soviet dogma in the process) by granting the working class a kind of mythical status, as the sole possessor of an authenticity and solidarity missing in every other segment of society. Cesare Pavese's often-quoted 1945 article "Ritorno all'uomo" ("Return to Man"), published by the PCI newspaper *L'Unità* and written while Pavese was already thinking about his novel *Il compagno*, is revealing in this respect:

We will not try to reach out toward the people. This is because we are already a part of the people, and nothing else exists. We will, if anything, try to reach out toward man. Because this is the obstacle, the shell that we must break through: the solitude of man, of ourselves and of others. . . . To suggest that we reach out toward the people is in essence to confess to a bad conscience. . . . We know that, in the social class that is customarily called "the people," laughter is more genuine, suffering is more vivid, speech is more sincere. And we ought to keep this in mind. But what else does this mean if not that in the life of the people solitude has already been overcome—or is on the way to being overcome? . . . These years of anguish and blood have taught us that anguish and blood are not the end of everything. Something is salvaged out of horror, and it is man's opening toward man. . . . Many barriers and stupid walls have fallen in recent days. . . . Truly man has revealed what is most profoundly alive in himself, and now waits for the rest of us to know how to understand and to speak (for it is up to us). . . . We all feel that we are living in a time in which words must be brought back to the solid and naked precision that they had when man first created them for his use.[66]

Written by Pavese in the final year of Fascism in Italy, this statement may be seen as the reversal of the desolate message implicit in two of the most poignant poems written by Eugenio Montale on the eve of the Fascist takeover: "Non chiederci la parola" ("Don't Ask for the Word") and "Meriggiare pallido e assorto" ("Pale and Absorbed Noon-Time Rest"). In the famous concluding stanza of the latter, Montale states: "E andando nel sole che abbaglia / sentire con triste meraviglia / com'è tutta la vita e il suo travaglio / in questo seguitare una muraglia / che ha in cima cocci aguzzi di bottiglia" ("And walking against the blinding sun / to feel with sad bewilderment how / all life and its travail / is like following a wall with pieces / of broken glass stuck to its top edge"). Here we see the coincidence between Pavese's views on literature and Sartre's, as well as the differences between them, most notably in the relationship between the writer and the masses, which for Pavese is (rather optimistically) a "given," as well as in the understanding of what *il popolo* is and what it signifies.

Pavese, Vittorini, and Sartre all belonged to the same generation (Sartre was born in 1905, Pavese and Vittorini in 1908), and while their experiences differed widely, the collapse of Fascism in Europe, the war, and the Resistance meant for all three the discovery of their own historicity. Montale's own poetry "opened up" to a new historical awareness with the war, although still characterized by his sense of skepticism and of the negative, as the section entitled "Dopo" ("After") in *La bufera e altro* indicates; even more emphatically to the point, the concluding line of the justly famous "Primavera hitleriana" reads, "e più nessuno è incolpevole" ("and no one is not guilty any more"). In his reply to the 1951 survey on neorealism, Montale, while expressing some reservations about the general quality of neorealist fiction, pointed out that the changes in the political climate after 1943 allowed Italian writers a greater freedom of action and creation.[67]

Sartre's *What Is Literature?* provides the most compelling description of how the intellectuals of his generation found themselves forcibly standing face to face with history:

> Our life as an individual which had seemed to depend upon our efforts, our virtues, and our faults, on our good and bad luck, on the good and bad will of a very small number of people, seemed governed down to its minutest details by obscure and collective forces, and its most private circumstances seemed to reflect the state of the whole world. All at once we felt ourselves abruptly *situated*.
>
> The detachment which our predecessors were so fond of practicing had become impossible. There was a collective adventure which was taking form in the future and which would be *our* adventure. . . .
>
> Historicity flowed in upon us; in everything we touched, in the air we breathed, in the page we read, in the one we wrote; in love itself we discovered, like a taste of history, so to speak, a bitter and ambiguous mixture of the absolute and the transitory. What need had we patiently to construct self-destructive objects since each of the moments of our life was subtly whisked away from us at the very time that we were enjoying it, since each *present* that we lived with gusto, like an absolute, was struck with a secret death, seemed to us to have its meaning outside of itself, for other eyes which had not yet seen the light, and, in a way, to be *already* past in its very presence? (*What Is Literature?*, p. 213)

For writers of Calvino's and Fenoglio's generation (Calvino was born in 1923, Fenoglio in 1922), the postwar situation was a somewhat different one. Unlike their predecessors, they had never patiently constructed self-destructing or self-consuming artifacts, for they started writing during the war and the Resistance, in which both participated as partisans—Calvino in a communist "Garibaldi" brigade in the Ligurian mountains behind Genoa and San Remo (where he grew up), Fenoglio near his hometown of Alba in Piedmont, as a member of the "autonomous" patriot bands made up of *sbandati* (disbanded soldiers).[68] The very first things they wrote were probably notes and diary entries, jotted down during intervals in the fighting.[69] Theirs was not so much a rediscovery of history, and of their own historicity, as an experience of being "thrown" directly into history at the very moment of their beginning as writers.

In an important article written in 1949 about the literature of the Resistance, Calvino remarks that for writers whose formation preceded the war years, the Resistance was but "the term of an antithesis." Their works are "the document of their position as individual intellectuals vis-à-vis the struggle"; the Resistance is not in itself the subject of their works.[70] Both Elio Vittorini's *Uomini e no* and Pavese's *La casa in collina* correspond to this same description (Fenoglio's works remained unpublished until the 1950's). Although in his article Calvino refrains from referring to his own novel, *Il sentiero dei nidi di ragno* is indeed the only neorealist work in which the historical reality of the Resistance emerges in all its problematic complexity without being subordinated—as it is in the fiction of Vittorini and Pavese—to the anguished self-questioning of the author or of his persona. While Fenoglio's narratives about the Resistance share some of the insights of Calvino's novel and have a compelling narrative rhythm for which Calvino himself later expressed his admiration,[71] Fenoglio's relative cultural "innocence" and isolation, and above all his inability and unwillingness to tackle the political and ideological issues involved in the Italian Resistance, prevented him from achieving the breadth and depth of Calvino's remarkable first novel. As the Italian historian Paolo Spriano has recently pointed out, Calvino had a considerable advantage over his contemporaries and—despite his youth—even over his predecessors: "He was the most cultured. He had not only read Hemingway, Steinbeck, Faulkner, Sartre and Vittorini, like all of us. He had a thorough knowledge of literature, of the great works of Russian, English, French and Italian literature; he also had a scientifically-oriented way of thinking."[72]

Calvino and the Call for a New Realism

The experience of the war and the Resistance led to a new sense of time itself, one in which the history of individuals and the history of humanity no longer seemed separated or separable. This experience of historical time immediately posed for neorealist writers the problem of its representation or, rather, its narration. The very magnitude of the forces involved seemed almost to dictate a return to an epic mode of realist narration, and neorealism is often charged with having failed to produce a truly "mass" epic of Italian life.[73] But Sartre's description of the position of the writer vis-à-vis history tells us why this was never a possibility and why a dramatic literature of "extreme situations" developed instead. Referring to the work of Camus, Malraux, and Koestler, Sartre notes that "their characters are at the height of power or in prison cells, on the eve of death or of being tortured or of killing. Wars, coups d'état, revolutionary action, bombardments, massacres. There you have their everyday life. On every page, in every line, it is always the whole man who is in question" (*What Is Literature?*, p. 223). In Italy, the autobiographical/historical novels by Vittorini and Beppe Fenoglio represent this literature of extreme situations, but it is mostly in the vast outpouring of docufiction and *memorialistica*, two key genres of the neorealist movement, and in neorealist film that this mode of narration emerges as dominant. The most celebrated example of the latter is, without a doubt, Rossellini's *Rome Open City*.

For Sartre, the first question that the modern narrator has to face is that of narrative form itself. Epic realism, or the "high" realism of Lukács's model, and the fiction of the omniscient narrator are not viable options for Sartre, for those who choose to narrate from the viewpoint of past history "seek to deny their body, their historicity, and the irreversibility of time" (*What Is Literature?*, pp. 229–30). Sartre advocates instead a narration *without* a stable, comprehensive, and all-knowing point of view, using characters

whose reality would be the tangled and contradictory tissue of each one's evaluations of all other characters . . . and who could never decide from within whether the changes of their destinies came from their own efforts, from their own faults, or from the course of the universe. . . . We had to leave doubts, expectations, and the unachieved throughout our works, leaving it up to the reader to conjecture for himself by giving him the feeling, without giving him or letting him guess our feeling, that his view of the plot and the characters were merely one among many others. . . . We were convinced that no art could really be ours if it did not restore to the event its brutal freshness, its ambiguity, its unforseeability, if it did not restore to time its actual course, to the world its rich and threatening opacity. . . . Let [the reader] be uncertain of the very uncertainty of the heroes, disturbed by their disturbances, flooded with their present. (*What Is Literature?*, pp. 224–26)

The problem is, therefore, to find a strategy for "the orchestration of consciousness" capable of fully rendering the multidimensionality of the event. While Joyce has taught us—Sartre writes—another kind of realism, a "new realism of subjectivity without mediation or distance," a third kind of realism is now necessary, which is "that of temporality" (*What Is Literature?*, p. 228). To focus exclusively on the subjective time of individual consciousness and to pack an entire epic into 24 hours is not—notwithstanding the great achievement of *Ulysses*—"desirable," Sartre argues, for it denies the reader a means to survey the whole, foreclosing true communication, and therefore "the reader jumps out of the book" (*What Is Literature?*, p. 228). While Sartre advocates the use of literature as a means to unsettle the reader's perceptions and to generate uncertainty about his own historical reality, then, he opposes the complete relativization of time and perspective. A story must still have a relatively perceptible order, albeit an order as subject to multiple interpretations as is the temporal succession of human events. Calvino's *The Path* realizes—more than any other neorealist work—Sartre's ideal of an "estranging" realism.

Calvino discovered his own voice and identity as a writer in trying to retell a story which was not only his own, but the (hi)story of a nation at a moment which was universally—if incorrectly—felt to have acquired the aura of a foundational epic. Calvino found himself emerging and "situated" as a writer at a seemingly transitional moment in Italian history, on the border between two epochs, in which history itself appeared to be narratable for the first time in a particular way. The time of this history is the privileged time of the realistic *Bildungsroman* for Bakhtin, a time in which individual and collective history come together in a single narrative. It is also the privileged time of authentically realistic, epic narrative for Lukács, in which the emergence of new social forces makes possible the meaningful articulation of the present with the past and the future through his telling of a single story in which the collectivity recognizes itself and discerns a "necessary" truth. Finally, it is the time, according to Sartre, in which a new realism of temporality is called for in literary discourse. "Saremo come Omero" ("We Will Be like Homer") is the title of an article Calvino published in the PCI journal *Rinascita* in December 1948. In spite of its PCI imprimatur, this article reveals how deeply aware Calvino was of the ambiguity of the claim implicit in his title. His text is in fact an ironic response to a prior critical intervention by Emilio Sereni—the head of the cultural office of the PCI—who had exhorted writers to abandon their individualism and to become "like Homer," that is, the epic poets of the working class's heroism in its history-making struggle.[74]

Calvino's article is a characteristically lucid assessment of the problems faced by neorealism. Sereni's idea that, in dealing with the "new" reality disclosed by the war and the Resistance, literature should free itself of the heritage of bourgeois art and pursue the new ideological direction dictated by the masses as historical protagonists is, Calvino argues, both abstract and incompatible with the way literature actually "works." While Calvino acknowledges—like Sartre—that a writer is never "free" of ideology, which is simultaneously "the objective limit and the instrument of his freedom," he nevertheless points out that a writer can never directly approach the historical and social. Literature has its own history, its own tradition, and its own discourse, and it is always in relation to these that the writer orients his own work and expresses himself ("Saremo come Omero," p. 448). The problem of choice for the writer is that of the choice of a language, and this language can never be the language of the real in the sense of Virgil's proverbial *sunt lachrimae rerum*. The language a writer has at his disposal is already charged with prior connotations, alive with the resonances of the literary past, laced with intertextual echoes: "It is only by working on the tradition that we can renew ourselves" ("Saremo come Omero," p. 448). Calvino may well be alluding here to T. S. Eliot's famous 1919 essay "Tradition and the Individual Talent," which he doubtless knew, since he had a degree in English literature from the University of Turin, earned with a dissertation on Conrad. Within the context of literary modernity, this dialectic of tradition and innovation is, Calvino notes, determined by the presence of "that immensely cumbersome character" of the author's self ("Saremo come Omero," p. 448). It is impossible simply to dispose of this "character," erase it, or pretend it is not there. The imperative, "be like Homer"—be, that is, an epic poet able "to write poetry as if it were born directly from nature and history, 'as if the author were not there'")—is a deluded one for the modern writer ("Saremo come Omero," p. 448), for the epic chorality of Homer and Virgil corresponds to a historical situation that is irrecoverably lost.

The emergence of the author's own "I" as a character in the scene of writing and the concomitant shift from the art of telling everyone's story to that of telling one's own story—no matter how sublimated or depersonalized—corresponds to the historical rise of the "I," of the single individual aware of his own subjectivity and isolation from the other (nature, history, the collectivity). Telling one's own story means to know that there is no such thing as objectivity and that a story is therefore always subjective and always entails a point of view, or an "eye" that is also an "I." While this "I" is in itself a historical construct, "the 'I' that lives and sees and transforms and improves itself in its contact with history and mankind," its historical transformation is by no means immediately coextensive with the historical transformations of society at large ("Saremo come Omero," p. 448).

Calvino points out that, in the struggle to transform society, the question of the individual subject cannot simply be wished away, nor will changes at the level of socioeconomic infrastructures automatically trigger a transformation of the individual subject. Thus to "write like a Marxist" when one is not a Marxist and to "discipline" the "I that writes" by repressing the conflicts within the writer's self can only lead—according to Calvino—to inauthentic literature. Whatever the writer chooses to do with the "I" in the act of writing—whether representing it "autobiographically or symbolically, or transfiguring it into a hero, or . . . succeeding in pretending it is not there"—he cannot circumvent it ("Saremo come Omero," p. 448). The modern writer always writes in the first person; only if he becomes conscious of this position can he begin to "engage" himself in his own time. Then "even if he will start narrating *his* novel, this novel will become the patrimony of many" ("Saremo come Omero," p. 448). For Calvino, as for Sartre, only in a future classless society will there be no opposition between the writer and his audience, the "particular and the universal." While "in some moments of plenitude" the poet may have indeed been "the direct voice of a whole society and epoch," today we are, Calvino continues, "at the opposite extreme" ("Saremo come Omero," p. 448). Even the "realistic chorality" and "historicity" that Marxist critics admire in masters of high realism such as Balzac and Tolstoy are perspectives that are simply "not yet" recoverable for the modern writer.

In another article of the same period, entitled "Ingegneri e demolitori" ("Engineers and Demolishers"), Calvino posits a double function for literature: a negative or destructive function and a positive or constructive one. Calvino points out that the bourgeois literature of negativity and "crisis" already has a long and complex tradition, which he traces back to Flaubert or, more specifically, to *Madame Bovary*. But while Flaubert describes the hollow and alienated fantasies of the petit bourgeois world, his own work is not in itself a challenge to alienation. "The consciousness of the negativity of our society has penetrated us down to the marrow but it has remained stagnant; the assiduous study of this negativity has bound us to it through a secret or open affection" ("Ingegneri," p. 400). This is still the situation most writers and intellectuals find themselves in, Calvino argues, and it is a situation from which there is no simple way out. Even though some of the Italian neorealists—unlike Flaubert— may have located the source of alienation in the totalizing logic of capitalism and have brought the proletariat to the center of the historical stage, the extreme contradictions of bourgeois culture are still "within us," Calvino argues. To pretend that this is not the case is only a form of "ambitious hypocrisy" leading to the transformation of the proletariat into a "moralistic myth." Unlike Pavese, Calvino does not seek to minimize the gap that separates the writer-intellectual from *il popolo*, nor does he see the working class as possessing a nonalienated consciousness and a nonreified relation with the real; such a "full" civilization is, Calvino writes, still only a "fascinating presage" ("Ingegneri," p. 400). Literature thus becomes a kind of utopian space, motivated not by a desire to escape the real but by a lucid dissatisfaction with the present and a longing for a different future: "It will be necessary to give birth to a range of characters who will unveil a whole world of new fantasies, of new contacts with life, death, love, the city, nature; a range of characters that will be positive but neither rigid nor rhetorical. If we want them to be paradigmatic for a new kind of man, if we want this new man to criticize himself, to improve himself and to recognize himself in these characters, it should be possible to make fun of these characters and to take pity on them as much as to admire them" ("Ingegneri," p. 400).

The world of Calvino's ironic imagination, with its playful defamiliarization of the real that constantly opens up new ways of looking and understanding through literary discourse, is sketched out for us in these few lines. Although Calvino's work undergoes a series of metamorphoses over the course of four decades and is tirelessly experimental in its pursuit of new narrative strategies, it never renounces this *impegno* to engage the reader in a critical reflection on the real that exposes its negativity, while disclosing the possibility—no matter how remote or elusive—of change. Calvino's decision to write narrative fiction is directly linked to his own desire to represent human time, and historical time, as man-made constructs. The agility of Calvino's plots, with their focus on adventures rather than description or in-depth psychological analysis, and his preference for the structure of the fairy tale and the quest-romance reflect Calvino's understanding of history as human action and his passionate involvement in it. His imaginative deployment of relatively traditional forms of narrative such as the fairy tale, the adventure story, and the quest-romance appears to him to be a solution to the problem of communicating with as large an audience as possible, a problem that seems so urgent both to Sartre and the neorealists. Calvino's recourse to these forms is a strategy for cutting the modern epic down to size, for stripping away the melodramatic effects of the "literature of extreme situations," and for dissolving the lyrical subjectivism of autobiographically inspired narratives.

While Calvino's strategy resembles Sartre's in many ways, it is closer to the substance of Roland Barthes's famous 1953 critique of *What Is Literature?*, entitled *Writing Degree Zero*. Barthes's vision of literature is not wholly incompatible with Sartre's, but, like Calvino, he sees the problem of commitment in a different light. For Barthes, as for Calvino, literary writing (*écriture*) can never be "prose" in Sartre's sense of the direct, intersubjective communication of meaning. Instead, all writing involves a three-tiered linguistic reality. The first level is a subjective, individual language which corresponds to the labyrinth of the author's own self, his subconscious, and his body. This language is the most ambiguous of all, for it remains outside the realm of communication, or it emerges only in the form of fragments and traces. Yet it is there, and it "mysteriously" makes for the idiosyncrasy of what Barthes calls the writer's "style" (*Writing Degree Zero*, pp. 10–12). The second level is language itself, in the sense of "the undivided property of men," but this language is—for the writer—"nothing but a human horizon which provides a distant setting of *familiarity*" (*Writing Degree Zero*, p. 10). The writer, Barthes contends, can engage himself only by choosing a mode of writ-

ing from within the tradition in which he finds himself historically inserted:

The choice of, and afterwards the responsibility for, a mode of writing
point to the presence of Freedom, but this Freedom has not the same
limits at different moments of History. It is not granted to the writer to
choose his mode of writing from a kind of a-temporal store of literary
forms. It is under the pressure of History and Tradition that the possible modes of writing for a given writer are established; there is a History of Writing. But this History is dual: at the very moment when general History proposes—or imposes—new problematics of the literary
language, writing still remains full of the recollection of previous usage,
for language is never innocent: words have a second-order memory
which mysteriously persists in the midst of new meanings. Writing is
precisely this compromise between freedom and remembrance. (*Writing Degree Zero*, pp. 16–17)

Thus the writer's commitment requires a delicate negotiation of
three "histories" and of three languages: the language of the
self, the language of tradition, and the language of historical
events. For Barthes, as for Calvino, the seemingly revolutionary
content of a work may be undermined, as in the case of socialist
realism, by "the adoption of a conventional mode of writing, to
which is assigned the task of signifying a content which is
powerless to impose itself without a form to identify it" (*Writing
Degree Zero*, p. 70). Paradoxically, then, "Communist writers are
the only ones who go on imperturbably keeping alive a bourgeois writing which bourgeois writers have themselves condemned long ago" (*Writing Degree Zero*, p. 73).

Calvino, however, does not share the skeptical conclusion
at which Barthes arrives. For the latter, the "Flaubertization"
of writing, or its transformation into an essentially formal craft,
has definitely detached the literary sign from its sociohistorical
context. At the very moment in which literature becomes self-
justified as form and thus "redeems itself" from its bourgeois af-
filiations, literary history becomes a kind of trap or double bind
for the writer: "History has brought about an obvious disjunction between the social vocation of the writer and the instrument which he has inherited from Tradition" (*Writing Degree
Zero*, p. 64). Sartre's novels do not escape from this tragic predic-

ament of inauthenticity, according to Barthes. A novel like *The Reprieve* (the second of the trilogy *Les Chemins de la Liberté*, written in 1945), with its attempt to fuse the private and the public, the individual and the historical, falls, according to Barthes, entirely within the realm of belles lettres, as it is wholly subordinated to the traditional device of the time of the narrator "whose particular voice, defined by highly recognizable contingent features, burdens the unfolding of History with a parasitical unity" (*Writing Degree Zero*, p. 85). Barthes concludes that

a modern masterpiece is impossible, since the writer is forced by his writing into a cleft stick: either the object of the work is naively attuned to the conventions of its form, Literature remaining deaf to our present History, and not going beyond the literary myth; or else the writer acknowledges the vast novelty of the present world, but finds that in order to express it he has at his disposal only a language which is splendid but lifeless. In front of the virgin sheet of paper, at the moment of choosing the words which must frankly signify his place in History, and testify that he assumes its data, he observes a tragic disparity between what he does and what he sees. Before his eyes, the world of society now exists as a veritable Nature, and this Nature speaks, elaborating living languages from which the writer is excluded: on the contrary, History puts in his hands a decorative and compromising instrument, a writing inherited from a previous and different History, for which he is not responsible and yet which is the only one he can use. . . . It is this stale language, closed by the immense pressure of all the men who do not speak it, which he must continue to use. Writing is therefore in a blind alley. The writers of today feel this; for them, the search for a non-style or an oral style, for a zero level or a spoken level of writing is, all things considered, the anticipation of a homogeneous social state; most of them understand that there can be no universal language outside a concrete, and no longer a mystical or merely nominal, universality of society. (*Writing Degree Zero*, pp. 86–87)

For Calvino, in the specific historical context which defines his own *Bildung* as a writer, the facts of history appear indeed as inescapable and as pressing as if they were a part of nature instead. As he writes in the 1964 preface to *The Path*, "The extra-literary elements stood there so massive and so indisputable that they seemed a fact of nature" (p. vii; 8). Calvino does not, on the other hand, feel literary tradition as a burden incompatible with his engagement as a writer, nor does he—unlike many other neorealist writers—fall prey to the illusion that a zero degree of writing is an objective possibility for literary discourse. While sharing the general neorealist perception that the transformation of literary language is a political project, he enters into the quest for a new mode of writing guided by the belief—however deluded it may appear to us today—that the formal resources of literary language might still yield an authentic mode of signification of the real: "To us the whole problem was one of poetics; how to transform into a literary work that world which for us was *the* world" (p. vii; 9). The use of the plural "we" has a particular significance in this last statement. Calvino finds himself, from the very beginning of his quest, in a position quite different from Flaubert's solitary contemplation of the blank page, for he is driven by a desire altogether different from Flaubert's wish to write a book built "on nothing" and held up entirely and exclusively by the ruses of style.[75] Calvino instead comes to the act of writing, as do many of his contemporaries, with the axiom in mind that every experience of recent history is a story waiting to be written down and read.

2 • Modes of Neorealist Narrative

The Voices of the Real: Writing the Resistance and the Resistance to Writing

Writing in Medias Res: Partisan Chronicles

From the first, the war and the Resistance in Italy were accompanied by specific practices of narration. Along with war bulletins, information on developments in guerrilla warfare, political editorials and messages, and practical information of every kind, the partisan broadsheets and the clandestine press printed a variety of very short narrative texts, often anonymous, which reported episodes of the struggle, recounted the exploits of particular individuals, or commemorated partisans who had lost their lives. Eyewitness accounts and extracts from personal diaries and notes were also often included. These texts oscillate between the bare sequential chronicle of facts and more articulate narrative microstructures which organize events into a plot. This first, spontaneous kind of Resistance writing sought to contribute to the success of the struggle by fostering a collective sense of solidarity and identity among its readers. The pervasive use of a nominal style, of paratactic syntax, of direct narrative discourse, and the mimetic representation of dialogue give this writing a tone of immediacy and urgency—aimed at recovering the referential and communicative functions of language—which reemerge in neorealist fiction. In a passage from a partisan diary published by the newspaper of one of the *Giustizia e Libertà* brigades in 1944, some of the most typical traits of Resistance writing may be clearly discerned:

Four of us sleep in the woods; the others have gone up to the Donna Morta. We eat cheese bought from the shepherds. We take turns keeping watch until nighttime.

At seven o'clock one of our comrades arrives: his face wan. Bad news. Today I am in a good mood; everything seems easy to me, even what is said does not make me afraid.

The Germans have attacked; at the Donna Morta at noon they captured our mules. Our comrades have withdrawn into the woods; then at night a patrol goes down to the Capannine to explore; a shoot-out awaits them. One man wounded. Nothing serious, fortunately. The men disperse in the woods again.

Shortly after the messenger, about ten of them arrive. And the others . . . ?

But time is short. We cannot delay. We leave immediately for Pratignano, leaving a man to wait for the others to join us.

It's already dark.

We go by the Bagnatori, the Acero; we go up to the Riva. Another band welcomes us, gives us warm milk, a bed of hay. "I have found a . . . double bed," I tell the captain. As soon as we lie down, we fall asleep. We are very tired.

Only a few minutes later a voice shouts: "We must leave! Order to go to Fanano!" What? Leaving? But they are crazy! And yet tired, sleepy, we leave again, we go down to the bottom of the valley. We find another division that is also going towards Fanano; heavily armed.

Towards ten o'clock, after a twelve-hour march, we arrive at C.

A plentiful *polenta*, some good wine, three hours' sleep and we are again ready to go. I go on patrol with Lello. It's a foggy day. The area is swarming with Germans: but the fog protects us. All of a sudden the wind blows, and we find ourselves exposed.

Two men under a beach umbrella, but we can't make them out. I shout: "Halt! Who goes there?" They stop, but no answer. I shout again, "Who goes there?" Meanwhile one of the two slowly raises a machine gun and aims at us. Hold on a moment: they're Germans. We shoot, the men fall down. Turned upside down on the path, the umbrella flaps in the wind.[1]

These diary pages clearly exhibit the structure of a short adventure story with an organic plot containing a beginning, a middle, and an end. It invites an analysis, though, not so much in terms of Aristotle's *Poetics* as in terms of the narrative functions discussed by Vladimir Propp in his classic study, *Morphology of the Folktale*. The reason is that this text makes schematic use of a series of types and archetypes, as well as of a minimal (but visible) set of narrative functions that derive from folk and fairy tales, on the one hand, and from quest-narrative on the other. The opening section establishes the setting (the spatiotemporal determination of the story) and introduces the protagonists. The second section introduces "the villains" and their evil doings (reported by the messenger) and sets the challenge for the hero. The third and fourth sections tell of the hero and his comrades setting out on their quest. The narrative traces the phases of their travel through a space in which every step is essential, space itself being articulated directly with time through a few, essential notations. These notations are concrete (names of real places, exact time of the day), and yet they assume a symbolic resonance through their very essentiality. The woods, the valley, the dwelling with the hay and the good food, the cycle of day and night, resting and setting out again towards an uncertain destiny: all these elements gather up the image of the space and time of the fairy tale and the epic quest-romance, abstract and universal.[2] Donors appear to assist in the quest; the fog, for instance, seems magically to protect the hero and his comrade from the villains. In the last section the story reaches its climax in the final confrontation with the enemy.

Notwithstanding its organicity as a narrative, this story is in turn part of a larger ongoing narrative, just as the anonymous author's own diary is in turn part of the epic story of the Resistance as a whole. The names of geographical locations, valleys, and villages are the signs of the real; they refer to the actual locations of the fight and therefore "anchor" the story to the bedrock of history itself. But the name of the protagonist (who also narrates the story) is not given; he simply signs himself "Alpino," one of the many members of the Alpine corps who deserted the army to join the partisans. The story is implicitly offered to the reader as "typical," standing for many other similar stories that remain untold. The immediacy of the narrative, its rapid characterization of the protagonists through a few brief notations, the agility of the plot entirely geared to the representation of action and movement, and the telegraphic and paratactic construction are all traits which will reemerge in the postwar genre of partisan short stories and which Calvino exploits with powerful effect in *The Path*.

Resistance writing and the oral folk tradition behind it are indeed, as Maria Corti has cogently argued (developing Calvino's own suggestion), one of the fundamental matrices of neorealist literature at the level of style as well as that of thematic and narrative structures.[3] The neorealist poetics of *"le cose che si raccontano da sole"* takes the telegraphic eyewitness report of events in Resistance writing as one of its bases (just as neorealist film absorbs and transforms the conventions of the newsreel). For the partisan chroniclers, events themselves unfold with the dramatic evidence of the "literature of extreme situations" and seem to eliminate any need for invention (the classical rhetorical *inventio*). If they make no attempt to reconstruct the historical background behind the stories of individuals and their acts, it is because the two are inextricably interwoven for them. Storytelling, and the telling of history, become one and the same, the *histor* being (as in the etymological meaning of the word) one and the same as the eyewitness. The texts of Resistance writing recount episodes and scenes of what is implicitly a single narrative; they are subplots that converge ideally into a single governing plot, which is that of history itself. The teleological perspective of the Liberation as the end of the conflict is what gives these mini-narratives the sense of an ending; it allows the partisans themselves to narrate the immediate past and the present as causally motivated and oriented towards a meaningful conclusion. The structural principle of causality which motivates Resistance narrative and informs the plot coincides with the partisan *cause* itself, that is, the *mythos* whereby historical time, geographical space, and human action are imaginatively grasped together in the form of a tale unfolding towards the recovery of (lost) freedom. This *mythos* is in turn what motivates the very act of writing as a perlocutionary speech act,[4] intended to elicit action on the part of the reader in the form of solidarity and participation in the partisan struggle.

The short narrative "L'orfanello" ("The Little Orphan"), which appeared in *Il Partigiano*, the broadsheet of the Third "Chichero" partisan division, is typical in this regard. It tells its readers about the daily reconnaissance flight of a German airplane over partisan-held territory. The airplane is portrayed at first as a dark threat hanging over the partisan outposts, but the text goes on to explain how the partisans dispel their fear of the airplane by derisively calling it the "little orphan" (implying that it is all alone and will not be followed by a larger show of air power). It becomes the symbol of a kind of power that seems to dominate everything from its lofty position but is in fact without any solid foundation or connection to the ground. The text's conclusion points out the final narrative meaning of the anecdote and its historical significance: "And in the cool nights of a time which is now forthcoming, we will go outside—having driven out the invader—to eat our bread on the thresholds of our homes, no longer bothered by the unpleasant sound of the little orphan."[5] Here, as in the story previously cited, the narrator/eyewitness/protagonist hardly distinguishes himself from his comrades; he narrates from the point of view of the collectivity and addresses himself to it.

The Partisan Short Story

As Calvino writes in his 1949 article on Resistance literature, entitled "La letteratura italiana sulla Resistenza" ("Italian Literature about the Resistance"), short stories inspired by these kinds of partisan narratives written in medias res were published on the third or "cultural" page of many Italian national and small-town newspapers and in many Italian journals after the war:

An interesting phenomenon of "mass literature" can be seen [in the partisan narrative], which perhaps has been unknown in Italy (excluding dialect poetry) since the days of the chivalric epics and classic *novelle*. Often truculent and charged with pathos, the partisan narrative is born from an oral tradition (an episode which someone has experienced, and told to others, little by little reaches every valley and every unit) and has as its transcribers an extremely large number of young people scattered all over Italy, who often lack all literary instinct or cunning, or at other times have too much of the same, but who are able to create poetry only when they succeed in playing the part of the anonymous poet.[6]

Angelo Del Boca, Silvio Micheli, and Marcello Venturi were among the most widely published narrators who specialized in this genre.[7] More than neorealist novels, and perhaps even film, this kind of Resistance writing was able actually to reach the wider and more diverse audience that was the "virtual," ideal public that neorealism sought to address.

Yet although they share the topoi, themes, and often the paratactic syntax of the partisans' eyewitness narratives, Resistance short stories have their own specific style and generic traits.[8] The Resistance short story is, for the most part, clearly fictional, even though it is often based on actual facts and events. The device of the omniscient narrator who "fills in the gaps," reveals the inner thoughts of the characters, or narrates a series of events leading to the death of a character who was the event's sole eyewitness reveals the transition from straightforward documentary or "journalistic" prose to imaginative reconstruction or, in other words, to the production of the verisimilar (the "probable," or that which happens generally, but not always).

The hybrid mixture of actual facts and probabilistic fiction that Manzoni had come to consider a kind of deception of the reader (he renounced altogether the genre of the historical novel and retrospectively disowned his *I promessi sposi*) does not seem to trouble the authors of these short stories.[9] Clearly the resistance to fictionalization cannot be the reason why the literature of the Resistance produced very few novels compared to the large number of short stories.[10] These storytellers share with the partisan chroniclers the sense that what matters is the historical exemplarity of their narratives, for they relate not so much specific events as the significance of those events in terms of the overall development of the Resistance struggle. But while the Resistance chroniclers write from within the struggle itself, with a sense of living through an epic-in-the-making, the short-story writers look back on the Resistance as a tale that is already over, having reached its triumphant conclusion with the Liberation. As a consequence, their stories tend more to be a celebration of the sacrifices and achievements of the Resistance. As Calvino notes in the preface to *The Path*, soon after the Liberation the rhetoric of the Resistance developed in the direction of a kind of hagiography.[11] Although the genre of the partisan short story was, as Calvino indicates in his 1949 article, a unique phenomenon in Italian literary history because of the direct contact that it encouraged between writers and their sociohistorical context, as well as the link it established between author and public, the texts themselves appear flawed by their idealized portrayal of the partisan struggle.[12]

Even the stories by one of the best among these storytellers, Marcello Venturi, exhibit a "tendentiousness" and a sentimentality that are almost totally absent in the short narratives of the partisan chroniclers:

> Just think: men and women went down to meet the Americans. On their shoulders, hanging from a stick, they brought their homes, their furniture, their dead. And it hadn't been the sun that had done this to them. But the flame-throwers of the German ravagers. And the peasant who from the threshold used to look at the German soldier fixing his tire expected the locusts to swarm over his fields any day now, destroying them, and over his house, reducing it to rubble. . . .
> Friends, we cannot forget that white summer of '44. And the bundle hanging from the stick. Inside that bundle there was a house, a bed, a grave. And the fir-trees were our fir-trees. The wheat was our wheat. The men who hung, their neck stretched, from the branch of a tree, were our brothers. Let us think, friends, of how many of our fathers have been killed. Of how many times we—the survivors—have been killed.[13]

The hortatory tone of Venturi's prose, which appeals to the reader to remember and reflect, signals an essential shift in the addresser/addressee relation away from the immediacy of the partisan chronicles. In the former we find, to use Ranke's phrase, a narrative telling us not "what really happened," but rather "how it shall be remembered."[14] The narrator, furthermore, states what happened but does not provide a direct presentation of it. Venturi does have many stories which are entirely in the "showing" rather than the "telling" mode of narration, but his scenes are always set in an implicitly hagiographic frame: "A blast hit him like an explosion of convulsive laughter. He fell slowly on his side, lightly grazing the damp leaves of the chestnut trees. The dogs suddenly stopped barking. And there was deep silence in the whole valley."[15] Thus while the topoi, the motifs, and even the scenes are taken directly from the epos of the Resistance, often through a kind of formulaic repetition (which varies slightly from author to author), the narrative practice of neorealist storytellers such as Venturi is a kind of epic writing that has become ossified and crystallized into pious stereotypes; the shift from a predominance of the present tense in the work of the chroniclers to a predominance of the past tense in short fiction of this sort is but the most obvious sign of this transformation.

In the Resistance short story, the partisan struggle has become a myth, but not in the sense of the living *mythos* that animates the partisan chronicles and fills those texts with a future-oriented perspective of the purposiveness of human action. The Resistance has, rather, become a myth in the sense of a firmly held conviction based on a set of unquestioned and unquestionable assumptions. This myth of the "sanctity" of the Resistance has its roots in the postwar thwarting of private and collective desire for change. As Calvino points out in his preface, immediately after the Liberation the Resistance already had its detractors; "right-minded respectability" (p. xii) in Italy exploited the political turmoil of the time to make partisan acts of violence and the ideals of its left-wing protagonists appear criminally irresponsible. As even Ferruccio Parri—one of the Action Party leaders of the Resistance and the first prime minister of liberated Italy, who led a coalition government which included all the anti-Fascist parties (Communists and Socialists were excluded only after May 1947 by the new Christian Democrat prime minister, Alcide De Gasperi)—pointed out in an address in Rome, "In the partisan movement there were the good and the bad, the heroes and the looters, the generous and the cruel; there was a people with its virtues and vices. Then there were the eleventh-hour partisans, in general a detestable lot."[16] These "eleventh-hour" partisans took advantage of the general chaos to carry out private vendettas. A dozen or more bodies were found nightly in the streets of Milan during the first few days after the Liberation, according to Allied reports.[17] Those who, like Venturi, had been "good" partisans, writing about the Resistance meant to defend it against its detractors, even if this also meant denying (in the face of facts) the existence of its "vices."

Where Parri takes a balanced view of the pluses and minuses of the partisan movement, many Italian writers like Venturi seek a justification for the Resistance that would explain it as a rite of passage into adulthood and political maturity and therefore, underneath surface appearances, wholly necessary and wholly positive. The Resistance is, in this perspective, a rite of passage not only for individuals but for the Italian people as a whole (in accordance with the formula: Fascism = juvenile politics; Marxism = mature politics). The desire to narrate leads, in this case, to the configuration of individual and collective experience in the shape of a *Bildungsroman*. "Ci siamo svegliati adulti" ("We Woke Up to Find Ourselves Adults") is the title of one of Venturi's stories: "So we passed from a period of life to the other. And we wore down the soles of our shoes pacing the sidewalks of the cities, searching for a truck to set fire to, for young men for whom to set an example."[18] The seamless, individual, and universal quality of this *Bildung* is, needless to say, a problematic one. Although the body of short stories about the Resistance does in its entirety constitute a kind of fragmentary epic of self and nation, it is an epic in the sense indicated by Bakhtin as the "other" of the dialogical novel, namely a grandiloquent epic, where the past appears irretrievably determined and closed-off in a mythic time of heroes.[19] To portray the reality of the Resistance in its full complexity (rather than just in fragmentary scenes or episodes) and to do justice both to its contradictions and ambiguities and to the political conflicts which pervaded it requires a more heterogeneous—and more "realistic"—narrative approach. Calvino alone among his contemporaries was up to this task, and *The Path to the Nest of Spiders* stands today as the most successfully "realistic" text of Resistance literature and of neorealism itself.

Memorialistica and Moralism: In the Shadow of Croce

The years between 1945 and 1948 saw the largest outpouring of retrospective chronicles, *memorialistica*, and diaries related to the war and the Resistance. One of the most eloquent examples of this paraliterary genre in that period is Nuto Revelli's *Mai Tardi* (*Never Too Late*, 1946), a memoir of the author's experience on the Russian front. In his review of Revelli's memoir, the Communist critic Carlo Muscetta compared the brutal immediacy of some of its sequences to the effect achieved by Rossellini in some episodes of *Paisà*.[20] Giorgia Bocca's *Partigiani della montagna* (*Partisans in the Mountains*, 1945) and Roberto Battaglia's *Un uomo: un partigiano* (*A Man: A Partisan*, 1945) are among the most compelling personal accounts of partisan warfare. Bocca later went on to become one of the most well known "independent" political commentators and journalists in Italy, while Battaglia became the most important Communist historian of the Resistance, publishing his *Storia della Resistenza italiana* in 1953, a work that is still fundamental to any study of Resistance historiography in Italy. (The importance of both his and Bocca's texts for the interpretation of *The Path* will be explored in Chapters 3 and 4.) Battaglia's history was republished—in slightly revised form—in 1964, when the second edition of *The Path* was published, just prior to the twentieth anniversary of the Liberation.

In the vast output of war and Resistance diaries and *memorialistica*, a tendency to put forward a tendentious, hagiographic portrayal of the partisan movement emerges, as it does in the Resistance short story. The diary of one of the most famous Action Party political commissars of the *Giustizia e Libertà* brigades in Piedmont, Dante Livio Bianco, is a typical example of this kind of writing, in which the Resistance is presented in the Manichaean terms of a struggle between good and evil. The partisan movement signifies, according to Bianco, "a deep fracture between the world of Mussolini and Hitler, a world of barbarity and darkness, and a just and free world, the world of democracy."[21] In his preface to Bianco's text (written toward the end of 1945), the historian Franco Venturi uses the metaphor of the body politic to describe Fascism in the same tone as Bianco. Franco Venturi depicts Fascism as a disease which contaminated the Italian body politic and nearly killed it; the Resistance leaders and their followers formed the head of a new living organism, a "new creature" which was born from the will of the entire Italian people to live and regenerate. Although the Resistance was indeed violent, this violence was necessary—as a *pharmakos* or cure—to rid the body of the disease. The regeneration of the body politic, however, was not completed with the return of democracy. Despite the Liberation, Franco Venturi says, the remains of the corrupt body of Fascism were never completely buried, and "we all find ourselves looking back nostalgically on the time when divisions were clear, when the burned-down houses separated death from life, when the 'no-man's-land' was a dangerous area, but neither ambiguous nor uncertain."[22] The beginnings of the retroactive mythification of the Resistance are already clearly visible in these statements by Bianco and Franco Venturi; in the light of the present, the recent past is endowed by them with a stability that makes it the storehouse of absolute values. The phrase "the spirit of the Resistance," which is repeated ad infinitum in postwar Italian literature, *saggistica,* and historiography about the Resistance, is grounded in this Manichaean view of recent history.

Significantly, Franco Venturi's diagnostic metaphor coincides with that of the single most influential and representative Italian intellectual of the period between the two world wars: Benedetto Croce. Croce's 1927 *Storia d'Italia* presents a classic view of Fascism as a "moral disease" which suddenly contaminated a healthy body politic and led to an escalation of "irrational violence." Although Croce was the spokesman in Italy for the traditional values of liberal humanism and a resolute opponent of Marxism, his idealist theory that—because freedom and justice are the permanent aims of mankind—despotism is always a transient phase of a nation's history eminently suited the political climate of the first few years after the Liberation.[23] Notwithstanding some vigorous protests, the policy of the leftist parties during this period was one of cooperation and compromise with the more conservative parties, in the interest of a peaceful transition to a democratic state that would resemble the former Italian parliamentary system. In the eyes of moderate and conservative anti-Fascists, the Italian state—prior to Mussolini's seizure of power in 1922—had indeed been a basically healthy body politic, which Fascism had only temporarily contaminated. (The fact that, in the 1946 referendum, the monarchy was abolished by only the narrowest of margins shows—among other things—how deeply rooted this belief was in postwar Italy.) While his views on Fascism were well-known and his opposition to Mussolini universally admired, Croce never actually performed a historical analysis of Fascism itself; his 1927 *History of*

Italy covers only the period between 1871 and 1915. He deliberately refrained from writing the history of the Fascist period because—as he told the students of his Istituto Italiano per gli Studi Storici in Naples—he found that epoch morally repugnant.[24] One should oppose Fascism, Croce argued, by imitating Boethius, who in another Dark Age had sought refuge in contemplative life and scholarly endeavors.[25] Croce's moralistic vision of the aberrant "disease" of Fascism was enormously influential among Italians, far more so than is usually thought to be the case today.

After the war, with the reemergence of Marxism as not only a political ideology and a philosophy of history but also a language of Italian cultural life that deeply influenced the discourse of Marxist and non-Marxist intellectuals alike, Croce's liberal idealism slowly lost its hegemonic role. Notwithstanding the open attacks on Croce's thought by the Left and the increasing influence of Gramsci's work,[26] it proved difficult for the Italian intelligentsia to free itself from the influence of Croce's position on Fascism. The PCI, motivated by its then-current policy of collaboration and solidarity with all the "democratic forces" (whose unity was thought essential for the reconstruction of the country), must be considered largely responsible for the continued currency of what was essentially a Crocean notion of Fascism, even among the most ardently anti-Crocean intellectuals. Angelo Tasca, Antonio Gramsci, and Palmiro Togliatti had all already outlined, in the 1920's and 1930's, an analysis of Italian Fascism as an outgrowth of the Italian liberal state, explaining how Fascism was able to form a consensus from a variety of lower social strata, while serving at the same time the interests of the great northern industrialists, southern landowners, and bankers.[27] There was, in their eyes, nothing "irrational" or exceptional either in the violence of the Fascists or in the increasing transformation of the regime into a totalitarian state; contrary to Croce's view, Fascism was not a temporary moral aberration but a part of a vast class struggle. Yet even Togliatti himself, during the Resistance and after the Liberation, upheld this "moralistic" interpretation of Fascism, because it was the only interpretation which could be universally accepted by the moderate and conservative political forces with which the PCI sought to ally itself in its efforts to appear as a legitimate democratic party. If the essence of Fascism was the negation of human reason, the irrational use of violence, and the perversion of the natural moral values of man, then the Resistance could be interpreted as a struggle to restore reason and morality through an ethically justifiable use of violence. While the illusion that the Liberation had "suddenly expunged Italy's twenty-year record of tyranny"[28] and that a new Italy had been reborn like a phoenix from its own ashes was—as Franco Venturi indicates—a short-lived one, the mythic image of Fascism and the "spirit" of the Resistance locked in a mortal struggle between good and evil retained its power in the collective imaginary and permeated all levels of political and cultural discourse in Italy in the years between 1945 and 1948. Only with the ouster of the PCI from the government in May 1947, beginning a period of an open confrontation between the Right and the Left, did the Crocean vision of Fascism as a "temporary illness" begin to give way to a less mystified vision of recent Italian history.

Truth-Bound Fiction

Another kind of writing also emerged between 1945 and 1948 on the threshold between fiction and nonfiction, which may be called docufiction or "truth-bound" fiction. Pino Levi Cavaglione's *Guerriglia nei Castelli Romani* (*Guerrilla Warfare in the "Castelli Romani"*), Luciano Bolis's *Il mio granello di sabbia* (*My Grain of Sand*), and Pietro Chiodi's *Banditi* (*Bandits*) are examples of what cannot be considered a subliterary or paraliterary genre, but rather a literary subgenre.[29] These works, and others like them, all share a strictly documentary intent and are written to bear witness to the recent history of Italy and to contribute to its rebirth. However, the events they narrate retrospectively, often—as in Chiodi's case—on the basis of notes and diaries written almost at the same time in which the narrated events occurred, have an inherently dramatic quality unlike that of the postwar *memorialistica* or *saggistica*, for the reality that they report is, intrinsically, a *realtà romanzesca*. These works have, as Calvino says, "a natural capacity to stir the reader's emotions."[30]

Paradoxically, though, these writers persistently deny the fictionality of their texts: "This is neither a novel nor a fictionalized account"—Chiodi writes—"it is a historical document, in the sense that characters, events and emotions have all actually *been*." [31] This is the distinguishing mark of the entire subgenre of "truth-bound fiction."

Bolis's book, for instance, is an account of the tortures inflicted on him in prison, his attempted suicide in order not to betray his partisan comrades, and his rescue in extremis. In the prefatory note Bolis writes:

> This chronicle . . . has no literary pretensions . . . or polemical intent. The only value of this story lies, then, in the absolute authenticity of what it narrates. . . . If I have used many superlatives, that is in part justified by the inadequacy of my means of expression, and in part by an absolute desire for truth. . . . I attribute to the same desire for truth the use of the narrative first person . . . seeming to me a useless rhetorical artifice to make something that only I could have written, because only I could have known about it, appear to have been written by others. This work had precisely the task of fixing on paper those facts that time might contest with memory. . . . I . . . am aware that my sacrifice is nothing but a grain of sand in the desert, and my story only represents the endeavor and suffering of one man among the endeavors and suffering of a multitude of other men . . . the best of whom certainly are today not in a position to write stories at all.
>
> I also maintain that it is the survivors' duty to tell the story of their own "grain of sand" because even those who—because of circumstances, or their own insensitivity—were not a part of that . . . "multitude" should know what a high price, in sacrifices of blood and will, this Liberation of ours has cost. [32]

The avoidance of any "literary artifice," the moral commitment of the author to disclose to the reader an authentic reality where the individual is represented as a historical being engaged in a quest for freedom, and the very appeal to the reader's critical faculty make Bolis's work a kind of "engaged" literature in the Sartrean sense (as well as a literature of "extreme situations"). It is this sense of commitment that leads Bolis, and others, to claim nonfictional status for their writing, as if fiction were a degraded way of retelling this tale, or a "betrayal" of the real.

The anti-fictional bias of the writers of *memorialistica* reflects a naive notion of the difference between literature and history (or chronicle). Yet works such as *Banditi, Il mio granello di sabbia*, and *Guerriglia nei Castelli Romani* possess a formal unity of plot structure which makes them—in Aristotelian terms—fictions rather than chronicles, at least inasmuch as they order events within the logic of a single narrative action, rather than register them as a discontinuous series of occurrences (as a chronicle does). Calvino himself notes that the best neorealist narrators do not share this deluded belief: "[What] animated the young writers," he points out in the preface to *The Path*, "was not so much the wish to document or to inform as it was [their] desire to *express*. . . . We knew all too well that what counted was the music and not the libretto. Though we were supposed to be concerned with content, there were never more dogged formalists than we; and never were lyric poets as effusive as those objective reporters we were supposed to be" (pp. vi–vii; 8–9). In his review of *Guerriglia nei Castelli Romani*, Cesare Pavese praises Levi Cavaglione's work for its staccato narrative rhythm and for its success at conveying the adventure and the sense of freedom in the partisans' life *alla macchia*. Despite its nonfictional pretenses, Pavese notes, the text shows the sure signs of a literary style.[33] Bolis's, Chiodi's, and Levi Cavaglione's works are noteworthy because they "spontaneously" achieve a considerable level of aesthetic control of their material despite the poverty of their narrative language and the bare sequentiality of their plots. The raw material on which they are based has clearly been subjected to a process of literary mediation; the events are selected, organized, and reconfigured with a narrative logic, not merely accumulated in a heap of details and anecdotes, and are therefore not mere chronicles or histories in the Aristotelian sense. Rather, they are truth-bound narratives whose "low"—but tangible—degree of fictionality coincides with their subjective organization (perspective, focus, selection, and linking of specific events). The fictionality of such works is, like that of traditional narrative historiography, limited by the constraints of available evidence, which in this case coincides with the *histor'*s own recollections and with the material gathered directly from other eyewitnesses.

In this subgenre, unlike the partisan short story, we find no tendency to portray the Resistance in moralistic or idealized terms. Pavese points out that Levi Cavaglione's *Guerriglia* "does not preach, does not try to teach lessons of history or heroism" (p. 242). The perlocutionary force of the fictional text, in other words, resides entirely in the "realistic" emplotment of events, so that the "inner life" of the narrative "I" is correspondingly "reduced to a minimum," and no analysis or explanation is offered to the reader as a comment on the action as it unfolds (p. 242). In *The Path*, Calvino recaptures the tone of immediacy and spontaneity of this truth-bound fiction, even though his emplotment of history is based on a far more elaborate deployment of the strategies of literary fiction.

Chronicle Versus History

The Terms of a Debate and a Narrative Practice

The editors of one of the most significant cultural journals to emerge after the Liberation, *Società*, consistently argued that the task of the postwar writer in Italy was to chronicle the experiences of individuals who lived through the war and the Resistance and to put forward a theory to accompany that practice of writing. Funded in Florence between 1945 and 1946 by a group of politically "moderate" intellectuals, including the novelist Romano Bilenchi, *Società* regularly published eyewitness accounts and documentary notes in a series entitled *Documenti* (edited by Bilenchi), organized by general thematic categories such as "Florence During the Occupation," "Italians in Yugoslavia," and "Prisoners and Refugees." [34] The journal opted, unlike *Rinascita* and *Il Politecnico*, for a documentary reevocation of the recent past, intended to be free of all ideological and political colorings; the facts themselves would speak eloquently through the voices of those who had experienced history.

The uncertain political and cultural situation of the immediate postwar period, *Società* contended, allowed for no clear-cut interpretive agenda. Instead, the only possible option for the Italian intelligentsia was to explore tentatively all interpretive possibilities, based on the factual reconstruction of the recent past; hence the need to be "chroniclers" who believed in the primacy of the historical real but were politically uncommitted. *Società's* notion of postwar literature was therefore fundamentally opposed to the "literature of extreme situations" advocated by Sartre and to the Sartrean view of engagement in general. Implicitly, it was also opposed to the kind of epic realism advocated by Lukács as the paradigm of all authentic narrative. To narrate, for the *Società* group, meant to *chronicle* a sheer continuum of facts and events, a narrative mode that Lukács condemns as shallow and uncritical and that Sartre and Calvino stigmatize as a kind of "simple description" that avoids the historical necessity of judging the present in the name of the future.

"Necessità di una cronaca" ("The Necessity of a Chronicle") is the title of a key editorial by Gianfranco Piazzesi, published in the third issue of *Società*:

A chronicle is necessary for this reason: the immediate evidence of facts has always frightened historians and artists, because they cannot yet have that sense of distance which is necessary, as it were, in order to see things. But a chronicle—this nearly-forgotten narrative genre—is still possible, and *socially* speaking, has an unforeseeable importance: for it means to narrate facts, to yield oneself up to the violence that today they do to us, with that indispensable reserve that the chronicler must have if he is to respect them completely, or rather, to eliminate any alteration that may have deformed the event in the excited memory of witnesses.[35]

From this perspective, the work of recording the recent past in a chronicle means first and foremost a documentary reconstruction by "gathering" evidence, thus making the chronicle a necessary preliminary step in the work of both the historian and the narrator of the real. An interpretive reconfiguration of the real in narrative form can only be attempted after an objective and thorough exposition of all known facts and events, which must be carefully purged of any subjective viewpoint that may have "deformed" them. Eyewitness acounts are, therefore, not entirely reliable; the truth in what they relate must be carefully filtered out of them and separated from the passions and partisan judgments of individuals.

Behind *Società's* theory of the chronicle looms, once again, the shadow of Croce. For the latter, historiography— no less than art—is a kind of knowledge of the real in its concrete particularity, but history cannot begin to be narrated until the sifting of documents and evidence has been completed. The only epistemological basis for historiography is a solid empiricism (or, as in Ranke's motto, "wie es eigentlich war"), but since its aim is the clear and accurate representation of the real, historiography must be purged of all ideological and political bias. Only a chronicle is possible, according to Croce, until the historian has been able to gain a serene perspective of the whole by disentangling himself from any moral, political, or ideological concern, that is, from any passion that may contaminate the neutrality of his analysis. Although a history of the immediate past is, in principle, not impossible, the difficulty of transcending all emotion and belief that might prevent the historian from grasping the overall coherence and necessity of events renders such a history an extremely problematic project at best. As already pointed out, Croce did not write the history of Italian Fascism because, he claimed, Fascism itself was morally repugnant to him, and he could not free himself from this bias, making proper historical judgment impossible. The historian must be able to grasp the real in its necessary positivity, since human history is and must be represented as something beyond good and evil: "What matter to the historian blows received and given, shouts raised, outcry of mutual accusations? He sees emerging out of these conflicts the lines of a new political, social, and moral formation, of a new institution with which reality was pregnant, and that this could be brought into the world only by means of this laborious process. All those who, in whatever manner, took part in it, gentlemen and scum, intelligent and stupid, the historian recognizes as positively and negatively (and in the last analysis, always positively) necessary."[36] To acquire the proper perspective on a historical epoch and to discern its narratable order, the historian must, like the artist, contemplate the real dispassionately. History is therefore, like art, utterly "disinterested"; it is a cathartic knowledge of the real, Croce concludes. Art and history differ only insofar as art is the intuition of the possible, while history is the intuition of the actual. But no such intuition is possible, he concludes, unless historian and artist alike raise themselves above the chaos of contemporary strife.

This Crocean perspective on both history and art lies behind the position of the *Società* group, who believed that the trauma of the war had created such a "crisis" in individual consciousness that the serenity necessary for the writing of "true" history and literature was no longer possible to attain in Italy. Hence the need for the chronicle, which would take upon itself the task of representing the real, but only in the form of a "low" mimetic literature, compromised with what Croce calls the field of the practical and the immediate (and its contradictions). It would be, in other words, a provisional and transitional literature, or, in other words, a *letteratura d'occasione*, devoid of any claim to "universality" and, most of all, to either a total synthesis of the historical past or a prophetic forecast of the future: "We say these words without shame because, in this case, they signify a particular moment, in which only 'occasions' make some sense, and culture is inevitably improvised on the basis of fortuitous and unforeseen events."[37] As a mode of literary narration, however, the chronicle is not just a record of the random order of events, because the latter must be disposed in such a way as to make them "come alive." The literariness of the chronicle consists in "respecting the facts while simultaneously setting them in a particular space and time capable of giving them life," writes Piazzesi, "and it seems to me . . . that the similarity with film montage is more than just a chance analogy."[38] Much of neorealist narrative adopts this stance toward the *dispositio* of the raw material of history. Cesare Zavattini and Vittorio De Sica, whose teamwork produced some of the most important neorealist films, subscribed—at least in theory—to a "poetics of the chronicle."[39] Zavattini later became, indeed, the most radical theoretician of an objective presentation of real events as the only true basis for a neorealist cinema, distancing himself from the more poetically (and politically) inclined De Sica and rejecting the idea of traditional narration altogether as a falsification of the real.[40]

Il Politecnico, the journal founded by Vittorini in 1945, also published documents, eyewitness accounts, and chronicles similar to those that appeared in *Società*. Among them was Vasco Pratolini's "Cronache fiorentine 20$_0$ Sec." ("Florentine Chronicles of the Twentieth Century"), which attempted to reconstruct the customs and beliefs of the Florentines through a series of loosely connected anecdotes and scenes taken from everyday life. Pratolini's text refers specifically to the medieval and Renaissance tradition of Florentine chronicles, those lively accounts of the daily life of the city written by ordinary citizens and merchants who often turned out to be colorful and insightful narrators. There is, according to Pratolini, a Florentine "nature" which can emerge only in the chronicle form itself: "It is a people forged by an experience of sacrifice and betrayal over the centuries. Its chronicles register a sequence of personal facts, women's quarrels, rivalries between *quartieri* and parties which engage the Universe: the *Divine Comedy* is the private invective of an exile against the dominating faction."[41] In order to understand why Florence was one of the cities in Italy that most strongly supported Fascism and later become one of its most courageous opponents, Pratolini argues, traditional methods of historical inquiry are not enough. "Marxist analysis is good only to a point. . . . It is always to the human origin of things that we must return" (p. 286). For Pratolini, as for the *Società* group, the chronicle discloses the underside of history by focusing on what Fernand Braudel called in 1949 "a history of gentle rhythms, of groups and groupings" rather than on the *histoire événementielle* with its "surface disturbance, the waves stirred up by the powerful movements of the tides."[42]

Pratolini goes one step further than the *Società* group, however, by putting into practice a kind of writing that incorporates the chronicle into the more conventional historical novel. *Cronache di poveri amanti* is, in this sense, the best example of Pratolini's interest in representing "a history of gentle rhythms, of groups and groupings." It studies the daily life of a social microcosm, focusing on traditional patterns of behavior and ritual and the values and sentiments of individuals, with the aim of showing how the dramatic events of the Fascist rise to power are refracted at the level of the day-to-day interaction between the members of the community. A considerable amount of neorealist narrative is in this vein. De Sica's *Sciuscià*, *Bicycle Thieves*, and *Umberto D*, for instance, although they deal with the Recon-

struction rather than with Fascism, are studies in the trauma of
the war and its aftermath, as seen through events in the daily
lives of the poor and the down-and-out in Rome (in one episode
in *Bicycle Thieves*, we see the riot squad dispatched from a police
station to quell a demonstration that De Sica never shows us;
historical events—"the powerful movements of the tides"—are
always elsewhere and always unavailable to the camera and to
the spectator alike).

In an article published in 1948, the year after *Cronache di poveri
amanti* first appeared, Pratolini stressed the "elective affinity"
between the narrative strategy of the novel-as-chronicle and that
of neorealist cinema, pointing out that film could provide an
"unadorned chronicle" of the quotidian but is endowed with a
direct spatiotemporal immediacy that the novel could achieve
only indirectly, through the mediation of words and the "complicity" of the reader's imagination.[43] Pratolini was an enthusiast
of the neorealist cinema; he had collaborated with Rossellini on
the screenplay for *Paisà* and later worked as both a *soggettista*
and scriptwriter on—among other films—Visconti's *Rocco e i
suoi fratelli* (*Rocco and His Brothers*, 1960). Although in his novel
Pratolini employs the traditional device of the omniscient narrator, much like Manzoni does, his characters are mostly portrayed from the outside, through brief notations on their physical appearances and gestures on which the eye of the narrator
pauses briefly, like the eye of De Sica's camera in *Bicycle Thieves*
and *Umberto D.*[44] This incorporation into the narrative of descriptive details that are inessential to the coherence of the narrative
plot and whose only function is to signify the real—what Barthes
refers to as the "reality effect"—is common to both Pratolini and
De Sica, as is the use of dialects and regional variants of spoken
Italian, which is one of the characteristic stylistic features of all
neorealist narrative chronicles. Dialect is, however, almost never
"unfiltered" in neorealism; not even De Sica's little Bruno speaks
a "real" *romanesco* in *Bicycle Thieves* (and neorealist films on
the whole rarely if ever use "live" sound, preferring to dub
the dialogue in a studio; for instance, the voice of Lamberto
Maggiorani—who plays the unforgettable protagonist, Antonio
Ricci—is that of a professional actor who could speak a more

comprehensible mixture of Italian and Roman dialect). The dialect and vernacular expressions which are interspersed in otherwise standard colloquial Italian dialogues in neorealist works
have the same "reality effect" of the inessential detail; they
"connote" the linguistic reality of the characters and their social
status. There is one notable exception to this general rule: Visconti's *La terra trema* was originally shot entirely in Sicilian dialect, and a voice-over commentary was added to summarize and
explain the action in Italian; later, Italian subtitles were added to
the film for mainland audiences.[45]

•

Although it gave ample space to *memorialistica*, neorealist docufiction, partisan short stories, and literary *cronache, Il Politecnico*
embarked from the very beginning on a critique of these modes
of writing, attempting to chart a new and different itinerary for
the development of cultural and literary discourse in Italy. A
short editorial published in May 1946 indirectly criticized the *Società* group in this regard: "Writers who today express themselves as they did during Fascism, 'who write as they did then,'
are to be pitied and avoided, to say the least."[46] *Società* replied
shortly thereafter by pointing out that a writer simply could not
change his mode of writing from one day to the next, no matter
what the "new contents" and new realities presented by the historical situation were.[47] No one in Italy knew better than Vittorini, however, that literature has its own memory and its own
rhythm of development, and it was precisely his sense of the
relative aesthetic autonomy of literature which led him in turn to
oppose the increasing pressures for an openly politicized realism in art which came from the PCI and its most important journal, *Rinascita*. Vittorini fought his own personal battle on two related fronts; on the one hand, he argued against the "neutrality"
of the chroniclers and, on the other hand, against the propagandistic tendencies of party literature. The general philosophy of *Il
Politecnico* was that literature and culture should participate in
the general movement for the renewal of Italian society, but in
an indirect way; culture and literature, for Vittorini, obey their

own internal dynamics and should not be directly involved in party politics. The political function of literature would be to reflect the struggle for a new society undertaken by the masses and their parties but not to intervene openly in that process.[48]

The "horizon of expectations" of *Il Politecnico's* readership was oriented, though, toward a literature that would address the facts and issues of the immediate political and historical context—a literature at once "true" to life and to the collective experience of recent history. In prefacing a short narrative piece (in the February 23, 1946, issue) entitled "Fear at Dawn," by and about a Neopolitan factory worker (Giuseppe Grieco), Vittorini states that this kind of writing has only the value of a chronicle and no intrinsic aesthetic interest. The preface provoked a flood of protest letters attributing to Grieco's text the value of "social art, the only kind of art we should have today."[49] In replying to the readers' letters, Franco Fortini points out that "those readers who prefer the immediacy of documents have found in *Il Politecnico* a journal that has acknowledged the historical importance of these documents. . . . But they remain indeed documents; they are not works of art."[50] In yet another reply to readers' letters which either blamed or praised *Il Politecnico* for not endorsing the PCI, Vittorini draws a distinction between the politics of literature and party politics. He begins with an act of rhetorical *captatio benevolentiae* by confirming his personal adherence to the PCI political positions and acknowledging the flexibility and openness of the party's cultural policy. Those intellectuals who, like Arthur Koestler, have left the Communist Party have committed not only a political mistake, Vittorini argues, but have also betrayed their role as "men of culture." But Vittorini goes on to state that while party politics operate on the immediate level of what is to be done now (the level of the chronicle), culture and literature search for a truth that cannot be compromised by tactical or strategic needs of the present historical moment.

Vittorini's faith in the possibility of remaining an active member of the PCI while at the same time pursuing a literary career free of all compromises with the Party's strategic needs sharply contrasts Sartre's views in this regard (and his own withdrawal from the "public scene" after 1947 confirms the accuracy of Sartre's diagnosis). Vittorini's postwar opposition between politics as chronicle and literature as prophecy was not at all a new one for him; as early as 1931, he had drawn the same distinction in reference to the literature of socialist realism in the Soviet Union.[51] At about the same time, Vittorini had acknowledged the modernists Proust, Valéry, and Svevo as the source of his inspiration as a writer.[52] It was a poetic genealogy that he would never disown, and its traces are visible in all his works, including *Uomini e no.* While *Uomini e no* does indeed "indulge" in the chronicle of Vittorini's actual experiences as a partisan, it is also a novel in which his Proustian recollection of childhood plays an important role, as does his typically Proustian use of discontinuous narrative time. *Uomini e no* is a unique example of "modernist" neorealism in this respect, but what makes *Uomini e no* a work bearing Vittorini's unmistakable signature is the prophetic tension and quasi-Biblical, allegorical tone of some of its passages. In its prophetic stance, *Uomini e no* aims at a total transcendence not only of politics as chronicle but also of history itself. No less than in Vittorini's masterpiece *Conversazione in Sicilia* (*Conversation in Sicily*, 1941), Fascism is a manifestation of absolute evil in *Uomini e no,* and its victims are a metaphor for all those who are victimized by evil in the world (suffering is what makes man human, and the infliction of suffering is what makes them inhuman). The chief defect in the chronicle as a literary strategy, for Vittorini, is its constitutive lack of this tension towards a totalizing synthesis of mankind's destiny.

The most interesting critique in the postwar period in Italy of the poetics of the chronicle, however, is found in an article by Franco Calamandrei, published by *Il Politecnico* in March 1946, entitled "Narrativa vince cronaca" ("Narrative Wins Out over Chronicle"). Calamandrei argues that the chronicle is filled with the innumerable threads of individual stories, which constantly overlap and become entangled with one another. Individual characters are caught in a maze of intersecting facts and events, so that it is impossible to distinguish what in their existence depends on their individual inclinations or choices and what depends on something else; the characters have no clear sense of their individual responsibility and wander aimlessly with no definite sense of purpose. "Real" narrative, on the contrary, extracts an order from this maze and reconstructs the logic of each character's itinerary, freeing it from digressions, inessential details, dead ends, deceptions, and even "lies."[53] Controlled by the narrator, stories recuperate their "truth," Calamandrei contends, for they show human beings at the crucial moments of their existence, which are inevitably moments of choice (which, as Aristotle notes in the *Poetics*, always reveal character). This narrative mode sets an itinerary for the characters that shapes their existence and propels it forward in time. The "illusion of time," but of a time freed from the chaos of the chronicle, is the achievement of the great realists; Calamandrei offers a critique of the *cronaca* as a mode of narration on the grounds that, however accurate and close to the real it may be, the chronicle fails to provide the reader with a symbolic model through which to understand history as essentially man-made and thus rooted in human choice and action. Calamandrei therefore proposes a mode of narrative realism along the same lines as Lukács's and Sartre's respective theories, without, however, prescribing what shape narrative time should take in its imaginative emplotment. As examples of great realists he cites, together with Manzoni and Verga, Proust and Conrad.[54] Thus, although he offers no specific formula for the production of the plot, Calamandrei—like Calvino—sees in plot itself the principal ordering force of those meanings that the writer (novelist or historian or both) seeks to extract from the experience of temporality.[55] Conrad's fiction, with its reliance on and (at the same time) suspicion of the ordering and organizing power of traditional nineteenth-century plots,[56] is indeed one of Calvino's discursive models in *The Path*.

The Resistance to Modernism: Il Politecnico, Rinascita

In its short life between September 1945 and December 1947, *Il Politecnico* launched a campaign to open up Italian culture in what Gramsci would have called a "cosmopolitan" rather than "national-popular" direction, publishing articles, debates, and interviews on major European trends in psychoanalysis, exis-

tentialism, and modernist literature. Translations of literary texts
by T. S. Eliot, Auden, Brecht, Eluard, and Malraux appeared together with reproductions of works by Grosz, Man Ray, Max
Ernst, and Picasso and essays by Brecht, Sartre, and Lukács
(among many others); Hemingway's *For Whom the Bell Tolls* (1940)
was published in installments. Cut off (culturally speaking) from
the rest of Europe during the 21-year Fascist interregnum, Italian intellectuals were anxious to rediscover what had been denied to them during that period. On the whole, the policy of *Il
Politecnico* was to be extremely eclectic, tending on the one hand
towards "high culture" and on the other hand towards popularization (*divulgazione*). Elementary introductions to the work
of contemporary thinkers and writers appeared side-by-side
with in-depth analyses of important theoretical and literary problems. Considerable space was devoted to poetry by Montale,
Umberto Saba, Alfonso Gatto, Vittorio Sereni, and Fortini himself, among others, along with more "readerly" narratives. Yet
this eclecticism and this two-pronged editorial policy mark the
limits of *Il Politecnico*'s direct political commitment as well.

Chiefly because of Franco Fortini's influence, the journal devoted considerable attention to symbolist and surrealist poetry
(both vehemently attacked by Sartre in *What Is Literature?*). Fortini's view of modern and modernist literature resembles that of
Bloch and Adorno. The formal harmony of the literary artifact,
he repeatedly argues, is implicitly a message of freedom, a kind
of utopian figure which is symbolically set against the alienation
of the modern historical condition. Fortini finds positive political value even in the poetry of the hermetic Italian tradition (he
cites Ungaretti and Montale as examples).[57]

Fortini's essay on Kafka, published only two months before *Il
Politecnico* closed down, is in effect a defense of Kafka against his
Marxist critics. Kafka, Fortini argues, is a revolutionary writer
not only because of his modernist style, but also because his
work exposes—and criticizes—the reification of human relations in the modern world. Kafka is neither a "symptom" of the
utter isolation of bourgeois intellectuals from the concrete reality
of history nor a nihilist. Like Sartre, who in *What Is Literature?*
writes that through Kafka "we recognize history and ourselves

in history" as in a "trial perpetually in session" (p. 227), Fortini argues that Kafka's work possesses—in its analysis of the alienation of the modern subject—a lucidity and rigor comparable to certain passages in *The German Ideology*. But "the innumerable figurations of this degradation would be impossible without the myth of freedom, emancipation, and resurrection. Paradox and absurdity are not the last words of Kafka's world, which is rigorously coherent and self-enclosed but seen with the remote eye of grace and liberation."[58] This is the point of contact between Kafka and the vision that the revolutionary must have in the modern world. Contrary to Sartre, Fortini points to the figural, evocative, and visionary power of literary discourse, rather than to its literal meaning, as the source of literature's commitment: Kafka as a writer in his text "expresses something *other* than what he seems to say" ("Capoversi su Kafka," p. 16). Kafka's texts reveal to readers something that his own characters are unable to see, namely that "every man, thing or act is the sign of something else, a revelation of the other" ("Capoversi su Kafka," p. 17). To illustrate this notion of the dislocation of meaning in a visionary sense, that pointing to "the total liberation of man," Fortini refers to Sartre's existentialist psychoanalysis which (as Sartre says in *Being and Nothingness*) recognizes nothing before the original upsurge of human freedom.

In Fortini's essay, as in Sartre's own postwar writing, we can see an attempt to integrate the codes of existentialism, psychoanalysis, and Marxism. Yet the resistance to such an integration in Italy, caused by the increasing hegemony of the PCI's "orthodox" version of Marx, is visible on the very pages of *Il Politecnico*. In his famous letter to Vittorini, published in the September-December 1946 issue, Palmiro Togliatti launches his first attack against *Il Politecnico*, echoing a previous *Rinascita* editorial by Mario Alicata which vehemently criticized the cosmopolitanism of Vittorini's journal, particularly the space allotted to a "decadent" and "useless" writer like Hemingway.[59] Togliatti rejects Vittorini's distinction between the politics of culture and party politics, arguing that *Il Politecnico*'s "abstract and superficial" search for the aesthetically new and different is objectively a choice against the PCI's policies. In his reply, Vittorini points once again to the revolutionary potential inherent in the so-called "literature of crisis" of modernist and avant-garde writers. The ability of aesthetic discourse to explore cognitive possibilities in human experience that are either marginalized or ignored in political discourse gives literature its revolutionary power as a critique of the modern historical experience.[60] Yet Vittorini and the other members of the *Il Politecnico* group clearly find themselves caught up in a dilemma from which there is no easy way out. In the issue following Vittorini's impassioned defense of the literature of crisis, an article by Fabrizio Onofri (a militant PCI intellectual) reiterates Togliatti's litany of accusations against decadent art, using arguments homologous to Lukács's (even though Onofri cites Gramsci as his only authority). Sartre in particular, Onofri argues, is a "dangerous" writer, since he appropriates and falsifies the discourse of Marxism.[61] In a review of *Uomini e no* published in *L'Unità*, Onofri severely criticizes Vittorini's novel as "the book of an intellectual with all the flaws and contradictions of the society in which he has lived, a society in which culture is the privilege of a few, and itself an instrument of discrimination."[62] Togliatti felt compelled to write Vittorini a letter of disavowal, praising *Uomini e no* as a work of art that is deeply moving in its representation of a drama involving not only a solitary individual but also humankind as a whole.[63] Paolo Spriano, the Italian historian who recently unearthed and published Togliatti's letter, doubts Togliatti's sincerity and attributes its motivation to Togliatti's desire to gather the support of intellectuals in that early period of postwar "democratic" hopes. In 1951, Spriano points out, Togliatti published in *Rinascita* a fierce critique of Vittorini, referring to *Uomini e no* as a "debatable book, for its morbid need to present the heroes of that struggle through a turgid literary disguise, when they were, instead, clear and simple men."[64]

Rinascita began to introduce Gramsci's work and to publish extracts from his *Letters* and *Prison Notebooks* as early as 1944, while embarking on a campaign against all literary avant-gardes and even against those Italian critics who, like Francesco Flora, undertook a serious critical analysis of surrealist and hermetic poetry and contemporary poetry in general.[65] *Rinascita* called for a socially and politically committed "national-popular" literature, defining writers like Valéry as "useless" in contrast to truly committed ones like Romain Rolland. Between 1944 and 1947 *Rinascita* also regularly published profiles of "Martyrs" of the Resistance, war *memorialistica*, and docufiction, as well as neorealist short stories about the Resistance and the war. The famous "last letter" of Giaime Pintor, the young literary critic who was killed by a bomb while on his way to join the partisans (after having fought with the British army in the south of Italy), was published in June 1946, followed by a profile written by his brother in March 1947. Giaime Pintor became the symbol of what a truly committed intellectual should be, and his last letter served as a kind of manifesto of Resistance rhetoric: "Musicians and writers, we must all today renounce our privileges and contribute to everyone's liberation. . . . Today the possibilities of the Risorgimento are open once again for the Italian people: no gesture is aimless, as long as it is not an end in itself."[66]

The Ideology of Form in Neorealist Fiction and Film: Brena and Rossellini

Neorealism, between 1945 and 1948, reflects the tensions and contradictions in the debate between *Il Politecnico*, *Rinascita*, and *Società*, as well as the difficulty involved in translating the various "voices of the real" into a literary style. As Calvino recalls in the preface to *The Path*, the historical events of the recent past, the oral and written tradition of storytelling, and the whole repertoire of themes and images which emerged from the experience of the war were still only "raw material" for postwar Italian narrators: "But the secret of how one wrote then did not lie only in this elementary universality of content. . . . On the contrary, it had never been so clear that the stories were raw material. . . . Characters, landscapes, shooting, political slogans, jargon, curses, lyric flights, weapons, and love-making were only colors on the palette, notes of the scale. . . . To us the whole problem was one of poetics; how to transform into a literary work that world which for us was *the* world" (pp. vi–vii; 8–9). Calvino's words confirm that, in their quest for new forms, neorealist narrators sought to find new ways of disclosing the nature of the real by estranging the familiar conventions of narrative realism. While Pavese, Vittorini, Fenoglio, and Calvino, each in his own way, concentrated on a renewal of narrative forms through a creative dialogue with the tradition and with contemporary European culture, others fell captive to their "raw material" and remained imprisoned within conventional form.

As "raw material," Resistance writing, *memorialistica*, docufiction, and truth-bound fiction proved to be both a source of inspiration and a "trap" not only for neorealist writers but for filmmakers as well. The scenes of torture at Gestapo headquarters in *Roma città aperta* are comparable in their intensity and power to Bolis's description of his experience in the Fascist prison in *Il mio granello di sabbia*. The rapid narrative pace of *Guerriglia nei Castelli Romani*, with its tone of adventurous romance, reemerges in Giorgio Ferrari's 1947 film *Pian delle stelle*, which is about the partisans' life in the mountains (the only postwar film devoted to this theme). As has already been pointed out, Resistance writing, *memorialistica*, docufiction, and truth-bound fiction are thematic and linguistic models above all for the short fiction of Venturi, Del Boca, and Micheli. These writers' "undoing" of literary Italian syntax, their use of nominal style and parataxis, the large space that they devote to dialogue as a direct mimesis of the real, and the incorporation of dialects and vernacular expressions are directly derived from these models. The latter, however, are also the source of a series of stylistic and ideological traits which neorealist fiction and film often tend to incorporate uncritically. Chief among these traits is the assumption that personal experience can somehow be seen as "exemplary" and endowed with a universal relevance. But the spontaneous autobiographical mode of works such as Del Boca's *Dentro mi è nato l'uomo* (*The Man Within Me Has Been Born*) makes them of purely documentary interest. Notwithstanding their sincerity, these narratives lack aesthetic verisimilitude in the Aristotelian sense of a coherent emplotment of events. Neorealist novels about the war and the Resistance such as Arrigo Benedetti's *Paura all'alba* (*Fear at Dawn*), Oreste Del Buono's *La parte difficile* (*The Difficult Part*), and Giuseppe Berto's *Il cielo è rosso* (*The Sky Is Red*) are all in varying degrees fragmented by a "rhetoric of facts" and of autobiographical confession.[67]

The neorealist tendency to narrate by non-integrated episodes and scenes can also be traced back to the influence of Resistance writing. Corollary to this lack of aesthetic motivation is the implicit assumption of the fixedness and stability of the "self," which acts as both protagonist and narrator, and of history itself, which is taken to be the unproblematic referential horizon of the narrative. As Carlo Emilio Gadda observes with regard to neorealist "mannerism," "No expectancy or mystery emanates from the crudely objectivist chain-sequences of neorealist narrative chronicles. . . . Each fact, each scene . . . is like a rosary bead, with all the beads juxtaposed on the same level of expression. Facts are enumerated as part of a series, joined to each other by 'asyndeton.' They are not coordinated with a consequentiality capable of motivating them more deeply, to dispose them in an architectural form, which is the form they really had. . . . The neorealist poetics generates a fragmentary, a-structural kind of narration."[68]

The best examples of this neorealist conventional "mannerism" may be found in the works of the *minori*, texts today all but forgotten but nevertheless invaluable for any reconstruction of the generic traits of the neorealist narrative code. Stefano Brena's *Bandengebiet* is typical in this respect. A series of "authentic" scenes and episodes of partisan warfare are presented in fictionalized form through the eyes of an imaginary alter ego of the author, Sandro, a "young man like any other." The novel is not only, says the author in the preface, a "storia di formazione" (a "story of formation," that is, a *Bildungsroman*) but also a "fragment of everyone's life." Sandro is presented as the partisan Everyman and the novel as an attempt to make known the "authentic partisan epic."[69] The novel tells of Sandro's increasing involvement in the partisan units near Turin, through a series of scenes and episodes recounted partly through the pages of Sandro's diary and partly through an omniscient third-person narrator. The only connection among the various scenes is provided by punctual references to historical dates and events: July

25, September 8, and April 25 are the major temporal junctures coordinating Sandro's story, which is interrupted at various points to clarify the historical background. Historical events, Sandro's adventures as a partisan, and his idyll with a young partisan named Lisa are all presented as following the same ascending parabola towards a single happy ending, but the three story lines never intersect at the level of either structure or language and appear as a pastiche of literary codes. Brena's hagiographic treatment of the Resistance is also typical of neorealist "mannerism," using capital letters to emphasize certain concepts ("Destiny," "Faith," "Freedom"), referring repeatedly to the Resistance as a new Risorgimento, and setting up a Manichaean opposition between Resistance fighters and the Fascists as a conflict of absolute good versus absolute evil.

Furthermore, and perhaps even more tellingly, no particular political interpretation of the Resistance is provided by Brena. Sandro is a young Catholic physician with generic "socialist" feelings, and the Resistance for him means above all the liberation of the fatherland—*La Patria*—from the foreigners and from Fascist oppression. Brena's neorealist representation of the Resistance reflects most of all the conventional image of the Resistance itself found in contemporary nonfictional writing. Throughout the early postwar years, Resistance hagiography could be found everywhere in Italian newspapers, and even the first full-length history of the Resistance, Luigi Longo's *Un popolo alla macchia*, portrays it as a holy war of patriots and humanitarians of all political persuasions against the inhuman barbarism of the Fascists and Nazis.[70]

Even in the works of the acknowledged "masters" of neorealism, such a conventional representation of the war and of the Resistance figures prominently. Rossellini's war trilogy of films (*Rome Open City, Paisan,* and *Germany—Year Zero*) is perhaps the most obvious example of this tendency toward stereotypes. *Rome Open City* is in many ways a formally innovative, even radical film; breaking away from the conventions of "white-telephone" Fascist-era Italian cinema, Rossellini achieved an effect of immediacy—despite his extensive use of melodramatic devices—by limiting studio sets and costumes to a minimum and shooting with fast stock on location, where the ravages of the war were still visible.[71] Rossellini, a Catholic intellectual who had lived through the German occupation of Rome, opposed Fascism at an existential, apolitical level, as did many other Italians at the time. In few other neorealist works is the Resistance portrayed in a more sanctifying light than in *Rome Open City* and, of course, it is to this conventionality that the film's success with the public both in Italy and abroad may to a large degree be attributed. Men, women, and children of all walks of life and convictions are represented as taking part in a unanimous defense of human dignity against the degenerate Nazis and Fascists, who are portrayed as sadists, sexual deviants, and drug addicts. At the level of its *fabula*, *Rome Open City* is somewhat reminiscent of Manzoni's *The Betrothed* (much admired by Lukács): a man and a woman (both lower-class) about to be married are torn apart by the foreign forces of oppression. Although Rossellini's film is set in the mode of tragedy rather than romance, the story of Pina (Anna Magnani) and Francesco (F. Grand-Jacquet) is, like the story of Lucia and Renzo, meant to be a metaphor for the plight of the entire Italian nation. The war and its miseries are explicitly compared by the priest, Don Pietro, to a plague that has been visited on Italy: "Are we sure we didn't deserve this plague? Are we sure we have always lived according to the Lord's laws?" Don Pietro's words echo Padre Cristoforo's allusion to the plague as a manifestation of divine justice in *The Betrothed*, during his dialogue with Renzo in the Milan *lazzaretto*. Likewise, in Rossellini's film the hagiographic interpretation of the Resistance clearly assumes religious overtones. Manfredi (Marcello Pagliero) is an archetypal Resistance hero whose martyrdom also makes him a Christ figure. Although Francesco survives, presumably to carry on the struggle, Rossellini's overall vision of the war is that of a tragic conflict between good and evil in which the heroes are victims whose sacrifice will bring about a final catharsis. The final sequence is an image of innocence and hope: a group of children (always a privileged theme in neorealism, since they represent a new and unfallen world) walk off together from the site of Don Pietro's execution, whistling a partisan song, while Rome, with the prominent silhouette of the

Manfredi as a Christ figure in *Rome Open City*. Photo courtesy of Cineteca Nazionale, Rome.

dome of St. Peter's at its center, is visible in the background behind them.

The second film of Rossellini's war trilogy, *Paisà*, is in most respects a veritable summa of the narrative poetics of the first phase of Italian neorealism. *Paisà*, divided into six episodes, tells the epic tale of the Liberation from the Allied landing in Sicily in July 1943 to the last heroic efforts of the partisans in the North prior to the end of the fighting in the spring of 1945. Rossellini presents six "typical" stories whose protagonists are individuals from all social strata and are from all parts of the Italian peninsula.

The neorealist chronotope emerges in *Paisà* in paradigmatic form; the time and space of the war are represented as one and the same with the time and space of individual life-sequences; historical events are interwoven with private events, and history itself appears as a unified master-narrative in which the mini-narratives of each episode are inserted as so many sequences of the same plot leading to the Liberation. (Rossellini's repeated use of a map charting the northward movement of the Allied forces, as a means of bridging the gap between one episode and the next, emphasizes this point.) The six episodes follow each other, then, in a sequential order of time and space; the narrative moves forward into time while taking the viewer from south to north up the Italian peninsula with the war itself, with stops in Sicily, Naples, Rome, Florence, the Apennines near Bologna, and finally in the delta of the Po river. Each of the episodes is self-contained from a narrative standpoint, but all are linked by the same collective chronotope. *Paisà* fully displays the neorealist tendency to narrate by juxtaposing scenes and sequences without an "architectural" structure (as Gadda points out), relying on the "natural" sequential order of real historical time. Unlike most partisan stories, *memorialistica*, and neorealist docufiction, however, *Paisà* does not limit itself to relying implicitly on the order of real historical time. This order is, on the contrary, made explicit through the use of newsreel footage to introduce each episode, while a voice-over has the function of scanning the rhythm of the historical narrative structure. The stock documentary shots and the speaker's commentary insert each episode in its proper historical frame: the landing of the Allies in Sicily, the September 8 armistice, the retreat of Kesselring's troops from Rome, the arrival of the American troops on June 4, 1944, and so forth.

The device of inserting real historical documents into a work of fiction in order to enhance its historical verisimilitude is not new; Manzoni's novel is once again the archetype behind Rossellini's work. (It is perhaps not entirely coincidental that Rossellini, like Manzoni, ended up devoting himself almost entirely to historical research in the last years of his life, abandoning commercial filmmaking and directing a long series of historical documentaries and docufiction for television.) Rossellini, like Manzoni, focuses on the impact of great historical events on the lives of common people and brings them as protagonists onto the stage of his historical narrative, but *Paisà* lacks the critical irony of Manzoni's novel and the grasp of the social and economic power conflicts which earned *I promessi sposi* Lukács's as well as Calvino's admiration.[72] Rossellini's *pietas*, his compassionate vi-

Paisà, the last episode. Photo courtesy of Cineteca Nazionale, Rome.

sion of human suffering, resembles more Edmondo De Amicis's sentimental paternalism than Manzoni's lucid political vision of the lower classes' struggle to survive. As Calvino points out, what makes *I promessi sposi* a great political novel, despite its decidedly anti-political vision of history as the product of a providential design, is Manzoni's rejection of religion as a power through which the conflicts of the social and historical world may be transcended. Precisely this transcendental vision, on the contrary, emerges as the key to Rossellini's worldview in the fifth episode of *Paisà* (scripted by Federico Fellini), which takes place in an isolated monastery in the Apennines somewhere near the Gothic line. The innocent faith of the monks in their mountain retreat is presented as the only possible way to transcend the tragedy of history and to recover "the peace of mind lost in the horror and the trials of the war."[73] Although there is a good deal of irony in this episode, the purely meditative life of the monks nonetheless appears as an ideal mode of existence in contrast to secular power struggles.

History for Rossellini is ironic and catastrophic, and nowhere is this clearer than in the final episode of *Paisà*, where partisan combat is portrayed as the final act of a collective tragedy. A rag-tag group of partisans, British flyers, and American O.S.S. men are surrounded by the Nazis in the marshlands of the Po delta and are cut off from help after General Alexander's order to the partisans to cease all hostilities. The entire episode is shot from the point of view of the trapped men, with the camera never peering above the lagoon's reeds behind which the men try to hide from the enemy; entirely dependent on the benevolence of nature (another neorealist theme), they risk death every time that they come out of the reeds, which function much like the fog in the narrative of the anonymous "Alpino."[74] After their capture, the partisans are executed one by one in front of the captive Allied officers. The last shot shows the corpses of the partisans floating in the water, while a voice-over announces, "This happened in the winter of 1944. At the beginning of Spring, the war was over," unveiling the full and bitter irony of their sacrifice.[75]

In *Germany—Year Zero* (1947), the third film of Rossellini's war trilogy, the limits of his vision of history and of European Fas-cism appear even more clearly. Set in the haunting ruins of post-war Berlin, the film's protagonist is a thirteen-year-old German boy, and the corruption of his innocence by a family and a social environment saturated with sexual and moral degeneracy (which for Rossellini represent the essence of Nazism) is the basis of the film's narrative. One of the most disturbing—and stereotypi-cal—aspects of both *Rome Open City* and *Germany—Year Zero* is indeed the parallel that Rossellini draws between homosexuality and Nazism as two facets of the same perversion of human na-ture. A homosexual schoolmaster corrupts little Edmund and fi-nally leads him—with a radical inversion of the idyllic *Bildungs-roman* conventions—*out* of the world rather than into the world. In an Oedipal allegory of the self-destructive violence of the Thousand-Year Reich, Edmund ends up killing his own father and then committing suicide.

As this film—the least successful of the trilogy with both the critics and the public—makes all too clear, the traditional moral values pertaining to sexuality, education, the role of women, and the patriarchal family are never challenged by Rossellini;

they constitute, on the contrary, the basic ideological framework of all his films. His tendency to represent Fascism as the negation of every essential moral value points to the fact that Fascism as a form of coercion deeply sedimented at all levels of Italian life is the repressed of neorealism itself. While the specifically Catholic perspective that animates Rossellini's films is not widespread in neorealist narrative, the sentimental humanitarianism and the tendency to simplify historical and political issues to moral oppositions is a neorealist constant. We find it in Stefano Brena no less than in Vittorini, Pavese, and Fenoglio; even in De Sica's poetic chronicle of the impact of the war on the life of *gli umili*, *Shoeshine*, the myth of childhood innocence is set in a binary opposition to the brutality of history. The real children on which the story is based were thought "too ugly" and "deformed" to play themselves in the film (despite De Sica's much-publicized insistence on the use of non-professional actors in his neorealist films), so the director opted instead for two more "acceptable"-looking boys to play the dirt-poor but well-scrubbed and sensitive protagonists of the film.[76] Indeed, most of neorealism differs markedly from nineteenth-century realist narrative (such as Stendhal, Balzac, and Dickens, for example) in what Bakhtin would call its "monologism." Notwithstanding the plurality of languages and kinds of speech found in the neorealist representation of social groups, this plurality does not imply a plurality of points of view and perspectives which would allow for a problematization or, as Bakhtin terms it, a "dialogization" of meaning.[77] Compared to the plurality of perspectives subsumed by the voice of the narrator in *I promessi sposi*, for instance, Rossellini's *Rome Open City* appears entirely univocal. While nineteenth-century narrative realism recognizes that no single perspective is adequate for the representation of reality,[78] Italian neorealism in general relies on a single, stable narrative perspective which is assumed to reflect the "truth" of the real itself.

Although specific ideological and political orientations vary widely, ranging from Rossellini's Catholicism to Pavese's Communism, neorealist narrative tends in general to employ a basic framework of values taken entirely from the traditional conventions of Italian patriarchal culture. The neorealists seek to endow their narrative representation of the real with a stable meaning that all can recognize as inherently true, fulfilling a collective need for certainty and stability in both the reconstruction of the past and in the projection of the future.[79] The recourse to traditional patriarchal roles, the deployment of value-charged oppositions concerning sexuality and family, the homeland, and human "nature" itself reflect the neorealists' attempt to make their representation of the world appear as non-ideological and "commonsensical" as possible. By appealing to the most deeply sedimented and universal "truths" of the Italians, neorealism sought a "catholic" consensus, above and beyond party differences.

The bracketing of the lesson of the avant-gardes and of modernism may be better understood in this light. Modernism in general involves a dissolution of those very certainties that neorealism wishes to restore, and it reveals them to be ideological categories open to deconstruction. The neorealists' return to nineteenth-century realism (most notably Manzoni and Verga) as a privileged model, and the simultaneous rigidification of the model into a monological mode of representation, belong to the same logic. Manzoni's epic becomes Rossellini's melodrama; Verga's choral storytelling turns into Vergano's and De Santis's feuilletons. Although Calvino takes the dialogism of *I promessi sposi* and *I Malavoglia* as a narrative model for *The Path*, he also in turn dialogizes the work of Manzoni and Verga in his novel by setting them side by side with a multitude of other, more "modern" models of fictional discourse.

The Neorealist Ethics of Representation and the Question of Psychoanalysis: Moravia, Viganò, Vergano, Pavese, Debenedetti

No Italian neorealist works, with the exception of *Cronache di poveri amanti* and *Il compagno*, attempt to analyze the effects of Fascism on everyday life under the regime itself.[80] Alberto Moravia's first novel, *Gli indifferenti* (*The Indifferent Ones*, 1929), a phenomenological and psychological study of the *fascistizzazione* of the Italian bourgeoisie and a forerunner of neorealist narrative, remains the most ambitious experiment in this regard. Like *Madame Bovary*, however, Moravia's novel is saturated with the worldview of its protagonists; it is a claustrophobic text, as monological in its study of "indifference" (the total lack of desire, rather than Emma Bovary's desire to desire) as Pavese's *Il compagno* is in its presentation of Pablo's political initiation. In his later, truly neorealist works, such as *I racconti romani* (*Roman Tales*, 1946), *La romana* (*Woman of Rome*, 1947), and *La ciociara* (*Two Women*, 1957), we hear, as Calvino notes in his 1959 assessment of contemporary Italian fiction, the "lazy, indolent voice" of the rural and urban lower classes in and around Rome. Contrary to the work of Carlo Emilio Gadda, though, there is no "tension" in Moravia's stylized Roman vernacular, according to Calvino, only a "cold faithfulness" to the spoken language of the lower classes.[81] Moreover, Moravia's diagnosis of the malaise that afflicts Italian society remains essentially the same in the prewar and postwar periods. Although with the war came his discovery of the conditions of everyday life among the workers and peasants,[82] there is no idealization of them to be found in Moravia's work. His commitment to Marxism and his support of the PCI have always been "with reservations," thanks to his equally strong beliefs in the principles of psychoanalysis and existentialism. For Moravia, Marxism, psychoanalysis, and existentialism—when taken together—reveal the fundamental conflictuality in the existence of the modern subject; the "empty indifference" of his characters' world is but the expression of a chronic, incurable sense of alienation. However, in most of Moravia's writing (with a few notable exceptions, such as *Il conformista*; *The Conformist*, 1951), this malaise of modernity is represented only in the most schematic fashion, in which Marxism, psychoanalysis, and existentialism are all condensed to a handful of notions and stereotypes. In particular, Moravia's use of the discourse of psychoanalysis—as in his 1944 *Bildungsroman*, *Agostino* (the story of a middle-class boy's coming of age)—tends to be extremely reductive, and his more recent works have simply demonstrated more openly what was already implicit in his earlier writing. Unlike Calvino, Moravia is unable or unwilling to face the full complexity of the relationship between sexuality and desire (including political desire); he in effect reduces all forms of desire to sexual drives, or libido.

Carlo Emilio Gadda observes in his 1946 article on literature and psychoanalysis that the foregrounding by psychoanalysis of the role of human sexuality in the formation of the subject, and its *smontaggio* of the "synthetic idea" we form of ourselves, was perceived by the prewar Italian intelligentsia largely as a menace from the "forces of barbarism" to the integrity of Latin culture. Fascist culture, Gadda continues, saw psychoanalysis as a "foreign" attack against the moral foundations and the most sacred values of the Italian nation, that is, the institution of the family, for psychoanalysis "defames" the innocence of childhood and of parent-child relations.[83] This resistance to psychoanalysis did not disappear with the fall of Fascism, however. On the contrary, it may be registered at all levels of neorealist narrative and of its cultural subtext (e.g., the mythification of childhood innocence). Ironically, both Togliatti and Croce openly and unconditionally condemned both psychoanalysis and modernist aesthetics. For Croce, psychoanalysis, like Marxism, represented the negation of the "ideality of life." Vehement attacks against both punctuate his writings in *La Fiera letteraria* and elsewhere after the war.[84] For Croce, as for Togliatti, neither Valéry nor Mallarmé were real poets, while contemporary French literature—contaminated by existentialism—appeared "decadent" (a key word in the Marxist critiques of literary modernism) to Croce.[85] The PCI was, on the other hand, rather more tolerant of both psychoanalysis and modernism in the immediate postwar period. A respected Communist intellectual and film critic, Umberto Barbaro, translated and edited a collection of essays by Freud with a long critical introduction after the Liberation. He soon became an *intellettuale scomodo* for the PCI, though, and psychoanalysis fell completely out of favor with the Party's cultural policymakers by the late 1940's.[86]

In Renata Viganò's *L'Agnese va a morire* (1949), a deliberate suppression of both modernist and psychoanalytic views of human identity is clearly visible. The novel exploits a range of conventional moral assumptions about the "natural" role of women as maternal, faithful, and above all selfless beings. (Agnese's figure and physiognomy are associated throughout the text with images of earth and water from the Po valley landscape in which the story is set, and the recurrent association becomes a symbolic motif, suggesting Agnese's naturality as an archetypal mother figure.) The narrative covers a time span from September 1943 to the winter of 1945 and traces the history of the Resistance through Agnese's paradigmatic story. Agnese's decision to join the partisans is an instinctive one, born out of her hatred for the Nazis who have taken away her husband.[87] Her role within the partisan group is that of a mother and nurse; not having children of her own, she "adopts" the partisans of the band near her village. She feeds them, sews their clothes, takes care of them when they are sick, and becomes their most trusted agent. As she becomes more and more involved with the Resistance organization, she also develops a political consciousness and starts to understand what she previously regarded as "mens' things" (*L'Agnese*, p. 166). Agnese, however, has no clear understanding of the principles of Marxism; she "instinctively" grasps their essence, letting herself be guided by the wisdom of the band's *comandante* (an "educated" man from the city who represents the PCI political cadre) and by the constant memory of her husband, who appears in her dreams to console her and give her strength. While she develops the endurance and courage of a man in carrying out the Comandante's orders and exhibits a seemingly inexhaustible physical resistance to hardship and privation (analogous to the Resistance itself), Agnese is also repeatedly portrayed as "tired" or incapable of thinking on her own (*L'Agnese*, pp. 124, 152, 222, 227). She therefore not only embodies the spirit of the Resistance but also the Italian peasantry, as seen from an orthodox PCI perspective. "Mamma" Agnese's exemplary virtue is contrasted by Viganò to the degeneracy of her neighbors, the Minghinas. The two daughters are the most "assiduous and avid" among the village women who prostitute themselves to the Fascists. The money they earn allows them to usurp the role of head of the family. The mother becomes their accomplice and "quiets down" the father who, although irritated by the women's dominance, is happy to be able to work less and eat well. The theme of the "bad" woman who sells herself to the Fascists or Nazis is a recurrent topos in all neorealist narrative about the war and the Resistance. The girls and their parents, consistent with the conventions of Resistance rhetoric, are of course punished for their actions in the end (although they have taken enemy soldiers as guests into their home for a whole summer, they fall victim to a savage Nazi reprisal). Agnese's death—already announced in the title—is, on the contrary, a life-giving self-sacrifice. As mythic mother of the Resistance, her winter death grants the spring rebirth which comes with the Liberation.[88]

The same symbolic representation of the role of women informs Aldo Vergano's 1946 film about the Resistance, *Il sole sorge ancora*. Like Viganò's novel, Vergano's film tells the story of a political education through the Resistance. Cesare, a young soldier who has returned to his native village in Lombardy after the disbanding of his regiment, is torn between two women. Laura, a refugee who takes care of her dead sister's children, symbolizes the moral values of the Resistance. Her father, a brick maker, is the partisan leader in the village. The rich and sensual Donna Matilde, married to the owner of the brick kiln, symbolizes on the other hand the irresponsibility of the upper classes unwilling to cut off their ties to the Fascists. Cesare is seduced by Matilde at first, but after witnessing a skirmish between Fascists and partisans in the village he decides to go into the hills. All the traditional topoi of Resistance narrative appear in the film, but unlike *L'Agnese* the film has a happy ending. Matilde is killed during a partisan uprising which prevents the destruction of the village in a German reprisal, and Laura and Cesare are reunited as "the sun rises once more" on the eve of the Liberation.

Vergano's efforts to make the village into a microcosm of Italian society as a whole, the use of "typical" characters (in the Lukácsian sense of the term), and the abundance of combat scenes alternating with the story of Cesare's and Laura's romance all contribute to make *Il sole sorge ancora* a full-scale epic work. The film—predictably enough—met with the approval of the PCI. The most famous scene of the film shows the execution of a Catholic priest who is, along with Laura's father, one of the principal leaders of the partisan movement in the village. The critic Dario Puccini, in his review of the film published in *Vie nuove*—a weekly founded by Luigi Longo in 1946—calls attention to precisely this scene as an example of the film's ability to capture the spirit of the Resistance and to convey it with astonishing immediacy. There is no need to comment on scenes such as this one, or that of Pina's death in *Roma città aperta*, argues Puccini: "Their logic is the evidence of history itself."[89] Ironically, however, the scene from *Il sole sorge ancora* praised by Puccini in fact "cites" Alessandro Blasetti's 1934 historical film, *1860*, about Garibaldi and the *Risorgimento*. Vergano's reference to Blasetti reveals an interesting continuity between Fascist rhetoric and the left-wing "patriotic" rhetoric of the Resistance. Virtually the same tone of nationalistic fervor that pervades Blasetti's celebration of Garibaldi's liberation of Sicily is echoed in Vergano's celebration of the Resistance and of the liberation of Italy from Nazi occupation and Fascist dictatorship. The most politically tendentious texts of neorealist narrative consistently attempt to legitimate their revolutionary message by deploying not only conventional moral categories but also by adopting the very same patriotic and nationalistic tone exploited by Fascist propaganda (although for quite different ends). The Fascist regime commonly associated the Fascist "revolution" with Garibaldi. The final sequence of Blasetti's film (cut from the version distributed after the war) was set in Mussolini's Rome, with Mussolini himself being hailed as the hero who fulfilled Garibaldi's revolutionary dreams.

•

Pavese's return to the tradition of Italian and European nineteenth-century naturalism via the mediation of the American realists of the 1920's and 1930's is one of the most intriguing episodes of the neorealist quest. Pavese's *Paesi tuoi*, like Visconti's *Ossessione*, is influenced by Italian *verismo* and by the American novelist James M. Cain. In the very same years in which he read and translated his beloved Sherwood Anderson, Sinclair Lewis, and John Dos Passos, Pavese also read and translated James

Joyce, Gertrude Stein, and William Faulkner. He had an unconditionally negative opinion of the latter three writers, which
helps us to understand the genesis of neorealism's widespread
resistance to modernism.[90]

In a 1931 essay, Pavese observes that Anderson's great strength
is *il racconto*, or his ability to tell realistic stories in the European
nineteenth-century tradition.[91] For Pavese, as for Anderson, to
be a storyteller means to "bring order where there was chaos."[92]
Pavese admires Anderson's ability to grasp and reconfigure in
his stories the specific American experience of the fundamental
modern conflict between industrialization and rural economy,
city and country, while recounting the private destinies of individuals in a language that translates the living American vernacular into a "healthy and vital" poetic style.[93] In drawing Anderson's profile, Pavese clearly sketches a self-portrait of sorts.
The notion that Anderson is an admirer and sometimes imitator
of Joyce's *Ulysses* is pure legend, Pavese argues, for Joyce does
not know how to tell a story. The attraction felt by American
writers for Joyce and for Freud, Pavese continues, is purely a
misguided reaction to American puritanism in sexual matters.
Joyce's passages on sex "are endless grey swamps of notation
after notation, from which a single note rarely emerges, if not
only for its own sake, singularly, bringing no contribution to
the construction of character, and independently of the whole
ponderous narrative apparatus which is Joyce's new 'method'"
("Sherwood Anderson," pp. 42–43). Gertrude Stein's word-
games make her, Pavese adds, totally unbearable as a writer.
Pavese resists, then, modernism's undoing of conventional plot
and narrative time, the decomposition of character, and the subversion—through the play of language and the slippage of sig-
nifiers—of the notion of any stable and fixed identity.

Even more revealing, though, is the way in which he lumps
these literary strategies together with psychoanalysis. The rejection of modernism, for Pavese, implies a rejection of psychoanalysis as well. Ironically, he attributes Anderson's interest in
Joyce and Freud to an American puritanism from which European culture, which has produced Boccaccio and Rabelais, is im-
mune. Yet his argument reveals precisely a kind of puritanism of

its own, a resistance to the "scandal" caused by psychoanalysis's undoing not only of the traditional subject but of the traditional definition of sexual difference as well.

The fundamental theme of Pavese's short novel *Paesi tuoi*, whose style and restricted narrative focalization are, as Calvino remarks in the 1964 preface, key reference points for Italian neorealism, is sexuality, but a sexuality seen within an anthropological perspective of human nature and culture as essentially unchanging structures.[94] The analysis of the individual's historical and biographical formation from within a specific cultural and social context and the notion of sexuality as historically constructed have little or no place in Pavese's narratives. Pavese's characters and stories tend to be configured as archetypes of an eternally recurrent dialectic of human alienation. Woman is always, in Pavese's novels, the negative principle, an archetypal embodiment of each and every force that works against man. Woman takes man away from himself; she "un-mans" him. Even in *Il compagno* the protagonist's conquest of a political consciousness and of a sense of identity can take place only after he has successfully exorcised the female presence that haunted his life. Gina, the woman who becomes his new companion, is not only totally submissive and unthreatening, but she also shares the "positive" features perennially associated with masculinity by Pavese. She is a hard worker, disciplined and methodical. She is, in fact, literally a man's replacement, since she has taken over her dead husband's job and even wears his work-clothes. She is, above all, entirely trustworthy, and therefore the exact opposite of the rest of Pavese's eternally scheming, promiscuous, and treacherous women.[95]

Nowhere is the timeless logic of this male-female antagonism clearer than in *Paesi tuoi*. The central conflict appears to be at first the traditional one of city versus country, embodied by the tension between Berto, a mechanic from Turin, and Talino, a peasant from the Langhe foothills of Piedmont. As the narrative unfolds, however, it becomes increasingly clear that the story rotates around the motif of man's undoing by the raw, destructive force of feminine sexuality, of which Gisella, Talino's sister, is the novel's ambiguous representative. In the first chapter, the figure of Michela, the lover of Berto's partner Pieretto, serves to introduce the theme of the destructiveness of woman's sexuality. Pieretto, who has to support his lazy and indolent lover, is caught by the police during an attempted robbery. To avoid imprisonment, he accuses the innocent Berto, who is arrested and spends time in prison for a crime about which he knew nothing. The day he is released from prison, Berto proceeds in turn to betray his friend with Michela, although her infidelity and promiscuity disgust him. "They deserve guys like Talino," he thinks.[96] This phrase, while establishing the general theme of misogyny that characterizes the discourse of all of Pavese's heroes, points to the plot's direction of development, since Talino will take on the role of symbolic controller of the forces of feminine sexuality. Berto justifies his own betrayal by attributing it once again to the degrading sexual drive that debases man but defines woman's nature: "If Pieretto knew he would be sorry for me rather than for you, because it was all the prison's fault; only women don't need to go to prison to betray a friend" (*Paesi*, p. 13).

When he first arrives at the farm, Berto is struck by the landscape which surrounds it; the hills on both sides of the valley have the shape of two maternal breasts (a recurring image in Pavese's poetry and narrative). The peasants, however, seem indifferent to the raw sensuality emanating from the earth that they work every day. Talino's family farm is a microcosm where the patriarchal order of peasant life appears in its most brutal form. The women are slaves of the family, their bodies broken and deformed by endless childbearing and by hard physical labor in the home and in the fields. Among all of them, Gisella alone seems different to Berto. Her body still retains its youthful form, and she possesses an untamed vitality that the other women do not have or have lost. Talino, the oldest son, is also a slave to the father, Vinverra, but he shares with him the privilege of brutalizing the women. When Gisella looks at Berto with obvious interest during the first meal that the family shares with him, while he is engaged as a mechanic in charge of the threshing machine, Talino grabs her in a seemingly playful way; the entire family laughs as he rubs some hot peppers on her mouth while reciting an obscene joke (*Paesi*, p. 26). As soon as she is able to free herself, Gisella covers her brother with insults, accusing him of cowardice and of having brought Berto there only in order to protect himself from his enemies on the neighboring farm. The father intervenes and gives Gisella a beating with his belt before turning on Talino who, unlike his sister, runs away after the first blow. The scene is, like the rest of the narrative, focalized through Berto's restricted perspective; since the latter is also the narrator, the reader is provided with no superior or different vision of the events and of their meaning. The signs of authorial presence are limited to the unobtrusive stylization of Berto's vernacular (whose lexicon and syntax are skillfully fused with literary Italian despite some excesses of "local color") and Pavese's implicit control of the plot's dramatic unity. Description, characterization, and dialogue are maintained within the scope of what might likely have been the interests and world-view of a northern worker in the late 1930's. While the beating that Gisella receives may be seen as a display of patriarchal power at its most elementary and literal level, Berto interprets it simply as another sign of the peasants' ignorance and cultural subalternity.

Berto falls increasingly under the sensual spell cast by the natural world around him, with the heat of the summer and the fields filled with ripe crops about to be harvested; his attraction for Gisella grows correspondingly. A symbolic correspondence between the rural landscape and Gisella's body systematically but unobtrusively is established over the course of the narrative. Berto discovers, however, that Gisella's body is marred by a scar, the sign of a former wound (*piaga*). The feminine *piaga* is a literary topos that runs through Italian literature from Dante to D'Annunzio, functioning as a figure for the female genitalia. It connotes both woman's imperfection—the "impure," contaminated nature of her sexuality from a masculine point of view—and the threat of castration that she poses. But Gisella's wound, while retaining this traditional symbolic meaning, assumes a series of other functions within the economy of Pavese's narrative. For Berto, it is a clue to Gisella's past; she is not a virgin, he deduces, and the scar shows that she has already had a child. Gisella denies this, claiming instead that she injured herself when she was a child. The scar is indeed a clue, but to a different kind of transgression of the patriarchal order than the one envisioned by Berto. For Berto the scar simply means that Gisella is not completely under the family's control and that she will let him secretly make love with her. As Berto starts to learn more about the family, however, he comes to realize that Gisella's scar is in fact a mark of ownership; like an animal, she has been branded as the exclusive property of her brother.

The series of feuds and vendettas which Berto discovers behind the apparently "normal" life of the farm originated in a single act of transgression against the patriarchal order, namely the breaking of the incest taboo. This transgression, originating in the destructive force of feminine sexuality, brings about the collapse of that order, for, according to the rules of patriarchy, women are to be kept not only in the service of the family but are also to serve as a means of social exchange. Speaking in today's terms, we may say that in *Paesi tuoi* Pavese combines a Lévi-Straussian anthropological perspective with a Girardian notion of the logic of violence.[97] The exchange of women through the institution of marriage—at least in principle (if not always in practice)—mitigates the rivalry of men and eliminates potentially violent competition for the same woman. The exchange of women is essential to sustain the reciprocal bonds of the community, to prevent civil strife, and to allow for the trade of labor and goods, on which the community's economic well-being is based. Led by his desire to keep Gisella as his exclusive property, Talino takes revenge on a rival by setting fire to his farm, thus disclosing the essential disorder caused by his transgression of the patriarchal order. He is released from prison for lack of evidence, but his return to the family farm is clouded by the prospect of retaliation by his rival. Berto's initial feeling that Talino is only an ignorant peasant is reversed as he slowly realizes that he is being manipulated by Talino and the family, who plan to make him take the blame for Talino's crime.

Violence cannot, however, be deflected or deferred here; it is bound to perpetuate itself unless "order" is restored through a ritual sacrifice. Since she is at the origin of the chain of violence, Gisella is bound to be its last victim as well. The scar on her body

marks her as the sacrificial scapegoat who will expiate all trans-
gressions of the social order that stem from uncontrollable desire. Talino's last crime is also the act that restores the rule of
patriarchy. Gisella is killed by her brother in the *aia* (threshing-
floor) in front of the farm, a symbolic "public" space on the
border between nature—the fields surrounded by the breast-
shaped hills—and culture, the family home and *focolare*. Unlike
the last scene of Verga's "La Lupa" ("The She-Wolf"), on which
this scene and Pavese's novel may be partly modelled, the narrative does not stop before the man's "phallic" weapon—an axe
in Verga's story, a hayfork in Pavese's—slays the woman like a
Gorgon.[98] The other members of the family, the day laborers,
and Berto are the powerless and horrified spectators of this murder, which takes place while they are unloading the ripe wheat
for threshing. Neither the ambiguity nor the tragic restraint of
Verga's story are to be found in Pavese's novel; the death of Gisella is clearly linked to the restoration of the patriarchal order.
As Gisella lies dying in her bed, the family seems fully resigned
to the necessity of her death. The threshing takes place as if
nothing had happened. Berto expects that Talino will be surely
"put away for life" for his crime (*Paesi*, p. 80). Ironically, though,
this is exactly what does not happen. Talino comes back to look
for his father just as two *carabinieri* arrive, apparently to arrest
him. But old Vinverra warns his son off, and the two disappear
together in the fields before the *carabinieri* have stepped into the
aia. When the *carabinieri* approach him on the *aia*, Berto learns
they have come only to give him his mechanic's work-permit;
they will never inquire into the circumstances of Gisella's death.
This ironic twist of the plot reveals the "law and order" of the
Fascist regime (as Girard argues is the case for the entire judi-
ciary system of modern Western civilization) to be only a state-
sponsored and institutionalized duplication of the original
scapegoat mechanism.[99]

Throughout *Paesi tuoi*, Gisella is given an aura of innocence,
and the innocence of the victim is, according to Girard's analysis
of ritual sacrifice, essential for the collective exorcism of violence. But, as a woman, Gisella is also necessarily the victim, insofar as—contrary to Girard's reading of the scapegoat mecha-

nism's social function—the destructive force that threatens the patriarchal order is not "pure" violence but rather that generated by uncontrolled feminine sexuality. Pavese's novel is clearly not, unlike Verga's "La Lupa," a celebration of the ancient Mediterranean or modern Italian modes of patriarchy. The narrative exposes patriarchy as a system of social coercion that generates violence and institutionalizes it, rather than controls it; it is simply displaced from one level to another. The story that Berto tells, which he interprets as a symptom of the peasants' subhuman conditions of existence, emerges through the symbolic motifs interwoven in the narrative as the reenactment of the story of the primordial act of violence that lies at the very foundations of Western civilization. The thematic opposition between country and city that seems to control the narrative is an illusory one, because there is always only the same story to tell; acts of transgression are destined to occur again elsewhere, and this story of violence and the ritual sacrifice that it brings in its wake will continue to repeat itself. In Pavese's last novel, *La luna e i falò*, as in *Paesi tuoi*, a symbolic parallel is drawn between the killing of a woman who has triggered an act of violence in the community and an ancient peasant fertility ritual—the setting of bonfires in the fields to ensure the return of life-giving rain. This time, however, feminine sexuality is associated directly with the violence of history itself. Santina (literally "little saint"), the innocent girl that the protagonist remembers from his childhood, has become a fallen woman, a spy, and a Fascist collaborator. Santina is executed by the partisans and her body burned on a bonfire because it has not ceased to be the object of men's desire even in death, just as Berto continues to desire Gisella even in her final agony. The desire for the body of woman is, in the last analysis, for Pavese a perpetually fatal desire (even in political terms); as he writes in perhaps his most famous poem, "Verrà la morte e avrà i tuoi occhi" ("Death will come and she will have your eyes").

Although *Paesi tuoi* undermines Fascist rhetoric exalting the vitality and moral fortitude of the peasant "backbone" of the nation, as well as the notion of the sanctity of familial ties, it is a novel that puts history into parentheses. Pavese's narrative is pervaded by a nostalgia for origins and by an ethic of the archaic as the "truth" of existence; it paradoxically remains within the patriarchal logic it seeks to expose and to criticize. Among these archaic peasants of "our" *paesi*, Pavese locates—as Lévi-Strauss does with primitive cultures—a kind of raw authenticity that "civilized man" must face and recognize as the inalienable and necessary truth of human nature. Although Pavese's vision of this original truth is, unlike Lévi-Strauss's, an essentially tragic one, it nevertheless relies on the very same patriarchal myth that is central to Lévi-Strauss's analytical system. As Jacques Derrida has observed, however, the *factum* of the incest prohibition is scandalous only if conceived within the traditional philosophical conceptualization of a nature/culture opposition. "The 'scandal' is designed to leave in the domain of the unthinkable the very thing that makes this conceptualization possible: the origin of the prohibition of incest." [100] Pavese accepts the prohibition or taboo as fatally necessary rather than probe its own origin and purpose, for that would be the task not only of anthropology but also psychoanalysis—that "dark science" of origins—and Pavese has no use for anything other than a notion of the unconscious as a set of collective archetypes.

•

Even a journal as open to the ideas of both psychoanalysis and existentialism as *Il Politecnico* bears the traces of this cultural resistance. Remo Cantoni's essay on *Notes from the Underground* locates in Dostoyevsky's work (as Lukács did) the prophetic expression of a "philosophy of crisis," which corresponds to the radical deconstruction of "human nature" and of the Enlightenment heritage undertaken by Nietzsche, Freud, and Heidegger. None of these modes of thought can be simply dismissed, Cantoni acknowledges, for their dismantling of traditional metaphysics is a necessary achievement of modern culture. But "the philosophy of crisis should not be the crisis of philosophy," he concludes, and goes back to what he calls Dostoyevsky's Nietzschean dialectic, his "deep and profound search for positive values" and for a tragic catharsis. [101] Characteristically, Vittorini adds a brief note to Cantoni's article, which must have seemed too lenient to him, and argues a point that could have been made by Lukács: Dostoyevsky's underground—in Cantoni's terms, the unconscious and its conflicts—is an arbitrary and absurd construct, damaging to the "progress" of human reason and knowledge.

In an introductory note to a poem by Umberto Saba in *Il Politecnico*, Giansiro Ferrata refers to Saba's poetry, and to his *Storia e cronistoria del Canzoniere*, as unduly influenced by the "silly fantasies of psychoanalysis."[102] Yet Giacomo Debenedetti, in the same postwar period, offers a far less reductive reading of Saba and of the intersections between the discourse of psychoanalysis and the discourse of literature. Debenedetti's "Probabile autobiografia di una generazione" ("Probable Autobiography of a Generation," 1949), written to introduce a collection of his early essays, is a subtly ironic analysis of Croce's influence on the critical discourse of Debenedetti's generation and of Croce's own repression of all in literature or culture that cannot be assimilated to the categories of spirit and reason. "The scandal of what was unmanageable, deviant, irreducible to the healthy and reassuring systems of reason, appeared put to rest. They were proper people, our fathers. . . . Human destiny itself resembled a dignified, conformist gentleman."[103] But, notes Debenedetti, precisely those areas that Croce had foreclosed and forbidden entrance into represented a potential challenge by "modernist" generations against the (intellectual) father.[104] In his "Probable Autobiography," Debenedetti holds an imaginary dialogue with a professor of belles lettres who is certainly meant to be none other than Croce himself. In the course of this dialogue, "Croce" calls Debenedetti "an incorrigible romantic," who has nonetheless provided his readers with "some passionate demonstrations—rigorous and implacable," although these are "undertaken with the tenacity of a critic engaged in a struggle with pale myths, rather than a living reality" (Debenedetti, p. 13). Although Debenedetti's work has its strong points, "Croce" admits, so far he has been able only "to compose a kind of apology in which the complexity of a work and the destiny of a life are fused in a unity which allows for no respite, no way out" (Debenedetti, p. 13). For Croce, of course, Debenedetti's kind of criticism ("criticism" being in itself a suspect activity) could only have been anathema, since, as he reiterates in his essay on psychoanalysis and literature, "poetry has nothing to do with psychoanalytic theories, because poetry is, as is well known, a matter of love . . . but of a love which is fully transcended into religious and moral life." [105] "Love, *che detta dentro,*" Croce writes (citing Dante), "is uniquely that of the individualized spirit or 'genius' of an artist . . . who creates a time superior to his own time and epoch: an eternal time and eternal art. . . . What exists for the artist is not 'the reality of the outside world' . . . but only his own soul, which he must transfigure in artistic vision, a form of beauty." [106]

Croce is, says Debenedetti in his "Probable Autobiography," "neither a real antagonist nor a real demon, but of the former he has the provocatory nature, and of the latter the influential, parental one" (Debenedetti, p. 9). Debenedetti's essay is far too complex to be summarized here, for it traces all the various ramifications of Croce's influence on Italian criticism between the two world wars, but his main point is that postwar Italian criticism in general still has not "gone beyond" Croce. This is because the project of "overcoming" Croce's monumental influence, he points out, has been doomed by the very notion of *superamento,* which implies that to attempt to exit from Croce's thought-system means to pass through the paths traced by Croce himself: "Always, no matter what turn events took, he had already seen it all, had already been there" (Debenedetti, p. 28). Croce has already been everywhere that his own paths could lead; the impeccable harmony and total closure of his system allow for no way out for those who are inside of it (Debenedetti, pp. 22–23). Debenedetti points out that even Gramsci, alone in prison and about to develop his own autonomous philosophy of praxis, still relied on Croce's aesthetic categories to express his own ideas on art. The anti-Croce movement of the 1930's and 1940's in Italy, Debenedetti concludes, has thus far ended up looking like "a letter we composed with great diligence, but— through a well-known mechanism—forgot to put a stamp on" (Debenedetti, p. 23). At last, he observes, Croce's intellectual heirs are starting to undermine successfully the foundations of his idealism. Suddenly a new time and space are opening up, thanks to psychoanalysis and its discovery of the historicity of the subject and of the unconscious, and a sense of an ending, or at least a provisional one, is now conceivable for the Crocean phase in the history of Italian thought. As in the ending of *Les Misèrables* (and all those romances whose plots are intricately entwined), "la chose simplement d'elle-même arriva" (Debenedetti, p. 33).

Debenedetti does not identify the postwar collapse of Croce's authority exclusively with the end of the illusion of the liberal pre-Fascist state's "restoration"; rather, the reason for the displacement of Croce's metaphysics is to be found in a more fundamental epistemic shift. Croce's rigorous separation of the various "forms of the spirit" (his so-called "*dialettica dei distinti*") takes the oppositions that articulate each form (beautiful/ugly in art, true/false in conceptual thought, useful/useless in economics and the field of the practical in general, good/bad in ethics) and makes them relevant only within that form, outside of which they are inapplicable. This, Debenedetti protests, precludes that osmosis and interchange between the various representations of man and of the world which are critical to modern thought. Croce's absolute idealism and absolute historicism are—despite all his protestations to the contrary—essentially metaphysical or, as Debenedetti says (quoting Gramsci), ideological, for they are centered on absolute oppositions without either questioning the validity of these oppositions or situating them in a historical process of change (Debenedetti, p. 34). Moreover, Croce severs historiography from any possible participation in the effort to construct a general science of man, for although historiography shows how all historical facts fulfill a function in the development of the spirit, it can never provide a perspective on the true nature of the current social and historical situation, for historical facts represent only the particular, not the universal. Yet, Debenedetti argues, precisely such a general science of man is now emerging through the work of those who probe structural questions and problems and who increasingly discover analogies in their points of view (Debenedetti, p. 34), envisioning in effect the advent of structuralism and semiotics as (in Umberto Eco's words) "a general logic of culture." [107] Nor is it surprising that he should look to psychoanalysis as a way out of Croce's metaphysical idealism, since psychoanalysis stands at the crossroads of all the branches of knowledge investigating man and is based on "a perpetual principle of dissatisfaction, of calling into question, of criticism and contestation of what may seem, in other respects, established." [108] It is in this sense that Calvino's own deployment of the discourse of psychoanalysis functions in *The Path*.

Visconti, the *Cinema* Group, and the Ideology of Form

Like Pavese's *Paesi tuoi*, Visconti's *Ossessione* is centered around the theme of sexuality but moves toward a critique of the patriarchal order as seen in its specific contemporary historical and social manifestations. Visconti's film was heavily censored by the regime (Visconti was able to rescue only one of the original negatives from complete destruction); after the war, *Ossessione* continued to meet in Italy with the opposition of the "moralità benpensante," the Church, and even the American occupying forces. The version which finally emerged some years after the Liberation was severely mutilated, and to this day it is nearly impossible to see the film in its original form. [109] Visconti cannot take exclusive credit for *Ossessione*, which was the result of the work of a group of intellectuals, filmmakers, and critics centered around the Roman journal *Cinema* and the *Centro sperimentale di cinematografia*, headed by Luigi Chiarini and Umberto Barbaro. Even Visconti's famous early articles, "Cadaveri" ("Corpses") [110] and "Cinema antropomorfico" ("An Anthropomorphic Cinema"), which attack the then-current conventions of Italian commercial cinema and propose a new "committed" cinema in its place, are—like most of the theoretical essays published by *Cinema*—the result of a concerted group discussion and critical reflection. [111] The coauthors of *Ossessione*'s screenplay, Mario Alicata, Gianni Puccini, and Giuseppe De Santis (who was also an assistant director, together with Antonio Pietrangeli), produced

Luchino Visconti and Clara Calamai on the set of *Ossessione*. Photo courtesy of Cineteca Nazionale, Rome.

a series of articles which are essential to understanding the complex of critical ideas and aspirations that led to *Ossessione* and opened the way for neorealist cinema.

In spite of the persistence of a Crocean view of aesthetics among some members of the *Cinema* group, Visconti's collaborators on the whole take a resolutely anti-Crocean position in these essays. Cinema should not and cannot be "disinterested," writes Gianni Puccini; like all aesthetic discourse, film cannot be (as Croce maintains) concerned only with the beautiful, for it is bound up with truth and history.[112] For the makers of *Ossessione*, cinematic art assumes the epistemic function which for Croce is instead confined—according to the logic of "*i distinti*"—exclusively to philosophical discourse. Since film (given the indexical function of the emulsion process itself) usually engages in representing the reality of the "outside world," its time cannot be the eternal time of art envisioned by Croce, but rather must be a historical time. The epistemic function of film within the historical context of the late Fascist era, Puccini concludes, is therefore to demystify the ideal of the timelessness of truth and beauty. This evokes in turn a moral and political function for art, for by representing the individual as a being whose ethical behavior is neither the result of a categorical imperative (an absolute opposition of good and bad) nor the expression of a transcendental human nature, but rather the articulation of specific material and historical circumstances, art reformulates the notion of morality in terms of a question for which there are no ready-made answers. In the absence of absolute principles of good and bad, morality ultimately involves an individual commitment or choice at each and every turn of one's social and historical existence. This view of morality as "*al di qua del bene e del male*" is embodied in the characters of *Ossessione*.[113] This relatively complex view of morality does not, as we have already seen, survive in the main body of neorealist art and thought. Nevertheless, at least in *Ossessione*, art enters the territory of human praxis (one of Croce's *sensi vietati*) by collapsing the distinction between ethics and politics.[114]

The story of Gino, Giovanna, Bragana, and Lo Spagnolo—the protagonists of *Ossessione*—is not only purged of the crudely arbitrary and melodramatic elements of Cain's plot (such as having the man acquitted of the real murder but sentenced to death for the accident);[115] it is also inserted in a far more specific social setting. *Ossessione* was shot on location for the most part; the film exploits both the somewhat bleak rural landscape around Ferrara and the run-down outskirts of a large city, "where each stone, each corner, each courtyard tells the story of the daily toil of mankind."[116] The eye of Visconti's camera reaches out to include within its frame "real people," such as peasants in the fields, fishermen on the river, the crowd at the fair in Ancona, the pathetic audience and the singers at the opera contest, women and children in the seedy park in Ferrara, or the gossipy villagers who congregate at the inn. The movement and animation of the communal forms of existence, labor, and socialization in these sequences—which Visconti would turn to again in *La terra trema*—underscore the concrete historical situation of the char-

Ossessione: "Real people" are included in the frame, behind the figures of the village priest and Giovanna's husband. Photo courtesy of Cineteca Nazionale, Rome.

acters and the progressive isolation of the lovers, alienated from the community and, finally, from each other as well.

The most scandalous aspect of *Ossessione* is, however, its "realistic" representation of eroticism and both heterosexual and homosexual desire. The camera's foregrounding of the body—the point of view shots that place the viewer in the position of the desiring subject (e.g., Gino looking at Giovanna's bare leg, or Giovanna transfixed by Gino's naked shoulders)—represents an inversion of that transcendence of the body and its desire into the life of the spirit which for Croce defines the very essence of aesthetic contemplation. There is no such contemplation in Visconti's film; looking and seeing always mean desiring the other and, in the process, destroying the other's freedom. The triangulations of desire in *Ossessione* define this alienating dialectic in social terms. Sexual desire is not a force for cultural dissolution, as it is in Pavese, nor is the feminine itself the cause and means of man's undoing. On the contrary, Giovanna is the prisoner of a social and economic system whose rules she has internalized and whose logic has made her what she is, while

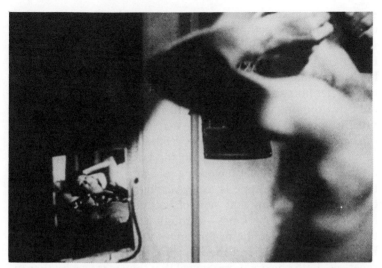

Ossessione: Foregrounding of the body. Giovanna is seen in a mirror as she looks at Gino's bare back. Photo courtesy of Cineteca Nazionale, Rome.

Ossessione: Doubling of the lovers' images. Photo courtesy of Cineteca Nazionale, Rome.

sexual desire instead corresponds to an impulse toward an anarchic freedom. The pathos of this conflict is captured in the scene where Giovanna cannot keep up with Gino's pace during their first attempt to get away, staggering along the dusty road in high heels, and finally falling and getting up again, only to turn back toward her home and husband. Giovanna sees herself as having only two options in life: namely, to return to the life of quasi-prostitution that she lived before marriage or to submit to her husband's brutal rule. Whore or wife: there is no alternative. She cannot have the freedom that Gino and Lo Spagnolo have, living on the margins of society, working odd jobs, and constantly on the move. Her one hope is to replace her husband with Gino; the gold watch-chain that symbolizes her enslavement to her husband's money becomes—through a metonymic substitution—the chain that she in turn gives to Gino, hoping to keep him tied to both her and the inn. But, in a specular system of reversals, both she and Gino reveal that they want each other to be the opposite of what they really are. While Giovanna would like Gino to be a stable bread-earner like her husband Bragana (but without the latter's flaws), Gino would like Giovanna to be like Lo Spagnolo, a travelling companion for whom money, home, and family have no meaning or value (but to retain her woman's body). The doubling of the lovers' images, who see each other and are seen through mirror reflections in several scenes, underscores the theme of desire as distortion and alienation. The seashell Gino picks up in Giovanna's bedroom after they have made love and he has promised never to leave her symbolizes his desire for her (for her sexuality), but as he raises it and holds it against his ear, no longer listening to Giovanna's words, the seashell suggests a Ulysses-like yearning to depart and to resume a nomadic life. Lo Spagnolo, another nomad of desire, is also associated in the film with the mythic theme of wandering, as well as the political ideal of a humanity free from moral and economic oppression, but also desires Gino to be the opposite of what he is sexually, and his jealousy finally leads him to betray Gino to the police. Family, marital fidelity, machismo, the "difference" between masculine and feminine, the power of desire: all are probed and dissected by Visconti and his

Ossessione: Gino and Lo Spagnolo, nomads of desire, surrounded by "real people." Photo courtesy of Cineteca Nazionale, Rome.

co-filmmakers, and their conventional definitions placed in doubt.

Ossessione is more than a critique of idealism, though, for it also breaks sharply with the dominant cinematic practices of its time. The new realists of the *Cinema* group opposed both the aesthetics and politics of contemporary filmmaking in Fascist Italy[117] and looked to the tradition of realist narrative in both literature and film as offering a solution to the problem of mediation between fiction and the reality they wanted it to represent. Alicata's and De Santis's idea that film is a kind of literature is not, though, meant to deprive the cinematic code of its autonomy. Rather, it is intended to emphasize the point that film shares many strategies of narration with the novel. Their call to take the camera out of the studio and into the streets is not, however, a call to shoot only documentary films: "When some of its theoretical problems became prominently visible, the cinema was transformed from 'documentary' to 'narrative,' and it understood that its destiny was linked to literature. In spite of the stupid pretentions of 'purist' filmmakers, from that day on there was the closest of relationships between cinema and literature, to the point that the history of cinema suddenly appeared to be an integral chapter in the history of literary and artistic taste in the twentieth century." [118]

Film is, according to Alicata and De Santis, a narrative mode par excellence, and realism, when understood as the imaginative construction of a (hi)story of people and events, is the only valid paradigm for any authentic narrative expression. The development of modern realist film in its various forms is based, they contend, on the legacy of the "perfect psychological syntax" and the poetic rendering of contemporary society found in nineteenth-century realist fiction and drama. This view of realism, however, although reminiscent of Lukács's, entails neither a dismissal of naturalism nor a rejection of modernism per se. Kafka, Faulkner, and the surrealists are favorably mentioned several times in the essays of the *Cinema* group, although the nineteenth-century naturalist tradition is by far their most privileged point of reference. The work of René Clair, Dupont, Pabst, Marcel Carné, and Jean Renoir (with whom Visconti worked as assistant director during his self-imposed exile from Fascist Italy between 1936 and 1940), Alicata and De Santis claim, is based on a freely creative rereading of the European naturalist tradition from Flaubert to Maupassant, Zola, Chekhov, and Ibsen. Their study of various pathological aspects of the human personality and of society itself, so typical of Zola's naturalism, often gives Carné's and Renoir's respective films the appearance of a "frantic chronicle" lacking the aesthetic control and coherence of true realism. [119] But the violence of Carné's and Renoir's films cannot, Alicata and De Santis argue, be interpreted as a mere symptom of the decadence and corruption of French society on the eve of World War II. In the "coded" language that characterizes the writing of the *Cinema* group, unable to address specific issues of the day (because of the constant threat of censorship), this is meant to suggest that these French films assume a political dimension as well. *Ossessione*, filmed as Italy was beginning to lose the war, is clearly intended both to represent and to criticize the violence at the very roots of Fascism and the corruption of Mussolini's faltering regime.

American narrative often appears as a mythic "other" for both writers and filmmakers of the 1930's and 1940's. This is linked both to a desire to emerge from the asphyxiating cultural atmosphere of Italy and to a question of form. The inspiration Pavese and Vittorini drew from American literature is well known, particularly in terms of a simplification of syntax and emphasis on direct discourse. Sartre observes in *What Is Literature?* that the fascination Faulkner, Hemingway, and Dos Passos held for French writers in the 1930's was caused by the same desire to break with previous forms of expression.[120] The point of Alicata's and De Santis's essay—a point which holds for literature as well as film—is that American realism offers in fact a path back to the Italian tradition of realist and naturalist narrative, in the aftermath of the various twentieth-century formal experiments.

In his 1959 essay on contemporary Italian fiction (originally a lecture delivered at Columbia University), Calvino explicitly connects the Italian "discovery" of American literature to the rediscovery of Verga, stressing at the same time the ideological and political implications of both, not only for his own writing but for Pavese's and Vittorini's as well:

For Pavese, America was the country that had created a literature linked to human praxis . . . creating new myths of modern life that had the force of primordial symbols of consciousness. . . . For Vittorini, American literature was an unlimited reserve of natural vitality, an ideal battlefield for the struggle between stylistic invention and academic tradition, between the sincerity of the passions . . . and the weight of conventional hypocrisy and morality. American literature, so far from our own tradition, was a means that allowed us to approach our tradition with a new spirit: with new eyes we reread Giovanni Verga, the late-nineteenth-century Sicilian novelist. . . . In the final years of Fascism, political themes mixed with literary ones: America was a gigantic allegory of our own problems, of the Italians of that time, of our good and evil, of our conservatism and sense of rebellion, of our South and North, of our mosaic of peoples and dialects, of Pavese's Piedmont and Vittorini's Sicily. It was a theater where a drama was played out, in explicit and extreme forms, that was not dissimilar from our own hidden drama, about which we were forbidden to speak. We younger writers, who began our literary studies during Fascism's final years with a sense of opposition to the official climate of that time, feel linked to this image of America. We grew up in tragic times, and it was only natural that our passion for literature would become one and the same with our passionate concern for the fate of the world.[121]

Verga's influence may be detected in Calvino's choice of a subproletarian boy as the protagonist of *The Path* (one who is in turn surrounded by individuals and groups belonging to the most marginal sectors of Italian society), as well as in his deliberate literary refraction of colloquial speech. Although extremely simplified and condensed through a process of stylization that is suggestive of the work of the early Hemingway (a writer whom Calvino admired throughout his literary career), Calvino's narrative language in *The Path*, particularly his representation of speech, reflects an attentive study of Verga, whose own narrative language Calvino defines as "miraculously modern" in the same 1959 essay.[122] While Calvino, like Visconti and the *Cinema* group, finds in Verga a unique and fundamental model for the sociohistorical representation of Italian workers and peasants, though, he radically alters the ideological framework of the model, giving his own novel a decidedly Marxian orientation.

In a 1950 interview on neorealism, Pavese substantially confirms Alicata's and De Santis's genealogical analysis of the bond between modern American literature and European naturalism, both old and new. While he does not deny the influence that American writers had on him, Pavese points out in fact that those writers "learned their narrative neo-realism" from nineteenth-century European writers but absorbed only their literary strategies and not their "spirit."[123] Pavese, however, never acknowledges that his own blend of realism and myth, his interest in the conflict between the peasant world and capitalism, and his tragic vision of "passion" all make him as deeply indebted to Verga as any other modern Italian writer.[124] In *The Path*, on the other hand, Calvino openly emulates Verga by taking on the voice of a *"historicus infante e popolare"* ("an infant folk *historicus"*).[125] Through the "artifice of regression,"[126] in other words, Calvino intends to bracket his own "bourgeois" voice, letting his characters tell their own (hi)story "in their own voice" without the populist tone that mars Pavese's use of the same kind of narrative device (i.e., the "lowering" of the narrative point of view to that of a working-class protagonist) in *Il compagno*. Furthermore, as does Visconti in *Ossessione*, Calvino derives from Verga a rhetorical strategy for the representation of the unconscious and its drives through an "external," choral perspective on the actions, gestures, and words of the main characters; although deeply interested in the psychological and social study of workers and peasants, Calvino chooses a "symptomatological" rather than psychological portrayal of their world. Like Visconti in *Ossessione*, Calvino's perspective on the drives and desires of the characters in *The Path* is coextensive with a critique of the patriarchal structure.

According to Alicata and De Santis, Verga's *I Malavoglia, Mastro don Gesualdo*, "L'amante di Gramigna," and "Jeli il pastore" provide the most promising models for the future development of the realist imagination and for "a revolutionary art inspired by a humanity that suffers and hopes" (Alicata and De Santis, p. 205). What is revolutionary in the adoption of Verga's work as a formal model for a new art lies in its potential to disrupt dominant cinematic and literary conventions. Verga shows his Italian followers how a story can be anchored in historical space and time, in contrast to the "false rhetoric" and the "shallow bourgeois manner" that afflict the contemporary Italian cinema (Alicata and De Santis, p. 205). Verga's lesson, however, is not purely a formal one; his representation of a humanity that is oppressed, yet hopes for freedom, appears to the *Cinema* group particularly relevant in the present historical circumstance. James M. Cain's novel is only used as a kind of narrative scaffolding in *Ossessione*; the real narrative model is Verga, as can be seen from the terms used by Pietrangeli to describe the "humanity" portrayed in Visconti's film:

A bare, avid, sensual and enraged humanity—which had become this way through the daily struggle for survival and for satisfaction of its uncontrollable instincts; a humanity that bursts forward into action, without the corrective stage of thought itself, but with that impetuous impulse for which desiring and having constitute a single spontaneous act. . . . Because their acts are born in these remote and uncontrolled recesses of consciousness, the protagonists appear as the pure of heart, as the innocent, as the victims, even in the unfolding of passion, betrayal, crime. . . . Wherever a psychic microscope is at work, one which is capable of capturing the minute reflection of the most hidden movements of the mind . . . every feature of a face reveals secrets and mysteries, just like the lines on the palm of one's hand.[127]

Pietrangeli's argument is a synoptic condensation of a series of statements found in Verga's preface to "L'amante di Gramigna" (whose adaptation was Visconti's first film project) and in his preface to *I Malavoglia*. Even the reference to the unconscious may be found in Verga's preface to "L'amante di Gramigna," reflecting Verga's own interest in late nineteenth-century behavioral psychology: "The simple human fact will always make one think; it will always have the force of what *has really been*, of true tears, of the fevers and sensations that have passed through the flesh. The mysterious process by which passions tie themselves together . . . in their subterranean journey . . . will still constitute for a long time the powerful attraction of that psychological phenomenon which forms the subject of a story, and which modern analysis endeavors to follow with scientific precision." [128] Although Verga's work serves as a touchstone for neorealism, he himself was, however, entirely unreceptive to socialism. He did not believe in the possibility of social progress and held fast to a tragic vision of modern history as fatally determined by Darwinian logic. Verga's theory of impersonality and absolute objectivity in art also runs counter to the new realists' belief in a committed art. According to Verga's *verista* tenets, art must be utterly dispassionate in depicting the passions and conflicts of individuals and social groups. The artist who observes the spectacle of human history—"the struggle for existence, for material well-being, or for ambition"—does not have the right to express a judgment. He must place himself "outside" the field of struggle and be rigorously impartial. [129] While the new realists adopt (with varying degrees of consistency and success) *verista* stylistic strategies for the effacement of the author's presence, they do not for the most part subscribe to Verga's position of artistic neutrality. As Alicata observes in his 1942 article "Ambiente e società nel racconto cinematografico" ("Milieu and Society in Film Narrative"), any *racconto* presupposes an authorial judgment and an authorial position that constitute the ideological matrix of narrative expression. To narrate means to articulate a motivated perception of human history through the use of form, which is always, as a consequence, a rhetorical act of persuasion. [130] Alicata and De Santis deduce from this that film can therefore never be simply documentary, even though it retains a documentary function by systematically setting the story in the actual social and historical circumstances of which the invented story is a creative and critical interpretation.[131]

For Verga, the advent of capitalism and economic "progress" in nineteenth-century Italy unleashes a desire for material wealth and well-being, which—as in the story of the Malavoglia's deal to transport and sell the lupines, thus breaking with their age-old *mestiere* and the folk wisdom of their proverbs—inevitably leads in the short term to alienation and degradation, rather than improvement, in the living conditions of the workers and peasants. Verga's narrative provides a powerful critique of the dehumanization brought by capitalism, which *Ossessione* clearly echoes and thematizes in building an opposition between Giovanna on the one hand—chained to her husband's money and to the inn—and Gino and Lo Spagnolo on the other hand. But for Verga the unleashing of desire is never a positive force in the history of subjects; it is the symptom of a "dis-order" which always must be contained, just as the novelist must contain his own passions and judgments. As pointed out earlier, though, Visconti's use of point-of-view shots in *Ossessione* has the effect of placing the viewer in the position of the desiring subject rather than of an external, superior or "disinterested" observer. The explosion of desire—restless, nomadic, amoral—signifies for him the untenable nature of the present order, which has its basis in repression and coercion. Desire for Visconti is a figure of hope, for it points to the need for a new and different order. Nearly all the institutions idealized by Verga as the essential elements of the patriarchal order, whose maintenance is the only hope for a harmonious communal existence, come under attack in *Ossessione* (family, work, home, etc.). But Verga is clearly not the chief target of Visconti's attack. That is instead, as pointed out by one critic, the topology of traditional patriarchal and petit-bourgeois values ingrained in the conventional Italian cinema of the 1930's:

All the *topoi* of the nineteen-thirties' cinematic Imaginary were taken up and reversed: sex, instead of an ethereal spiritual sublimation, becomes a dense physiological carnality; the family, instead of the very nucleus of the "social," becomes an inhuman prison; the people, instead of a sanctifying chorus, become an aggregate of bitter individual solitude; the peasant world, rather than the center of unity, becomes the center of fragmentation; the landscape, from an idyllic backdrop, becomes a turbid stage set; crime goes from being an infraction that is set right to a negation brought into closeup view; life goes from being the site of gratification to the site of desire.[132]

If *Ossessione* offers such a scathing critique of the conventional— not to mention political—Italian cinema of its own time, this reflects the fact that the film was conceived and produced by an intellectual movement that sought to dismantle the present cultural order, not to define a mode of commitment or "constructive" action. Yet, as Calvino observes in a 1976 essay entitled "Right and Wrong Political Uses of Literature," "This is the paradox of the power of literature: it seems that only when it is persecuted does it show its true powers, challenging authority."[133] For this reason, *Ossessione*, like *Paesi tuoi*, remains in the prehistory of neorealism proper, lacking the element of more explicitly "constructive" and future-oriented political commitment that will emerge with *La terra trema* for Visconti and *Il compagno* for Pavese.

●

In 1945, Visconti and De Santis, together with Marcello Pagliero and Mario Serandrei, worked on a documentary about the Resistance entitled *Giorni di Gloria (Days of Glory)*. The documentary tells the story of the *Resistenza armata* as the epic tale of the uprising of the entire Italian populace against the Fascists and Nazis. Footage of partisan attacks and of acts of sabotage is juxtaposed in a progressive crescendo, leading to the climactic discovery in a cave near Rome (the "Fosse Ardeatine") of the corpses of 335 victims of a Nazi reprisal, which had been ordered by Hitler after a partisan attack upon a detachment of German security police which killed 33 Germans. Visconti contributed the sequences of the September 1944 trial of Pietro Caruso, Rome's Fascist chief of police, who was accused of having turned over to the Germans more than fifty of the doomed hostages and who had been responsible for Visconti's arrest as a partisan (Visconti was condemned to death but never executed). The emotional power of the central episodes about the Ardeatine atrocity (filmed by Pagliero) and the trial of Caruso compensates only in part for the documentary's lack of structure and stylistic shortcomings; the scenes of partisans in action are for the most part reconstructed and on the whole are awkwardly rhetorical, as is the voice-over commentary. The documentary employs in effect a solemn and celebratory visual style and a resonantly patriotic tone in the commentary which closely resemble those of Fascist documentaries and newsreels.[134] *Giorni di Gloria*, even in its very title, may be one of the first examples of that rhetoric which would soon permeate fictional and nonfictional treatments of the Resistance alike.

After his work on *Giorni di Gloria*, Visconti gave up filmmaking and turned to the theater for the next few years. His next film project, begun only in 1947, was originally conceived as a cycle of three documentaries devoted to the fishermen, farmers, and miners of Sicily. Each was to illustrate different aspects of the life of workers and peasants in the *Mezzogiorno* and its struggle to emerge from a condition of poverty and subalternity, a situation which neither the kingdom of Italy nor the Fascist regime had substantially altered. The so-called "southern question" was one of the most important issues in Italian politics after the Liberation. The disparity between the far more economically and socially dynamic North and the backward South amounted at the time (as is still the case today) to the division of Italy into two separate nations.[135] Starting in February 1945, *Rinascita* began to publish Gramsci's writings specifically devoted to the "southern question," in which he argues that the industrial working class of the North should ally itself with the workers and peasants of the South as the only feasible means for a general mobilization of the Italian masses. While the PCI never abandoned its view that Italy was not yet ready for a socialist state, it consistently sought to transform the southern workers and peasants into a political force capable of urging a rapid solution to their economic problems. A series of peasant uprisings and demonstrations calling for land reform in 1945 and 1946 and the occupation of many of the vast *latifundia* in 1946 forced the new Italian coalition government to assign 50,000 hectares of land to cooperative farms. These actions and others like them appeared at the time to confirm the PCI's hypothesis regarding the politicization of the masses in the South. The revolutionary fervor Visconti brought to his original project, hoping to make it both a document of the present and a call to arms (the ending envisioned for the three interlinked episodes was to be a unified uprising of fishermen, farmers, and miners against their oppressors) cannot be understood unless these specific historical circumstances are borne in mind.[136]

Visconti stayed in Sicily for six months, at first with the funding and support of the PCI (later he financed part of the film's expenses himself), but his plans dramatically changed as he came to realize that his Gramsci-inspired ideals did not correspond to the current social and political reality of the island. In the end, he made only one episode of his trilogy, whose subject was the fishermen of Aci Trezza, the same town where Verga's *I Malavoglia* is set; the film, entitled *La terra trema*, was not only an adaptation of Verga's novel for the screen but also perhaps the most aesthetically rigorous neorealist narrative film ever made. Although he radically reverses the ideological framework of Verga's novel, making young 'Ntoni's struggle to oppose the wholesalers' exploitation of the fishermen the focus of the narrative, Visconti's film is not—as some critics have claimed— simply an act of naive political wish fulfillment.[137] *La terra trema* is, on the contrary, politically realistic, and it makes no concessions to the tenets of socialist realism. 'Ntoni's defeat, and the story of the tragic disintegration of the Malavoglia family, are set by Visconti in the context of the current situation in Sicily. As Visconti worked on the film with his assistants Francesco Rosi and Franco Zeffirelli, assaults against sections of the PCI and of the labor unions, organized by the landowners, took place all over Sicily, apparently with the tacit consent of the police.[138] After the success of the Left during the regional Sicilian elections of April 1947, the support that it had temporarily gained during the peasant uprisings gradually failed, and power passed back to the conservatives.[139]

Like *Ossessione*, *La terra trema* is formally complex and can be viewed in many ways. The composition of the images in a series of visually striking deep-focus shots, the dialogue in Sicilian dialect, and the commentary of an invisible but omniscient narrator constitute three conflicting levels of discourse whose tension Visconti orchestrates skillfully. Contrary to *I Malavoglia*, in which the use of free indirect discourse and the fusion of sayings, proverbs, idiomatic expressions, and dialect-forms with literary Italian allow Verga to play the role of a "folk" historian and storyteller speaking from within the community itself, *La terra trema* accentuates the "anthropological" distance between the vision and voice of the community and the narrator (sometimes giving the latter a paternalistic tone from today's vantage point). The incomprehensibility of the dialect—even for other Italians— stresses the "otherness" of the community and the fact that it belongs to a culture and a historical reality that the filmmaker (a Milanese aristocrat) can only view and represent through a perspective which is entirely alien to the community's mentality. The voice of the narrator is in effect the voice of a "revolutionary" consciousness that has yet to emerge within the fishing community, and therefore is alien to it and "outside" of it. The quality of Visconti's compositions and montage, as in the renowned sequence of the women on the rocks during the storm or the opening sequence of the fishing fleet's return to the harbor at dawn, gives the film the character of an epic (even if Visconti has also sometimes been criticized for "aestheticizing" the villagers' poverty). The chorality that is developed by the use of deep focus and long, slow pans adds to the sense of a communal "epic."

In contrast to the film's visual quality, however, there are no epic heroes, only victims, in the narrative itself. Even 'Ntoni (the protagonist) is repeatedly victimized by his own deluded desire for economic—but not political—progress, which leads to a series of setbacks and hardships, and finally to the dissolution of the patriarchal family, but leaves him with the seeds of a revolutionary vision of his world. Desire and consciousness must now be joined, unlike in *Ossessione*; the desire for better material conditions of existence must be integrated with political consciousness or, as happens in 'Ntoni's case, the former will never be fully realized. Visconti does not idealize the patriarchal family itself or the rustic communal existence of the village; the Grandfather's wisdom—which in Verga represents the fundamental values of patriarchy—is but a set of empty proverbs which have lost all meaning, and the villagers are venal and politically apathetic, leaving themselves open to manipulation by the capitalists.

The principle difference between *Ossessione* and *La terra trema* lies in Visconti's shift to a committed cinema, openly political and pragmatic but still formally uncompromising. The arc that his work traces between 1942 and 1947 (although the film was released only in 1948) shows how the transition from a negative to a constructive social critique could be achieved in the Italian cinema, even if intermingled with Visconti's other preferred themes of "decadence" and "decline" (in the case of *La terra trema*, the "decline" of an ancient way of life). Unlike many other neorealist films, which either explicitly avoid politics altogether (as in De Sica's and Zavattini's case) or tend towards socialist realism (as in De Santis's and Lizzani's case), Visconti's *La terra trema* conveys a political message without either overly simplifying its aesthetic discourse or obscuring the complexity of the issues involved.

Visconti's former fellow member of the *Cinema* group, De Santis, turned to another, more typical solution. De Santis co-wrote *Il sole sorge ancora* (with Guido Aristarco and Carlo Lizzani) in 1946 and directed *Caccia Tragica* (*Tragic Pursuit*) in 1947. *Caccia Tragica* is a neorealist film that exploits conventional commercial genres—melodramas, American gangster films, and Westerns— to tell the story of the struggle between the peasants of a collective farm in the Romagna region of north-central Italy and a gang of sinister henchmen hired by the local absentee landlords to crush the peasants' efforts to free themselves economically. Like *Il sole sorge ancora*, *Caccia Tragica* was produced by the National Association of Italian Patriots (ANPI), a PCI-controlled organization formed after the demobilization to help those partisans who were not entitled to the benefits normally granted to regular army veterans. *Caccia Tragica* is one of the most successful cinematic examples of socialist realism in the postwar Italian tradition. The simple, effective plot is filled with dramatic action sequences and crowd scenes, developing the central theme of class solidarity through the portrayal of a group of characters whose private passions intersect with the larger social and economic conflicts of the day. Like *Il sole sorge ancora*, the film's outlook on the prospect for political change after the Liberation is optimistic. In particular, the notion of class solidarity as the necessary premise for social and political change is developed by De Santis through the conflict between the two male protagonists, Michele and Alberto. The two first met and became friends in a German prison camp, but while Michele and his wife Giovanna try to build a new life by starting a collective farm with a group of peasants who have succeeded in saving enough money to buy their own land, Alberto enters into the service of the landowners and falls in love with the gang leader, a woman named Daniela, whose association with the Germans during the Occupation earned her the nickname of "Lili Marlene." On their way to the site where they plan to start their collective farm, the peasants are ambushed and robbed by the gang, and Giovanna is kidnapped. In the course of the long "tragic pursuit" that follows, Alberto begins to regret his actions, and when Michele finally tracks him down, the repentant Alberto leads him to the gang's hideout and "redeems himself" by shooting Daniela dead. Put on trial by a tribunal appointed by the peasants, Alberto is spared thanks to Michele and Giovanna, who speak in his defense. In the closing sequence Alberto walks off alone, while the peasants gently throw clods of earth at his feet in an act symbolizing hope for regeneration.

A similar symbolic act closes De Santis's most famous neorealist film, *Riso amaro* (*Bitter Rice*, 1949), scripted together with Gianni Puccini and Carlo Lizzani. The film is a melodrama about the *mondine*—or women rice-gatherers—of the Po valley and their difficult working and living conditions. The *mondine* scatter handfuls of rice on the corpse of Silvana (Silvana Mangano),[140] who has killed herself out of remorse for her betrayal of them, after having been seduced by a swindler. To the class-solidarity theme of *Caccia Tragica*, *Riso amaro* adds an indictment of the values of consumer society, as represented by pulp fiction, *fumetti*, and commercial Hollywood films, all of which have "corrupted" Silvana and turned her into a subproletarian Madame Bovary.

(Ironically, the film owed its immense success precisely to Silvana's pin-up sex appeal and to the spectacle of hundreds of half-naked women singing in perfect harmony as they worked in the rice fields.) In both films De Santis uses the conventional devices of melodrama and the cliché antitheses that typify feuilletons, although he claims to do so with full critical awareness: "I like to immerse myself in tradition, express the current aspirations of the people through its traditions. Besides, all of us, from time to time, happen to rediscover the Italian tradition of melodrama. And of course that applies to me in particular." [141] The audiences who deserted *La terra trema, Umberto D,* and *Germania anno zero* flocked to see De Santis's films; for better or for worse, the style and themes of his filmmaking far more accurately summarize those of the majority of so-called "neorealist" films of the period (many of which were just conventional "B" movies which appropriated a few of the critically fashionable stylistic markers of De Sica or Rossellini).

Calvino's Choice

In July 1948 Calvino—then twenty-five years old—went to the rice field in the Vercelli area, where De Santis was shooting *Riso amaro,* in order to write an article on the making of the film for *L'Unità.* He was—reports Paolo Spriano—"dazzled" by Silvana Mangano, and in his article he not only commended the film's thematics of commitment but also wrote a kind of madrigal praising the beauty of the eighteen-year-old actress and predicting the success of the film on account of it. What makes this episode more than a mere curiosity are the circumstances in which Calvino's article was published and the events that followed its publication. Calvino's article appeared on July 14, 1948, the same day as the attempt on Togliatti's life. Three months earlier the Christian Democrats had defeated the Communist-Socialist coalition in the national elections, gaining a solid majority in the Chamber of Deputies. Backed by the United States and the Catholic Church, the Christian Democrats had made their campaign into a crusade against Communism. The Vatican mobilized the clergy, despite the Lateran agreements (which forbade it to interfere in the internal politics of the Italian state), and threatened excommunication for all those who voted for the Left. Catholic organizations all over Italy rallied to bring to the polls all potential anticommunists, including many of the destitute and diseased who traditionally could rely only on the network of Catholic health and charitable organizations for care and support. The number of voters reached an unprecedented level: 92.1 percent.[142] The shooting and wounding of Togliatti—the act of a fanatic, which, however, reflected the tension of the electoral campaign and its Cold War context—triggered a series of protests and strikes, and a number of factories, town halls, and state offices in the northern cities were occupied by angry workers. Ex-partisans brought out the weapons they had hidden after the war and the conviction spread among the strikers, left-wing militants, and even among party officials, including members of the PCI Central Committee, that the hour of revolution had struck. When the PCI and the Union finally called off the strikes, disturbances continued for several days afterward, before dissolving in frustration. Many left-wing militants realized only after this episode that Togliatti's promise to respect the rules of democracy was not just a Machiavellian maneuver on his part. In the superheated insurrectional atmosphere of the four days following the assassination attempt, Calvino devoted himself to chronicling the progress of the strikes. His reports appeared in a small newspaper belonging to *La Camera del lavoro*, because all other newspapers had temporarily suspended publication.

Calvino was extremely active between 1947 and 1956 as a journalist and political commentator sympathetic to the PCI and its policies. His articles focused on specific issues regarding firings, wages, salaries, contracts, inflation, unemployment compensation, and other economic matters throughout the various stages of labor relations during the Reconstruction period. Unwilling to become an apologist for the PCI, Calvino chose instead to report about postwar Italy in newspapers, journals, and magazines, as his own mode of political—if not in terms of a party program—commitment. Calvino nonetheless often found himself in the position of having to justify his political "reticence." In his 1950 letter written to Valentino Gerratana after Pavese's suicide, Calvino refers to a series of reports he sent to *L'Unità* about a recent confrontation between the police and the striking peasants of the Vercelli area—the very same ones who figure as the protagonists of *Riso amaro*—as an example of his own positive political commitment. Although written on his own initiative (like the reports on the 1948 strikes), the articles were— Calvino points out—"useful to the newspaper (as usual lacking both in information and communication), the Party and public opinion, and to some extent, to the general strike of solidarity which followed." [143] Although he gave up this form of political activity after 1957 and published articles on social and political questions only sporadically in the 1960's, [144] Calvino never regretted his militancy on the side of the PCI. A few months before his death, he asked Paolo Spriano how he might be able to track down a copy of the *Camera del lavoro* paper where his reports on the 1948 strikes had appeared, perhaps intending to republish them along with other early essays and articles. [145] Unlike most PCI militant intellectuals, however, Calvino clearly saw that fiction writing devoted to chronicle, sociological analysis, criticism of the government's policies, denunciation of social and economic injustices, and political education could do only imperfectly what could be better done with other kinds of discourse, including journalism. His views on the politics of literature were, in this period, closer to Vittorini's than to those of Alicata and other PCI militants. But unlike Vittorini, who in his own literary work consistently envisioned modernity as a cosmic tragedy, adopting the voice of a disillusioned prophet whose ideal was the impossible "restoration" of pre-capitalist communal values, Calvino has a far less apocalyptic vision of contemporary history and of the role of literature in its making. Although, like Vittorini, he believes in the specificity of literature, literature appears to him from the very first as a discourse committed to contemporaneity. Literature may assume a political role in contemporary society by addressing those issues that other forms of contemporary discourse are unable or unwilling to confront. The literary imagination does not seek a visionary transcendence of the here and now, but rather the disclosure of perspectives and possibilities that generate a critical understanding of the present reality and of its full range of potential meanings. Calvino's 1976 statement entitled "Right and Wrong Political Uses of Literature" substantially confirms this position as the same that he held throughout his four decades of work as a writer.[146] Literature, if conceived as a mode of discourse that "voices a truth already possessed by politics," is as a consequence reduced to no more than an ornament; such a notion, moreover, relies on a deluded idea of politics as "fixed and self-confident. . . . Such a pedagogical function for politics could only be imagined at the level of bad literature and bad politics" ("Political Uses," p. 97). According to Calvino, a second and equally erroneous view of the relation between literature and politics assigns to literature the function of containing and expressing "eternal human sentiments," those values and truths "that politics tends to overlook" ("Political Uses," p. 97). While this concept apparently leaves literature more freedom and gives it more power, it in fact at the same time restricts literature "to a function of consolation, preservation, and regression" ("Political Uses," pp. 97–98). Calvino then goes on to suggest two more productive ways of thinking about the political uses of literature:

Literature is necessary to politics above all when it gives a voice to whatever is without a voice, when it gives a name to what as yet has no name, especially to what the language of politics excludes or attempts to exclude. I mean aspects, situations, and languages both of the outer and of the inner world, the tendencies repressed both in individuals and in society. Literature is like an ear that can hear things beyond the understanding of the language of politics; it is like an eye that can see beyond the color spectrum perceived by politics. Simply because of the solitary individualism of his work, the writer may happen to explore areas that no one has explored before, within himself or outside, and to make discoveries that sooner or later turn out to be vital areas of collective awareness. ("Political Uses," p. 98)

The indirect political dimension of literature, Calvino points out, is in fact often totally unintentional and may have little or nothing to do with the writer's own political beliefs; the classic example is perhaps still Balzac's revolutionary realism and reactionary politics. A more intentional politicization of literature—

the kind discernible in Calvino's own works of the neorealist era—consists in the writer's decision "to impose patterns of language, of vision, of imagination, of mental effort, of the correlation of facts . . . in short the creation (and by creation I mean selection and organization) of a model of values that is at the same time aesthetic and ethical, essential to any play of action, especially in political life" ("Political Uses," p. 99). The symbolic order that literature must strive for, if it is to become a model for human action, must be systematic enough to be "firm ground for all practical activities," and at the same time "complex enough to contain the disorder of the world within itself . . . [and] to be the same thing as an absence of any method whatever" ("Political Uses," p. 99). Calvino's ideas on the politics of literature do not adhere either to the philosophy of commitment discussed earlier in this chapter or to the various filmic and fictional practices of engagement developed by other neorealists, for he does not seek to define a direct link between political praxis (that of parties and groups) and writing itself. Calvino's notion of a politically empowered literature takes neorealism far beyond the limits explored here. Both grounded and groundless, ordered and disordering, unable to ignore its own figurality and yet still "the only way of starting to invent a new way of being" ("Political Uses," p. 100), literature for Calvino is "condemned (or privileged) to be forever the most rigorous and, consequently, the most unreliable language in terms of which man names and transforms himself." [147] *The Path to the Nest of Spiders* is Calvino's response—or rather, the first in his series of attempts to respond—to the challenge laid down by literature to politics, and to the writer, in the postwar world.

3 • The Narrative Paths of Memory and History

The Path to *The Path*

After the end of the war, Calvino began writing and publishing short stories about the Resistance. He also wrote editorial notes and book reviews for the northern editions of *L'Unità* and became a PCI activist, doing political work among the students at the University of Turin and in the province of Imperia. Vittorini published one of his partisan stories, "Andato al comando" ("Gone to Headquarters"), and three short "Cronache" on the history and social problems of Liguria.[1] Both Pavese and the communist critic Giansiro Ferrata—the editor of the Milan edition of *L'Unità*, in which several of Calvino's early stories first appeared—encouraged Calvino to write a novel. When the latter had finally finished *Il sentiero dei nidi di ragno*, he entered the contest for unpublished novels by first-time authors sponsored by the Mondadori publishing house in Milan. Neither Ferrata nor Vittorini—the heads of the jury—liked it, though, and the novel did not win the prize. Calvino then sent his manuscript to Pavese, who, although not without reservations, passed it along to Giulio Einaudi. Einaudi was so impressed with *Il sentiero dei nidi di ragno* that he not only decided to publish the work but also promoted it with an extensive advertising campaign. Six thousand copies were sold; this figure represented rather a success for the times, as Calvino himself points out.[2]

In 1947 (the year of *The Path*), Calvino began working for

Einaudi part-time in Turin. From April 1948 through the summer of 1949 he was also coeditor of the cultural section of the Turin edition of *L'Unità*. He also became in this period a journalist, writing articles on trade-union, industrial, and agricultural issues. Calvino's eventual decision to leave his job with *L'Unità*, however, and to accept a full-time position as literary editor for Einaudi in 1949 (a position he held for most of the rest of his life)[3] was motivated by more than one factor. He had understood that, as he himself later admitted, he was not particularly gifted either as a journalist or as a professional politician.[4] Moreover, Enrico Berlinguer (later to become head of the PCI), in offering him the directorship of a Party weekly, had warned him that a political career in the PCI would have been incompatible with "writing novels."[5] Calvino clearly preferred to write novels. Throughout the early and mid-1940's, Calvino continued to support the PCI and its policies and continued to write part-time for *L'Unità*, even as he was preparing his great allegorical trilogy, *I nostri antenati* (*Our Ancestors*). In his articles he concentrated almost exclusively on economic and social issues and generally abstained from the cultural debate of the period. No other Italian writer or intellectual of Calvino's stature, one recent historian has observed, followed the life of the working class in Italy as closely as he did in those years.[6] His first major essay on literature, entitled "Il midollo del leone" ("The Lion's Marrow"), appeared only in 1955. After the events of 1956, Calvino broke with the PCI altogether, which led to a bitter public exchange between himself and Togliatti. The latter accused Calvino of being "the '*letterato*' who yesterday refused to write something that would have meant a political commitment to, and support for, the noble battles fought by the Party."[7] In a letter written immediately following his break with the PCI, though, Calvino expressed his sense of "relief" for no longer being in the position of having to endorse the Party's policies.[8]

●

Calvino was among the draft evaders who failed to report for duty in Mussolini's new Republican army. To avoid conscription, he and his sixteen-year-old brother went into hiding at the family country estate near San Remo, living with the peasants.[9] To force him and his brother to report for duty, the Fascist police arrested their mother and held her as a hostage. Calvino turned himself in and was sent under armed guard to a local army barracks to await assignment to a unit of the Fascist army. During a transfer from one barracks to another, Calvino was able to escape and reach a partisan camp in the mountains; his father—who had taken his own wife's place as hostage—had been freed just before his son's escape became known to the Fascist police, and no harm came to him. Calvino joined a communist partisan unit and saw action in the rugged, parched mountains of Liguria until April 1945. Like so many other partisans turned writers, Calvino began by "telling his own story" to bear witness to the reality of the recent past. Three short stories written in 1945, "La stessa cosa del sangue" ("The Same Thing as Blood"), "Attesa della morte in albergo" ("Waiting for Death at a Hotel"), and "Angoscia in caserma" ("Anxiety in the Barracks"), recount in fictionalized form episodes from Calvino's own life between 1943 and 1944. These are today chiefly of biographical interest, and Calvino himself later disowned them.[10] The non-autobiographical partisan stories written between 1945 and 1946, on the other hand, represent a noteworthy departure from these early experiments in a confessional mode of narration. At least two of them, "Paura sul sentiero" ("Fear on the Footpath") and "Ultimo viene il corvo" ("Last Comes the Crow"), are small masterpieces; in them Calvino takes some of the familiar topoi of Resistance literature and turns them into fables of estrangement in which the Resistance and its representation are redefined. Turning away from the epic, rhetorically inflated representation of the Resistance, Calvino in many of his early stories that "write" the Resistance instead adopts the literary strategies of the fairy tale and the *racconto d'avventure* as forms with which to erode and undermine the dominant discursive logic of the epic.[11]

Taking partisan narratives and diaries and the "oral tradition" of a multicolored universe of stories as his basis, Calvino constructs a practice of writing which also represents—in his eyes—a "critical position." In his 1946 review of Stefano Terra's *Rancore*,

Calvino argues that the postwar writer's commitment requires the choice of a style that is anything but "neutral," "impersonal," or "documentary" in intent:

> From a writer like Terra . . . one would expect . . . the incisiveness of a new moral and social evaluation. Why is this not the case? Precisely for this unwillingness of his to compromise himself, his letting men and facts tell their own story rather than telling it himself, thus analyzing them, criticizing them, judging them. By refusing to assume a critical position through the elaboration of his own discourse—a language constructed by himself—the writer gives up an instrument of inquiry, criticism, and action. This refusal is a form of self-indulgence rather than an act of solidarity toward other men, a surrender to the approximate, imprecise language of mere communication.[12]

The writer's construction of a narrative order of fiction openly foregrounds a possible interpretive configuration of human experience and human action and functions as a potential epistemological and pragmatic paradigm. This is why writing must serve as "an instrument of inquiry, criticism, and action" and not "refuse" to "assume" such a position. Calvino's poetics is in this sense rigorously classical: to delight *and* instruct is the function of poetry. The politics of narrative is, however, neither a matter of mere didacticism nor of persuasion per se. The storyteller tells tales that are memorable and can be repeated, retold, and disseminated, becoming the starting point for other stories and other symbolic reconfigurations of human experience and human action.[13] Storytelling, as an endless dissemination of other stories, is a constant motif of Calvino's fiction, most clearly thematized in the elaborate narratological games of *Il castello dei destini incrociati*, *Le città invisibili*, and *Se una notte d'inverno un viaggiatore*. The relative brevity of Calvino's novels (they are, for the most part, "short novels") and the often-noted lack of any detailed psychological analysis of characters may be attributed to a degree to this need to make the story line memorable for the reader. As Benjamin observes, "There is nothing that commends a story to memory more effectively than that chaste compactness which precludes psychological analysis. And the more natural the process by which the storyteller foregoes psychological shading, the greater becomes the story's claim to a place in the memory of the listener, the more completely is it integrated into his own experience, the greater will be his inclination to repeat it to someone else someday, sooner or later."[14] Calvino is, in the terms of Benjamin's definition, a real storyteller, for the style that he adopts is designed to integrate itself into the experience of the reader and to claim a place for itself in memory, where it may serve as a model for action.

"Paura sul sentiero" is an early example of perhaps the fundamental narrative strategy of Calvino's entire body of work, which he describes as follows:

For Calvino, what matters most is a geometrical design, a *combinatoire*, a structure of symmetries and oppositions, a chess-board on which the black squares and the white squares exchange places in accordance with a very simple mechanism. . . . Should we conclude that while, for the nineteenth-century writer, the story was a "slice of life," for today's writer it is above all a written page, a world in which only autonomous forces are at work? . . . Let us rather say that, in constructing a story (i.e. establishing a model of relations between narrative functions), the writer foregrounds a logical procedure that can *also* be used to establish relations between the facts of experience.[15]

Although this statement dates from 1970, it offers a vision of narrative as "symbolic action" which is to be found in Calvino's fiction from the very beginning.[16]

Binda, the protagonist of "Paura sul sentiero," is a partisan folk hero whose speed as a courier has made him a local legend: "At a quarter past nine, just as the moon was getting up, he reached Colla Bracca; at twenty past he was already at the crossroads of the two trees; by half past nine he'd be at the fountain. He would have been within sight of San Faustino before ten, at Perallo by half past ten, Creppo at midnight; he might reach Vedetta at Castagna by one—ten hours of walking at a normal speed, but six hours at the most for Binda, the fastest courier in the brigade."[17] The names and indications of geographical locations in this paragraph presuppose a partisan audience, one familiar with the topography of the Ligurian *entroterra*. Binda's story is a local story—a tale that goes from mouth to mouth among the various battalions of the partisan brigade (which has itself traveled across this space)—and the reader is drawn into the same community of listeners, who are aware of the distance between the various points of this space and the time that it takes to get from one point to the next. The opening paragraphs of "Paura sul sentiero" define Binda's story as a quest but not as an epic in the conventional sense. The goal of the quest is Vedetta's camp, which Binda must reach as fast as he can by traversing a familiar terrain. The object of the quest is not immediately defined; it appears at first as a challenge that Binda sets to himself—a kind of sporting challenge to reach his destination faster than any other courier: "He went hard at it, did Binda, flinging himself headlong down short cuts, never making a mistake at turnings which all looked alike, recognizing stones and bushes in the dark, racing uphill, never changing the rhythm of his breathing—his legs went like pistons. 'Go Binda!' his comrades would say as they saw him from a distance climbing up toward their camp" (p. 47; 110—here and throughout the remainder of the book, a second page number refers to a quote's location in the Italian edition). Binda, however, is an authentic hero of the Resistance, of the kind celebrated in the partisan broadsheets. Binda's tale is told by a fusion of private and public history, and of individual and collective memory, which is altogether characteristic of the neorealist chronotope:

> But it was the natural job for him, as he never got lost in the woods and knew all the paths, from having led goats about them or gone for wood or hay since he was a child. . . . A chestnut tree with a hollow trunk, blue lichen on a stone, the bare space around a charcoal pit—a strange and unfamiliar setting for anyone else—linked themselves in his mind to his remotest memories. . . . And now new memories were added to those, memories of the war in these parts—a continuation of his story. Work, play, hunting, all turned to war. (p. 48; 111)

The fundamental motif of the landscape's familiarity links the site of partisan warfare to Binda's "remotest memories" of childhood. Indeed, the war seems to take Binda back to his childhood games and away from the routines of his adult life, but it is also what turns the familiar into the unfamiliar, the known into the unknown.[18] The central theme of "Paura sul sentiero" is precisely this opposition, with its doubling of the *heimlich* into the *unheimlich*, and the way in which his legendary speed as a courier is motivated by something deeper than devotion to the partisan cause.

Landscape and social life—space and human time—are represented as a collective reality in the story. Binda's personal life and his experience of the war are linked to the life and experience of the community, which is made up of both the civilian population—for example, Binda's lover and his mother, who live in the village—and the partisan brigade with which Binda fights against the Fascists and Germans. The geometry of the relations among individuals and groups and the alternate positionings of the opposing factions on the scene of combat are drawn by Calvino with the rigorous and economic precision of a tridimensional *combinatoire*:

The war turned round and round in those valleys . . . partisans elbow to elbow with Bersaglieri and Fascist militia; each side alternating between mountain and valley, making wide turns round the crests so as not to run into each other and find themselves fired on; and always someone killed, either on hill or valley. Binda's village, San Faustino, was down among the fields, three groups of houses on each side of the valley. Regina hung out sheets from her window on days when there were round ups. Binda's village was a short halt on his way up and down; a sip of milk, a clean shirt ready washed by his mother; then off he had to hurry, in case the Fascists suddenly arrived. . . . Winter was a game of hide and seek; the Bersaglieri at Baiardo, the Militia at Molini, the Germans at Briga, and in the middle of them the partisans squeezed into two corners of the valley, avoiding the round ups by moving from one to the other during the night (p. 48; 111–12)

From the maddening and apparently endless hide-and-seek game which informs the narrative *combinatoire* of "Paura sul sentiero," Binda's behavior emerges as a model means for dealing with experience, in order to master the rules of the game rather than be mastered by it.

In the third section of the story, the task of Binda's quest is specifically defined: "That very night a German column was marching on Briga, had perhaps already reached Carmo, and the Militia were getting ready to reinforce from the Molini. The partisan detachments were sleeping in stalls around half-spent braziers; Binda marched along in the dark woods, with their salvation in his legs, for the order he carried was: 'Evacuate all the valleys at once. Entire battalion and heavy machine guns to be on Mount Pellegrino by dawn'" (p. 49; 112). Binda is—like the quintessential hero of the fairy tale—"the figure of the man who sets out to learn what fear is (and) . . . shows us that things we are afraid of can be seen through."[19] Thus Calvino tells us what his fears, desires, and fantasies are as Binda makes his way through the dark and threatening landscape towards the goal of his quest—namely, the rescue of his endangered comrades. Binda must battle with his own sense of fear as well as with the enemy. Although filtered through the perspective of an omniscient narrator, even the descriptions of Binda's fears stay within the basic outline of the fairy tale, which frames the story of his civil war of the self. As in *The Path*, Calvino draws a psychosocial portrait entirely through dialogue, the actions of the character, and the order of events, rather than through the use of a narrative point of view that details for the reader the inner workings of the character's mind.[20] During his long journey through the night, Binda longs for supernatural powers; for instance, he wishes that he were able to pull himself up to the top of the mountain as if by magic: "Binda felt anxiety fluttering in his lungs like bats' wings; he longed to grasp the slope two miles away, pull himself up it, whisper the order like a breath of wind into the grass and hear it floating off. . . . Binda would have liked to lose the path, plunge into a sea of dry leaves and swim in them until they submerged him" (p. 49; 112). Every tree, every stone, and every shadow on the path turns into a ghostly image of an enemy, the spectral sign of a trap lying just ahead, a terrifying omen. Binda's fears become fused with his childhood nightmares and superstitions and finally coalesce into the image of a beast pursuing him relentlessly: "Following on Binda's tracks was an animal raised from deep back in his childhood; it was coming after him, would soon catch him up. . . . Those lights were the Germans searching Tumena, bush by bush, in battalions. Impossible, Binda knew that, although it would be almost pleasant to believe it, to abandon himself to the blandishments of that animal from childhood which was following him so close" (p. 50; 113). The animal subsequently undergoes a series of metamorphoses in Binda's imagination, until it becomes the monstrous image of a German soldier: "Gund . . . with a terrible white smile under his helmet, would stretch out huge hands to seize him" (p. 51; 115). The familiar path is simultaneously transformed into a maze as if by a magic spell, and Binda turns into an archetypal Theseus figure, struggling against a Minotaur who is actually a projection of his own unconscious, a monstrous double of himself: "Suddenly he thought he had missed the way; and yet he recognized the path, the stones, the trees, the smell of musk. But they were stones, trees, musk from another place far away, from a thousand different far away places. . . . It was a trick of the Germans waiting in ambush, and he'd suddenly fall into their hands, find himself facing the big German called Gund who is deep down in all of us" (pp. 51–52; 115).

No celebration awaits the hero when he finally reaches his destination, however. Binda delivers his message, and while the partisans get ready to evacuate the camp he eats some boiled chestnuts left over from their spartan meal. As he resumes his nocturnal journey, setting foot once more on the trial-filled path, Gund rises up one more time from the bushes along the path and starts to follow Binda with his giant's stride. Binda's story is therefore revealed to be only a segment of a continuing narrative: it is this that propels him from one camp to the next with such superhuman speed. This narrative is not only a part of the history of the war and of the Resistance—the tales which went from mouth to mouth among the partisans and helped them make sense of the small and large events they lived through as protagonists and victims—but of an individual reality whose surface is deceptively simple. Binda's is a story which will be followed by other stories, similar and yet different, familiar and unfamiliar, repeating the same pattern with new dramatis personae, new scenarios and settings, as long as there will be destinations to reach, labyrinths to challenge, and monsters to slay. "Every real storyteller," observes Benjamin, "has counsel for his readers." This counsel, woven into the fabric of the story, "is less an answer to a question than a proposal concerning the continuation of a story that is just unfolding."[21]

"Ultimo viene il corvo," one of Calvino's most admired short stories, has its source in a story by Flaubert, "La Légende de saint Julien l'Hospitalier."[22] Flaubert's story was inspired in turn by the medieval folk tradition of storytelling, narrative iconography, and saints' legends, as pointed out with exquisite irony in the story's closing sentence: "and that is the story of St. Julian Hospitator, more or less as it is depicted on a stained-glass window in a church in my part of the world."[23] The preface for the 1893 illustrated edition of the story was written by another master storyteller, Marcel Schwob, who used the occasion to trace the story's genealogy back to a vast constellation of legends, folk narratives, fairy tales, literary texts, and myths which include the *Legenda Aurea*, *The Thousand and One Nights*, *The Decameron*, fables by the brothers Grimm and by La Fontaine, and the myth of Oedipus. Schwob's preface is in effect another story, an imaginary biography not of a person but of the legend itself and its amazing series of transformations over the centuries and across the world. In his preface, Schwob points to the key opposition which is the structural matrix of Flaubert's story, an opposition which reappears—albeit entirely transformed—in Calvino's story. Julien, writes Schwob, "has a sort of destructive faith. This truly touches on the sacred mystery that will make him a saint; for are not destruction and creation sisters?"[24] The dialectic of destruction and creation that transforms Julien into a saint is the same that transforms the protagonist of "Ultimo viene il corvo" into a "partisan hero" through a bloody rite of passage.

From Flaubert's elaborate tale, which traces the course of Julien's life from birth to death, Calvino takes only the key sequence about young Julien's uncontrollable passion for hunting and his superhuman marksmanship. In "Ultimo viene il corvo," the nameless boy protagonist meets by chance a group of partisans by a stream teeming with trout. The partisans are contemplating the possibility of throwing a hand grenade into the stream to catch the fish. The boy, "a mountaineer with an apple face" (p. 68; 133), approaches them, demands to be given a rifle, and then takes one without hesitation from one of the men. One of the partisans warns him that he will never get a fish with a rifle, but the boy has already taken aim at a target: "If you fire into the water you'll frighten the fish, that's all," the man tried to say, but he didn't even finish. A trout had surfaced with a flash, and the boy fired a shot and hit it as if expecting it at that very spot" (p. 68; 133). To the men's amazement, the boy repeats his feat several times, displaying truly unusual skill with the rifle. The partisans ask him to join them and he readily agrees, delighted to be able to keep the rifle. As he marches along a path with the partisans, everything he sees becomes a potential target in his eyes: "It was fine going off because there were new things to be seen at every turn, trees with cones, birds flying from branches, lichen on stones" (p. 69; 134). The partisans explain to him, however, that he cannot shoot at random, for "these parts were to be passed in silence and the cartridges were needed for the war" (p. 69; 134). The temptation is too strong, though, and when the boy sees a hare running across the path he cannot resist shooting it. The partisans' leader praises his sharpshooting but forbids him to fire again: "We're not out hunting here. You mustn't fire again even if you see a pheasant" (p. 70; 135). At the next infraction—partridges this time—the rifle is taken away from him. The boy grumbles a bit, but he stays with the partisans, hoping to get the rifle back. He gets his chance early the next morning. While the partisans are still asleep, he takes the best rifle and sneaks out of the shepherd's hut where they have spent the night. Pinecones, mushrooms, snails, frogs, lizards, mice, jays: the boy walks along shooting at everything that attracts his attention. The crescendo of destructive frenzy is, however, comic rather than tragic (unlike Flaubert's tale). While Julien derives a morbid erotic pleasure from killing,[25] the game of the apple-cheeked boy appears entirely innocent: "It was a lovely game going like this from one target to another; perhaps he could go round the world doing it" (p. 70; 135). For both the boy and Julien, the hunt coincides with a quest whose ultimate goal is unknown. Julien's own quest unfolds under a curse, though, and its power dooms him to kill his own father and mother—the very beings who have given him life—before he can discover, through expiation and sacrifice, the true purpose and meaning of his existence.[26] Calvino's story, on the contrary, articulates a model of human time which is es-

sentially future-oriented, thus reversing the oedipal structure
of Flaubert's narrative. Rather than an epic hero, the apple-
cheeked boy is a fairy-tale hero, and the governing principle of
Calvino's narrative is indeed that naive wish fulfillment which is
inscribed in the mode of the fairy tale and makes it the dialogical
other of the past-oriented heroic saga.[27]

Calvino's "deconstruction" of Flaubert's story implies in turn
a deconstruction of the Resistance mystique. Rather than tell
once again the epic tale of the partisan heroes whose sacrifice
redeems the Italian people of its original crime and tragic fate—
that is, their "irrational" submission to the corruption and degenerate violence of the Fascist "monster"—Calvino offers the
simple story of a boy who joins the partisans only to be able to
play with a rifle and go in search of adventure. This ironic inversion is not in turn a mystification of the reality of the partisan
struggle or a transfiguration of historical truth into an escapist
fantasy. On the contrary, many members of the younger generation joined the partisans out of a simple desire for weapons and
adventures—as is apparent in Levi Cavaglione's memoir, *Guerriglia nei Castelli Romani*, for example (this accounts to a degree for
the phenomenon usually labelled "spontaneous anti-Fascism"
by Resistance historians). Equally estranging with respect to Resistance rhetoric is Calvino's depiction of the boy's transformation into a "partisan hero." As he walks down the path with his
rifle, firing at random, the boy suddenly runs into a group of
German soldiers, who immediately aim their guns at him:

But the boy had already picked out some gilt buttons on one of their
chests and fired at a button. . . . He was now lying stretched on the
ground behind a heap of stones on the edge of the road, under cover. It
was a long heap, and he could move about, peep over in some unexpected part, see the gleam on the barrels of the soldiers' weapons, the
grey and glittering parts of their uniforms, shoot at a stripe, a badge.
Then back he'd drop to the ground and slide quickly over to another side
to fire. After a bit he heard bursts from behind firing over his head and
hitting the soldiers; these were his comrades coming to reinforce him
with machine guns. "If that boy hadn't woken us with his shots. . . ,"
they were saying (p. 71; 136).

A hero *malgré soi*, having saved his comrades' lives, the boy
is still shooting in the woods as if this was simply some sort

of game. Rather than aim at their most vulnerable points, he picks in fact the smallest and most difficult-to-hit targets on the bodies of the soldiers. Forced to abandon his hiding place when a bullet grazes his cheek and he sees that a German has reached the road above him, the boy jumps up and runs after the soldier, whose gun is now jammed. The pursuit takes him away from his comrades and into the woods; each time the German appears through the trees he nicks off some part of his uniform with another shot, until the soldier hides behind a rock in the middle of a clearing.

At this point there is a radical shift in point of view, as the ingenuous, apple-cheeked boy turns into an uncanny avenger. While the narrative was first focused through the eyes of the partisans amazed at the boy's skill and then through the eyes of the boy exhilarated by the effect of his shooting on the objects around him, the concluding sequence places the reader in the position of the German soldier. The reader thus suddenly finds himself on the other side of the boy's rifle, face to face with its threat of death, rather than looking down through its sights. The German is at the same time transformed from an anonymous uniform—a synecdoche of the enemy for the partisans, a mere moving target for the boy—into a human subject faced with imminent death. The German's thoughts and fears, his increasingly desperate attempts to save himself, and his ultimate resignation to the fate that awaits him occupy the rest of the story. The boy's shooting, seen from the German's perspective, turns from an innocent into a deadly game:

How long would the boy stay there? And would he never lower that gun? The soldier decided to make a test; he put his helmet on the point of his bayonet and hoisted it slightly above the rock. A shot rang out and the helmet rolled to the ground, pierced through. The soldier did not lose heart. It was obviously easy to aim at the edges of the rock, but if he moved quickly it should be impossible to hit him. At the moment a bird winged quickly across the sky, a pigeon perhaps. A shot and it fell. The soldier dried the sweat on his neck. Another bird passed, a thrush; that fell too. The soldier swallowed saliva. This must be a place of passage; birds went on flying over head, all of them different, and the boy went on shooting and bringing them down. . . . Now the soldier felt a taste of lead in his mouth. . . . He must not hurry things, anyway; he was safe behind the rock, with his grenades. And why not try and get him with a grenade, while staying under cover? He stretched back on the ground, drew his arm out behind him, taking care not to show himself, gathered up all his strength and threw the grenade. A good effort; it would have gone a long way; but in the middle of its flight a shot exploded it in mid-air. . . . When he raised his head the crow had come. (p. 72; 137–38)

The crow is, like the great stag in Flaubert's story, a magic animal whose appearance coincides with a crucial moment of revelation. He is the bearer of a prophetic message that discloses the true meaning of the hero's hunt by erasing the illusion of his innocence. But while the great stag reveals to Julien his tragic fate determined by a curse whose reason remains shrouded in the mystery of origins ("Accursed, accursed, accursed! One day, cruel heart, you will kill your father and mother!"),[28] the appearance of the crow marks the boy's initiation into history through the killing of the German. The appearance of the crow is ambiguous, for the bird may be a hallucination in the mind of the German soldier, or the boy may be pretending to be momentarily distracted in order to trick the German. The crow is in either case an omen of death, and time seems to stop as the bird circles over the scene of the life-and-death confrontation between the two characters:

It was swinging slowly around in the sky above him. . . . Now the boy would be certain to shoot it down. But the shot seemed to be a long time in coming. Perhaps the crow was flying too high? And yet he had hit other birds flying higher and faster. . . . Surely it was impossible the boy hadn't seen it? Perhaps the crow did not exist? . . . Perhaps when one is about to die one sees every kind of bird pass; when one sees the crow it means one's time has come. He must warn the boy . . . so the soldier got to his feet and pointed at the black bird. "There's a crow!" he shouted in his own language. The bullet hit him in the middle of the eagle with spread wings embroidered on his tunic.
Slowly the crow came circling down. (p. 73; 138–39)

The pause—the interval between the coming of the raven and the last shot—signals a disjunction in temporal levels, the symbolic crossing from the time of the fairy tale and childhood innocence into the time of history, a history which lacks all innocence and sets insurmountable limits to individual fantasies and desires. Despite its pathos, the killing of the German hides no mystery or absent cause; its referent is the historical fact of the German occupation and of the war in Italy. Thus the final bullet, hitting the Nazi "Kriegsadler" embroidered on the soldier's uniform, signifies the end of the boy's arbitrary hunt and is a fully motivated sign, pointing to both the boy's and the soldier's symbolic roles in the scene of history.[29]

●

With *The Path to the Nest of Spiders*, Calvino finally sets himself the task of problematizing Resistance history in a novel. Unlike most of the partisan stories of *Ultimo viene il corvo*, which provide limited, fragmentary insights into some of the more disturbing and repressed aspects of the war and of partisan life but carefully avoid any autobiographical element, *The Path* attempts to convey both the overall sense of Calvino's personal experience of the Resistance and his intellectual assessment of it.

In his preface to *The Path*, Calvino remarks that when he was originally trying to narrate the partisan experience by using the first person singular or a character similar to himself as the main focalizer, the results were disappointingly poor. Only when he distanced the narrative from his personal perception of "what happened" by approaching his subject obliquely, namely from the point of view of a child on the margins of the partisan struggle, did he feel able to convey "the color, the flavor and pace" of his own experience of the Resistance. "Everything would be seen through the eyes of a child, in an atmosphere of urchins and tramps. I invented a story that would remain at the edge of the partisan war, its heroism and sacrifices, but at the same time would convey its color, its harsh flavor, its pace" (p. xii; 13). San Remo and the Ligurian mountains—the setting of Calvino's experience as a partisan—provide the backdrop for the story of *The Path*.[30] Pin, an eleven- or twelve-year-old orphan from one of the poorest parts of San Remo, lives with his sister Rina and works as an apprentice cobbler. One day an envoy of a partisan organization comes to the local tavern, seeking to mobilize the men who usually gather there, with whom Pin spends long hours when he is not working or roaming the streets. The men in turn talk Pin into stealing a pistol for them from one of his sister's clients (Rina is a prostitute and a Fascist collaborator). Pin steals the pistol and hides it in a place known only to him ("the place where the spiders make their nests") outside of town, but he is quickly arrested by the Fascist police. In jail, he meets a young partisan named Red Wolf, with whom he makes a daring escape. Unable to return home, Pin wanders alone in the woods on the edge of town until he runs into another partisan, the legendary Cousin, who takes him to a partisan encampment in the mountains. This partisan detachment turns out to be made up of all the rejects from the other partisan units; they are a motley crew of army and militia deserters, psychopaths, Trotskyites, and so on. Their leader, the apolitical Dritto (an ex-waiter), succeeds in keeping his men under control, but partisan headquarters does not trust either him or his men, and they are usually left out of any major combat engagements. Pin becomes a part of the unit, although he carries no weapon, working as the cook's helper and entertaining the men with his pranks and songs. One night, though, while flirting with the cook's wife, Giglia, Dritto absentmindedly sets the partisans' cabin on fire, destroying their ammunition and supplies. Although certain to face severe disciplinary action from headquarters, Dritto is left in command of the unit by two of the partisan leaders, Kim (a student) and Ferriera (a factory worker). Finally Dritto's unit is called upon to join in an ambush of the Germans; however, when the day arrives for the men to move out, Dritto stays behind in order to make love to Giglia, and Pin remains to keep an eye on them. The ambush does not go well, the men have to retreat, Dritto is arrested, and the unit disbanded by partisan headquarters. Alone once again, Pin returns to his sister's apartment in town. She has recovered the pistol that Pin originally stole, but Pin takes it away from her and flees back to "the place where the spiders make their nests." There he runs into the solitary Cousin once again, who borrows the pistol to go into town and settle an old score; when he returns, Pin goes off with him to become a real Resistance fighter, happy to have at last found a friend whom he can trust.

Although Calvino's first novel is about his involvement as a young bourgeois intellectual in the partisan struggle, the Resistance as a historical event, and the epic dimensions of the struggle for the liberation of Italy, these subjects are represented indirectly rather than directly; they constitute a kind of "referential horizon" behind the text. The most interesting features of the novel are in fact the distancing of the narrative from the author's autobiographical experience, the decentering of the scene of history through the setting of the narrative on the margins of the partisan struggle, and the defamiliarization of the conventions of neorealist literature and Resistance historiography. Oddly enough, these features of Calvino's novel have received relatively little critical attention, yet they are the rhetorical strategies that allow Calvino to weave his textual web and thus deserve closer scrutiny.

The Path is a study of memory but not in the sense of memory as the accurate retention of the past. Memory is inevitably rooted in the desire to recover the origin; often this takes the form of a desire to retain the past exactly as it was and to make the present the fulfillment of the past. In memory, however, as Calvino remarks in his preface, the past never returns exactly as it was but only in the form of fragmentary, often elusive, and sometimes incomprehensible traces. When an author (novelist or historian or both) sets out to write in order to recover the past, a complex process of replacement and supplementarity is set in motion. The conflicting memory-traces of past events are reworked, rewritten, and rearranged in a way that endows them with an order and a meaning and identifies them as narrative functions. Narrative always makes the implicit claim to be a mode of repetition, a going over once again (or doubling) of a ground already covered in real life.[31] However, the very possibility of narrative form—that is, meaning plotted over and through time—depends on a type of repetition that implies difference. Narrative representation is not the "re-presentation" of real events, no matter what it may claim to be or to do; it employs modes of textual repetition (such as symmetry and parallelism) to create a plot, which is always a significant interconnection of events. It is therefore always also a (trans)figuration of reality or a "reality effect" (Barthes), even in what seem to be its most simple and spontaneous forms. The transfiguration of past events into a narrative structure, which is the act of comprehending the past, refers at the same time to the present needs and desires of the author (novelist or historian), who inevitably also composes the history of his own present in the act of "writing the past."[32] Narrative, more than any other kind of writing, is the place of a perpetual interference between what is and what has been. While the moment of writing is itself already a "historical" moment, bearing within itself the traces of the author's cultural past and present, our sense of the tangled "historicity" of writing is greatly intensified in any narrative which specifically seeks to capture and convey the essence of a past event.[33] Indeed, Calvino is well aware that this kind of superimposition is unavoidable even in the most spontaneous of narratives about the past, whose proximity to the past may be a matter of days, hours, or even moments: "During the partisan war, stories just experienced were transformed and transfigured into tales" (p. vi; 8). Historical events can never be portrayed in a narrative as they actually occurred, precisely because they are continually interwoven with the images, verbal echoes, and cultural memories that come to the writer's mind at the moment of writing. The historical referent, as a result, may be assumed within the confines of the text only as the locus of an interpretive act and forever eludes exact reproduction within the text itself.

The Modern Epic

By the time Calvino began to write his partisan stories, the historical events of the Resistance had already been encoded into a narrative. Resistance rhetoric celebrated a heroic and necessary triumph of good over evil, and the historical events of the struggle quickly took on the configuration of an epic tale: "It seemed to us then, a few months after the Liberation, that everyone was talking about the Resistance in the wrong way, a bombast was growing up, hiding its true essence, its basic character. . . . I remember only our constant argument against all mythicized images. . . . It became the key to present and future history" (p. xviii; 18). The actual experience of the Resistance was, according to Calvino, much more chaotic and fragmentary than official rhetoric would allow for: "For many of my contemporaries chance alone had determined the side for which they were to fight. Often roles were abruptly reversed: a die-hard Fascist became a partisan, or vice versa. Whatever side they were on, they shot and were shot at; only death gave their choice an irrevocable mark" (p. xix; 18–19). In writing *The Path*, then, the principal problem for Calvino is to find a narrative strategy that can reconstruct and convey to his readers the fragmentary, chaotic reality of the Resistance. At the same time, though, this narrative strategy must itself—for reasons that will become clearer shortly—avoid either being fragmentary and chaotic in form, on the one hand, or imposing on the reality of the Resistance a fictitious and arbitrarily totalizing narrative order, on the other hand.

While he senses that the Resistance is indeed an event of epic dimensions, Calvino opposes the epic as a mode for the mythic transfiguration of history and for the idealization of the recent past. In particular, he resists what Bakhtin calls the epic's "transferral of the world it describes to an absolute past of national beginnings and peak times." [34] The world of the epic is often perceived, according to Bakhtin, as the national heroic past, distanced and crystallized in the language of myth. In the Italian cultural context of the period immediately after the Liberation and the proclamation of the new Republic in 1946, the events of the Resistance appear particularly well-suited for this kind of epic transfiguration. Yet in his partisan stories as well as *The Path*, Calvino rejects any such transformation of the history of the Resistance into a foundational myth and instead tries to abolish what Bakhtin calls "epic distance." [35] Calvino's polemic against "the positive hero" required by so-called "left-wing culture" in Italy is a direct consequence of his opposition to the epic aggrandizement of the events of the war. The choice of Pin—an illiterate young boy without the slightest hint of "class consciousness"—as the central figure of *The Path* is Calvino's answer to the dogmatic aesthetic prescriptions of socialist realism for the contemporary "epic" and to the heroic distancing of the

past: "The danger of the new literature's being assigned a celebratory, didactic function was in the air. . . . My reaction at that
time could be expressed thus: 'Ah, so you want the "socialist
hero," eh? . . . Well, I'll write you a partisan story in which nobody is a hero, nobody has any class consciousness'" (p. xiv; 14).
In a number of ways, the modern "epic" quality of Calvino's
novel and the "anti-heroic" character of its protagonist stand in
marked contrast to the modern epic as Georg Lukács defines it
in his 1937 study of the historical novel. What Lukács admires in
the classical historical novels by Scott, Manzoni, Pushkin, and
Tolstoy and sees as the "heritage" informing the "concrete historicism" of the new Soviet literature[36] is the ability to select
characters and plots which are typical and paradigmatic of the
economic and sociopolitical conflicts of the organic totality of a
particular historical age. The epic character of Scott's works—
which are, according to Lukács, the prototype of the modern
historical novel—is intimately connected with Scott's conception
of the hero:

> In the entire history of the novel there are scarcely any other works . . .
> which come so near to the character of the old epos. . . . [Scott selects]
> those periods and those strata of society which embody the old epic
> self-activity of man, the old epic directness of social life, its public spon-
> taneity. This is what makes Scott a great epic portrayer of the "age of
> heroes." . . . Nevertheless, Scott's works are in no way modern at-
> tempts to galvanize the old epic artificially into new life, they are real
> and genuine novels. Even if his themes are very often drawn from the
> "age of heroes," from the infancy of mankind, the spirit of his writing is
> nevertheless that of man's maturity, the age of triumphing "prose." . . .
> Scott's novel hero is in his way just as typical for this genre as Achilles
> and Odysseus were for the real epopee. The difference between the
> two hero types illustrates very sharply the fundamental difference be-
> tween epic and novel, moreover in a case where the novel reaches its
> closest point to the epic. The heroes of the epic are, as Hegel says,
> "total individuals who magnificently concentrate within themselves
> what is otherwise dispersed in the national character, and in this they
> remain great, free and noble human characters." Thereby "these prin-
> cipal characters acquire the right to be placed at the summit and to see
> the principal event in connection with their individual persons." The
> principal figures of Scott's novels are also typical characters nationally,
> but in the sense of the decent and average, rather than eminent and all-
> embracing. . . . It is their task to bring the extremes whose struggle fills

the novel, whose clash expresses artistically a great crisis in society, into contact with one another. Through the plot, at whose center stands this hero, a neutral ground is sought and found upon which the extreme, opposing social forces can be brought into a human relation with one another.[37]

Compared to the "real epopee" as Hegel defines it and to the modern one as Lukács (following Hegel) defines it, Calvino's is clearly an epic without a real hero, or rather, it is the epic of an anti-hero. Pin is definitely not free, not noble, and not even a total individual; finding out what these things may mean is indeed part of his quest. While he is unquestionably at the center of the plot, Calvino's anti-heroic hero is highly decentered in relation to the historical process itself. Compared to Scott's modern hero, Pin is also an anti-hero because he is neither typical nor average; he is not a "world-historical individual" but rather a marginal figure who cannot claim to embody fully the sociopolitical dialectic of the Resistance as a crucial phase in modern Italian history. As a subproletarian boy living on the margins of society, Pin is also not in any position to assume the function of mediator or catalyst in the class struggle, which Lukács envisions as the key role for the hero of the modern epic. Furthermore, given that the governing perspective through which historical events are represented in Calvino's novel is that of a child's imagination, *The Path* seems to represent a regression to the older epic mode, that of the poetic fantasy of the "infancy of mankind," rather than the triumphal "prose" (and, implicitly, the "rationality") of "man's maturity."

However, the representation of a key moment in the history of the Italian nation—the Resistance—remains the chief concern of the novel, and the struggle between the partisans and the Fascists is the principal event we are made to see in connection with Pin. This struggle undoubtedly did offer to many individuals the chance to perform heroic and courageous deeds that were entirely out of keeping with the routine of everyday life before the war. Combat involving the partisans took place for the most part in the wildest and most impervious locations on the peninsula, far away from the civilized world. The war required the partisans to exercise great ingenuity in order to survive, to organize themselves, and to fight the enemy in quite primitive conditions of material and social existence. In many ways, then, the partisan movement in Italy did revive precisely what Lukács calls the "old epic self-activity of man, the old epic directness of social life," and the "public spontaneity" of an ancient "age of heroes." This epic quality of the Resistance is conveyed by Calvino particularly in the account of Pin's experience in the camp of Dritto's detachment, where Pin witnesses the material difficulties, the often brutal internal conflicts, and the constant threat of anarchy which permeate the partisans' precarious life and social organization, almost as if indeed they had regressed to an earlier, more primitive stage in the evolution of mankind.

While in many ways it seems to recapture the spirit of a more ancient epic mode, *The Path* does nevertheless fulfill some of Lukács's requirements for the historical novel as a modern epic. *The Path* may be defined in Lukács's terms as "an attempt to portray historical reality as it actually was, so that it could be both humanly authentic and yet be re-livable by the reader of a later age." In *The Path*, as in the works of Scott and Manzoni, "the personal destinies of a number of human beings coincide and interweave within the determining context of an historical crisis." [38] *The Path* shows, furthermore, "how important historical changes affect everyday life, the effect of material and psychological changes upon people who react immediately and violently to them, without understanding their causes." [39] In one fundamental way, though, *The Path* is irreconcilable with the principles of Lukács's modern epic, for it does not take as its principal assumption and ideological matrix the neo-Hegelian, Marxist, or generally "pan-determinist" notion of "historical necessity." Rather, it persistently questions and problematizes this notion. The modern epic must, according to Lukács, "render visible the *generally progressive* features of the whole society, of the whole age." [40] *The Path*, on the contrary, not only focuses on a marginal segment of Italian society and of the Resistance struggle itself but also consistently raises doubts as to the possibility of discerning progressive features in the overall historical process; the novel places under close scrutiny the very idea of history as a global, positive, and necessary progress toward

emancipation.[41] Above all, Calvino rejects the idea that a historical phase such as that of the war and the civil war in Italy before
the Liberation could be represented as an organic whole, a self-
enclosed totality with an intrinsic and discernible order and purpose that logically leads to the following phase (i.e. the present
historical order of the "new" Italy), as if history were somehow a
chain of causally related sequences within a single metanarrative. The narrative transfiguration of the Resistance into such
an organic and rational "epic" totality is precisely what Calvino
sets out to demythify in his novel.

The Naive Focalizer and the
Bracketing of the Empirical Self

The selection of Pin as protagonist and focalizer solves for Calvino the problem of representing a linguistic consciousness in
The Path. Illiterate and naive in most things, Pin's character functions as a narrative device that allows the author/narrator to withhold his comprehensive, retrospective knowledge of the Resistance and to convey the sense of what it was like to become
involved in the partisan struggle at a time when the meaning of
that struggle was still tentative and ambiguous. Paradoxically, by
"bracketing" his empirical self and by imagining a fictional character, Calvino observes in his 1964 preface, the author may succeed in representing his own lived experience more accurately:
"This was *my* experience. . . . The relationship between the character of the boy Pin and the partisan war corresponded symbolically to the relationship with that war that I myself had come
to have" (p. xx; 19). The narrative device of internal focalization,[42]
which makes Pin both a participant in the represented events and
the central consciousness whose perceptions orient the representation, allows for a verisimilar restriction of knowledge about
the events of the novel. Being a part of the represented world,
Pin cannot by definition know everything about it. Unlike the
narrator who tells us his story (but whose role remains implicit
for the most part), Pin could not possibly know in advance how
that same story will end. This restriction of knowledge is aug-

mented by the youth and naiveté of the character-focalizer. Like little Sartoris Snopes in Faulkner's "Barn Burning" or Pip the child in many parts of Dickens's *Great Expectations*, Pin's understanding of the events he experiences and of their implications is a strictly limited one. Even when the focalization shifts to a level external to Pin's consciousness and the narrator's presence becomes less covert, the representation is still "colored" by Pin's perceptions and remains consistent with his worldview.

The choice of a boy as a focalizer also allows Calvino to "let the events speak for themselves," thus avoiding any explicit reference to the bitter political and ideological controversy about the Resistance which took place in Italy while Calvino was writing his novel.[43] In selecting Pin as a focalizer, Calvino consciously chooses to bracket as much as possible the historical and ideological framework that inevitably must orient the point of view of any "adult" focalizer, opting instead for the perspective of a fictional Everyman, a character whose constitutive naiveté makes him almost the lowest common denominator among all possible perspectives on the Resistance. Pin is indeed a latter-day version of Candide; everything he encounters on his adventurous path is new and surprising to him and often eludes his understanding. This does not, of course, render equally innocent Calvino's decision to narrate through the eyes of Pin; on the contrary, this narrative strategy has deep political and ideological implications of its own, whose full importance will be discussed in Chapter 4.

In representing Pin's consciousness, Calvino strives for an effect of elemental simplicity. Pin's experience of the world and of the Resistance is represented in *The Path* as taking place (as far as possible) at the level of immediate phenomenal perceptions of objects, people, and space itself, which Pin seeks to organize into a comprehensive and comprehensible whole.[44] In his attempt to make some sense of the events he witnesses throughout the narrative, Pin resorts to the only interpretive code he has: a heterogeneous and fragmentary oral repertoire made up of childhood stories and fables, plots of films and comic-strip adventure stories, folk songs, and various more or less legendary anecdotes that he has gathered—one assumes—from the most diverse sources over the course of his life as a street urchin. Seen through Pin's eyes, the men and events of the partisan struggle become the protagonists and the adventures of a fantastic narrative, whose multiple threads Pin is always trying to unravel in his mind. For Pin, his "friends" Red Wolf (the young *gappista*[45] Pin meets in prison), Pelle (the ex-Fascist in love with his weapons), and even Cousin exist together in an undifferentiated, fabulous temporal dimension, along with Tarzan, Little Red Riding Hood, Hansel and Gretel, and the characters of the anecdotes, folktales, and adventure stories that he has heard in the alleys of the old city.

When he first has the pistol, for example, Pin looks at it as an object whose shape and function are entirely unfamiliar to him. He proceeds to make a careful examination of the object's physical appearance, using all of his senses; his understanding of the pistol is based on a boy's code of perception and instinct for imitation and play:

Pin unrolls the belt, opens the holster, and with a gesture as if he were taking a cat by the neck pulls out the pistol. . . . Pin first points it at the gutter-pipe, right up against the metal, then at a finger, making a fierce face, drawing back his head and hissing, "Your money or your life"; then he finds an old shoe and points it against that, first the heel, then the inside; then he pushes the barrel down into the toe. What fun! A shoe, such an ordinary object, particularly for a cobbler's apprentice like him, and a pistol, such a mysterious, almost unreal thing; by putting them up against each other he can do wonders, make them tell marvellous tales. (p. 15; 45–46)

Pin is an innocent *homo ludens*, or rather, a *bricoleur* whose game has to do with "whatever is at hand"[46] (in this case, an old shoe) and with his own mythopoetic imagination (his "marvellous tales"). Its purpose is to grasp the use and function of the pistol, which is a privileged signifier in *The Path* in more ways than one.

Red Wolf appears as a picaresque or comic-book hero to Pin, a cross between the Scarlet Pimpernel, Robin Hood, and Batman: " 'Red Wolf!' Who hasn't heard of Red Wolf? Every time there's an attack against the Fascists, at every bomb that explodes in one of their headquarters, at every spy who vanishes without anyone knowing what has happened to him, people whisper the name of Red Wolf. . . . [Pin] has always wanted to meet Red Wolf, to see him appear one night in the alleys of the Old Town" (pp. 30–31; 63–64). Pin's fable-like vision of Red Wolf and of all the people and situations that he encounters on his quest is consistently motivated by wish fulfillment, namely the desire to escape from the dreary reality of his daily life and to enter a world of high adventure. Everything about the partisan struggle, its protagonists and places, turns into a strange and wonderful game for Pin: "How wonderful it would be to go around in a band with Red Wolf and make explosives big enough to blow up bridges and walk through towns firing machine gun bursts against patrols" (p. 34; 67). Pin and Red Wolf's swashbuckling escape from prison does indeed seem to fulfill Pin's fantasy, but it also has a parodic effect for the reader, since it undermines the epic portrayal of the *gappisti*. After their escape from prison, Pin and Red Wolf hide from the Fascist guards who are chasing them. For Pin, it is another wonderful and strange game: "It's wonderful to be sitting with him behind the water-tank, like playing hide-and-seek; except that there is no difference between the game and real life, and it has to be played seriously, which Pin likes" (p. 42; 77).

Calvino plays with this dialectic between Pin's games of make believe and the real war games in which he finds himself increasingly involved over the course of the novel, insinuating that the difference between the two may be less real than apparent. Pin seeks to discover the secret rules of the adults' war games (and all the other games that they play) by comparing them to the games that he knows. When this procedure fails to work, though, he finds himself in uncharted territory, which turns out to be the endless space of the quest-romance and the fairy tale: "Pin can only see mountains around him, and huge valleys with invisible depths, and high rocky slopes black with woods, then mountains again, row after row of them, into the infinite distance" (p. 120; 166).

The fairy-tale optic through which Pin sees both the landscape and the people in it works to defamiliarize even the most apparently normal aspects of partisan life, as in the following dialogue between Pin and Cousin:

"Cousin, what are the trucks coming up for?"
"To hunt for us, that's what they're coming for. But we'll go out and hunt them. That's life."

"Are you going too, Cousin?"
"Of course, I must go."
"Aren't you tired of walking?"
"I have been walking and sleeping with my boots on for the last seven years." (p. 55; 92)

Here Pin learns one of the most fundamental rules of the game of war from Cousin, who in turn presents war itself as a fundamental rule of human existence ("that's life"). But the image that Cousin, the gentle giant, draws of himself also summons up a fabulous or fairy-tale image, that of Puss in Boots and the magic seven-league boots. On first meeting Mancino, the Trotskyite who works as a cook in Dritto's partisan band, Pin once again has the impression of being in a fairy tale: "He is a tiny little man, dressed in a sailor's jersey and a cap made of rabbit fur on his bald head. Pin thinks he must be a gnome living in this little house in the middle of the woods" (p. 54; 91). The spectacle of the partisans is particularly amazing, for to Pin they look like warriors or errant knights: "Pin has always wanted to set eyes on partisans. Now he is standing open-mouthed in the middle of the clearing in front of the hut, and no sooner has he begun staring at one of them than another two or three arrive, all looking different and all hung with weapons and machine-gun belts. They might also be soldiers, a company of soldiers who had disappeared during a war many years ago and been wandering in the forests ever since without finding their way back" (p. 61; 98).

The four Calabrian brothers-in-law in Dritto's partisan detachment, nicknamed "Duke, Marquis, Count, and Baron," also possess a fairy-tale dimension. These characters, who "left their own parts to come and marry four sisters" (p. 72; 111), resemble many similar fairy-tale characters—usually brothers—who set out together on a journey or quest where each will try to make his own fortune and prove himself worthy of inheriting the kingdom. In the light of this allusion, their involvement in partisan warfare appears to Pin as a mythic struggle whose deepest motives go back to an ancient tale of violence and revenge: "Often they go off, all four of them, down towards the valley and the carnation plantations where the sisters, their wives, live. And there they have mysterious duels with the Black Brigade, ambushes and vendettas, as if they were waging, on their own, a war caused by ancient family feuds" (p. 72; 111). This allusion to a violence that seems to have roots—like the violence found in certain fairy tales and legends—in an ancient past of rival clans and ritual sacrifices takes a more tangible form in the episode of the execution of two Fascist prisoners in reprisal for the killing of one of the four brothers. The remaining three brothers carry out their reprisal in cold blood, ignoring the pleas of the two prisoners, who had been captured in action the day before and are desperately trying to explain "for the hundredth time to anyone near them that they had enlisted only because they were forced to" (p. 76; 116). Before killing their victims, the brothers-in-law force them to dig an enormous grave for Marquis and for themselves, in a grotesque and blasphemous funeral: "Duke begins reciting prayers for the dead; the Latin words sound heavy with anger in his mouth, like curses; the two brothers-in-law intone the responses, with their pistols always cocked" (p. 76; 117). This ritual execution and the entire episode throw a disquieting light on so-called "partisan justice." The ritual appears as one of those adult games whose logic Pin is unable to fathom because the rules seem to make no sense at all, or rather, because they are so arbitrary: "game upon game, so that one can never understand which one is the real game" (p. 17; 49).

Partisan Justice and Resistance Historiography

In his memoir, *Un uomo: un partigiano*, Roberto Battaglia devotes an entire chapter to partisan justice. Battaglia was (like Kim in *The Path*) the political commissar of a partisan brigade, and he was responsible for the brigade's relations with the CLN command in the Garfagnana region of Tuscany (originally a member of the Partito d'Azione, Battaglia joined the PCI after the Liberation). The chapter on partisan justice foregrounds the uncertain nature of partisan warfare to which Calvino refers both in the episode of the four brothers-in-law and again at the end of the novel, when Pin finally reaches the end of his quest. Battaglia's reflections resemble those of Kim on such related issues as the necessity of violence, sacrifice, and historical judgment:

This is the chapter of partisan life that has left in me—and will leave forever—a deeper impression than any other and to which my memories often return, as to an argument still deserving of further reflection and anguish. . . . To have killed men in combat, or to have ordered them killed, is an experience that millions of others have also had during this partisan war that probably will, in a few years' time, weigh only lightly on our minds. . . . Quite different instead is the case of partisan warfare, where the unarmed are killed as well. This necessity is the darkest aspect of the struggle that, inevitably, because of its very nature, leads to civil war. . . . It would seem to be the same problem as that faced by military tribunals that must try deserters or enemy spies; but in this case the judges are officers who have the full weight and authority of the Army behind them to grant certainty to their decision; they must interpret the law, not create it, and may send the guilty to prison rather than to their deaths; whatever their sentence may be, it is ratified by a legal system, which the sentence serves (quite normally) to express. In a partisan tribunal, on the other hand, everything is different: the judges are, legally speaking, men like any other . . . who must pass judgment without the support of a body of law, and whose authority is recognized only by themselves and their comrades. One might argue that such a judge will use his own conscience as a guide; but this is true only up to a certain point, because there is no such thing as a rigid moral conscience in the abstract, but, according to the circumstances, it may be animated by pity or rigor, by the acuity or uncertainty of the inquiry. To isolate it in itself, to achieve an awareness of being simply just, free of any sentimental feeling, is one of the most difficult, almost desperately so, tasks that one can undertake.[47]

Battaglia's text has a distinctly existentialist tone, expressing a sense of the arbitrary nature of justice and the absence of an absolute moral or legal code that relieves the individual of all personal responsibility in choosing and judging. This same existentialist problematic is thematized in chapter 9 of *The Path*; elsewhere in the novel, Calvino dramatizes the same dilemma in terms of Pin's inability to understand what is happening around him with any degree of certainty.

For Battaglia, those condemned to death by the partisan tribunals are at once guilty and innocent, for they are afflicted by a blindness in regard to history and to the responsibility of the historical subject that in a sense explains their actions. These same traits characterize Pin's own experience of partisan life (and account for Rina's collaboration with the enemy). Battaglia continues:

> The guilty party is an unfortunate peasant who guided the Germans during a round-up, in order to get a little more money, and now stammers, saying that he too knew nothing . . . or it is a woman who lived with the Germans and turned in the townspeople who slandered her . . . without knowing that they would have been arrested and shot. No one knows anything, no one is guilty. Everyone was forced to do as they did, no one knew what the consequences of their own actions would have been. . . . Can I shoot them because they did not have— like almost all Italians—such a sense of conscience? . . . They die with their eyes closed (I too could have been one of them), without understanding . . . what the word "betrayal" means. (pp. 248–49)

Battaglia's text is striking, at least from the point of view of the present study, for his ambivalent feelings about the violence of guerrilla warfare and the justice meted out by the partisans lead the author to question how the story of the Resistance itself can be truthfully emplotted and narrated, or, in other words, represented. Moreover, Battaglia questions not only the way in which the events of recent history can be truthfully represented but even what meaning can possibly be assigned to them:

> It is well-known that everyone fights wars with their own feelings . . . but this is of no concern for those interested only in the results of a war: they want to know only the technique with which so many deaths and so much destruction were produced on one side and on the other. . . . Once all this has been clearly stated, and without taking into account whatever concerns the life of the individual, can we be sure that we have achieved our goal? That is what one asks oneself, re-reading this report, or any other report on the partisan movement. Did the events really occur according to that well-ordered plan, those lucidly-stated paragraphs? Were those four or five thousand men really united in those months under the command of headquarters, and did they act in one way rather than another because they were directed to do so by exact orders? Is this history, or that part of history that concerns them, truly authentic? I who commanded them, and during that time was certain that I could answer such questions in the affirmative, now feel my certainty wavering. . . . I do not . . . raise questions or doubts about the truthfulness of the facts contained in this report . . . but rather am concerned with the very nature of what happened then. What is needed is no longer the kind of truth to be found in a military report, or

a lively documentary of the events themselves, but rather a truth like that of life itself in all its uncertainty, in which we might find the main motive, and which cannot be found in official explanations . . . for once again the same sincere question must be asked: "what is the truth?" (pp. 159–64)

Battaglia's memoir would not be the poignant document that it is, nor would it be as enlightening in terms of Calvino's novel, if not for his return to the same questions in his later *Storia della Resistenza italiana*. In his monumental and pivotal 1953 study, Battaglia does a dramatic about-face from his earlier position on the representation of the Resistance and produces a veritable summa of Resistance hagiography instead.

Although they vary in political point of view from left-wing to moderate, the histories of the Italian Resistance through the first decade after the war ended consistently reflect the same tendency to transform the story of the Resistance into an epic, justifying it in terms of patriotic and moral values, that is to be found in neorealist literature and film.[48] The collection of essays entitled *Il Secondo Risorgimento (The Second "Risorgimento")*, published in 1955 with the sponsorship of the government (led by the Christian Democrats), reflects the general tendency to transform the Resistance into a patriotic myth, devoid of all partisan political thrust: "It is hardly surprising that most of these authors try to use the Resistance as a kind of national flag . . . insisting on the definition of it as a 'second Risorgimento.'"[49] While wholly subscribing to the PCI's point of view, Battaglia's history also reinterprets the Resistance as an epic tale of the masses taking charge of Italian history under the guidance of the PCI and the various CLN's. Although its scholarly apparatus is most impressive, Battaglia's history does not—in its essence—differ substantially from the history published by Luigi Longo, *Un popolo alla macchia*. In contrast to his 1945 *Un uomo*, Battaglia stresses in his subsequent work the unanimity of the partisan movement and its "mass heroism." The only meaning of the Resistance, Battaglia states, was the "cause of oppressed humanity" and the "bene della patria." No uncertainty stood in the way of the Italians' "clear rejection of Fascism," for, he explains, "liberty was opposed to tyranny," and partisan justice becomes "the morality of history itself."[50] Battaglia's narrative of the history of the Resistance is, like Longo's, configured as a unilinear plot unfolding from July 25 to the final uprising in April 1945 ("the point of arrival") and the day of Liberation. Its center ("the maturity of the Resistance") is the "high season" of the partisan campaign, namely the summer of 1944.

The "value attached to narrativity," observes Hayden White, "in the representation of real events arises out of a desire to have real events display the coherence, integrity, fullness, and closure of an image of life that is and can only be imaginary."[51] Nowhere is this any more visible than in Longo's and Battaglia's respective histories of the Resistance. Despite their claims to the contrary, the political and ideological motivations behind Longo's and Battaglia's work lead them, beyond the shadow of a doubt, to overlook—or even, at times, repress—the very same contradictions and conflicts in the partisan movement that, as Marxist historians, they should have sought to expose.[52] Longo, in fact, entirely dismisses the question of partisan justice and attributes all criticism of it to (neo)Fascist propaganda.[53] Calvino, on the other hand, shows himself—both in *The Path* and elsewhere—to be painfully aware of the unresolvable nature of this conflict between a particular political and ideological agenda and the demands of historiography for objectivity. In chapter 9, for example, Kim must agonize over his decision to execute Dritto, while seeking at the same time to rationalize the sacrifice of his men's lives for the cause.

Calvino's Estrangement of the Resistance Epic

The use of a naive focalizer in *The Path* allows Calvino to present certain essential, elementary facts of the Resistance as discoveries. From the partisan sympathizers in the tavern where he spends endless hours, Pin learns of the existence of the CLN, which his imagination transforms into a mythical, all-powerful man named "Committee." From them he also learns the "mysterious word: GAP," which binds them to a pact of secrecy. In prison, he discovers who the "political prisoners" are, namely the inmates who have already been there for many years because their Resistance started long before the partisan struggle itself. Red Wolf introduces him to the ABC of Marxism, mentioning "capitalism" to him and using expressions like "proletariat without class consciousness." At the partisan camp Pin learns to sing the communist song "Bandiera Rossa," and through Mancino he first hears about the Trotskyite "heresy," the proletariat, and the International. He sees Fascist spies killed and hears from the members of Dritto's band the various motives which led them to join the Resistance. He witnesses the preparation for a major action of the partisan brigade against a German column. Finally, he gets his own weapon and goes off to fight together with one of the bravest of all the partisans, Cousin.

The device of internal focalization, moreover, serves a specific function in the novel's structure of temporality: it allows Calvino to create for the reader the illusion of the experience of "real time." The narrator's implicit knowledge of the entire sequence of the story's fictional events, as well as of the events which constitute its historical setting, is purposely withheld throughout most of the novel in order to make the reader's perception of both the narrative and historical events synchronous with Pin's. There are no prolepses which allow us to glimpse another temporal order (i.e. the narrator's omniscient and retrospective one) from within the narrative itself. This particular narrative strategy has a defamiliarizing effect on the reader: the epic reality of the Resistance is "made strange" by being focalized through the eyes of a character who, unlike the reader, has neither an overall grasp of the Resistance as history nor an established understanding of what the Resistance "meant." Pin's perspective places the reader in the position of looking at the Resistance as if "for the first time," of not knowing "how it turned out" or what its consequences and meaning are in relation to the history of Italy.[54] Through Pin, the narrative conveys to the reader certain elementary features of the Resistance as an immediate human experience: the sense of adventure, the strangeness and the fear, the excitement of seeing incredible things happen or of having to deal with the unknown and the bewildering, and the undergoing of a series of trials in a quest for both survival and understanding. Pin's experience of the Resistance, in other words, deprives the "epos" of its distance; it reinscribes it within the experience of a fabulous "present" which for the reader is the experience of reading itself.

Part of the narrative's defamiliarizing effect is achieved through the representation of Pin's experience in the present tense. Calvino's choice of the present tense has a polemical target: the novel and history have always been closely linked to each other by the use of the preterite in narrative. Roland Barthes explains the part the preterite plays in the following way:

> [The preterite serves] to reduce reality to a point of time, and to abstract, from the depth of a multiplicity of experiences, a pure verbal act, freed from the existential roots of knowledge, and directed towards a logical link with other acts. . . . Through the preterite, the verb implicitly belongs in a causal chain, it partakes of a set of related and oriented actions. . . . Allowing as it does an ambiguity between temporality and causality, it calls for a sequence of events, that is, for an intelligible Narrative . . . [namely] the unreal time of cosmogonies, myths, History and Novels. It presupposes a world which is constructed, elaborated, self-sufficient, reduced to significant lines.[55]

Narrative language in general always implies a temporal distancing from the epistemological uncertainty of the present; it is a means of correcting and making sense out of the initially disordered nature of experience, usually by imposing an origin and an end where in reality there are only many conflicting ones. Historical narrative, as Barthes points out, cannot evade this same gesture, for it too puts into a temporal sequence or order what is initially disordered in the "present moment" of experience. Pin's world, on the other hand, is deliberately *not* reduced by Calvino to "significant lines." The metaphoric title of the novel suggests, among other things, the mazelike intricacy of historical events and facts as yet uncharted by an interpretive path. Throughout *The Path*, Pin constantly experiences a sense of uncertainty; he is faced with a conflictual reality, a multiplicity of facts that lack any visible order or causal interconnection. Through Pin's eyes we see the world as a fantastic maze of meanings, as "games . . . so complicated and involved that it's difficult to discover what the real one is" (p. 17; 49). The use of the present tense thus helps to give *The Path* its uncanny narrative rhythm, for it creates within the narrative a sense of radical proximity to Pin's perceptions of a reality that he cannot comprehend. It allows the text to become a kind of extension of Pin's existence, which unfolds simultaneously with it and which is equally devoid of a sense of causal logic. Calvino's use of the present tense and the simple, paratactic sentence structure recapture the tone of immediacy and the sense of closeness to the events themselves that we find in Battaglia's 1945 memoir (written mostly in the present tense, or the *passato prossimo*) and in many partisan diaries and brief episodic accounts written while the Resistance was still a lived experience that had not been crystallized into a metanarrative.[56]

Throughout *The Path* the progress of the reader's knowledge—or, in other words, the expansion of his field of vision as the story unfolds—is made to coincide with the itinerary of Pin's quest and discovery. Calvino does not rely only on the use of the present narrative tense, however, in order to achieve this effect. In the opening section of the novel, for example, Pin frequents a seedy tavern in the old town and comes into contact with its denizens. The men in the tavern are presented from Pin's point of view as a homogeneous group of derelicts who spend endless hours drinking, smoking, and telling stories about sex, violence, and prison. Pin knows only their nicknames: Michel the Frenchy, Giraffe, Gian the driver. Theirs is a kind of "choral" collective identity, represented in the text through the popular songs Pin sings to them (which they themselves have taught him):

"Sing, Pin" they say. And Pin begins singing, seriously, tensely, in that hoarse childish voice of his. He sings a song called "The Four Seasons":

> When I think of the future
> And the liberty I have lost
> I'd like to kiss her and then die
> While she sleeps . . . and never knows.

The men sit listening in silence, with their eyes lowered, as if to a hymn. All of them have been to prison; no-one is a real man unless he has. (p. 4; 32)

In this passage the reader hears the men's voices filtered through Pin's voice and perspective. The statement about prison and "real men" is an instance of how Calvino achieves an effect

of "double-voicedness" through the use of free indirect discourse.[57] In *The Path*, this narrative device requires an almost
total bracketing of the authorial voice and perspective in the representation of the men's conditions of existence and system of
beliefs. In this manner Calvino's text successfully avoids (like
Verga) the awkward populist overtones which the representation of lower-class speech assumes—for example—in a novel
like Cesare Pavese's *Il compagno*, where the image of the authorial bourgeois and intellectual consciousness constantly in-
terferes with that of the proletarian narrator-protagonist.

A further instance of this same strategy, which is so crucial to
Calvino's purpose of enmeshing the reader's perspective with
Pin's, is found in the middle section of the novel, where Pin lives
alla macchia with the partisans. The past experiences of the men
in Dritto's band and the motives that led them to join the Resistance are discovered by Pin in the course of dialogues with the
men themselves; alternately, they are narrated in the form of ci-
tational free indirect speech. In the latter case, the reader infers
that the information he is given about the characters has for the
most part probably been gathered by Pin from various conversa-
tions and from listening to the men talk during his stay at the
camp. A typical example of this strategy can be found in chapter 8, in presenting the character of a partisan nicknamed Carabiniere, who—after the armistice of September 8, 1943—had deserted from the regular state police when he learned that he was
about to be deported to a forced-labor camp in Germany. The
explanation of Carabiniere's reasons for joining the partisans is
provided in conjunction with an account of his past but filtered
through Pin's primitive linguistic consciousness:

Pin does not know the difference between when there's war and when
there isn't. He seems to have heard people talking about war ever since
he was born. . . .
    "I know who wanted it! I have seen them!" a man called Carabiniere
suddenly says, "It was the students!"
    Carabiniere is even more ignorant than Duke and lazier than Long
Zena; his father was a peasant who, realising he would never get his
son to wield a spade, said to him: "Join the Carabinieri"; so the son
joined and was given a black uniform with a white bandolier and carried out his duties in town and country without ever realising what he

was doing. After the 8th of September he was told to arrest the parents of deserters, then one day he heard that he was going to be deported himself as he was for the King; so he escaped. First the partisans had wanted to make him dig his own grave, because of those parents of deserters he had arrested; then they realised that he was just a poor wretch and sent him to Dritto's detachment, as no one wanted him in any of the others. (pp. 87–88; 129)

The colloquial simplicity of the narrator's discourse here corresponds to Pin's linguistic consciousness, through which the voices of the various partisans are refracted.[58] The historical events of the Resistance are reflected through the lives of the partisans themselves and then refracted by Pin's own thoughts and words, so that history is available in Calvino's novel only through the mediation of this double filter. Throughout *The Path*, as we have seen, the narrator programmatically refrains from stepping back to give a synthesizing and integrated image of Pin's deeds and of the experiences he goes through. As Bakhtin points out, "Such a generalizing image would . . . lie outside the hero's own field of vision, and on the whole such images presume some stable position on the outside."[59] This "stable position on the outside" assumes the possibility of a knowledge of events that would transcend the limited vision of the protagonist and that could organize those same events into a coherent narrative. If Calvino does not posit any such stable position for the narrator and instead promotes the reader's empathetic identification with Pin's character, it is because this "outside" is precisely what he is questioning in writing *The Path*.

Calvino's strategy of withholding the narrator's panchronic knowledge poses no real challenge to the reader's interpretive codes. It is in fact a fairly traditional device for the creation of suspense and a sense of surprise or discovery in narrative; such enigmas form an integral part of the pleasure of reading fictional narratives. In the case of *The Path*, however, the situation is complicated by the interweaving of the fictional events of Pin's story with specific references to the real events and circumstances of the Resistance. If, from the point of view of narrative conventions, it is perfectly plausible that the reader should not know until the final page how Pin's fictional story turns out, it is certainly not plausible that the reader should, like Pin, not know how the history of the Resistance developed and what its "significant lines" were (even if only in the most general sense of knowing who the "winners" and "losers" were). It is in this regard that *The Path* poses its most significant challenge to the reader, for Calvino asks us to bracket our historical knowledge, as well as our political and ideological assumptions, and to pretend that we are, like Pin, wholly innocent of them.

•

Defamiliarization through the use of a naive focalizer is a narrative device that Calvino appropriates from nineteenth-century models of the historical novel and romance. As Calvino acknowledges in the 1964 preface, for example, the figure of Pin is at least in part modelled on the character of Carlino in the first section of Ippolito Nievo's *Confessioni di un Italiano* (*Confessions of an Italian*, 1867): "I had wanted secretly to pay homage to Nievo by modelling Pin's meeting with Cousin on Carlino's meeting with Spaccafumo in *Confessions of an Italian*." [60] Stendhal's depiction of Fabrizio del Dongo's experience at Waterloo in *The Charterhouse of Parma* may also have served Calvino as a model for the defamiliarization of historical events through the use of a naive focalizer. [61] Calvino was also influenced by Alessandro Manzoni's work, particularly the chapters on Renzo's involvement in the 1628 bread riots in Milan in *I promessi sposi*.

In a 1958 essay, "Natura e storia nel romanzo" ("Nature and History in the Novel"), Calvino makes some interesting remarks concerning the use of the viewpoint of young or very young protagonists by Nievo, Stendhal, and other nineteenth-century writers. These remarks indirectly clarify the reasons for his own choice of a child as the protagonist of *The Path*:

The character of the boy had entered nineteenth-century literature because of a need to keep offering to mankind the model of an attitude of quest and discovery, the possibility of transforming every experience into a triumph, as is possible only for a young person. . . . The élan of the Italian Risorgimento found only one truly poetic echo in literature: the adventurous days of Nievo's Carlino among the bastions and ditches of the decrepit Fratta castle. It is Carlino's and Pisana's childhood that illuminates for us the movement of the entire text of *Confessions of an Italian*, as the passage about Carlino's first discovery of the sea, seen from Attila's bastion, makes sufficiently clear. In the third decade of the century, Stendhal had already had his seventeen-year-old Fabrizio del Dongo experience the battle of Waterloo, when he still didn't know how to shoot, and had to be told what to do by a vivandière. That great precursor of the modern sensibility had already understood that the attitude of the adult towards military glory cannot escape the deception of rhetoric, and that the genuine emotion of ancient epic can be found again—mixed with an irony which, however, does not destroy it—through the eyes of someone who discovers life for the first time.[62]

In the context of this essay by Calvino, the term "epic" refers to a narrative mode representing "man" on a quest during which he interrogates both nature and history. In ancient epic, at the "beginning of poetry," this kind of narration was—Calvino claims—simply a direct representation of the real conditions of human praxis: "To propitiate the success of their undertakings, men celebrated the first to overcome difficulties, namely the hero: not a god but a man, though related to the gods; he is a man inasmuch as his destiny is on earth, as a trial-ridden itinerary. Ancient epic narrated the first act performed by man to emerge from the chaos of indistinctness, the struggle against a primeval nature, still populated by monsters" (p. 21). While the genuine emotion of ancient epic cannot be duplicated in the modern novel, Calvino argues that certain novelists in the nineteenth century succeed in giving their works the character of a "modern epic" by adopting narrative strategies that provide the reader with a means by which to see the real as something that has yet to be mastered and understood: "In the modern epic man is represented as having with nature and history a relationship which is free, and not ideological, unlike that of someone who sees in the world a predetermined design, whether immanent or transcendent; it is, in short, a relationship of interrogation" (p. 23). The use of a child as a focalizer, or of a character who is presumed to be "innocent" of all dominant cultural and ideological presuppositions, therefore becomes a way to induce the reader to divest himself—if only temporarily and with the ironic knowledge that this is indeed a fictional game the "adult" narrator is inviting him to play—of his own "adult" and historically determined cultural and ideological identity. The reader is invited to assume a naive, questioning attitude toward reality and to regress (as it were) to a primitive stage of imaginary openness and uncertainty vis-à-vis the phenomenal and historical world.

In a famous and controversial passage in the *Grundrisse*, Marx hypothesizes that the appeal which Greek epic poetry and art still hold for the modern sensibility (to the point that they have become an absolute aesthetic ideal) may be caused by what—at least to the moderns—appears to be their "childlike" quality. Marx's argument is very close to Calvino's, and it can be used to bring out some of the implications of the latter. The appeal of ancient epic is, for Marx, closely linked to its having been produced in what we now perceive as "the historical childhood of humanity."[63] Its charm, Marx continues, "does not conflict with the immature stage of the society in which it originated. On the contrary, its charm is a consequence of this and is inseparably linked with the fact that the immature social conditions which gave rise, and which alone gave rise, to this art cannot recur." While the conditions of existence that made possible the flourishing of the epic in its "epoch-making, classic form" (p. 216) are beyond recovery, the perceptual and epistemological inquisitiveness, the freedom from alienation and ideological overdeterminations, and the positive human resourcefulness that we somewhat nostalgically and perhaps even sentimentally associate with the epic world lead us to look at our own historical condition with different eyes. For the young Marx, the epic model becomes a valuable alienation device, and the epic world turns into a figure through which the ideal of a nonalienated society of the future is projected. It is in attempting to recover the "lost horizon" of the epic creative imagination in our own representation of the real that we can break the automatism of our perceptions and ideology. "An adult cannot become a child again, or he becomes childish. But does the naiveté of the child not give him pleasure, and does he not himself endeavour to reproduce the child's veracity on a higher level?" (p. 217). According to Marx, then, the impulse to reproduce the epic "truth" or, in Calvino's terms, its "genuine emotion" is not a nostalgic or sentimental relapse into childhood. It is rather the attempt to give form in the aesthetic object to an effort to transmute everything we know into what we would like to know and to experience knowledge as discovery. The fictional frame of mind that we are invited to assume through the device of the naive focalizer and/or protagonist, then, is "epic" almost in a Brechtian sense. It is a positive "alienation effect" which destabilizes the reader's vision of the natural and historical world by showing us the familiar in an unfamiliar light and by restoring to the reader a sense of reality as something that must still be discovered and understood in its changing and often discontinuous manifestations.

Both the Waterloo episode in *The Charterhouse of Parma* and the passage on Carlino's discovery of the sea in *Confessions of an Italian* are classic examples of "epic" defamiliarization through the use of a childlike focalizer, as Calvino himself observes. Nievo and Stendhal succeed in making the familiar seem strange by focalizing the object (the battle of Waterloo in Stendhal's case, the sea in Nievo's case) through a novel point of view provided by a naive character who shares none of our commonplace, habitual perceptions and notions about the object itself. But, as Calvino remarks in his discussion of Stendhal, a certain type of irony is an essential component of defamiliarization. It is an irony that allows the reader to perceive the difference between the perspective of the implicit narrator and the naive point of view of the focalizer without, however, distancing the focalizer to the point of making him appear altogether "inferior" to the narrator and to the reader. Irony thus prevents the naive focalizer from appearing as the victim of a conspicuous blindness or innate lack of understanding. Indeed, while the implicit authorial consciousness in *Confessions of an Italian* and in *The Charterhouse of Parma* makes us aware of Carlino's and Fabrizio's naiveté, these same characters are never treated in a patronizing manner. On the contrary, built into these narratives is a sense that the protagonists' youthful "innocence" can alone provide the reader with a means to lift himself out of his own perceptual and ideological framework and to engage in a game of rediscovery.

In the same essay on the modern epic novel, Calvino cites a passage from Alessandro Manzoni's *The Betrothed* in which Renzo's perceptions and feelings—as he walks alone in the night, trying to reach the Adda river in order to escape from the dangerous territory of Milan—are poetically represented as the perceptions and feelings of a child afraid of the dark and of the unknown. This is, Calvino says, one of his favorite passages in the whole novel,[64] particularly "the lovely passage about the entrance into the woods, and Renzo's fear of the shapes of the trees in the dark." In *The Path*, the sequence following Pin's escape from the Fascist prison and his first encounter with the bewildering realities of the war closely resembles Renzo's escape from the riots in Milan:

Every shadow takes on a strange shape, every noise sounds like a footstep coming nearer. . . . He is alone now, alone in the whole world. He walks off through the serried rows of carnations and of *calendule*, then makes for the higher slopes of the hills, to keep above the military area. Later he will come down to the river-bed and the parts which are his own.

He's hungry. The cherries are ripe at this season. Here's a tree, far from any house. Has it grown there by magic? . . .

When he has taken the edge off his hunger he fills his pockets with cherries and climbs down from the tree, then walks on again spitting out cherry-stones. Then he thinks the Fascists might follow the track of the stones and catch him up. But no one in all the world would be clever enough to think of a thing like that, no one except Red Wolf! He decides to drop a cherry-stone every twenty yards. . . . But long before he has reached the river-bed the cherries are finished. . . . Now there is nothing left for him to do but wander aimlessly about in the countryside. . . . Tears well over and cloud his pupils. (pp. 46–49; 82–85)

Both Manzoni and Calvino represent their young protagonists in an archetypal escape from a dangerous situation, facing the unknown as they make their way along a mysterious and trial-ridden nocturnal path in the hope of reaching a safer place. Both protagonists are bewildered by historical events whose violence has touched them directly but whose meaning escapes them. In both texts, a landscape that is perceived by the protagonists as unfamiliar and menacing symbolically serves to articulate their sense of anxiety over the as-yet-undetermined future that awaits them. Finally, both Renzo and Pin devise naive or even mythic stratagems to dispel their fears and to keep going through the nighttime landscape. Renzo recites the prayers of the dead as if their spirits could magically dispel the threat that—under the influence of the ghost stories that he heard as a child—looms before him in his imagination; Pin hopes that by reenacting the fable of Hansel and Gretel the young partisan Red Wolf will come to his rescue. It is precisely their childlike naiveté that makes both these characters "universal heroes," for they represent the essential human dialectic of innocence and experience; theirs is the parable of the human quest as a perilous journey through a dark wood toward an uncertain destiny. It is also the search of the desiring self for a mastery of reality that will deliver it from its state of anxiety and uncertainty. Both Manzoni and Calvino use the same basic structure of the quest-journey found in epic romances and in fairy tales to articulate the relationship of their protagonists to nature and to history.

However, in light of the outcome of Renzo's nocturnal escape, Calvino remarks that Manzoni's text cannot—unlike Stendhal's—be cited as an example "of this modern epic we are now trying to define." When he finally finds a hut where he can spend the rest of the night before crossing the border to safety, Renzo thanks God and Divine Providence for having assisted him throughout his journey.[65] Renzo's journey, then, is in Calvino's view no longer an epic one; it is no longer a quest or an interrogation of the real. The outcome of Renzo's quest is in fact ideologically predetermined by Manzoni, who reinscribes the sense of Renzo's journey within the dominant logic of Divine Providence. The power of this logic asserts itself through the conspicuous presence of its interpreter in the novel, namely the omniscient narrator. It pervades the whole narrative and ultimately accounts for the shape of the story as an organic part of the course of human history. Renzo's childlike vision of the world implicitly becomes the object of an ironic demystification "from above," for it is shown by Manzoni to be superstitious and immature in the light of a higher providential design. Although Pin and Renzo share the qualities that characterize the archetypal hero of quest narratives, Calvino consciously refuses to assert his authorial power over his character, suspending as much as possible the traditional role of the omniscient narrator put into practice by Manzoni. The point that Calvino aims to convey in *The Path* is in fact that a predetermined scheme is lacking both in human history and in the story that unfolds before the reader's eyes. Pin's sense of bewilderment is consequently and consistently not reinscribed into an explicit and "higher" narrative order by the author. On the contrary, Calvino strives to erase himself from the text (or rather, to disguise his presence by reducing authorial intervention and commentary to a minimal degree) and to make Pin's perspective stand alone with a phenomenological immediacy which undermines any sense of preordained narrative closure or stability for the reader. The experience of reading *The Path* must be, like its protagonist's experience of the historical world, a quest in its own right.

•

The basic literary way of seeing any object anew is, according to Victor Shklovsky, to place the object in a new semantic row, that is, in a row of concepts that belong to another category.[66] Shklovsky calls this a strategy of *ostranenie*, meaning estrangement or defamiliarization. Tolstoy, for example, in his late works depicts certain religious dogmas by substituting common speech for the customary religious terms used in church rituals: "Many persons were painfully wounded by this," comments Shklovsky, for "they considered it blasphemy to present as strange and monstrous what they accepted as sacred."[67] Shklovsky also refers to Tolstoy's use of *ostranenie* in the descriptions of battles in *War and Peace*, intended to alter the traditional perception of the historical reality of Russia in 1812.[68] As in Nievo's, Stendhal's, and Tolstoy's novels, defamiliarization in *The Path* functions as a device to make the reader reconsider his conventional view of history. Seen through Pin's eyes, the "familiar" history of the Resistance loses its familiarity and appears before us as an enigmatic, gap-riddled tale; in *The Path*, the history of the Resistance is defamiliarized by being placed within the "estranging" logic of Pin's childish imagination. Pin's estranging vision (which ignores the meaning of the most elementary facts about the war and the partisans) is intended by Calvino to renew our perception of historical events, not in terms of another authoritative "narrative" explanation of them but as an immediate phenomenological reality. Although it provides some considerable advantages, however, the choice of a child or of a naive, innocent character as a focalizer also apparently poses a problem in a narrative that deals with well-known historical facts. Our willingness to look anew at history through Pin's eyes is constantly accompanied by an awareness of the limitations of his vision, even if we do not feel our own understanding to be necessarily superior to his. How, then, does Calvino's narrative compel the reader to "suspend his belief" in a conventional view of history (as a *grand récit*) and share Pin's experience of time and history? How may the reader be persuaded to let himself be placed in the position of someone who does not yet know what the Resistance is?

One element that contributes to make Pin's perspective a compelling one for the reader, despite its apparent flaws, is of course the structure of the plot itself. The arrangement of the narrated events of *The Path*, however, is consistent with the chronology and causality that governs their temporal succession and logical sequence. There is no obvious discrepancy between the way the events may be logically inferred to take place sequentially in terms of the *story* of Pin (the *fabula* or *histoire* of the narrative) and the way they are made to follow one another in the plot (*sjuzet* or *récit*) of the novel.[69] There are no conspicuous anachronies in the plot and no anticipations of events to come. The few analepses (or "flashbacks") in the narrative, revealing events that took place prior to the time of the action, are entirely subordinate to the main story line; their only function is to provide the reader with information about the characters' past necessary to follow the logical development of the action.[70] The information provided through analepsis is, furthermore, almost always consistent with the focalization of the narrative from Pin's point of view. The narrative action of *The Path* is emplotted much like a fairy tale that employs the structure of a quest-journey; the reader has really no choice but to follow the progressive unfolding of each stage of the journey as it leads toward its conclusion.

A further, and equally powerful, persuasive factor is the archetypal nostalgic appeal that the child-protagonist holds for any reader. Prior to any psychological characterization (a narrative device Calvino generally resists in his writing), the child is always—generally speaking—readily granted the narrative status of a "hero" with whom the reader is immediately willing to identify. This occurs in literary works belonging to vastly different traditions, not only because the child represents a truly universal experience of being in time but also because of his very position in time: at the beginning of human life. The fascination that the child-protagonist of the literary work holds for the reader is the fascination of beginnings. It is not by chance that a child-protagonist often appears at the beginning of fairy tales and romances. As Walter Benjamin remarks in his essay "The Storyteller," "The fairy tale, which to this day is the first tutor of children . . . was once the first tutor of mankind. . . . The fairy tale tells us of the earliest arrangements that mankind made to shake off the nightmare which the myth had placed upon its chest. . . . The wisest thing—so the fairy tale taught mankind in olden times, and teaches children to this day—is to meet the forces of the mythical world with cunning and with high spirits." [71] The child is itself a metaphor for a story that has just begun and for the multiple possibilities of narrative development that mark every *incipit*, including that of human life itself. The archetypal appeal of childhood as a time of beginnings, of discovery, and of unlimited possibilities is not, however, simply a ruse on Calvino's part aimed at captivating the reader on an emotional or subconscious level. As Edward Said has observed in relation to Vico's own tireless thinking about the childhood of humanity, "A distant and irrecoverable origin is not yearned after fruitlessly, because the mind can reexperience its making power by forging novel connections again and again." [72] Pin's function in *The Path* is precisely that of making the reader forge "novel connections" about the history of the Resistance—and perhaps discover its unreliability in the process—by willingly "playing along" with Pin's estranging fantasies and his tentative and imaginative decoding of events as he progresses in his quest.

Pin's name alludes to the most proverbial of all Italian fairy tales, *Le avventure di Pinocchio*, a text which stands for Calvino as an exemplary model of narrative construction. Indeed *The Path* exhibits to a considerable extent the same stylistic features that Calvino admires in Carlo Collodi's masterful tale: "Each motif obeys an exemplary narrative rhythm and is sharply focused; each episode has a specific, necessary function within the overall design of the action; each character is made vividly visible and has a language of his own."[73] Like Pinocchio, Pin is a little rebel, an impish *discolo* who defies authority and runs away from home in search of adventure. In joining the partisans in the rugged mountains of Liguria, Pin—like Pinocchio—pursues the fantasy of a free life unconstrained by discipline and hard work but falls victim to a series of misfortunes, including imprisonment. Like Pinocchio, he uses cunning and deceit to get out of trouble, but he is in turn tricked, deceived, and humiliated by a series of characters whom he mistakes for friends. Like the fairy in *Pinocchio*, Cousin—the most courageous of all the partisans— materializes as if by magic to rescue Pin after Red Wolf has left him alone in the woods after their escape from prison, with the Fascists and Nazis in pursuit. It is Cousin who comes to Pin's rescue again in the end, and finally—like the fairy does with Pinocchio—teaches him how to be good. Pinocchio becomes human at the end of the story when he is reunited with his "father," Geppetto, and begins a new life under his guidance. Pin too finally finds a father figure at the end of *The Path*; it is none other than Cousin himself, the "great friend" Pin had been looking for all along in his quest. Under Cousin's guidance, Pin will also at last become a real human being by finding his place in the real world.

Obviously the thematic analogy with *Pinocchio* holds only to a limited degree. What the two stories have in common is in effect an elementary fairy-tale/folk-tale plot structure operating as a particularly seductive narrative prototype.[74] As Vladimir Propp has shown in his classic study, the fairy tale embodies primarily a syntagmatic, "horizontal" structuring, whereby the "act of a character is defined from the point of view of its significance for the course of the action."[75] What makes a fairy tale a fairy tale, Propp argues, is not its specific "fantastic" content (magic, talking animals, etc.), because a fairy tale may also deal with themes taken directly from everyday life. The fairy tale is instead perhaps—as many of Propp's structuralist followers have claimed—the fundamental prototype of *all* narrative.[76] More than any other kind of narrative (as Calvino points out in his description of *Pinocchio*), the fairy tale subordinates characterization, psychology, description, speech, and all the connotative aspects of the narration (which in other kinds of narrative project "vertical" associations, requiring the reader to resort to a multiplicity of interpretive codes from his cultural encyclopedia) to the single principle of the syntagmatic development of the action. The course of the action itself is what captivates the reader's attention as it unfolds horizontally through a series of limited and reciprocally bound motifs (or, in Propp's terminology, "functions"). The functions are "arranged in pairs: prohibition-violation, reconnaissance-delivery, struggle-victory, pursuit-deliverance, etc."[77] While the storyteller is free to select a group of functions, to repeat them, or to omit some of them, and can choose a potentially limitless number of characters and objects through which a function is realized, "he is constrained . . . in the overall sequence of functions." The series of functions develops according to a "fixed scheme," and the storyteller "is not at liberty to make substitutions for those functions bound by "absolute or relative dependence," such as interdiction/violation and other pairs that are reciprocally bound.[78] The "constraint" experienced by the storyteller runs parallel to the constraint experienced by the reader in decoding the story.

If we look now at *The Path* from this perspective, we see that the plot deploys 21 of the functions discussed by Propp in his study, articulating them into three "moves" or series of functions: 1–8; 9–15; 16–21. Each "move" corresponds to a new sequence of the story that is initiated each time there is "a new villainous act."[79] The plot of *The Path* can therefore be analyzed schematically as follows (Propp's general function definition and the relevant exemplification for each function precede the description of how the function appears in Calvino's text):

1. "Absentation." "Children, after the departure or death of their parents, are left on their own" (p. 27).

Pin's mother is dead; his father has abandoned the family. Pin's sister, a prostitute, pays little attention to him. Pin has to earn his living as a cobbler's apprentice.

2. "An Interdiction or Order Is Addressed to the Hero" (p. 26).

Pin is ordered by the men in the tavern to steal the gun from his sister's German lover if he wants to join their partisan group and fight the enemy: "you must steal the pistol from him" (p. 9; 38).

3. "Violation." "The fulfillment of the command implies a violation or misfortune which threatens the family. . . . The villain enters the tale" (p. 27).

Pin steals the gun while the German and his sister are making love and hides it in his secret place on the path to the nest of spiders; he cannot remain at home with his sister because the Nazis and the Fascist guards will surely arrest him.

4. "Villainy." "The villain causes harm to a member of the family . . . the villain abducts or imprisons a person . . . the villain causes bodily injury" (pp. 31–32).

The Fascist patrols catch Pin and put him in prison; they do not allow his sister to take him back home with her. A German officer beats Pin.

5. "Lack." "The hero lacks something (a talisman) or desires to have something." "Wondrous objects are lacking or without magical power" (p. 35).

Pin no longer has the gun with which he felt he could "do anything, like a grown-up" (p. 15; 45). He feels powerless. "Perhaps one day Pin will find a friend, who understands him and whom he can understand, and only to him will he show where the spiders have their lairs" (p. 19; 51).

6. "Mediation." "The opportunity for departure is given" (p. 38).

Pin discovers that one of the prison inmates, the legendary partisan guerrilla fighter Red Wolf, is planning to escape. Pin hopes to be able to escape with his help.

7. "First Function of the Donor." "The hero is tested . . . which prepares his way for receiving either a magical agent or helper. . . . A prisoner begs for his freedom" (pp. 39–40).

Red Wolf questions Pin and tests his loyalty to the partisan cause before agreeing to take Pin with him.

8. "The Initial Misfortune Is Liquidated." "A captive is freed" (pp. 53–55).

Pin escapes from prison with the help of Red Wolf.

9. "Pursuit." "Chase" (p. 56).

Pin, after Red Wolf's disappearance, is pursued by the Fascist patrols.

10. "Rescue of the Hero from Pursuit" (p. 56).

The partisan Cousin comes to Pin's rescue.

11. "The Hero is . . . Led to the Whereabouts of an Object of Search" (p. 50).

Cousin leads Pin to the partisan camp. "Pin is accepted as one of the band" (p. 66; 104).

12. "A Difficult Task Is Proposed to the Hero." "Test of strength, fortitude" (p. 60).

To become a partisan, Pin must prove that he is a man. The partisans challenge Pin "to go down into town, shoot an officer, then escape up here again" (p. 68; 107).

13. "Exposure." "The false hero or villain is exposed." "Exposure is the result of an uncompleted task" (p. 62).

Dritto—the band's leader—shows his weakness. He fails to go into battle and causes his men to disband.

14. "The Villain [or false hero] Is Punished" (p. 63).

Dritto is arrested by the partisan command. Pelle, the sometime Fascist collaborator who has tricked Pin into telling him where the gun is hidden, is killed by Red Wolf's group of partisan fighters.

15. "The Hero Returns" (p. 55).

Pin goes back to "his own kingdom in the river-bed, back to the magic spot . . . where the pistol is buried," but the gun—stolen by Pelle—is no longer there.

16. "The hero once more sets out in search of something. . . . He is the subject of actions leading to the receipt of a magical agent" (p. 59).

Pin goes to his sister's apartment; he discovers that she has the gun.

17. "A New Villainy Occurs" (p. 59). "The villain entices his victim" (p. 33).

Pin's sister tries to get Pin to become a Fascist collaborator.

18. "Struggle" (p. 51). "The hero wins with the help of cleverness" (p. 52).

Pin succeeds in taking the gun away from his sister and runs away.

19. "Lack" (same as no. 5).

Pin "feels as if he were back at the night when he stole the pistol. Now he has his pistol, but everything is just as it was; he is alone in all the world, and lonelier than ever" (p. 141; 191).

20. "Rescue" (same as no. 10).

Pin runs into Cousin again: "These are enchanted places, where magical things always happen. The pistol is enchanted too, like a magic wand. And Cousin is also like a great magician, with his tommy-gun" (p. 141; 191).

21. "Solution" (p. 62).

Cousin—who performs the Proppian functions of "helper" *and* of the "sought-after person"—is "the great friend Pin has sought for so long" (p. 143). They are finally reunited, and they go off together holding each other by the hand.

In part, then, it is because the novel adopts some of the most traditional features of the fairy tale that the reader is ready to accept the inner logic of the fictional plot; the familiar fairy-tale plot structure seduces the reader into sharing Pin's fantastic perception of the Resistance. This in turn works to persuade the reader to step out of his own framework for the decoding of history and to apply instead the peculiar logic of the fairy tale to the historical object. The act of having to adjust one's angle of vision to Pin's estranging perspective forces the reader to "step out" of his own original perspective, seeing it in turn precisely as a perspective. Pin's consciousness serves as a vehicle for the reader to look back at his own historical consciousness and to see it rather than through it. In much the same way, the peculiar logic of this fairy tale about the Resistance leads the reader to see the familiar narrative version of history as just another narrative and another version of a story. This process of historico-ideological self-estrangement, however, represents a rejection neither of history nor of ideology on Calvino's part. Rather, as Calvino observes with regard to the Waterloo episode in *The Charterhouse of Parma*, this kind of estrangement abolishes the epic distance that reduces history to the image of a frozen sequence in time, cut off from any possibility of change in its significant lines, and restores to the reader the "genuine emotion" felt by someone like Fabrizio, whose experience of momentous historical events has not yet crystallized into a "definitive" epic image or ideology. The point is to see history not as something absolute that has a "finalizable" (as Bakhtin would call it) shape and meaning but as something whose shape and meaning are perpetually subject to change in accordance with our particular imaginary representation of it. Although no reader may successfully bracket altogether the ideology that he brings to the scene of reading (nor does the device of the naive internal focalizer intend to achieve that effect), in assuming Fabrizio's or Pin's perspectives we do become aware of both their limits and the limits of our own original vision of history.

In rejecting the conventional epic celebration of the Resistance and the Liberation and in choosing instead to structure his narrative like a fairy tale, Calvino at first may seem to have opted for what is simply another mode of totalization, as ideologically overdetermined and arbitrary in its organic sequence of functions and in its teleological orientation as Lukács's modern epic. But as a fairy tale *The Path* makes no totalizing epistemological claims with regard to historical reality, and the fairy-tale structure does not represent Calvino's optimistic vision of the Resistance as a story with a happy ending. Rather, this structure may be shown to possess a code-switching rhetorical function in the novel which corresponds to another form of *ostranenie,* namely the "baring of the device" (Shklovsky). *The Path* not only defamiliarizes the reality of the Resistance, but it simultaneously "makes strange" for the reader its own mode of emplotment as a work of narrative fiction on the threshold of both fantasy and history.

This defamiliarization of form is carried out in two different but related ways: on the one hand, Calvino persistently calls the reader's attention to the conventional devices of the fairy-tale genre employed in the novel (consequently exposing the fictionality of the narrative); on the other hand, however, in writing his text he repeatedly breaks the familiar rules of the genre itself. Although it appropriates a number of the thematic and stylistic devices of the fairy tale, in fact, *The Path* does not allow for the easy accommodation of appearance and reality which above all else characterizes this genre. Pin's world is not simply an imaginary world with its own "unreal time" and fantastic logic, which can be seen as separate and distinct from real time and historical logic. Rather, "fantastic time" and "historical time," "fantastic logic" and "historical logic" constantly intersect and interrogate each other in the narrative. While preserving the appearance and the appeal of a fantastic quest-journey, then, the fairy-tale structure of the novel is constantly undermined by the "intrusion" of historical allusions which force a rapid shift in perspective. This process of code-switching remains operative throughout *The Path*. No reader who enters its textual labyrinth can rely exclusively on either a command of the generic code of fairy tales or on a command of history itself but must continuously adjust his angle of vision to accommodate the disturbance of the fantastic by the historical and vice versa.

As an integral part of the poetics of *The Path*, then, defamiliarization involves a kind of ironic doubling of the reader's self in the act of reading. The defamiliarized image is always an ironic or self-reflexive one, inasmuch as it foregrounds the "artificial" nature of the textual construct. An unfamiliar form will always remind us that we are reading a text and thus pull us out of the fictional reality in which the text simultaneously engages us; the reader is at once inside and outside of the text. In its more extreme forms, the "baring of the device" underscores the fundamentally ironic nature of the relationship (first discovered by the German Romantics) between the reader and the work of fiction—and between the spectator and the work of art in general. Fredric Jameson points out that "it is instructive to compare this ultimate form which defamiliarization takes for Shklovsky in the 'baring of the device' with the irony of the German Romantics, which in many ways resembles it. . . . Irony . . . characterizes our relationship to the work of art insofar as, knowing that the surface before us is an imaginary representation and the result of someone else's labor, we nonetheless consent to lose ourselves in it as though it were real." [80] Defamiliarization takes on an ironic function—as it does in *The Path*—inasmuch as it calls attention to the process of representation as the product of the author's creative imagination, reminding the reader that, as Shklovsky observes, "an image is not a permanent referent for those mutable complexities of life which are revealed through it; its purpose is not to make us perceive meaning, but *to create a special perception of the object—it creates a 'vision' of the object instead of serving as a means for knowing it.*" [81] The irony generated by the "baring of the device" does not destroy the illusion of representation. Rather, contrary to Manzoni's irony "from above" (which consistently stresses the author's superiority and totality of vision over his characters' limited insights), it seeks to delegitimize the absolute "author-ity" of the representation. The ironic "baring of the device," as Calvino demonstrates in *The Path*, shows representation to be a particular way of "imaging" the real, rather than a product of the author's superior knowledge of the real (or, to put it another way, of his access to a foundational *ontos on*).

Shklovsky's approach to literature through the heuristic device of *ostranenie* lacks—as has often been pointed out—the rigor of a consistent methodology. [82] The flexibility of the *ostranenie* concept is a consequence of Shklovsky's own intellectual evolution from an early "existential" view of art (as a practice that modifies habitual ways of seeing the world and "resurrects" things for us)[83] to a strictly formalist position privileging synchrony over diachrony (and isolating art from all other spheres of social life) to a more complex articulation of formalism, genre theory, and dialectical materialism in his 1928 book on Tolstoy's *War and Peace*.[84] His notion of *ostranenie*, however, can hardly be dismissed as a commonplace of aesthetic theory, as has been done by (among others) Victor Erlich. The latter argues—in his classic study of Russian formalism—that *ostranenie* is in effect not a definition of literariness at all but rather another in a long chain of "defenses of poesie" that runs from Aristotle through the Romantics to French surrealists and even T. S. Eliot. Erlich effectively reduces *ostranenie* to the recovery of the referentiality of literary discourse through the undoing of the linguistic stereotypes which "hide" the object of representation. He cites the following passage by Jean Cocteau, claiming that its description of what literary language does is "practically identical" with Shklovsky's: "Suddenly, as if in a flash, we *see* the dog, the coach, the house for the first time. . . . Such is the role of poetry. It takes off the veil, in the full sense of the word. It reveals . . . the amazing things which surround us. . . . Get hold of a commonplace, clean it, rub it. . . . *Tout le reste est littérature*."[85] Clearly, though, there is no more than a slight resemblance between Shklovsky's notion of *ostranenie* and Cocteau's neo-Romantic idea of artistic revelation. Although the former lays great emphasis on the role of art in the de-automatization and renewal of perception (particularly in his earlier work), he does not argue that art can make us see things, or reveal them, as they "really are" in their own essence. On the contrary, as is already apparent in the essay "Art as Technique" (1917), literature for him is the mode of a "special perception," or one possible vision of the object, and thus never points to "a permanent referent." What literature reveals, for him, are "the mutable complexities of life," that is, the ultimate unrepresentability of the real as an object in itself. Literature does not make us see the object "for the first time," as Cocteau claims, but rather—and the distinction is vitally important—*as if* for the first time. To be aware of the fictionality of any representational construct means to recognize the ironic (self-)consciousness of all literature: "le reste" is not "littérature" but the real itself, namely that which forever eludes codification.

In *The Path* the reader clearly cannot rely on Pin's particular way of "imaging" the real for a satisfactory understanding of the Resistance. On the contrary, the limits of Pin's vision and the precarious nature of Pin's naive attempts to make some sense of what he sees are made pellucidly clear in the work. The function of this partial unreliability of the main focalizer is to call attention to the process of focalization itself. Pin is able to make sense of what he sees by emplotting events into a narrative that belongs to the dimension of fairy tales and adventure stories. Yet, rather than supply the reader with a more reliable, satisfactory view of things (unlike, once again, Manzoni), the novel provocatively uses and presents Pin as the most reliable of witnesses. Even Kim, the partisan commissar and Marxist intellectual whose reflections on the historical meaning of the Resistance and on the role that Pin, Dritto, and his men play in it, are reported in chapter 9 of *The Path*, is clearly unable to give the reader a more comprehensive interpretation of events. Presented at first as the most enlightened interpreter of the historical process, with a complete command of the terminology and techniques of dialectical thought, Kim is ironically reduced at the end of chapter 9 to a position analogous to Pin's, and his version of events is ultimately exposed by Calvino as being an equally "fantastic" emplotment of the real. Indeed, the narrative specifically compares him to his namesake, Kipling's little Kim, lost in the middle of the vast Indian subcontinent. Thus the novel on the one hand "bares its devices"; on the other hand it suggests ironically that the focalization of the real in the novel through the wondering and naively imaginative gaze of a boy who "makes up stories" about what he sees is in effect less of a mystification than the vision we get through official historical accounts. Unlike Calvino's novel, in fact, traditional historiography employs a narrative emplotment of the real that hides its devices (and its subjective choice of focalization) behind the familiarity of an impersonal form and the narrative use of the preterite.

The Role of the Fantastic

"Le fiabe sono vere," Calvino writes in his introduction to the collection of Italian tales that he edited in 1956.[86] This phrase may be interpreted to mean both that "fairy tales (and folktales) tell the truth" and that "fairy tales (and folktales) are real." Calvino uses the term *fiaba* to refer to both fairy tales and folktales, the former being essentially a subcategory of the latter.[87] There are a number of different but complementary reasons that explain why Calvino makes this paradoxical attribution of reality and truthfulness to the most blatantly fictional of all narrative genres. Fairy tales (I will continue throughout to translate "fiaba" as "fairy tale"), in their always varied but essentially repetitive structure, provide us—Calvino argues—with an inexhaustible "catalogue" of the different shapes that the narrative representation of human life can take, particularly in that phase which more than any other determines the course of an individual existence, childhood and early youth, which stretches from the moment of birth—so often marked by a blessing or a curse—to the fated departure from home and the beginning of the odyssey that one must undergo in order to become an adult. "The technique with which a tale is constructed involves the deployment of conventions and a free inventiveness. Once the theme is laid out there are certain steps required to reach a solution; interchangeable 'motifs' appear in different 'types' of tales. . . . It is up to the narrator to organize these, to pile them up like the bricks in a wall."[88] Calvino's approach to the fairy tale, however, is not merely a formalist/structuralist one along the lines of Propp's 1928 *Morphology of the Folktale*. On the contrary, Calvino "reads" the fairy tale from a perspective influenced by Propp's later work, the 1946 *Historical Roots of the Fairy Tale*.[89]

Propp's 1946 study combines a synchronic analysis of plot types and narrative functions with the study of their historical transformation. His book is an attempt, as Calvino observes, to integrate an essentially Marxist approach with the methods and results of the "anthropological school."[90] Calvino's own reading of Italian fairy tales (both in the sense of his creative translation and rewriting of the tales and of his general introduction and commentary) attempts—although in an admittedly unscholarly way—a somewhat similar integration of synchronic and diachronic elements.[91] For him, fairy tales are "real" because their origins and subsequent transformations, as indicated by Propp, reflect specific changes in early modes of material production, social and cultural institutions, and myths and rituals. Certain aspects of the marvelous and of seemingly gratuitous acts of violence and cruelty in fairy tales refer back to earlier modes of cultural organization and discourse, whose traces remain inscribed in a society's folklore.[92] Calvino refers, for example, to Propp's ethnological interpretation of the Cupid-and-Psyche type of tale:

> Psyche is the girl who lives in a house where youths are segregated during the final phase of their initiation. She comes into contact with young men in the guise of animals, or in the dark, since they must be seen by no one. Hence it is as if only one invisible youth loved her. Once the period of initiation is over, the young men return home and forget the girl who lived segregated with them. They marry and begin new families. The story grows out of this crisis. It describes a love born during the initiation and doomed to destruction by religious laws, and shows how a woman rebels against the law and recovers her young lover. Although these customs have been forgotten for thousands of years now, the plot of the story still reflects the spirit of these laws and describes every love thwarted and forbidden by law, convention, or social disparity.[93]

The theme of a transgressive eros that challenges the laws of patriarchy emerges in the story of Pin's own initiation, which is, however, modeled on still another mythic tale that bears the traces of the institutionalization of patriarchy, namely the tale of Oedipus (which Propp analyzes as well in his study).[94] Pin's quest is in fact a variation on the motif of "the child-hero who does not know his father and sets out to find him."[95]

According to Calvino, however, the "reality" of fairy tales

does not depend exclusively on "historical roots" but also on historical transformation: "La novella nun è bella, se sopra nun ci si rappella" ("The tale is not beautiful if nothing is added to it"), he notes, citing a Tuscan proverb.[96] The tale's value "consists in what is woven and rewoven into it."[97] It is through whatever the storyteller adds, with reference to a specific historical situation, that "the timeless tale is linked with the world of its listeners and with History."[98] The socioeconomic situation of the teller of the tale, together with his own political and ideological desires, inform the tale and give it its particular configuration at a given moment in the history of its telling. The tale, and the very act of the telling of the tale, disclose—in a transfigured form—the hopes and aspirations of its narrators and audiences[99] as a kind of symbolic wish fulfillment. By the same token, universal motifs take on a solid concreteness when they refer to present conditions of existence: "In contrast to . . . [the] world of kings is that of the peasants. The 'realistic' foundation of many folktales, the point of departure spurred by dire need, hunger, or unemployment is typical of a large number of Italian popular narratives."[100] In the Sicilian tale "Sperso per il mondo" ("Out in the World"), for example, the initial situation is one of unemployment and hunger: "There was a widow with two daughters and a son named Peppi, who was at a loss to earn his bread."[101] The "realistic" situation is not, in fact, only an opening motif in Italian fairy tales, a sort of "springboard into wonderland," Calvino points out; on the contrary, "Magic powers are . . . complements to natural human strength and persistence."[102] Fairy tales often appear to be "fragments of an epic of laborers that never took place and which on occasion borrows its themes from episodes of chivalry, replacing deeds and tournaments to win princesses with mounds of earth to be moved by plow or spade."[103] Calvino, like Ernst Bloch, sees in fairy tales the expression of an authentic political desire, which makes the fairy tale the estranging other of the hegemonic modes of epic emplotment. For Calvino, as for Bloch, the fairy tale projects a different vision of history, one that expresses the desire to transform the conditions of existence of dominated or subaltern groups. Pin's story in *The Path* would appear to be precisely this kind of political fairy tale, while Pin's own constant urge to tell tales signals his desire for a different life.

In terms of Calvino's paradoxical argument ("le fiabe sono vere"), however, fairy tales are not only "real" but also "true," because they do not hide their fictionality; whether or not they arise out of a real historical situation and incorporate allusions to a specific social and economic context, fairy tales do not in any case pretend to reproduce the real except in a highly mediated symbolic form. These tales are, for Calvino, the expression of a self-conscious use of fantasy and invention; they construct an illusion without deception.[104] Through the use of blatantly fantastic images and an open display of the conventional signs of the marvellous (e.g., "once upon a time"), fairy tales—perhaps more than any other narrative form—acknowledge their status as fictions or, in other words, imaginative constructs. Once this is recognized, fairy tales always appear as ironic narratives precisely because they do not hide their fictionality. Yet, of course, it is by avoiding any such irony that traditional historiography disguises its own narrative status as a symbolic reconfiguration—rather than a reproduction—of human existence. This same lack of ironic self-reflexiveness characterizes most literary neorealism, which takes history as its subject and traditional historicist mimesis as its narrative model. Neorealist narrative claims to provide the reader with a faithful account of how things really happened in Italy in the 1940's, as can be seen in works ranging from partisan memoirs, short stories, and docufiction to novels such as Benedetti's *Paura all'alba*, Brena's *Bandengebiet*, Viganò's *L'Agnese va a morire* to films such as Rossellini's *Paisà*. While Calvino still takes history as his subject in *The Path*, he takes the fairy tale instead as his narrative model. This paradoxical strategy is designed to reveal—within the confines of *The Path*'s fictional discourse—how uncannily similar are the narrative modes of historicist mimesis, on the one hand, and the fairy tale, on the other hand, and Calvino does this with the intent of destabilizing the former's claims to truth. Despite their thematic and formal differences, both modes rely on the teleological unfolding of bound narrative functions in the construction of a compelling plot. While the former claims (either implicitly or explicitly) that its "plot" corresponds to the way actual events are configured in real historical time, however, the latter designates its time to be a mythic "once upon a time"—or, in other words, a time of the imagination.

The fairy-tale structure adopted by Calvino in *The Path* in order to demythify the rhetoric of historicist mimesis, however, is not without a problematic aspect. As a "closed" narrative space—that is, an organic plot structured through reciprocally bound motifs with an internal logic of cause and effect—the text tends to exclude all reference to what is outside of its borders. Although its subject is ostensibly the history of the Resistance, *The Path* as a fairy tale programmatically works against the depiction of historical reality. It thus appears as simply a mode of discourse of the unreal, or of unreal time, while the historicist mode retains the authority of the discourse of the real, of real time; this would seem to interfere with Calvino's desire to demythify Resistance rhetoric and to represent the non-narrative plurality of Italian history. *The Path*, however, is obviously not *just* a fairy tale, or rather—at least in Calvino's eyes—no fairy tale is purely and simply a fantastic tale. "Fairy tales tell the truth"; the construction of narratives and the weaving of plots may indeed be—as a 1967 essay of his, entitled "Cibernetica e fantasmi" ("Cybernetics and Ghosts"), suggests—the irreducible essence of all epistemological activity and therefore the ground for whatever truth may be available to man.[105] Fairy tales "tell the truth" of telling itself, or at least a part of that truth, and therefore possess a valuable epistemological function. It is this aspect of the fairy tale—as a mode of discovering the very essence of man's epistemological activity—which for Calvino legitimates its challenge in *The Path* to the historicist mode of emplotting experience.

It would be overly one-sided, however, not to see that the historicist mode of narration also presents a challenge of its own to the fairy-tale mode of *The Path*. In the novel there is a constant interplay—almost a textual "shuttle"—between the code of the fairy tale through which Pin's quest is emplotted and the code of historicist mimesis through which Pin's quest becomes projected onto the stage of real historical time. The realist-referential code is activated, for example, each time the narrative distances itself from Pin's perspective; we no longer see through Pin's eyes—we no longer see the Resistance as a strange and wonderful game— nor do we follow Pin's adventures as we would those of the hero in a fairy-tale quest journey. Rather, we are made to see Pin as a historical subject in the making, an individual involved in a se- ries of events which roughly correspond to the historical events narrated by Resistance historiography and neorealist literature about the Resistance. It is through the intersection of these per- spectives that Calvino succeeds in conveying the contradictory complexity of reality itself within the space of the text.

His project in *The Path* is not the simple "deconstruction" of the historicist mode, then, but rather something more complex. As Lotman shows in his study of the structure of artistic texts, a work of literature may succeed in conveying a sense of the real in all its indetermination even though the work itself is a highly structured whole in which nothing is accidental. Literature "imi- tates" by creating a model of the extra-systemic out of its inher- ently systemic material: "In order to appear 'accidental,' an ele- ment in a work of art must belong to at least two systems and must be located at their intersection. That aspect of the element which is systemic from the point of view of one structure will appear 'accidental' when viewed from the vantage point of the other." [106] The fairy-tale mode and the referential-mimetic mode function as two separate "systems" whose challenge to each other, and whose intersection, produce an effect of incongruous- ness and discontinuity in *The Path*. This strategy of double- exposure does not allow for a simultaneous, unified vision which would integrate Pin's quest with the sequence of historical events to which the narrative continually refers. The impossibility of a unified vision/meaning is thematized in the novel by Pin's con- stantly frustrated attempts to make sense of the reality of the partisan struggle in which he has become involved: "another mysterious word. *Sim*! *Gap*! What a lot of words there must be; Pin wishes he knew them all" (p. 32; 65).

Calvino gives no indication in the novel that Pin's naive at- tempts to understand what he sees in terms of his fragmentary

memories of adventure stories, fairy tales, and folk songs correspond to a flawed interpretive model. On the contrary, Pin's vision is presented throughout as paradigmatic of the way in
which subjects try to make sense of the real by making up stories
about it or, in other words, by ordering events into some kind of
narrative form. In "Cibernetica e fantasmi," Calvino—citing
Lévi-Strauss—remarks that fables and myths have a "different
logic," which is a logic nonetheless and which has been developed "to deduce an explanation of the world." [107] Indeed, the relationship between the child's imaginative vision and the "adult"
historicist vision in *The Path* is in some ways homologous to
the dialectic of mythic and scientific thought outlined by Lévi-
Strauss in *The Savage Mind*: they "are certainly not a function of
different stages of development of the human mind, but rather
of two strategic levels at which nature is accessible to scientific
inquiry: one roughly adapted to that of perception and the imagination; the other at a remove from it." [108] Pin is, in effect, a kind
of Lévi-Straussian *bricoleur*; he conceives his imaginative explanations of events "using the remains and debris of events" and
builds his "castles out of the remains of an ancient social discourse." [109] However, while for Lévi-Strauss the legitimacy of
mythic thought is linked to the notion of a single, totalizing epistemological project, insofar as mythic thought is always "a step
toward rational ordering" (p. 15), Calvino's novel instead implies that the modes of fantasy and historicist mimesis are uncannily similar but reciprocally irreducible (they "double" each
other but only as simulacra, not copies, of each other: they stand,
in other words, in a relationship of similarity-in-difference). *The
Path* builds its discourse around this very tension and this very
irreducibility.

While *The Path* may indeed be said to enact a dialectic of
mythic versus scientific thought, then, it does not sustain the illusion of a "total knowledge of the whole," nor does it strive for
the "balanced synthesis" that Lévi-Strauss envisions as the goal
of all aesthetic expression (*The Savage Mind*, pp. 24–25). The
mutual subversion of the mythic-fantastic and the historicist-
scientific modes is in fact explicitly thematized in chapter 9 of
the novel, which is the chapter that contributes most to disrupt

the illusion of narrative unity in both a formal and epistemological sense. However, this reciprocal undermining of the two modes—and the undecidability of meaning to which it leads—is not an expression of a radical historical skepticism on Calvino's part. Rather, the text is structured so as to provide us with a symbolic representation of "real history" as something that we can know only through a "story"—through, in other words, a set of figures and functions organized into a narrative whose shape and meaning are radically subject to reinterpretation. In *The Path*, the reader cannot but identify with Pin's sense of "wonder" and amazement at the seemingly strange events to which he is a witness. Pin's fragmentary vision of the Resistance and the alienation and pain that he experiences over the course of his odyssey motivate the reader both to fill in the gaps in Pin's vision by finding an explanation for what appears inexplicable to Pin and to find a rationale that will account for Pin's suffering in the context of the historical process of the Resistance. To do so, the reader is forced to re-examine his own understanding not only of the Resistance itself but also of the very logic of history and the way historical events make sense and fit together with the events of individual lives. Through Pin as focalizer, the reader of *The Path* is increasingly led to question the meaning of historical events in the novel and to interrogate the limits of a historical order that can be reproduced in an organically structured narrative.

In his still-fundamental structuralist analysis of the fantastic as a literary genre in the nineteenth century, Tzvetan Todorov argues that the fantastic was originally "nothing but the bad conscience" of positivism.[110] He notes that the symbolic function of the nineteenth-century fantastic is that of allowing the reader to think "the other" by widening the scope of what may be considered "real," "human," and "rational," rather than an aberration or a superstitious belief: "The fantastic questions precisely the existence of an irreducible opposition between real and unreal" (p. 167). The reader of fantastic tales, such as those of E. T. A. Hoffmann, is generally called upon to determine whether an event that appears strange or even inexplicable may or may not be accounted for in terms of the laws of reason and everyday life. The transgressive power of the nineteenth-century fantastic—the hesitation, or even the sense of undecidability, that it generates in the reader—is essentially linked to two different and equally powerful conventional beliefs. One is the steadfast belief in a reality that is immutable and fixed in its laws, and the other is the belief in literature's ability to represent reality as it "really is." While often availing itself of topoi and images drawn from the discourse of the marvelous, then, the fantastic as a genre also relies heavily on the conventions of mimetic realism. In order to produce its disconcerting "reality effect," the nineteenth-century fantastic must carefully avoid any explicit sign of its own fictionality. Unlike the fairy tale, it cannot say "once upon a time there was" but must instead say—like narrative history itself—"it was." Consequently, the nineteenth-century fantastic poses no evident epistemological threat to the mode of historicist mimesis and positivist thought. "Irrational" and "inexplicable" events or phenomena are implicitly assumed to be no more than material that may be added to that single repository of positive and rational knowledge that is the history of humanity.

According to Todorov, fairy tales cannot be considered fantastic texts precisely because they are openly fictional in nature. Fairy tales instead belong to a genre "adjacent" to the fantastic, namely the marvelous (such as Gautier's "La Morte Amoureuse"), in which strange or irrational events are represented without, however, placing the reader in a position of doubt or hesitation. "The fantastic confronts us with a dilemma 'to believe or not to believe?' The marvelous achieves this impossible union, proposing that the reader believe without really believing" (p. 82); "the marvelous implies that we are plunged into a world whose laws are totally different from what they are in our own" (p. 171). Therefore, Todorov contends, fairy tales lack the subversive power of truly fantastic texts. The same holds true for the other genre "adjacent to" the fantastic, which he calls the uncanny (exemplified by Edgar Allan Poe's "The Fall of the House of Usher"). In the latter, all hesitation is resolved through a rational explanation: the disturbing strangeness of the events experienced by the characters is revealed to be purely the product of an altered or abnormal state of mind caused by madness, hallucinations, or a general inability to distinguish between reality and illusion. The uncanny effect of a text is linked to the specific perceptions an individual character has of certain events rather than to the strangeness of the events in and of themselves. Some elements of the marvelous as described by Todorov are definitely present in *The Path*, for Pin is like the protagonist of a fairy tale who sees and experiences strange, inexplicable events, which in turn he attempts to understand in terms of the "marvelous" logic of myth and fairy tales. The focalization of the narrative through Pin's perspective plunges the reader into the marvelous world of Pin's imagination and places the reader in the position of "believing without believing" throughout most of the narrative. Some elements of the uncanny are present in *The Path* as well, since the focalization of the narrative through Pin's eyes and mind allows us to explain the strangeness of events in terms of the child's failure to distinguish between the real and the unreal. Since the novel also relies, as we have already seen, on the referential code of historicist mimesis for its estrangement effect, it is clearly neither a "purely marvelous" nor a "purely uncanny" text. Rather, *The Path* is a fantastic text (in Todorov's terms) which borders on both the marvelous and the uncanny.

Clearly *The Path* contradicts Todorov's claim that the fantastic is no longer a viable mode of writing in the twentieth century. Todorov bases his claim on a typically structuralist assumption: since we no longer believe either in the referentiality of language or in a reality which obeys a "fixed" rational order—he argues— the fantastic has lost its reason to be. The most inexplicable, impossible events represented in literary texts no longer have the power to make us hesitate when we attempt to interpret them, because we immediately recognize them as fictional, imaginary constructs. Whatever hesitation or undecidability the text may produce in the reader no longer concerns "reality" at all; it becomes, rather, simply a matter of literary interpretation. The reader no longer seeks to explain the events of a fantastic narrative or *any* narrative as he would events in real life. But Todorov— perhaps under the sway of a theory (i.e. structuralism) that seeks to reduce radically the agency of the subject in language—underestimates the power of the desire for a truthful and rational emplotment of the real in human discourse. This desire permeates the literature of neorealism, and it is this desire that continually informs the narrative discourse of historiography.[111]

In *The Path*, the undecidability generated by the text is directly linked to the reader's desire for a truthful and rational emplotment of the real. Calvino's text exploits this desire by deploying the conventions of neorealism while at the same time seeking to subvert them. The *incipit* of the text draws the reader in with a typically (neo)realist move, laying out the scene of the story in the old and decaying *carrugio* of the coastal city on the western Italian Riviera, introducing the customs and manners of the people who live there, and describing their environment and sociohistorical context, before proceeding to focus on Pin's character. In the opening page of *The Path*, Calvino employs a strictly external narrative focalization. Like the initial establishing long shot of a neorealist film (typically followed by a gradual focusing of the camera onto a specific location within the larger topographical context where the action of the narrative begins),[112] *The Path* starts with a view of the street from above, describing the trajectory the sunlight traces to reach the street through the narrow space between the houses. This establishing shot defines "the slice of life" the narrative is going to focus on, making it visible for the reader in an absolutely objective way, throwing light on it as naturally as do the sun's rays. The first few pages of the novel are descriptive; they tell of the usual, habitual things which make up Pin's life with his sister and the lives of the inhabitants of the *carrugio* under German occupation. The time of the narrative here can be described, in Gérard Genette's terms, as an "iterative" present; the narrative simply tells us once what happens every day in Pin's life.[113] The plot starts into motion with a clearly marked "singulative" (telling once what happened once): "That day . . ." It is the day in which Pin first comes into contact with the Resistance, when Comitato appears among the men in the tavern. From that point on, the referential-mimetic code loses its position of absolute dominance, and the code of Pin's fantasy starts to make the narrated events appear strange and inexplicable. Thus the discourse of neorealism is used at first by Calvino to "ground" the events narrated in the novel into the conventionally accepted order of the real and to sustain the belief in the objective truth and stability of that order, but he then proceeds to show how the conventions of neorealism—and the reader's belief in its objectivity—are actually groundless. In *The Path*, the order of the real eventually emerges through Pin's perspective as a precarious, shifting construct of the imagination.

While the weakening (but clearly not the collapse) of the positivist notions of objective representation and referentiality may have rendered the fantastic obsolete in its specific nineteenth-century form, the persistence of so-called objective modes of representation in the twentieth century opens up the possibility of a different kind of fantastic literature. In the nineteenth century, the fantastic challenged cultural codes by widening the scope of what could be considered "real" and "human." In *The Path*, Calvino's modern fantastic continues to have the same transgressive function, but rather than seek a broader description of the order of the real or of the historical order, his fantastic strategy instead pursues the delegitimation of the kind of totalizing discourse that claims to be able to provide us with such a description. Calvino's twentieth-century practice of the fantastic performs its transgressive function precisely by incorporating the explicit marks of fictionality—the "once upon a time" of the fairy tale—that the nineteenth-century fantastic had to repress. In the twentieth century, the border between the marvelous, the fantastic, and the uncanny is no longer insurmountable; on the contrary, it is by crossing that border that the fantastic renews itself as a genre.[114]

4 · The Politics of 'The Path'

The Politics of Fantasy

Calvino's portrayal of the partisan struggle through Pin's eyes allows him to recapture a number of its more radical and unsettling aspects, many of which are not to be found in the official rhetoric and retrospective historical accounts of the Resistance. The partisans who fought in the mountainous regions of central and northern Italy were cut off—often suddenly and dramatically—from the routines of their everyday lives, their jobs, and their families, as well as from the institutional control of the state, the Church, the army, the party, and the union. They were thrown into a more primitive and in many respects anarchic form of existence, living in direct contact with nature and the "wilderness" on the one hand and—in the face of violence and death—with the truth of the material reality and vulnerability of their own bodies on the other hand. Although this experience was in many ways a deeply disturbing one, as Roberto Battaglia observes in his 1945 memoir, it also had a positive effect on the men and women who shared it, for it offered something like a return to an essential and "earlier" human condition, with its ardent sense of wonder about the world:

Because this is . . . the first effect . . . of partisan guerrilla warfare: it takes man back to a primitive state of reflection and sensation, it makes him intensely aware—while stretched out flat on the ground, having discovered that the enemy is close by—of the trembling of a blade of grass, of the smell of the earth, of the sudden flight of a multi-colored insect, miraculous in its perfection. Never again will we be able to find in our normal lives that state of mind . . . in which one is happy simply to be alive and to be at one with the world."[1]

In this passage, Battaglia describes his impressions in a way that is strikingly similar to that used by Calvino in describing Pin's vision of the landscape surrounding the partisan camp in the mountains of Liguria: "Pin sings as he goes, looking at the sky and the clear morning world and the mountain butterflies of strange colours meandering over the meadows. . . . Now Pin has discovered all kinds of coloured things; yellow and brown mushrooms growing damp in the earth, red spiders on huge invisible nets, hares all legs and ears which appear suddenly on the path then leap zigzagging out of sight. . . . The new camp is surrounded by lovely places to explore" (pp. 84–86; 125–27).

According to the testimony (recorded in diaries or memoirs) of many of its participants, there was indeed something inherently marvelous, fantastic, or even pastoral in the partisan experience—despite the daily hardship and danger—that evoked the unreal atmosphere of a fairy tale, an adventure story, or an epic romance. In his *Partigiani della montagna*—an account of the life of a *Giustizia e libertà* partisan brigade in the mountains above Cuneo—Giorgio Bocca describes as follows his impressions of a secluded and deserted mountain village and of the fighting which went on around it: "This is the village I imagined as a child when I listened to tales about fairies and gnomes. An abandoned village, set in a narrow and deep little valley, near the snow beneath the peak of Mount Tibert. . . . The bands engaged in a constant criss-cross of fights which flared up suddenly; everywhere they entwined, they separated and entwined again. It was like a gigantic hunt, in which the knights—both the hunters and the hunted—were mixed together in an endless chase devoid of any sense of direction."[2] In the wartime diary of Pino Levi Cavaglione, we find a similar sense of estrangement and regression to an archaic state outside of real time, along with a feeling of taking part in a grotesque but exhilarating children's game. The Germans are often described in Cavaglione's diary as "puppets," and a train thrown off a bridge sabotaged by the partisans is seen "like a toy broken by a mischievous child."[3]

It is Roberto Battaglia's memoirs, though, that provide us with some of the most telling insights into the "marvelous" and estranging quality of the partisan experience in Italy. Like Bocca, he also alludes to the world of epic romance and adventure stories, as well as to the recovery of a childlike vision, in order to give his readers a sense of the strangeness of his partisan experience "[As] in some chivalric romance . . . when we made our weapons shine, there were Ariosto's woods and Angelicas and brigands. . . . Happy days, days of a new childhood for us and for our guerrilla warfare" (pp. 102–4). This sense of a return to the scene of childhood, with its unlimited potential for discovery and surprise, can be at once delightful and strangely grotesque for those who experience it, as Battaglia points out in the following passage from his memoirs: "I look at Tony who is advancing as if he were following imaginary tracks on the ground; it seems to me that he is smelling the wind suspiciously; I look at my comrades cautiously advancing behind me. The situation suddenly takes on a different color. I almost feel like laughing silently. In that line of men meandering through the meadow under the moon, moving forward in sudden bursts, I rediscover some faded images from the adventure stories I used to read when I was a boy" (p. 112). The tone of this passage from Battaglia's memoirs, which is equally to be found in many parts of Levi Cavaglione's diary, is linked to a sense of freedom from the constraints of the normal social order and its institutions while living out an adventure and pursuing a common quest. Simultaneously, as we have seen, this results in a sense of a return to a more authentic, direct relationship with both nature and a vanished form of communal life. The "comic" or "grotesque" connotations that this experience acquires in the very eyes of the people who live it and write about it is profoundly linked to the suspension of their customary forms of existence, or, in other words, to their estrangement from their familiar reality as historical beings. Hence the reason for the common feeling, repeatedly expressed in partisan diaries and memoirs, of being outside of history and of real time itself, and of having been thrust back into the mythic time of fables and epic romances (which is akin to what Marx calls "the childhood of humanity").

Battaglia points out how the very choice of names that the partisans gave themselves—he mentions Diavolo Nero ("Black Devil"), Drago ("Dragon"), Corsaro Rosso ("The Red Pirate"), Orlando, Achille, Tarzan, Siluro ("Torpedo")—were based on vague memories of the classical epics, adventure films, and popular novels. These nicknames not only reveal the partisans' "candid imagination," he notes, but also reflect a peculiar collective sense of rejuvenation: "This is what may be most surprising for an observer from outside the movement: to see how that primitive world had such a firm basis, and how its very tone of ingenuity was actually a positive force rather than a weakness: it is almost as if Italians needed—after so much indifference, pettiness and selfishness—to look at reality with the light and agile spirit of a child, in order to be able to live and die without rhetoric."[4]

In his "La storiografia della Resistenza," Battaglia himself subsequently criticizes the "ludic" character of Levi Cavaglione's diary as symptomatic of the "immaturity" of the Resistance movement in central Italy.[5] In the second part of his own narrative account, which describes the progressive militarization of the partisan divisions, Bocca remarks that through the new regimentation "the partisan struggle has emerged from its adolescence, it has entered the stage of virility and is about to become mature" (p. 64). His is, in a certain sense, a *Bildungsroman* of the partisan struggle; "maturity" means the triumph of the reality-principle for Bocca, the end of childish illusions, and the acceptance of a historical compromise after the Liberation with those same surviving reactionary institutions that the partisan struggle had originally dreamed of destroying, like an inspired but deluded knight errant. Attempts were made after the Liberation—Bocca says—to preserve the spirit of the armed *partigianato* through various clubs and associations, but to no avail:

In reality what was vital and alive in the partisan movement was spontaneously reinscribed into the fabric of civil society; it contributed to the transformation of the political spirit of the nation; it strengthened its organism like an injection of energy. The injection did not in and of itself have the power to make the organism healthy again: contrary to the hopes and plans of the people who had experienced the heroic enthu-

siasm of the partisan struggle and the isolation of clandestine existence, the democratic revolution failed to occur completely. The forces
which had nourished Fascism and the war were not wholly defeated.
This, however, does not diminish the importance of the work that they
accomplished. . . . The setback presently being experienced [by the
popular forces of the Resistance], due to the resurgence of an opposition that was too simplistically considered to have been vanquished, is
not in the last analysis totally negative. . . . It compels them to reex-
amine their ranks, to purge them of elements that might be superficial
or false, to correct those ideas born out of an initial enthusiasm which
was too impulsive and too naive. It turns them, in other words, into
conscious political forces, the way the trials of existence shape the character of a given individual. (pp. 112–13)

For Bocca, the fact that the Resistance failed to trigger a democratic revolution in Italy and the fact that the new Italy was in
effect still very much a conservative state—with ties to the former regime—despite the "interlude" of the partisan struggle are
part of a political reality which must be rationally accepted and
analyzed. The partisan movement itself, in this perspective,
needs to repress its original idealism and revolutionary fervor
and to allow itself to be reabsorbed into the organism of the
state.

The Path, however, rejects this pragmatic notion of "maturity"
and "reality." By focalizing his narrative in the way that he does
and by emplotting it in the form of a fairy tale, Calvino gives his
readers an image of the partisan struggle as an unleashing of human imagination and fantasy, as a projection of a desire for a
better and freer way of life leading to the possibility of an authentic emancipation of the subject. Precisely this side of the Resistance was, as we have seen, systematically repressed in the
reactionary backlash which followed the "Liberation" of Italy.
The nostalgic recollection of an imaginary state of freedom—
whose chief components would include the world of childhood
and of the infancy of mankind in general, together with the
themes and forms of fairy tales, epic romances, and adventure
stories—is an essential part of the partisan experience for Calvino. It is a utopian nostalgia which generates the desire for a
recovery of a lost sense of organic community, of common goals
and values, and of a more authentic relationship with the natu-

ral world. Walter Benjamin—who, like Calvino, held a lifelong fascination for fairy tales and children's books—sees the fairy tale as an inherently utopian genre: "The liberating magic which the fairy tale has at its disposal does not bring nature into play in a mythical way, but points to its complicity with liberated man. A mature man feels this complicity only occasionally, that is, when he is happy."[6] However, unlike many archaicizing nineteenth- and twentieth-century utopias, which imagine mankind's return to a more genuine and authentic (because supposedly more original) state of nature, there is nothing reactionary in the nostalgic utopianism of Calvino's fairy tale. "If nostalgia as a political motivation is most frequently associated with Fascism"— Jameson writes regarding Benjamin's own form of nostalgic utopianism—"there is no reason why a nostalgia conscious of itself, a lucid and remorseless dissatisfaction with the present on the ground of some remembered plenitude, cannot furnish as adequate a revolutionary stimulus as any other: the example of Benjamin is there to prove it."[7] In his "fairy tale," Calvino foregrounds the sense of "liberating magic," the strangely innocent delight the partisans felt in discovering their new mode of existence, despite the specter of violence and death that haunted their world. Fantasy therefore takes on a revolutionary political value in Calvino's novel. The world of childhood fantasy—with its sense of unlimited possibility and freedom from the social structure of domination—becomes a metaphor in *The Path* for a desire that will not let itself be easily mastered or repressed, a desire for a kind of liberation that goes far beyond the limited historical achievements of the Italian Resistance.

One of the foremost historians of the Italian Resistance, Guido Quazza, provides ample evidence, in his *Resistenza e storia d'Italia* (the product of three decades of study and research on the Resistance), that "none of the foremost political and social objectives of the Resistance" were achieved with the Liberation; indeed, the Liberation paradoxically constituted, according to him, a defeat for the Resistance movement.[8] Although criticism of the Resistance as a failed revolution may—Quazza notes— appear pointless, since "what never was a revolution cannot be a failed revolution," the question of the revolutionary potential of the partisan struggle cannot simply be dismissed on those grounds. Despite the great social diversity and varied political orientation of the partisan bands, he argues, the partisan experience on the whole constituted an episode of direct democracy unique in the history of Italy: "A new partisan would discover to his amazement a world ruled by sincerity, noble intentions, and disinterestedness, and devoid of either competitiveness or attachment to private property; a world, in short, that appears to him as a kind of 'city of the sun,' in which the first rule is the absolute equality of all its members."[9] Notwithstanding their differences in political orientation, background, and organization, the partisan bands and autonomous democratic governments in the zones liberated by the partisans were truly radical experiences in Italian history. The "utopian" democratic features of the partisan experience, in fact, constituted such a dramatic rupture with Italian history that, after the Liberation, they had to be eradicated and almost exorcised by the institutions of the new Italian state, including the PCI and the other left-wing parties. In fact, Palmiro Togliatti was Minister of Justice when the first partisans were arrested and brought to trial. Quazza comments in this regard that "an ethical and political patrimony of enormous potential value for an authentic renovation of the nation was thus rapidly squandered, almost in a kind of fearful haste to close the chapter of uncontrollable armed struggle, thus putting an end to a push from below, which was both genuine and self-propelled."[10] In August 1946, hundreds of partisans went back into the mountains to express their sense of frustration and betrayal, and above all to protest against the amnesty granted to the Fascists by the new government. The "rebels" were "pacified" with the help of Togliatti's diplomatic skills, as well as through the mediation of some of the most prestigious partisan leaders from the various Liberation Committees. However, as Quazza makes clear, "The rapid liquidation of the Resistance movement coincides with the equally rapid instauration of a relation of continuity between the new Italy and Fascist Italy; both show how meaningless it is—already in the first year after the liberation of Italy—to speak of 'anti-Fascist unity'" (p. 345). The radical character of Calvino's novel must be considered in this same context. *The Path* in no way represents the Liberation as something already accomplished, as a dream that the new Italy has realized in freeing itself—together with the Allies—from German occupation and from the official manifestations of Fascism. On the contrary, *The Path* represents the partisan experience as the expression of a radical form of political desire, a fantasy of human emancipation that is yet to come, and that must be sustained against the efforts of a more "rational" and "reasonable" approach to the real to suppress it or to curb its revolutionary potential.[11]

Although Quazza employs a loosely narrative structure and sequential chronological order, his *Resistenza e storia d'Italia* rejects the traditional "organic" narrative emplotment of Resistance history writing, opening up his inquiry in several directions at once. Quazza's work reflects the research done since the mid-1950's by a number of specialists on both the national and international context of the partisan movement, the different characteristics that it assumed in different parts of Italy, the diversity of the partisans' social and political backgrounds, the variety of internal and external relations (and tensions) between the different units, brigades, and CLN's, and the rapport between the partisans and the civilian population in both occupied and liberated territories.[12] Each of the sections of Quazza's history is organized around a series of related problems (economic, social, political, etc.), and thus is able to appear as a self-contained and autonomous narrative; there is no sequential or causal order that links them, only a transversal or diagonal "space" that cuts across all the different levels. His text breaks down the Resistance into a multiplicity of elements and sequences of different kinds of events which cannot necessarily be reconciled with each other or reduced to a single governing logic. Quazza focuses in particular on the problem of violence and what he sees as the misleading distinction between the "irrational" violence of Fascism and the "rational" violence of the partisans. He argues that this false dichotomy has consistently blinded historians to the elements of continuity between the pre-Fascist state, the Fascist state, and the post-Fascist state. In this perspective, with its far longer *durée*, the Resistance no longer appears as a separate chapter in the history of Italy and its masses of laborers, one which possesses its own epic logic of "beginnings" and "peak times" (in Bakhtin's terms), but rather as a part of a socioeconomic process that was already underway even before the Unification of Italy in the nineteenth century.[13]

Each of the questions raised by Battaglia in *Un uomo: un partigiano* (discussed earlier in Chapter 3) is explored by Quazza; these range from the question of legitimate violence to the lack of a truly unified "spirit of the Resistance" to collaborationism among civilians and the arbitrary nature of partisan "justice." Quazza observes in particular that the so-called *colpisti* ("hit men") tended to take justice into their own hands. In *The Path*, Cousin is a *colpista* who follows the questionable practice of acting as accuser, judge, and executioner. This points once again to the gap between the CLN command structure (including the leaders of the PCI) and the more radical impulses of the partisan base, something which is entirely repressed by both Longo and Battaglia. Calvino's novel anticipates the "decomposition" of the history of the Resistance performed by Quazza three decades later, for Calvino represents the history of the Resistance as a series of interpretive enigmas, and—like Battaglia in his 1945 memoir—portrays the "truth" of the Resistance as a question mark.

The Politics of Estrangement and the Decomposition of History

The fairy-tale emplotment of Pin's story is the projection of a utopian political desire; it represents Calvino's wish to promote historical action as a part of a positive quest for human happiness. But *The Path*, while affirming the value of embarking on a struggle against evil and searching for happiness, simultaneously discloses the illusory nature of this search. The positive meaning of Pin's quest is constantly undermined by the intrusion of references to the deeply ambiguous reality of the partisan struggle, a reality that contradicts Pin's fantasy of emancipation. Indeed, even the very heterogeneity of "historical time" in the novel—the sense conveyed by the narrative that historical time is constituted by a series of reciprocally incongruous levels or zones—contributes to render the meaning of Pin's quest problematic. However, there is nothing arbitrary about the kinds of people and events that Pin, and we along with him, encounter along his path in *The Path*. This is wholly in keeping with Calvino's design in inscribing his own political desire into the texture of the novel, for each character and event is carefully calculated to demythify an aspect of Resistance rhetoric.

First of all, the presence of an omniscient narrator is signaled each time that a historical allusion or a reference to one of the character's actions or thoughts occurs that could not possibly belong to the field of Pin's knowledge and understanding. This attenuation of the process of internal focalization, whereby the reader learns (or is reminded of) things that Pin does not know, is one of the forms that Calvino's irony assumes in the novel. It is dramatic irony in the sense that the reader is allowed insights into Pin's existence, and into the historical circumstances that shape his existence, which the protagonist himself is unable to see. This ironic framework is responsible for the pathos generated by the narrative, particularly in its memorable final sequence. As a rhetorical device, dramatic irony helps to account for the reader's tendency to empathize—in reading *The Path*— with Pin's illusions while at the same time recognizing their deluded nature.

The first crucial scene of Pin's initiation into the adult and historical world, found in the opening chapter, exemplifies this strategy. In this scene Pin encounters for the first time the open hostility of the group of men in the tavern he is desperately trying to join. The scene takes place in the presence of a secret envoy of the CLN. Although a number of interparty anti-Fascist committees had begun to form in Italy as early as 1942, the CLN was officially founded immediately after the September 1943 armistice, in the wake of the flight of King Victor Emmanuel III and of Badoglio's government to southern Italy, the proclamation of Mussolini's new "Social Republic" in northern Italy, and the beginning of the German military occupation of the peninsula. None of the dramatic events of 1943 are, however, referred to directly in *The Path*. We learn only that the CLN envoy has come to the tavern to convince the men to form a GAP, or "Group of Patriotic Action." In the spring of 1944 there was in fact a concentrated effort on the part of the CLN in northern Italy, and particularly on the part of the Italian Communist Party's secret committee, to gather strength and support for the Resistance movement and to promote the formation of guerrilla warfare groups (such as the GAP's) among the population of the occupied territories, regardless of political allegiance, party line, or social class. It is in this context, first and foremost, that the attempt of the secret envoy in the novel to mobilize a group of petty criminals and subproletarians—such as the men of the tavern—should be understood.[14]

From within the group of men in the tavern, two characters emerge who will play crucial roles both in Pin's education about the realities of adult life and in the novel's problematization of the historical reality of the Resistance. They are Michel the Frenchy and Gian the driver: "Michel is one of those people who used to work in hotels in France before the war; he'd had quite a good time there on the whole, though sometimes they would call him *macaroni* or *cochon fasciste*, then in '40 he began being put into concentration camps and everything had gone wrong with him since: unemployment, repatriation, lawbreaking" (p. 23; 56). Michel the Frenchy is indeed one of the darkest figures in *The Path*. After the Fascists round up the men in the tavern and arrest them, he enlists in the notorious Black Brigade. "Yes," he tells Pin, when the two meet again in prison. "I've asked to join the Black Brigade. They've told me what the advantages are and the pay they get. Then, you know, during round-ups one can snoop around people's houses and take what one wants. To-morrow they'll give me my weapons and uniform. Keep your chin up, Pin" (p. 26; 59). Michel represents the common attitude of many who—as PCI leader Giorgio Amendola acknowledged in his 1973 memoirs—were indifferent to the cause of the Resistance and to the CLN's call for action because they "no longer believed in anything" after their lives had been ruined by the collapse of the regime:

The Nazi maneuver was able to gain a much larger consensus than our propaganda still today would lead us to believe. . . . There was the support of groups of young people who had witnessed with disgust the collapse of all their hopes when the regime fell without the slightest defense or redeeming dignity; they had experienced the cynical double-dealing practiced by the monarchy and by Badoglio (and what appeared to be the betrayal constituted by the renewed commitment to the German allies) as a personal affront. And there were those who believed in an ultimate victory by the Germans with the appearance of the famous "secret weapon," and the desperate ones who no longer believed in anything at all, wanting only to avenge themselves for the failure of their lives as long as it was still possible.[15]

When Pin meets Gian the driver again in Dritto's partisan encampment, he learns that "he plays a double game, Michel does, with the Black Brigade and with the *Gap*; he hasn't decided yet which side to be on . . ." (p. 124; 172).

Gian the driver comes forward in the scene with Comitato in the tavern and declares: "I've been in Croatia and there a bloody German only had to go looking round a village for women, and he was never seen again, nor was his corpse" (p. 9; 38). Since he lacks the historical frame of reference required to interpret this statement, Pin registers it only as an indirect threat to himself, given that his sister sleeps with Germans, but the reader is provided here with a synoptic reference to a specific historical situation. Gian the driver was drafted by the Fascists and sent to join the German forces that occupied Croatia during the war. There he had occasion to witness the development of the Yugoslavian Resistance struggle. Gian is therefore one of the many soldiers who had to face alone the tumultuous days after the armistice, when all Italian troops were left to fend for themselves by the Badoglio government, and many Italian soldiers in Yugoslavia were immediately imprisoned and deported to Germany. As a war veteran in occupied Italy, Gian has a number of different options: he can join the Black Brigades of the new Fascist republic and continue fighting for Mussolini, join the Resistance and fight for the CLN, or hide out from the Fascist recruiters and do nothing at all, waiting for the war to end. This "wait-and-see" attitude (or so-called *attendismo*) constituted the most widespread popular form of "resistance to the Resistance" that the CLN had to contend with in northern Italy, particularly after the Allies' arrival and the beginning of the liberation of the South. Indeed, many draft-age men were induced to join the partisan groups in the mountains only out of the hope that they could hide up there, avoiding direct confrontations with the enemy and the Fascist patrols as far as possible while waiting for the war to end. Gian's potential motives for joining the armed Resistance have nothing to do with his political beliefs or with a sense of patriotism. In the same conversation with Gian, after running into him at Dritto's partisan encampment, Pin learns that Gian himself narrowly escaped arrest in another roundup at the tavern, when the men—including the double-crosser Michel—had finally decided to set in motion their plan to form a GAP. Thus Gian's decision to join the partisans in the mountains is motivated on the one hand by his need to hide out somewhere and on the other hand by his desire to take revenge on the Germans for their treatment of him on the Yugoslavian front.

While not explicitly thematized, the tenuous nature of the link that the CLN succeeded in establishing with those who were not already politicized activists in Marxist parties or groups is implicit in the dialogue among the men Pin hears after Comitato leaves the tavern:

"I wouldn't get too involved with those guys from the committee," says Michel the Frenchy to the others. "I don't feel like risking my life for their sake." "Well," says Gian the driver, "what have we done after all? We just said: we'll see. In the meantime it's a good idea to keep in contact with them without committing ourselves, in order to gain time. I myself have to get even with the Germans from when we were at the front together. If there's a chance, I'm willing to do it." "Look," says Michel, "fighting the Germans is no laughing matter. Who knows how it will end up. The committee wants us to form a *Gap*; all right, we'll form a *Gap* all of our own." "To start with," says Giraffe, "we behave as if we were on their side, and we arm ourselves. And once we are armed . . ."[16]

The themes of suspicion, intrigue, and double-crossing are explicit in this dialogue, and Calvino uses them here as a means to represent the disquieting atmosphere in Italy after Mussolini's arrest (described by Amendola above). This same uneasy sense of a duplicitous game being played out between the parties of the CLN and the most politicized activists of the partisan warfare emerges in Calvino's representation of two other characters that Pin runs into after his arrest and subsequent escape: the young *gappista* Red Wolf and the cook of Dritto's detachment, Mancino. Although the complex and often contradictory motives which led Italians to fight the Nazis and Fascists are only indirectly alluded to in the novel (chiefly through the use of concise dialogues and character sketches, such as those of Gian and Michel), the novel clearly distances itself from the celebration of the Resistance as a unanimous national and popular uprising against foreign occupation and political tyranny.

As with all the characters, words, and facts associated with the historical reality of the Resistance in *The Path*, Pin is unable to understand exactly who the CLN agent is, or what he is doing in the tavern. In Pin's childish imagination his name becomes simply "Comitato." This misunderstanding has a comic effect for the reader, which is one of Calvino's principal strategies for demythifying Resistance rhetoric. The men's way of giving the CLN envoy proof of their support is to turn on little Pin, insulting him and accusing him of being a Fascist sympathizer because his sister sells herself to the Germans: "You're a filthy little pimp. . . . With your contacts, you and your sister . . . you'll end up as important Fascists" (p. 8; 36–37). The man nicknamed Michel the Frenchy comes out with a threat addressed to Pin and his sister: "The day everything changes—you know what I mean—the day everything changes we'll send your sister round town with her head as shaved and bare as a plucked chicken . . . And for you . . . for you we'll think up something you haven't even dreamt of" (p. 8; 37). Thus Pin is introduced to the notion of the historical changes the Resistance movement will produce in Italian life through the image of one of the most infamous practices of the partisans, who often performed such rituals of symbolic castration on local women who had sexual relationships with Fascists or Germans. Pin's spirited reply to the threat addressed to both him and his sister—as if they were a single potential scapegoat figure—exposes Michel's and the others' hypocrisy and deluded machismo. At the same time, however, it shows Pin's progressive internalization of the men's way of thinking and behaving:

Pin does his best to look unconcerned, but is obviously suffering inwardly, and is biting his lips. "On the day when you get a bit brighter," he says, "I'll explain how things are. First, that I and my sister each go our own way, and as for pimping you can go and do it for her yourself if you feel like it. Second, that my sister doesn't go with the Germans because she particularly likes them, but because she is as international as the Red Cross; and the same way she goes with Germans now she'll go later with English, Negroes and anyone else who happens to turn up" . . . (all these are things Pin has learnt from listening to grown-ups, probably the very same ones he's talking to now. Why should he have to explain them?) "Third, the only dealings I've had with that German is getting cigarettes out of him, in return for which I've played tricks on him like the one I did to-day, which I won't tell you about as you've put me in a bad temper." (p. 8–9; 37)

Pin's puzzled reflection (which Calvino "objectifies" by using free indirect discourse, as he often does in *The Path* to report Pin's thoughts and impressions) expresses his amazement at having to tell the men something which they themselves have told him before. This poses a question for the reader: are the men simply putting on an act for the benefit of Comitato, or has Comitato actually been able to convince them to take sides and join the anti-Fascist armed struggle? No clear answer is provided until later in the narrative, but it is certain that in either case the men's brutal threat to Pin (whose implications will be explored in more detail in the next chapter) is not simply a reflection of their ignorance, deluded machismo, and subalternity. Rather, the threat is the expression of a will to power which is in turn generated by the men's reaction to Comitato's more sophisticated, impersonal, and less brutal exertion of ideological power, namely his attempt to make the men feel guilty for not taking part in the anti-Fascist movement. Thus, in defending himself against the threats of the men, Pin ironically speaks for them too, for he expresses the very thoughts the men are trying to hide from Comitato. Pin's little speech significantly fails to generate any reaction in Comitato, who listens and watches impassively without smiling or showing any sign of approval, like a silent and impartial judge.

Pin's speech offers a perspective on human life and history for which the idea of the Resistance as a national liberation movement is essentially alien. Pin, his sister, and the men in the tavern lack both the class consciousness and the patriotic ideals which allowed the CLN to gather strength and support for the

Resistance movement among widely different strata of the Italian populace and to expand the ranks of the armed Resistance. Calvino's choice of *lumpen* proletarians as protagonists in his novel is motivated in part, as we have seen, by his opposition to the tendency—particularly widespread among left-wing Italian intellectuals—to celebrate the Resistance as a "national and popular movement" in the Gramscian sense and to represent it as an apotheosis of the "socialist hero" required by the then-current cultural policy of the Communist Party. Calvino's unorthodox approach, however, does not imply a refutation of the notion of class consciousness as a crucial historical force behind the Resistance, nor does it, for that matter, skeptically call for a reduction of the heroic dimension granted to the liberation movement. At the time he was writing *The Path*, in fact, Calvino was still a member of the PCI and very much a Marxist intellectual. However, in *The Path* he is primarily interested in looking at class consciousness and at the "national-popular" development of the Resistance movement as complex and contradictory processes, rather than as abstract dialectical concepts. As Calvino states in his 1964 preface, he felt in 1946 that his was the most "positive, the most revolutionary of works," precisely because it described class consciousness and historical awareness in the process of being molded (p. xiv; 14).

The tavern scene is emblematic of this approach in *The Path*. Comitato comes to the tavern to deliver a call to action "from above." He is indifferent to, or unaware of, the reality "from below" which makes his appeal difficult or impossible to grasp and to respond to, except in the form of the men's brutal threat to Pin and his sister. Pin's identification of the agent with the organization that he represents ironically underscores the impersonality and remoteness of both in the world of the *carrugio*. Thus we find that two different but equally limited perspectives intersect and collide in the discourse of the novel: the "existential" and apparently ahistorical and apolitical perspective of both Pin and the men, on the one hand, and Comitato's abstract and pragmatic vision of "what has to be done" on the other hand. Pin's comic and chaotic enumeration of all the men with whom his sister will indiscriminately sleep reflects an instinctive sense of history as an undifferentiated continuum. In his short life, Pin has never known anything but the war; the sudden reversal on the front after the September 1943 armistice and the transformation of the Germans from allies into enemies means nothing to him. Major political conflicts and events generally identified with history itself because they effect significant changes in the life of a social group, a nation, or an entire continent appear in fact to lead to no change at all from the point of view of Pin and his sister. In their lives, Fascism, the war, the Allies' invasion, the German occupation, and the Resistance itself merely represent slight variations within the same repetitive pattern. The time they live by, it seems, is not historical in this sense, for so-called "historical events" filter down to their consciousness only in fragmentary form. They seem to have little or nothing to do with the events which make up their social existence, their daily life, and the facts of their material existence as a struggle for survival. The time Pin and his sister live by belongs to a slower kind of history, a history which is almost changeless in its everyday appearance. The foregrounding of Pin's perspective in Calvino's novel, therefore, performs the estranging function of "decomposing" historical time and of making traditional history (or *histoire événementielle*) appear as one level of history, but by no means as the only one or the one under which all other levels can be coherently subsumed.[17]

Calvino's decomposition of history in *The Path*, as might be suspected, has specific political implications, for it was precisely the CLN leadership's mistaken assumption that history was made of and with "major" political and military events and that the reality of social and material existence—as well as the Italian people's "mentality"—would have been transformed in accordance with the direction that these events would take that led the CLN to actively shape those events "from the top," while neglecting the complex and contradictory reality that lay "below" it. The "Jacobin" approach by the CLN, widely discussed and criticized during and after the Resistance, is thematized by Calvino in *The Path* through the quasi-allegorical figure of Comitato,[18] who takes on a meaning which goes beyond the immediate situation of the scene described in the novel. His silence, his indifference to the real conditions of existence of the men in the tavern, and his failure to communicate with them except by giving them orders represent the kind of blindness that helped to lead the CLN and the PCI to their eventual and paradoxical defeat.

One of the most hotly debated issues concerning the partisan struggle and the Resistance in Italy was (and still is) the political role played by the Communist Party and by the other Italian political parties in the national and local Liberation Committees. Although all the anti-Fascist parties were represented in the Committees at the national level, the left-wing parties generally played the leading role in them, as well as in the organization of the various partisan bands themselves. While it was a participant in this coalition group, the PCI opted for a decidedly moderate line. Rather than press for the revolutionary goal of a war of national liberation, the leadership of the PCI instead opted for a compromise with the more conservative anti-Fascist parties— the Liberals and the Christian Democrats—whose goal was simply a restoration of the pre-Fascist parliamentary regime.

There were considerable disagreements about this decision not only within the PCI itself but also between the CLNAI (the Committee for Northern Italy, which was more directly responsible for the strategic and military leadership of the partisan bands) and the Committee in Rome (which handled diplomatic relations with the Anglo-American forces, the King and his cabinet headed by Badoglio—still officially at the head of the Italian government in southern Italy—and the Soviet Union). The Communist Party's moderate stance, thanks chiefly to the influence of Togliatti, finally prevailed. By collaborating with the royal government and subordinating the Resistance to the policy of the Western allies and the Soviet Union, the PCI hoped to gain its own legal reinsertion into national life after the end of the war.[19] The PCI thus rejected the argument, put forth by some of its own members and by some of the more radical groups within the Socialist Party of Proletarian Unity and the Action Party, that called for it to isolate the King and Badoglio and to turn the CLN itself into the nucleus of a new provisional national government, while awaiting the opportunity to hold national elections and to form a constituent assembly after the end of the conflict. The PCI also refused to accept the idea that social revolution should be posited as the ultimate goal of the national struggle for liberation. As far as the Party's leadership was concerned, the immediate goal of the Resistance was to be the liberation of Italy from the Germans and the Fascists, and the restoration of the political conditions for a parliamentary democracy; the CLN was to draft no immediate programs for economic or social reforms in the country.[20] Only the short-term perspective of this "limited" liberation, it was thought, could truly unify all the anti-Fascist forces—conservatives and radicals alike—and receive the unqualified support of the Anglo-American forces and of the King. The Soviet Union had in 1943 reached a preliminary agreement with the Allies whereby both Italy and Yugoslavia were to be considered outside the Soviet sphere of interest. Unlike Tito, though, who refused to accept Stalin's directives and proceeded to turn the Yugoslavian Resistance into a socialist revolution, Togliatti—partly because of the very real presence of the Allies on Italian territory—complied with them and opted for a policy of "national unity."[21]

All calls for revolution coming from the militant base of the Communist Party, from the Communist peasants and factory workers, and from the other parties were therefore to be systematically discouraged or suppressed by the Central Committees. There was to be no political propaganda among the partisans. The Socialist Party and the Action party, however, were particularly dissatisfied with this policy. The Action Party argued that the partisan experience could be turned into the basis for a new kind of decentralized, direct democracy in Italy. The Socialists favored a clean break with all the individuals and institutions, including the monarchy, which had been accomplices of the Fascist regime. The PCI, however, was by far the strongest of the Italian left-wing parties, and none of the smaller parties could manage to alter its policy decisions. Ironically, the PCI owed most of its prestige to the myth of Stalin and of the Soviet Union among the working classes in Italy, but the partisans—after the initial period of anarchy and the spontaneous formation of the first armed bands—were asked never to mention Stalin's (or

Lenin's) name and to wear the Italian tricolor as an emblem of their cause rather than the red star.

While officially endorsing the policy of a "united front," however, the PCI continued to nourish among its supporters and sympathizers the myth of another, more radical liberation yet to come. Surely the liberation of the masses from the repressive institutions of the capitalist state would follow after the fulfillment of the more immediate goal of liberation from the Nazis and the Fascists.[22] Quazza defines the policy of the PCI as a rather ambiguous and deceptive form of mass manipulation: "This was indeed a duplicitous situation, because the [communist] activists were convinced for the most part that the policy of unity was just a tactic destined in the end to lead to the Party's final victory, a victory that the forward thrust of the masses and the support of the Soviet Union could not fail to bring about quickly" (p. 281). In speeches and writings dating as late as June 1945, Togliatti kept referring to a "new type of democracy" which would dismantle the old repressive institutions of the state after the Liberation: "The democracy that is taking shape today in our country must take a particular form. It cannot be purely and simply the old parliamentary regime we had before Fascism. . . . It must be an anti-Fascist, popular, progressive democracy."[23] However, Togliatti's call for a "popular" and "progressive" democracy was destined to remain but a hollow gesture, as the years following the Liberation witnessed the restoration of the traditional structure of the Italian economy—with its powerful privileged groups—and the reconstitution of the former centralized state.[24] Many of the Fascist laws were never repealed, and the bureaucratic state apparatus in all its forms remained basically unchanged after the Liberation. The new Italian constitution was itself a deeply ambiguous document—the product of several compromises among the political parties—which delegated all concrete possibilities of change to the legislative activity of the Parliament.[25] Even the same individuals who had held positions of responsibility in the Fascist state were largely able to keep their jobs or were at most moved to some other level or location in the bureaucracy.

Togliatti himself—after the disappointment of the 1946 elections, in which the PCI failed to gain the majority and the Christian Democrats emerged as the leading conservative party (one which was to play a crucial role in maintaining the economic and social structures of the prewar Italian state)—admitted the failure of his policy: "It was evident—and it was, we must admit, to be expected—that Italian conservatives would have endorsed the policy of the most advanced forces of the anti-Fascist bloc only if provided with clear guarantees. Italian conservatives had to make sure that the liquidation of Fascism . . . would not coincide with deeper or even revolutionary changes."[26] When Calvino wrote *The Path* it was already clear that Togliatti and the PCI had been far too optimistic about the possibility of "deep or even revolutionary changes" in Italy. Both the Communists and Socialists were able to participate in the first government of the new Republic in 1946, but the prime minister was a Christian Democrat, Alcide De Gasperi. The failure of his conservative policies in the implementation of any substantial social and economic reforms and the extremely precarious postwar economic situation of the country (which was plagued by inflation) contributed to weaken the support of the electorate for the Marxist parties. With the exclusion of the Communists and the Socialists from the coalition government in 1947—writes the British historian S. J. Woolf—"the hopes of the Resistance were finally buried."[27]

The PCI policy of compromise reflected in part the contradictions inherent in Gramsci's notion—implicit already in his work on the factory councils in the *Ordine Nuovo* days but elaborated mostly in his prison writings—that in Italy the struggle for a new order had to take place through the construction of a consensual hegemony, rather than through more violent forms of opposition that would attempt to dismantle directly the structure of the state. Togliatti without a doubt believed in the possibility of a parliamentary road to socialism in Italy. He believed, in other words, in the possibility of using the structures of the pre-Fascist parliamentary state, with its system of democratic elections and representation, in order to transform radically Italian society. "Progressive democracy," from his point of view, called for a progressive conversion of the masses to socialism

through the rallying of a consensus within the various mass social organizations—parties, trade unions, cultural associations—
until the conquest of a democratic majority in Parliament would
make possible a painless transition to socialism. According to
Gramsci, in fact, while the totalitarian state exerts its power
through coercion by abolishing all forms of autonomy within society, the bourgeois-democratic state allows different social organizations to exist outside the boundaries of the state system
proper and uses them as the means to exert its power through
cultural hegemony and consensus rather than coercion.[28] The
struggle for a new order within a non-totalitarian state must
therefore take the form of a "war of position" in the territory of
society itself, through the construction of a cultural and ideological hegemony and the unification of all the exploited classes
against the exploiters.[29]

Togliatti's view of the role that the PCI and the other leftist
parties were to play during the Resistance and in the construction of the new Italy was clearly influenced by Gramsci's ideas.
Togliatti believed that a compromise with the monarchy, the
Western allies, and the conservative parties was a necessary part
of a "war of position." Once the parliamentary regime was restored—he thought—and the fabric of Italian society reconstituted, the PCI would be able to establish the hegemony of the
working class in a democratic fashion. Thus the suppression of
all radical demands and "extremist" dissent during the Resistance, through an emphasis on party discipline and the postponement of the political education of the masses until after the
Liberation, was part of a general Gramscian strategy. In a rare
autobiographical statement, Calvino summarizes his own feelings, when he was a partisan, concerning Togliatti's wartime political strategy: "According to my frame of mind at the time, the
Party's policy of unity and peaceful change from within the system, and those addresses by Togliatti that I got a chance to read
in mimeographed copies, sometimes seemed to be the only
level-headed wisdom in a general climate of extremism, and
sometimes seemed to be incomprehensible and remote, far removed from the reality of blood and wrath which surrounded
us."[30] This in turn was linked, Calvino notes, to his equally con-

tradictory views—so widely shared—on the purpose of the partisan struggle itself, one of which was "legitimated" by the Party and the other of which was not: "One [view] was of the Resistance as advocating change from within the system, in opposition to Fascist subversion and violence; the other was of the Resistance as a revolutionary fact, as an impassioned identification with the rebellion of those who had always been the oppressed and the outlaws."[31]

Togliatti's strategy exacerbated two major conceptual problems which, as Perry Anderson has pointed out, were all along inherent in Gramsci's thought. Although Gramsci's concepts of hegemony and *la società civile* are asystematic and subject to different interpretations, Gramsci seems to have greatly underestimated the coercive nature of both social organizations and the ideological function of the parliamentary state system in Western democracies. The parliamentary system is not simply an "ideological" apparatus of bourgeois power, Anderson argues, because the juridical rights and the civic freedoms of bourgeois democracy are a genuinely positive reality whose loss would be "a momentous defeat for the working class." However, he observes in the following passage:

The bourgeois State . . . by definition "represents" the totality of the population, *abstracted* from its distribution into social classes, as individual and equal citizens. In other words, it presents to men and women their unequal positions in civil society as if they were equal in the State. Parliament, elected every four or five years as the sovereign expression of popular will, reflects the fictive unity of the nation back to the masses as if it were their own self-government. The economic divisions within the "citizenry" are masked by juridical parity between exploiters and exploited.[32]

Thus, Anderson contends, the parliamentary state is the formal framework of all ideological mechanisms of the ruling class, while the various apparatuses of civil society only extend and reinforce its central function. The idea—implicit in Gramsci's work—that the working class does not exercise its right to choose socialism through parliamentary elections simply because it is still subject to the cultural hegemony of the ruling class within civil society is a misleading one, according to Anderson, who comments: "In fact, it might be said that the truth if anything is the inverse: the general form of the representative State—bourgeois democracy—is itself the principal ideological linchpin of Western capitalism, whose very existence deprives the working class of the idea of socialism as *a different type of State*, and the means of communication and other mechanisms of cultural control thereafter clinch this central ideological 'effect'" (p. 28).

In Calvino's short novel, *La giornata di uno scrutatore (The Watcher)*, which takes place during the national elections of June 7, 1953, the skeptical ruminations of the protagonist (Amerigo Ormea, a PCI poll-watcher) on the democratic electoral process ("the bourgeois deceit of the whole business"),[33] and his nostalgia for the all-too-brief illusion of a "progressive democracy" after the Liberation, represent the culmination of a gradual process of political disillusionment already apparent in *The Path*:

> In those years, Amerigo's generation (or rather, that part of his generation that had lived in a certain way during the years after '40) had discovered the resources of a previously unknown attitude: nostalgia. And so, in his memory, he began to contrast the scene before his eyes with the atmosphere of Italy after the Liberation, in those few years whose most vivid recollection now was the way everyone had taken part in political affairs and actions. . . . He thought that only that newly born democracy deserved the name "democracy" . . . because that period was over now, and the field had slowly been occupied again by the gray shadow of the bureaucratic State, the same before, during, and after Fascism.[34]

Just how much the "new" Italian state represented the interests of capitalism and international imperialism did indeed become clear when De Gasperi was able to evict both the Communists and Socialists from the coalition government in 1947. Togliatti had firmly believed in the possibility of a coalition of the three major political parties—PCI, PSI, and DC—as a transitional united front from which the hegemony of the working class would emerge. But in fact, with the collapse of the Parri government six months after the Liberation (November 1945), the Christian Democrats (DC) instead emerged as the main conservative party precisely by setting themselves in opposition to the left-wing parties. Within the international situation (colored by

the Cold War), the DC represented the only political force capable of keeping Italy within the American sphere of influence,
while allowing Italian capitalism to recover its strength through
the support of the Marshall Plan and begin to take the offensive
against the unions. Through its allegiance with the oldest and
most repressive of all the institutions of Italian civil society, the
Church, the DC was able to receive the vast support of the
catholic masses while at the same time systematically absorbing
into its ranks the traditional liberal and conservative clienteles of
southern Italy.[35] By rejecting the call for a "different kind of
state" put forth by the Action Party during the Resistance and
by making its own hegemonic project dependent on the restoration of the pre-Fascist state, then, the PCI had placed itself in an
endgame situation.

Calvino dramatizes this paradoxical situation in *The Path*
chiefly through two characters, Red Wolf and Mancino (the
Trotskyite cook in Dritto's band). Red Wolf is a *gappista*, one of
those partisan "hit-men" who, acting either alone or in small
groups, carried out acts of guerrilla warfare in the cities during
the Resistance. Red Wolf's original battle name—Pin learns—
was "Ghepeu," and he always wore a Russian-style cap with a
red star, but he had to change his name to Red Wolf ("Wolf" being
a name associated with the world of fairy tales, but also with the
name of one of the Fascist youth organizations, the *Figli della Lupa*
or "Sons of the She-Wolf"). He also had to add two white and
green circles inside the red star—he tells Pin—"because we're
not out for social revolution now, but for national liberation.
When Italy's been liberated by the people, we'll nail the bourgeoisie down to their responsibilities." Pin is puzzled by this pe-
remptory statement. "How?" he asks. Red Wolf replies: "Just
that. We'll nail the bourgeoisie down to their responsibilities. The
brigade commissar explained it all to me" (p. 32; 65). Pin's innocent question and Red Wolf's reply are charged with dramatic
irony, for the reader is, unlike Pin, aware of their implications in
regard to the failure of the PCI's policy, and the ultimate failure of
the Resistance itself, to bring about a different society for people
such as Pin to live in.

When Pin wants to write "Long Live Lenin" on the water tank

behind which he is hiding with Red Wolf (he remembers having seen it written at night on the walls of the houses in his neighborhood and subsequently rubbed off by the Fascists every morning), Red Wolf corrects him, telling him to write "Long Live Italy" instead. But Pin doesn't like writing anyway, especially not that phrase (which for the reader is ironically reminiscent of nationalistic fascist rhetoric). Pin suddenly remembers his schoolteacher who used to smack him across the fingers while trying to teach him to write (before he dropped out of school). Then he writes something on the water tank anyway, which turns out to be a curse word. From Red Wolf, Pin also hears that the "ordinary criminals" who are in the fascist jail with them (among whom are several of Pin's acquaintances, including Pin's old boss Pietromagro) "aren't to be trusted" because "they are proletarians without class consciousness" (p. 34; 68). Precisely because Pin is also a proletarian without class consciousness, Red Wolf doesn't think twice about deserting him and leaving him alone to be hunted by the fascist patrols.

Pin runs into Red Wolf again near Dritto's camp, and Red Wolf reveals to him that Dritto's band has been put together by the brigade's commissar only in order to isolate the undesirables among the partisans, who might disrupt the order of the regular bands. Mancino in particular is an "extremist," Red Wolf says, a man afflicted by "an infantile disorder: left-wing Communism" (p. 64; 102). This is, like everything Red Wolf says, a staple phrase of communist propaganda (and an allusion to Lenin's famous 1920 pamphlet "Left-Wing Communism: An Infantile Disorder," in which Lenin rebukes the communists who protested against the subordination of the proletarian Soviets to the party apparatus). It is also a particularly ironic phrase because Red Wolf— barely an adolescent himself and until recently an "extremist" as well—addresses it to the innocent Pin to make sure that he does not catch Mancino's "infantile disorder."

Red Wolf is implicitly presented in the novel as a product of the kind of superficial indoctrination that the Communist Party deemed suitable for the Italian masses. The Gramscian project of making the masses more politically conscious and responsible, which was at the heart of his plan to work toward the creation of a new civil society by creating the conditions for democratic hegemony, could not be implemented—according to the Party's official policy—because of the priorities of the war. The Party's leaders had to maintain the hegemonic role in the decision-making process, at least until the immediate crisis was resolved. Until that time, the PCI would have to rely on the "spontaneous" anti-Fascism and the equally "spontaneous" socialism of the masses. (The Party paid dearly for this postponement in 1946, when the elections showed that it did not have as much popular support as it had hoped to have.) The younger generation in particular, born and raised under Fascism, could easily be deflected from its superficial attraction to socialist ideas and ideals. In *The Path*, Red Wolf belongs to this shallow younger generation who sees in the partisan struggle only an exciting adventure: "Red Wolf belongs to the generation brought up on strip-cartoons; he has taken them all seriously and life has not disproved them so far" (p. 39; 74).

The figure of Red Wolf is opposed to the general Resistance myth of the *gappista*, which the PCI historian Luigi Longo presents in the following way in his narrative apology of the Resistance:

In this atmosphere at once burning with hatred, passionately heroic and ennobled by an endless spirit of sacrifice, the GAP (Groups of Patriotic Action) were born and began operating. They were anonymous and merciless avengers. . . . They were young, for the most part very young. . . . They had grown up with an aversion for the establishment, an establishment they would have liked to eliminate at all costs, even at the cost of their own blood. They had joined the struggle on the basis of a reasoned and deeply moral imperative. They were not, therefore (as someone who never met them, or had perhaps observed their deeds with diffidence, might imagine), "musketeers," adventurers, fighters out of a novel. The most surprising aspect of this struggle to the death is precisely that it was undertaken by men who had come to it through a long, deeply rooted, deeply felt . . . love for truth, freedom, humanity, justice.[36]

Like Red Wolf, the characters of Pelle and Michel the Frenchy, with their "double-dealing" that takes them back and forth between the "black" and the "red" brigades and their total lack of cultural or moral orientation, point to the ideological and political void in which (contrary to Longo's claims) the younger partisans generally moved, joining the fight often out of an attraction for violence or simply—as in Michel's case—out of opportunism.[37]

All the characters who belong to Dritto's detachment are carefully chosen by Calvino for his ironic and often surreal mise-en-scène of the most deviant and contradictory aspects of the partisan bands. Dritto's band is the very antithesis of the partisan groups described by Longo: "homogeneous, solid, healthy bodies," led by political commissars who helped the partisans become fully conscious of the reasons and the goals of their struggle (Longo, pp. 118–19). Dritto in particular, an ex-waiter who liked his job because he "lived close to the rich," is described repeatedly as feeling "ill." Dritto is afflicted by a chronic malaise which is really a sense of indifference for the partisan cause, combined with a sense of resentment towards the brigade's commanders, who do not trust him enough to let him get involved in important actions with his men.

During his time as a partisan, Calvino actually belonged to one of the communist "Garibaldi Brigades," which were "model" brigades in all respects, but in *The Path* he chooses to represent "not the finest partisans, but the worst ones possible" (p. xiii; 13). To depict "realistically" this imaginary band of outcasts—Calvino says in the preface—he "decomposed" and "disfigured" the familiar physiognomies of his comrades: "I distorted the features and the character of people who had been my dearest companions, with whom for months and months I had shared a mess tin of chestnuts and the risk of death, for whose fate I had feared, whose nonchalance I had admired as they burned their bridges behind them, as I had admired their way of life free of egoisms; and I made them masks, contracted by constant grimaces, grotesque figures. I created dense chiaroscuro clouds . . . around their stories" (p. xv; 15). The reason for this calculated estrangement of his own lived experience, as well as of the familiar codes for the representation of the Resistance, Calvino explains, is a political one. *The Path*, he argues in the preface, is an example of "committed literature" but not in the sense of socialist realism or propagandistic art; it is not an illustration of some thesis that precedes and determines poetic expression. Calvino's political strategy in *The Path* is comparable to a Brechtian alienation-effect (or *Verfremdungseffekt*), for *The Path* "stages" a microscopic slice of the history of the Resistance in a polemically grotesque and expressionistic form intended to shock the reader accustomed to the conventional mimetic code of neorealist narrative and to the hagiographic tone of Resistance literature and historiography after the Liberation. In a 1984 interview conducted by Gregory Lucente, Calvino spoke of his preference for Brecht's idea of an estranged or distanced realism over the Lukácsian theory of realism as objective reflection:

I wrote a neorealist fiction because during the war I had experienced the everyday life of the people first hand. . . . Following an initial period during which I believed in a kind of objective realism, I quickly understood that in order to say something, including something that had to do with Italian society, it was necessary either to look within oneself or to expose social mechanisms through representations that might well *not* be realistic in the traditional sense. The method of Bertolt Brecht, for example, was extremely important for its demonstration that in order to represent the moral fabric of a social life, a determined set of historical processes, what is essential is to represent the basic mechanism. . . . [Brecht's notion of] the creation of distance . . . has been quite important for me, whereas I have never found Lukács's theories of reflection very interesting.[38]

But *The Path* is not—unlike Brecht's theater—intended to be didactic and makes no attempt to reduce its characters to allegories of social processes and actions on the assumption that the *fabula docet* will translate into political practice. Rather, *The Path* is indeed an example of "committed" literature in—as Calvino argues in the preface to the novel—"the most rich and full meaning of the word": namely, as "immagini a parola, scatto, piglio, stile, sprezzatura, sfida" ("images and words, pace, tone, style, *sprezzatura*, challenge"; p. xii; 13).

Theodor Adorno has argued along these lines that the autonomous form of a literary work is in itself a form of commitment, or rather, that form *is* commitment. A work whose form negates or disrupts the petrified system of representation of "the real" in a given cultural context is, in his analysis, a politically radical work. "The hostility to anything alien or alienating can accom-

modate itself much more easily to literary realism of any prove-
nance, even if it proclaims itself critical or socialist, than to works
that swear allegiance to no political slogans, but whose mere
guise is enough to disrupt the whole system." Yet the commitment of the autonomous work of art is inseparable from the *relativity* of its autonomy; the distance autonomous works of art
maintain from empirical reality "is in itself partly mediated by
that reality . . . it originates in that empirical reality from which
it breaks free." [39] It is this claim to freedom—that Calvino calls
scatto, piglio, stile, sprezzatura, sfida—that makes the work a political challenge. The very structure and inner aesthetic order of
a truly radical work, according to Adorno, convey the message
that "it should be otherwise": "As eminently constructed and
produced objects, works of art, even literary ones, point to a
practice from which they abstain: the creation of a just life." [40] In
The Path, however, Calvino does not rely exclusively on the estranging power of literary discourse, or the inner formal logic of
the work of art (its "negative" utopian configuration, in Adorno's
terms), in order to put forth his political critique. Unlike Adorno
(and Bloch), Calvino does not believe that the literature which is
revolutionary in terms of its form—or literature *tout court*—is
also necessarily revolutionary in political terms. On the contrary, for Calvino (as for Brecht and Sartre), any such work of
literature must situate itself historically by communicating specific political meanings to its readers and must for that reason
express its critique implicitly or explicitly in thematic form.

Calvino's defamiliarization of the Resistance and of its codification in the language of neorealist narrative and hagiographic
historiography is also aimed—in the immediate historical context
of postwar Italy—at another, somewhat different target. With the
writing of *The Path*, Calvino opposes the attempt by conservative
and reactionary forces to dismiss the Resistance as a mere aberration, an interlude of anarchy and chaos in Italian history: "Hardly
more than a year after the Liberation, 'right-minded respectability' was already on the upsurge again, exploiting every contingent aspect of that time—the confusion of postwar youth, the
recrudescence of crime, the difficulty of establishing a new legality—to exclaim: 'There, we said so all along; these Partisans,

they're all like that; they needn't come telling us tales of the Resistance; we know perfectly well the sort of ideals . . .'" (p. xiii; 13).

Faced with an ever-growing number of critics of the Resistance in the postwar period in Italy, Calvino launches an unexpected counterattack in *The Path*; in it he represents the partisans in a way which no one else had yet dared to do, namely as individuals on the fringes of legality and even, in some cases, as outlaws. One of the innumerable ironies of *The Path* is that it paints a darker portrait of the partisans than Italian conservatives had ever tried to do. The effect of this defamiliarization is to foreground what is for Calvino the authentic political essence of the Resistance, apart from any abstract ideals of patriotism, justice, and morality. The partisans—no matter how undefined their original motivations may have been—all share a single common denominator, "an elementary impulse of human emancipation," which alone makes them "active forces of history." The hope for an end to human suffering, through the will to make oneself the subject of one's own existence, is the only hope—and a minimal, barely discernible one at that—which *The Path* offers us in the form of Pin's story.

The notions of a collective "anti-Fascist unity," of a "spontaneous" and "heroic" insurrection against the enemy, and of the determining role played by the PCI in making the partisans conscious of the political meaning of their struggle are exposed one by one throughout *The Path* as retrospective mystifications. As Quazza points out in his landmark study, the pervasive postwar rhetoric of the Resistance tended to hide the fact that "after the explosion of enthusiasm in July, the strikes in August and the short-lived hope for peace of the 8th and 9th of September (1943), the great majority of the population lapsed into a state of uncertainty, which was either a product of inertia or of the simple desire to defend oneself, one's relatives, one's friends."[41] Many people joined the partisans in the mountains in order to avoid conscription into the new Fascist army (and Calvino was one of these) or deportation to Germany, others went up into the mountains with the partisans simply to hide out and wait for the arrival of the Allies, and still others were attracted by the chance to bear arms and to use them to get what they wanted. Car-

abiniere and Giacinto are examples of the first tendency; Long
Zena (who spends all his time at the camp reading American spy
thrillers and talking about America as a Land of Cockaygne
where everyone is free to get rich) and Dritto fit the description of
this second tendency; the Calabrian brothers are examples of the
third. Dritto himself, the day before the battle in which his band
will be directly involved in action for the first time, thinks "how
much he would like to leave the partisans and hide away in a
place he knows of, till the end of the war" (p. 98; 142). The presence in the novel of the four Calabrian brothers evokes, on the
other hand, the war-within-the-war carried out by the peasants
against the landowners during the partisan struggle in southern
Italy, where, according to the PCI historiographers, the Resistance remained in a "primitive" state of development.

For many partisans, the myth of Communism was directly associated with the myth of sudden, almost miraculous emancipation from the hunger and poverty that had haunted their lives as
workers and peasants. The power of this myth, which the Communist Party did nothing to dispel, played a significant role in
raising popular support for the PCI and for the Resistance itself
in Italy. The collapse of this illusion in the postwar years of severe economic depression, during the time that the PCI was still
in the coalition government, led many members of the base to
withhold their votes and their support from the party. In *The
Path*, Giacinto—who is supposed to be the political guide of
Dritto's band and the mediator between it and the political leaders of the brigade headquarters—accurately summarizes this
simplistic view of the purpose of Communism: "Communism
means going into a house and being given soup if they are eating
soup" (p. 92; 134). Mancino is the only member of the band who
has a political education, but his tirades against capitalism and
world imperialism and his constant complaints about the commissars' failure to help the partisans become more politically
enlightened only cause irritation and resentment among his
comrades. Mancino's pet hawk is named Babeuf, which is a
transparent allusion on Calvino's part to the eighteenth-century
French revolutionary François Noel Babeuf, whose radical views
on economic and political freedom and equality made him "the

first communist." Babeuf's "conspiracy of equals" was, however, crushed by the ruling revolutionary forces after he plotted
to overthrow the Directory in Paris, and Babeuf himself was executed. In *The Path*, the hawk who shares his name—and who
clearly represents his ideal of a "conspiracy of equals"—is also
executed. This execution becomes an emblem of the hopeless-
ness of the partisans' quest for self-fulfillment and freedom, and
the burial of the hawk is equally emblematic of the burial of the
highest hopes of the Resistance itself.

The night before the battle, Dritto's men express their ner-
vousness and fear by ganging up on Mancino, and they force
him to strangle Babeuf with his own hands. Dritto then orders
Pin to bury Babeuf; with a sense of solitude and revulsion, Pin
goes in search of a place in which to bury the hawk. But while he
is walking alone in the dark forest, suddenly Pin has a vision in
which the dead hawk is transformed into a magical animal out of
a fairy tale. His fantasy is that the hawk is the magical helper
who will lead Pin towards the goal of his quest: "At his feet lies
the dead hawk. . . . He feels an impulse to fling the hawk into
the great empty space above the valley and see its wings open,
then watch it raise in flight, circle above his head and fly off towards a distant peak. And then he would follow it as they do
in fairy stories, walking over mountains and plains until he
reached an enchanted village in which all the inhabitants were
good. But instead Pin now puts the hawk down into the grave
and rakes earth on it with the tip of the spade" (p. 121; 167). The
perspective of liberation—as is evident in the above passage—
remains an unfulfilled fantasy and an unfulfilled desire throughout *The Path*. Indeed, even at the end, when Pin finally finds his
great friend in Cousin, Pin's quest is not over; the text merely
suggests the possibility that Pin and Cousin together, as a minimal community of two, may start down a new path towards that
distant peak to which Babeuf has flown in Pin's imagination.

5 • Between the Imaginary and the Symbolic: History, the Subject, and Desire in 'The Path'

The Path as *Bildungsroman* and the Play of Metaphor

Pin's story in *The Path* appears to have a synecdochic relationship with the history of the Resistance itself. At least, this is the most evident way of interpreting the plot of the novel in referential terms. Notwithstanding all that *The Path* discloses about the contradictions and complexities of the Resistance as a historical phenomenon, the novel still implicitly offers a positive vision of the Resistance on the whole and as a whole. The heterogeneous agents, motives, and circumstances that Calvino brings into play in order to demythify the rhetoric of the Resistance are integrated into a meaningful and unified action, or, in other words, a "synthesis of the heterogeneous."[1] In *The Path* this synthesis corresponds to the very act of "emplotment," or the "grasping together" of events into a textual configuration. The plot of Calvino's novel is in this sense the realistic representation of an action in classic Aristotelian terms, for it functions as an organization of events into a whole, or rather, as an organic structuration of events.[2] The reader follows the narrative of *The Path* with a sense of progressive development, moving forward through the interconnected episodes and even the reversals or setbacks to which Pin is subjected, always guided by an expectation whose fulfillment is found in the fairy-tale conclusion. The configuration of the plot as an ordered and mimetic whole is governed by what Frank Kermode has called the "sense of an ending," namely the end point from which the story can retroactively be grasped in its totality. In *The Path*, this ending we both anticipate and recognize to be a reference to the Liberation.

Pin's "progress" in his quest coincides with the historical progress of the struggle for Liberation, and the unfolding of the narrative follows implicitly the chronological order of historical events. Although there are no specific dates given by Calvino in the text,[3] the story clearly begins sometime in early 1944, when—historically speaking—the GAP's began to form in Italian cities (as indicated by the scene with "Committee" in the tavern and by Pin's first encounter with Red Wolf), and the partisan bands were no longer just rebel groups hiding out in the mountains but were beginning to develop a full-fledged military organization coordinated by a central command. Red Wolf's reference to the policy of the "national front" and to the depoliticization of the Resistance alludes to the new course of the partisan struggle called for by Togliatti upon his return to Italy—after eighteen years of exile in the Soviet Union—at the end of March 1944.[4] Pin's arrival at Dritto's camp coincides with the "ascendant" phase of the partisan war between April and June 1944, when the many bands first became organized into "brigades" and assigned to a central brigade headquarters with a political commissar (in *The Path*, Kim) and a military commander (Ferriera), who relayed the orders of the national military headquarters of the northern CLN. The "decisive battle," in which Dritto's band is finally called on to participate, takes place during the phase of the general partisan offensive of the summer of 1944 across all of northern Italy; Roberto Battaglia has called this the "high season" of the Resistance, its moment of fullest maturity.[5] At this point, however, the direct chronological correspondence between the sequential development of Pin's story and the various phases of the development of the Resistance ends. The narrative closes with Pin's reunion with Cousin when it is still that same summer, as the final image of the flickering light of the fireflies indicates.

However, Calvino's description of the partial setback which

the partisans suffer in the battle and the subsequent disband-
ment of Dritto's detachment alludes to the crisis of the fall and
winter of 1944. Just when they appeared ready to break through
the Gothic Line and crush the German ground forces on the
peninsula, the Allies decided (mainly for political reasons) to
slow down their northward advance, suspending temporarily
both their offensive on the Italian front and the flow of provi-
sions and weapons to the partisans. Indeed, the partisan units
were requested to cease fighting and to hide out for the duration
of the winter of 1944–45.[6] This halt in the Allied offensive was
accompanied by an escalation on the part of the Germans against
the partisans during that same winter. A large number of the
partisan brigades were destroyed or forced to disband (see episode six of Rossellini's *Paisà*); many partisans abandoned the
mountains for the valleys, the plains, or the cities, where they
could find food and shelter with the help of the civilian population. In *The Path*, Pin too is forced to go back to his sister's apartment in the old city after the collapse of Dritto's band. But, as
Massimo Salvadori (somewhat hyperbolically) notes, "Like the
legendary phoenix, the partisan movement rose again from its
own ashes"[7] and embarked on the final, decisive phase of the
fighting in Italy. Pin's eventual reunion with Cousin and their
setting off together—Pin with his German P.38 and Cousin with
his tommy gun—to continue the fight refers to this concluding
phase of the Resistance. In the early spring of 1945 the partisan
movement gathered momentum again in different forms; new
acts of sabotage, attacks against German checkpoints and the
Fascist police, and a coordinated effort with the civilian population all helped to accelerate the Germans' now-impending retreat. Many of the liberated villages and communities which had
been reoccupied by the Germans during the winter were freed
by the partisans once again. After the Allies relaunched their offensive at the beginning of April and broke through the enemy
lines near Massa, the fifteen thousand German troops who still
occupied the region of Liguria—the setting of *The Path*—tried
to withdraw across the mountains towards Tortona, but they
found the roads blocked by the partisans and had to surrender
to the Liguria CLN command.[8]

Yet *The Path* is not only a tale of the Resistance. Its plot inter-
weaves the story of the formation, growth, and maturation of
the Resistance movement, and the trials and difficulties that the
latter faces, with the story of Pin's own formation, growth, and
maturation, and the trials and difficulties that he too must face.
Collective history intersects with the history of the formation
of an individual (which takes the form of the narration of his
"progress" through the world). Thus *The Path* is also a *Bildungsroman*, for it is an account of the young protagonist's "progress"
through the world. The theme of Pin's formation as an individual, however, brings into the text a series of problems connected
to the question of how one becomes a "subject" by entering the
realms of intersubjective communication and of history itself. As
a particular kind of *Bildungsroman*, with its focus on the end of
childhood and the rite of passage out of the child's world, it also
raises the issue of how the body and its desires come to be controlled and "productively" oriented within a given social and
historical context. It is no accident that it is precisely in connection with these issues that the plot of *The Path* appears most like
an impossible synthesis of what is irreducibly heterogeneous
and least like a classical Aristotelian plot. These problems are
initially signalled by a disturbance in the organic flow of the narration of Pin's progress in the novel. In the descriptions of Pin's
emerging subjectivity, historicity, and corporality, a series of
metaphors and figures also emerges, but only to call into question the very possibility of an organic *Bildung* (and the narrative
line upon which it depends). Despite the conventional promise
of its form as the narrative of an individual's development, *The
Path* ultimately questions—in its effort to represent the truth of
Pin's particular personal history—the coherence of this narrative
paradigm in its classical mode. It does this through its use of a
disruptive pattern of figural motifs, connoting sameness and
repetition, which are paradoxically related to the problems of
Pin's *Bildung*. By disrupting rather than integrating the unified
unfolding of the plot from beginning to end, the web of metaphoric motifs interwoven in the text implicitly negates the possibility of a simple, univocal, and literal reading of *The Path* as the
story of Pin's coming of age through the experience of the Resis-

tance or—in other words—about the necessary and natural unfolding of Pin's existence in a positive movement that leads from
childhood to maturity and historical understanding.

The "negative sense" of tropes and figures in literary discourse is often more subtle and less easy to recognize than the
(positive) linguistic and semantic "norm" that it opposes, yet at
times this sense may be so powerful as to subvert the literal and
referential meanings of a text altogether. *The Path*, indeed, is a
prime example of this power of literary discourse to subvert referential or conventional meaning and to problematize understanding through the use of figurality. There is, however, a difficulty with the "negative" use of figural rhetoric in a literary text
such as Calvino's; no matter how carefully the work orchestrates
the figural turnings of the text away from the literal and the referential, the risk always exists that a reader who approaches the
text through the "horizon of expectations" of the (neo)realist
mimetic code and its rhetoric of objectivity will see only the literal meaning of the story as it unfolds from beginning to end.[9]
Such a reader will "miss" the tropological detours and their
operations at another level of textual meaning. At most, this
literal-minded reader will see the tropes of the text as a sign of
its fragmentation, an unnecessary disruption of the coherence
and organic unity of the story. And this is exactly why so many
readers of *The Path* have objected to the presence of chapter 9
in the novel, with its elaborate political analysis, as well as to
Calvino's use of mythic images and allusions to fairy tales.[10]

The ambivalence generated in *The Path* by the tension between
the literal and the figural has, however, also left many readers
puzzled and has led in turn to a variety of misreadings. Many
commentators have attempted to do away with the text's constitutive ambivalence by either reducing it to a contradiction (as,
for example, in the case of chapter 9) or by simply neglecting
altogether the more disturbing aspects of the work.[11] Other readers—looking at Calvino's work from a biographical or sociological point of view—have assumed that it may most likely be
attributed to its author's extreme youth or to his lack of a coherent outlook on the world at the time.[12] The disruptive oppositions within the text have often been forcibly manipulated by

critics in order to supply a synthetic account of the supposed contradictions which "disfigure" the novel. According to one critic, for example, "*The Path*, as it unfolds between Pin's first escape and the final meeting with Cousin (which represents the definitive reconciliation with both nature . . . and man), appears as the fantastic projection of an optimistic vision of the world (man has become the force that dominates history) that Calvino expresses and proposes through the form he chooses to give to his text. . . . Here we find the signs of a whole generation's illusions." [13] Even when no detailed interpretation of the novel is offered by a given critic, the decision to classify *The Path* as a typical work of neorealist fiction allows for a reassuring historical explanation of its apparent contradictions. [14]

The unwillingness of most critics to read *The Path* metaphorically or, rather, to decipher the textual metaphors of *The Path* is partly caused by Calvino's particular use of poetic language in the novel. As he points out in the 1964 preface, the poetic "sense" of language for him always implies negativity and opposition. For this reason the tropological movement of *The Path*—configured in particular through the metaphor of "the path to the nest of spiders"—tends to work *against* the linear movement of the narrative, disrupting its causal unfolding and metonymic temporal sequence, and engendering a tension between opposite meanings. This in turn, though, makes it difficult, if not impossible, to reconcile the figural and the literal in the novel and still maintain a vision of the text as a coherent and unified whole. Both structuralist and Marxist critics of *The Path* tend to presuppose that every textual detail must work to confirm the governing logic or organic totality of the text. This basic aesthetic assumption leads such critics to ignore or exclude what does not fit into their interpretation of the text's (presumed) unity and coherence. While it is likely that—at one level or another—a function can be discovered for every detail in a literary text, this does not mean that every detail must necessarily work toward affirming the unity and coherence of the text to which it belongs. Indeed, once we are willing to recognize the conventional (and hence arbitrary) nature of such an assumption, then we may acknowledge that the notion of a literary work as a heterogeneous entity, all of whose elements need not be accommodated within any kind of organic structure, is at least as valid as any other notion of textuality. In *The Path* it is precisely the disunified and decentered nature of the narrative (riddled with tropological detours) that allows it to achieve a more complex representation of its subject matter than has generally been recognized by critics in Italy or elsewhere.

Even what Calvino calls in the preface "the exacerbation of the themes of violence and sex" (p. ix; 10), which he attributes to his own inexperience as a writer, does in fact perform a specific textual function in *The Path*. This "exacerbation" serves to dramatize the tension between the "history" of the individual (a history that is closely linked to the unconscious and its drives) and collective history, which is perceived as a dialectic of social conflicts between classes.[15] The "incongruous" use of snippets of popular songs, epithets, and so on—which critics have usually attributed to the young Calvino's taste for documentary effects (bordering at times on the folkloric)—appears in an altogether different light if we examine, for example, the figural function in *The Path* of the most important of these citations from popular culture and language, namely the strange folksong sung by Pin in the central section of the novel. This "truculent and macabre" song, called "Chi bussa alla mia porta" ("Who's That Knocking at My Door?"), tells a mythic tale of a mother murdered by her son when he returns from the war. As we shall see later in this chapter, Pin's song functions in *The Path* as an oedipal allegory, one whose ambiguity prefigures that of the novel's ending, for the latter allows for two irreconcilable interpretations, depending on whether we choose to read it literally or figuratively.

The syntagmatic order of the narrative, whose linear development defines Pin's own development in conjunction with the progress of the partisan struggle, is opposed in *The Path* by the web of metaphoric motifs woven around the image of the path to the nest of spiders. The reappearance of these motifs at each phase of the narrative continually takes us back to the beginning, suspending the diachronic and linear development of the story. Inserted—through the web of metaphoric motifs—into a motionless spatial dimension, Pin's story appears to obey a

different logic than that of a conventional *Bildung*. In the contra-
puntal figural logic of *The Path*, the idea of a possible progressive, forward movement towards "maturity" is openly questioned. The path to the nest of spiders is defined, from the very
first, as Pin's secret place of retreat into a natural setting far from
the pressure and turmoil of social existence (whether in the
city's old quarter or at the partisan encampment):

> Pin wanders along the paths which wind along the side of the torrent,
> stony parts which no one cultivates. Here there are paths which he
> alone knows and which the other boys would love to be told about.
> There is a place where spiders make their nests. Only Pin knows it. It's
> the only one in the whole valley, perhaps in the whole area. No other
> boy except Pin has ever heard of spiders that make nests. (p. 19; 51)

> No one knows the place, it is Pin's place, a magic place. (p. 128; 176)

> Now he will leave these windswept unknown parts and go far away,
> back to his own kingdom in the river-bed, back to the magic spot where
> the spiders make their nests. (p. 136; 185)

> Pin reaches his own river bed. . . . There, beyond the bamboos, begins
> the path of the spiders' nests, the magic place which only Pin knows.
> There he can weave strange spells, become a king, a god. (p. 138; 187)

The path to the nest of spiders gives Pin a sense of belonging to a
place and to an order; he discovers in it an identity that is both
natural and mythic. During the course of the novel, Pin returns
there, either in person or in his mind, to take shelter from and
seek comfort for the trials of his existence. Like nature itself, the
place is always the same; it has a reassuring sense of perma-
nence and stability for Pin. Its magical effect on him is linked to
the capacity of "the path to the nest of spiders" to dispel the
pain and anxiety that Pin experiences in his encounters with the
social and historical worlds. How, though, does this pattern of
repetition—or of a return to/of the same—constitute a pattern of
disruption in Calvino's narrative?

From the very beginning of *The Path*, Pin's natural and mythic
space is also linked to the process of his growing up and gradually becoming involved in social and historical events. At the
outset of the narrative, Pin is portrayed as a boy on the threshold of adolescence who is denied participation in either the normal life of other children or in the life of adults. His only social

habitat is the *carrugio*, a long and narrow alley typical of the poorest and oldest sections of the towns along the Ligurian coast. Pin lives with his older sister in one of the most run-down buildings of the *carrugio*. When his boss Pietromagro is in jail and his sister is busy with a client, Pin spends long hours loitering in the local tavern, where he listens to the conversation of the adults and watches them drink and smoke. From the men in the tavern and the motley crowd of the *carrugio*, Pin picks up "stories about men and women in bed, or men murdered or put in prison . . . the sorts of fables grown-ups tell among themselves" (p. 7; 35). Pin tries to imitate the adults in everything and even tries drinking, smoking, and swearing like them. He develops a repertoire of obscene jokes and "old songs which have been taught him by the men of the tavern, songs about violence and bloodshed" (p. 5; 33). He tries to entertain and provoke the grown-ups in the *carrugio* and the tavern by making bawdy or sarcastic remarks about everything they do or say, but no matter how hard he tries to "become one of them," the men in the tavern ridicule him as the prostitute's little brother and "little pimp." Because of his tough and aggressive style of speaking, with its constant references to the adult world, Pin is excluded from the world of innocent childhood games as well:

He longs to go off with a band of young companions to whom he could show the place where spiders make their nests, or with whom he could have battles among the bamboos in the river-bed. But Pin is not liked by the boys his own age; he is the friend of grown-ups, Pin is, he can say things to grown-ups that make them laugh or get angry, while other boys can't even understand what grown-ups say to each other. Pin sometimes feels a longing to ask boys of his own age to let him play with them, to show him the way into the underground passage that goes right under the Market Square. But the other boys avoid him; sometimes they even set on him, for Pin has tiny arms and is the weakest of them all. . . . So Pin is forced to take refuge again in the world of grown-ups, of men who turn their backs on him and are as incomprehensible and far removed from him as they are from the other little boys, but who are easier to make fun of, with their yearning for women and their terror of the police, till they tire of him and begin to slap him on the head. (pp. 6–7; 35–36)

In order for Pin to share the secret of the path to the nest of spiders with someone, whether child or adult, he would first have to be accepted into the social order to which the other person belongs: "Perhaps one day Pin will find a friend, a real friend, who understands him and whom he can understand, and then to him, only to him, will he show the place where the spiders have their lairs" (p. 19; 51). Once shared with someone, the place itself would no longer be a mythical one; it would no longer be the exclusive locus of the bond between Pin and the natural order, a bond that lies outside of history itself.

However, the place where the spiders make their nests is not itself in any sense a *locus amoenus* in *The Path*. It is not an idyllic setting of natural freedom and innocence, outside of the constraints of civilized life, where Pin could give free rein to his fantasies. He has instead conflicting feelings of fascination and revulsion toward the path to the nest of spiders:

It's on a stony little path which winds down to the torrent between earthy grassy slopes. There, in the grass, the spiders make their nests, in tunnels lined with dry grass. But the wonderful thing is that the nests have tiny doors, also made of dried grass, tiny round doors which can open and shut. . . . With a long stick he can probe right into the nests and skewer the spider, a small black spider with little grey markings on it, like those on the summer dresses of old village women.

It amuses Pin to break the doors of the nests down and skewer the spiders on sticks, and to catch grasshoppers and gaze close into their little horse-like faces, then cut them up into pieces and make strange designs with their legs on a smooth stone.

Pin is cruel to animals; to him they are monstrous and incomprehensible as grown-ups; it must be horrible to be an insect, to be green, and always to be frightened that a human being like him might come along, with a huge face full of red and black freckles and fingers that can pull grasshoppers to bits.

Pin is now alone among the spiders' nests, and around him is night, infinite as the chorus of the frogs. . . .

At that moment the spiders underground are gnawing away at flies or coupling together, males and females, giving out little threads of slime; they are as filthy as men are, Pin thinks. (pp. 19–20; 51–52)

This description of the childishly sadistic game Pin plays with the insects is charged with multiple, and somewhat contrasting, connotations.[16] As Calvino describes it in the above passage, Pin's game appears to represent the archetypal condition of man as a being engaged in the activity of exploring and mastering the natural world with the aim of finding a place and an identity for himself. Pin is depicted in this passage as possessing a sense of inquisitive wonder about the natural world as it is represented by the spiders' nests. By breaking through the doors of those nests, Pin symbolically opens for himself the doors of the natural world. He expresses his will to the knowledge and mastery of nature by probing and dissecting the bodies of his victims and by recomposing the fragments on top of the rocks in fantastic shapes, which take on the look of a kind of primitive script. Like Vico's first men, the "children of the human race" in the first "mute times," Pin's script is a fantastic code, making use of "signs, whether gestures or physical objects," and "imaginative characters of animate and mute substances" as in a kind of primitive and still natural hieroglyphic system incapable of "abstracting forms and properties from subjects." [17] Pin's discovery of the wonder of nature fills him with a sense of power and provides him with a tentative sense of identity; his very impulse to master nature through language is, in Vico's terms, what makes him human. Pin's solitary discovery nevertheless remains an unsatisfactory one for him unless it can be shared with others; Pin longs to tell his secret to a friend, whether child or adult. This goal, however, can only be accomplished through the use of a system of intersubjective communication which would report his findings back to a cultural context. At one level, this scene can thus be interpreted as an allegory of Vico's insight—fundamental for the Marxian vision of history—into the difference between history (which, being man-made, can always be understood) and nature, which remains alien to man unless it is humanized through a mythical (childlike) or rational (adult) discursive order. [18]

By probing the spiders' nests and breaking apart their bodies, though, Pin engages—at another level of meaning—in an act of infantile voyeurism and violence; the will to master is also a desire to destroy. This aggressivity is directly related to the spectacle of the spiders' coupling, as well as to the coupling of humans which comes to Pin's mind by association. It is not surprising that a Freudian scenario thus informs this passage in *The Path*. The transition from myth to history, and from nature to culture, also involves a transition from infantile to adult sexuality; Pin's cruel game with the spiders takes place on a symbolic threshold between childhood and adulthood. While what he does could take Pin back to the level of fantastic, make-believe war games with other children, "a band of young companions to whom he could show the place where spiders make their nests, or with whom he could have battles among the bamboos in the river-bed" (p. 6; 35), it could also signify his readiness to join in the seemingly more complicated games of the adult world. And yet, in the last analysis, Pin is unable to take either of these two paths. "Pin is a boy who does not know how to play games, and cannot take part in the games either of children or of grown-ups" (p. 18; 50). In fact, Pin's lonely game in the place where the spiders make their nests—if we look more closely at the text—raises a fundamental interpretive question for the reader. Whether it is understood to lead in the direction of either a regression to the ingenuous world of child-play or a leap forward into a new mode of adult social existence and historical consciousness, will the path really take Pin to some place that is "better" than his present one? Or rather will he follow it, over and over again, to the same familiar dead end? Despite *The Path*'s ostensible design as a *Bildungsroman*, and its fascination with fairy tales and myths, there are elements in the text that suggest that Pin's game is neither the expression of a tendency to regress to a symbiosis with the natural world through the power of a child's myth-making fantasy, nor a representation of an adult propensity to master fully the natural world through abstract conceptualization and history making. The path of Pin in *The Path* may turn out to be an unusual path which is circular in form and, since it goes neither forward nor backward, may be said not to lead anywhere at all.

As is explicit in the passage above, Pin's close-up vision of the spiders and grasshoppers makes them appear absurd and grotesque to him. This classic textual strategy of estrangement is used by Calvino to suggest, paradoxically, Pin's alienation from nature rather than his proximity to it. (One of the most famous literary examples of this same strategy of estrangement through an extreme "close-up" is found in Jonathan Swift's *Gulliver's Travels*, in which a woman's breast—magnified in enormous detail from Gulliver's point of view—suddenly appears monstrously deformed and repulsive.) Pin's own gaze, in the place where the spiders make their nests, tends to de-naturalize nature. He repeatedly looks at nature as if through a microscope, and in this way sees it as an external object which is totally alien to him. Yet he still identifies with it, taking on its point of view to the extent that he imagines his own body to be the very body of the spider or the grasshopper at which he is looking ("it must be horrible to be an insect, to be green"). Thus the estrangement of the natural object is reversed in a moment of self-estrangement or doubling of the perceiving subject. In identifying with the object, Pin elides his own gaze; he regresses—if only for a moment—to a state of imaginary oneness with the perceived object, or, to put it another way, he suspends his own being as a perceiving subject separate from the object of perception. Then, however, his own probing gaze becomes visible to him as a violent threat, for it appears from the point of view of an insect whose hidden world has been violated by the hand of man ("frightened that a human being like him might come along, with a huge face full of red and black freckles and fingers that can pull grasshoppers to bits"). The scene of Pin's game articulates the question of the subject as a position within the field of perception. The "I" which the eye discloses as an organizing center of consciousness proves, however, to be an unstable position, and the subject itself becomes aware of its own existence not by seeing the object but rather through the estranging experience of being seen by it; in other words, in this experience the subject discovers itself as an object for the other.

According to Jean-Paul Sartre, it is through the gaze of the other or through the experience of "being-seen-by-another" that one apprehends himself as an object for the other. Through the gaze, Sartre notes, "I apprehend that I am vulnerable, that I have a body which can be hurt, that I occupy a place and that I cannot in any case escape from the space in which I am without defense—in short, that *I am seen*." [19] The analysis of the "scene" of seeing, which is fundamental to our interpretation of "the place where the spiders make their nests" as the central metaphor of Calvino's novel, finds its most extensive elaboration,

however, in Jacques Lacan's psychoanalytic theory of the formation of the subject. Pin's specular game, as described above, resembles Lacan's notion of the "mirror phase" (or *le stade du
miroir*) that lies at the basis of the distinction between the Symbolic, the Imaginary, and the Real. The gaze that Pin elides by
identifying with the spiders, and that he subsequently perceives
as a threat, is in fact not the gaze of another human being but
rather his own gaze seeing itself as if in a mirror. "The gaze I
encounter," writes Lacan, "is not a seen gaze, but a gaze imagined by me in the field of the Other." [20] It is not by chance that
Calvino, later in life, became deeply interested in Lacan (as can
be seen most clearly in the most overtly "Lacanian" of Calvino's
works, *Invisible Cities*),[21] for this problematic, which so concerns
Lacan's work from the 1930's on, is a problematic which haunts
Calvino's writing from the 1940's on (although this fact has not
been generally acknowledged by critics), even in his first novel.

In Lacanian terms, the scene of Pin's game in *The Path* may be
understood to portray Pin's position as a subject at the crossroads between the order of the Imaginary and the order of the
Symbolic; the image of the spiders' nests becomes a metaphor of
the unconscious itself, with its conflicting drives. What Pin does
to the bodies of his victims in the place where the spiders make
their nests represents the primal aggressivity that for Lacan is
always associated with the Imaginary as "a kind of situational
experience of otherness as . . . struggle, violence, and antagonism, in which the child can occupy either term indifferently, or
indeed . . . both at once." [22] In the mirror phase, the child goes
from an intransitive relationship with the world, in which he
cannot distinguish himself from reality, to the discovery of his
corporeal being in the image of the mirror. The child's identification with the object prior to the mirror phase corresponds to a
pre-point-of-view stage; the child is "free" to assume a multiplicity of positions, to move back and forth in an endless play of
imaginary (self-)associations. Thus the image in the mirror appears to the child as an image of another human being, before he
himself identifies with it. Lacan argues that the child's fascination with the image of that "other" and the attempt to appropriate and control that image correspond to the creation of the ego

as a process of internalization of the other. The Imaginary construction of the ego inevitably involves a dual relationship of objectification and aggressivity, an indistinct rivalry between self and other. This primal experience of doubling is, according to Lacan, symptomatic of the formation of the subject as a process of estrangement or alienation of the self, even before the subject has entered into the social sphere of intersubjective communication through its insertion into the system of language and the dialectic of desire.[23]

With reference to Charlotte Buhler's work on the phenomenon of "transitivism" (the child's passage from an indifferentiation of subject and object, through the process of play, to an identification with the object, as Pin identifies with the spider), Lacan argues that the self is from the very first subject to "a veritable capture of the other" in a "primordial ambivalence which appears to us . . . 'as in a mirror,' in the sense that the subject identifies his sentiment of Self in the image of the other. . . . Thus, and this is essential, the first effect of the Imago which appears in human beings is *an effect of alienation in the subject. It is in the other that the subject identifies and even senses himself first.*"[24] Here at last we are in a position to see the cogency of Lacan's psychoanalytic theory for our interpretation of *The Path*'s central metaphor. This fundamental alienation, to which all human beings are "condemned,"[25] is evoked by the scene of Pin's game. His adoption of the insects' "point of view" and his identification with the spiders' bodies ("it must be horrible to be an insect, to be green, and always to be frightened that a human being like him might come along, with a huge face full of red and black freckles and fingers that can pull grasshoppers to bits") thematizes the resurfacing of the Imaginary, in the form of a lack of a separate sense of self. Pin's imaginary identification with the spiders, which at once attract and repel him, shows that the distinction between subject and object is—in this primal experience—always lost in a never-ending play of reflections. The sense of Lacan's definition of the Imaginary as a "dual relationship" is in fact "an ambiguous redoubling, a 'mirror' reflection, an immediate relationship between the subject and its other in which each term passes immediately into the other and is lost in a never-ending play of reflections."²⁶ By connecting Pin's formation as a human subject with his access to the position of historical subject, Calvino's fiction combines the discourse of psychoanalysis with elements of dialectical materialism. The latter can never be truly dialectical, he implies, nor can the fundamental issue of human alienation be addressed without interrogating the origins of alienation in the process of the child's emergence into subjectivity. Pin seeks to discover a path for himself in the labyrinth of the self, but this search cannot be isolated from the labyrinth of history and power relations, as the metaphor of "the path to the nest of spiders" suggests. For Calvino, the interpretive system of psychoanalysis is constructed not around sexuality per se, but rather around desire, which he sees as the dynamic force of human existence and the historical transformation of the subject.²⁷ It is this vision of psychoanalysis which allows *The Path* to incorporate elements of both Freudian and Marxist thought, for both disclose—although in distinctly different ways—the revolutionary potential of human desire.

•

Lacan defines the Imaginary as a precise stage in the early development of a child, yet even when the child is released from the specular, narcissistic dialectic of the mirror phase and learns through language to perceive himself as a separate subject (thus entering the order of the Symbolic), the Imaginary still continues to be present in the field of the subject. In point of fact, insofar as the subject's Ego is still captive to a fascination with an ideal self-image—or an alter ego who promises the restoration of a lost happiness—the order of the Imaginary is a permanent function in the "history" of the subject. Pin's fantasy of finding the great friend with whom alone he will share the secret of the path may be interpreted in light of this last remark, for it represents an attempt to restore a lost unity of self and to return to the magical circle of the path, undisturbed by the pain and violence of the outside world. Again and again, when Pin confronts the disturbing nature of the adult world and the partisan struggle, he fantasizes a return to his secret place: " 'No one knows that magic place but me.' This reassures him greatly. Whatever happens, there are still the spiders' nests" (p. 128; 176).

The theory of the mirror phase of the subject was first formulated by Lacan in 1936 and subsequently developed in a series of essays of the mid-to-late-1940's. Lacan's theory is both a radical interpretation of Freud's *Beyond the Pleasure Principle* (in particular the section on the *"Fort! Da!"* game of Freud's grandson Hans, which Freud interpreted as the child's initial attempt to master his environment through the use of speech)[28] and an elaboration of Melanie Klein's theories about the child's identification with fantasized objects; it is also a re-elaboration in psychoanalytic terms of Hegel's notion of alienation in the formation of the self. In the 1930's and 1940's in France, Alexandre Kojève's and Jean Hyppolite's teaching and commentaries on *The Phenomenology of the Spirit* contributed greatly to a revival of interest in Hegelian concepts not only in philosophy (Sartre) and psychoanalysis (Lacan) but in literature as well (Bataille and Klossowski). The emergence of neo-Hegelian and psychoanalytic notions of alienation in Calvino's early work is not a matter of demonstrable direct influence (even though this cannot be excluded, given the wide range of Calvino's reading).[29] Rather, it once again shows how, in dealing with the question of the individual's formation as a historical being in *The Path*, Calvino takes up—in the form of a fictional discourse—an essential problematic of postwar European culture; he enters, that is, a discursive "field" where psychoanalysis, philosophy, and literature mutually intersect with and interrogate one another.

Jean Hyppolite's analysis of Hegelian alienation, in his highly influential 1946 study of *The Phenomenology of the Spirit*, usefully defines the general scope of the problematic of the subject as it emerges in both Lacan's and Calvino's texts: "The two terms 'formation' [*culture*; *Bildung*] and 'alienation' [*Entäusserung*] have a very similar meaning [for Hegel]. It is through the alienation of his natural being that a determinate individual cultivates and forms himself for essentiality. . . . For Hegel self-formation is only conceivable through the mediation of alienation or estrangement [*Entfremdung*]. Self-formation is not to develop harmoniously as if by organic growth, but rather to become opposed to oneself through a splitting [*déchirement*] and a separation."[30] As Anthony Wilden has pointed out, the Lacanian notion of formation is very close to both the Hegelian *Bildung* and to the idea of the *Bildungsroman*.[31] Pin's story is a particular sort of *Bildungsroman*, or novel of formation, but, like Lacan's theory of the subject, it is radically anti-Romantic precisely because it foregrounds self-formation as a process of estrangement and alienation. "One has to admit that there is a lot of alienation about nowadays," Lacan writes in 1964. "Whatever one does, one is always a bit more alienated, whether in economics, politics, psycho-pathology, aesthetics, and so on. It may be no bad thing to see what the root of this celebrated alienation really is."[32] Thus while Lacan adopts the Hegelian concept of alienation (*Entäusserung*) rather than the Marxian one of *Entfremdung*, he posits the alienation or the splitting off of the self as the root of every form of alienation. Calvino, in *The Path*, appears to take a similar view of alienation as a process that coincides with the formation of the subject as such, rather than with that kind of human self-estrangement which—according to Marx and Lukács—is an inevitable product of the division of labor, commodification (the selling of human labor power in the capitalist mode of production), and reification (the reduction of social and human relations to relations between things and their prices).

Lacan's Imaginary is in many ways an outgrowth of Freud's concept of narcissism. The narcissistic "ego-libido" for Freud is a presexual identification with an ideal object of love; it is the desire for (re)union with the object of love, rather than the desire to possess the object of love. In his 1914 essay "On Narcissism," Freud develops the notion of the ego ideal as an object of love that becomes the target (by displacement) of original narcissistic love. He goes on to hypothesize that for an individual this object of love may be either the mother or "the man who protects him and the succession of substitutes who take his place."[33] Throughout the narrative, Pin is constantly in search of just such an ego ideal; the chain of figures whom he encounters in the course of his search includes the group of men in the tavern, Comitato, Red Wolf, the partisans in Dritto's band, Pelle, and finally Cousin. Even the German soldier who sleeps with his sister and the Fascist prison guards turn for a brief moment into fantasized objects of love for Pin. Paradoxically, narcissism—which is usually associated with an egotistic withdrawal from reality—becomes instead in *Civilization and Its Discontents* (1930) an all-encompassing Eros for Freud.[34] Freud's later view of narcissism depicts Eros as a powerful impulse to regain a lost happiness which is that of a self still undivided from the other and from the world. This original undivided and nonalienated self is clearly a mirage for him no less than it is for Lacan. Yet both narcissistic Eros in Freud and the Imaginary in Lacan point in the direction of an affective bond free from the constraints of the patriarchal order of Western society—an order whose fateful necessity Freud and Lacan never cease to affirm, serving perhaps as its most powerful apologists in the twentieth century. As Herbert Marcuse has observed, this resistance in Freud (and, one might add, Lacan) to the perspective offered by an Eros freed from the oedipal regime reflects an inability to see beyond the limits of the patriarchal order of modern Western society:

The Narcissistic phase of individual pre-genitality "recalls" the maternal phase of the history of the human race. . . . But in light of the paternal reality principle, the "maternal concept" of reality here emerging is immediately turned into something negative, dreadful. The impulse to re-establish the lost Narcissistic-maternal unity is interpreted as a "threat," namely, the threat of maternal engulfment by the overpowering womb. The hostile father is exonerated and reappears as a savior who, in punishing the incest wish, protects the ego from its annihilation in the mother. The question does not arise whether the Narcissistic-maternal attitude toward reality cannot "return" in less primordial, less devouring forms under the power of the mature ego and in a mature civilization. Instead, the necessity of suppressing this attitude once and for all is taken for granted. The patriarchal reality principle holds sway over the psychoanalytic interpretation. It is only beyond this reality principle that the "maternal" images of the super ego convey promises rather than memory traces—images of a free future rather than of a dark past.[35]

It is in this direction that Calvino polemically orients Pin's fantasy, namely in the direction of another kind of subjectivity that would be free from the constraints of the patriarchal order.

The Oedipal Path

Pin's erotic quest in *The Path*, and his inability to fit into the adult social order or to grasp the reality principles which organize it, place him in a position of liminality, neither fully in the realm of the Symbolic nor in that of the Imaginary. His ambivalent vision of sexuality is but one of the most evident ways in which this "neither/nor" condition manifests itself in the novel. The small and rather squalid apartment Pin shares with his sister is nevertheless for him an intimate and inviting space where he withdraws from the harsh street-life of the *carrugio*; this space is permeated by his sister's strangely sensual scent and is constantly disturbed by the presence of her clients. Although she is the only "parent" Pin has left, his sister Rina is not fully a maternal figure; rather, she is the last, tenuous link to the image of the maternal body that Pin possesses. Rina is, at the same time, a figure of loss, for the role that she plays in Pin's life serves as a constant reminder for him of the loss of his mother, his father's desertion of the family, and Pin's own loss of innocence:

When Pin was a baby and used to cry loudly in her arms, his head full of sores, she would leave him on a ledge of the wash-house and go off to skip with urchins around the chalk squares marked on the pavements. Every now and again their father's ship would return; all Pin could remember of him was being swung in the air in his big, bare arms, strong arms marked with black veins. But after their mother's death his visits became rarer and rarer, until he was never seen again; people said he had another family in a city beyond the sea. (pp. 11–12; 41)

This passage contains the only reference to Pin's father in the entire novel; it is, however, a particularly crucial reference, since it supplies a key to the underlying cause for Pin's liminal situation. Pin's was a "family romance" that did not fully unfold. The natural attachment to the mother, characteristic of the first phase of childhood, is displaced in Pin's case to his father as a consequence of his mother's death. His father's desertion in turn generates a search for a substitute father as an object of love and as an ego ideal, while it simultaneously "detains" Pin at a point of psychic development prior to the phase of the Oedipus complex. Yet it is only by going through the "rite of passage" of the Oedipus complex, Lacan argues, that the child enters the Symbolic.[36] The Imaginary identification with the love object or Imago—of which the mirror phase is the paradigmatic expression—is, in fact, a closed dialectic. It is a primary identification or, to put it another way, the original, pre-oedipal link of the Ego to the object of love (the mother's body or its substitute by displacement). As Lacan notes, this imaginary dialectic takes the form of a dizzying solitude. To break out of this alienating dialectic in order to "become human" (and thus become alienated in a "positive" way), the subject must enter into a triangular relation, in which what is desired—the restoration of a lost unity with the mother's body—is precisely what cannot be had because the Word of the Father forbids it. The reorientation of desire towards a different object, which itself can never be the primal object of imaginary love, establishes the subject as such. The subject must learn to say "I am," thus giving up all claims to imaginary identity with the mother and with the world. It is in the oedipal relation, according to Lacan, that the father appears as the symbolic embodiment of the Law by exercising the threat of castration and thus enforcing the incest prohibition:

The boy enters the Oedipus complex by a half-fraternal rivalry with his father. He manifests an aggressivity comparable to that revealed in the specular relation. . . . But the father appears in this game as the one who has the master trump and who knows it; in a word, he appears as the Symbolic father. The Symbolic father is to be distinguished from the Imaginary father (often . . . surprisingly distant from the real father) to whom is related the whole dialectic of aggressivity and identification. In all strictness the Symbolic father is to be conceived as "transcendent," as an irreducible given of the signifier. The Symbolic father—he who is ultimately capable of saying "I am who I am"—can only be imperfectly incarnate in the real father. He is nowhere. . . . The real father takes over from the Symbolic father. This is why the real father has a decisive function in castration which is always deeply marked by his intervention or thrown off balance by his absence.[37]

Pin's continued attempts to identify with a series of imaginary fathers, then, in the absence of the normalizing function of the symbolic castration threat by the symbolic father which "bears the transmission of culture,"[38] may be seen as a foreclosure of the whole symbolic order and an instinctive rejection of the patriarchal regime. Pin's liminal position at the crossroads of the Imaginary and the Symbolic thematizes in *The Path* the phallocentric control of erotic desire, which forms the basis of the rule of patriarchy and informs the very notion of sexual difference in patriarchal culture.

Living with his sister and looking through the cracks in the partition which separates his little "cubbyhole of a room" from her bedroom, Pin has become aware at a very young age of the "secrets of life." Yet he is incapable of recognizing and relating to the desire of the sexes for each other. The scene in his sister's bedroom is but a shadowy, dark vision for Pin:

The explanation of everything in the world is there, beyond that partition. Pin has spent hours and hours at those cracks ever since he was a baby, and he's trained his eyes to be like needle points; he knows everything that happens inside there, though the reasons for it all elude him. When, in the end, he curls up in his little bunk with his arms around his chest, the shadows of the tiny room transform themselves into strange dreams, of bodies chasing each other, hitting and embracing, till something big and hot and unknown comes over him, caresses him, and encloses him within its warmth; it seems the explanation of everything, the remote recollection of a long-forgotten happiness. (p. 12; 42)

The partition that prevents Pin from having a "clear vision" of the scene in his sister's bedroom is a textual metaphor for the borderline Pin still has to cross to gain access to adulthood and to the Symbolic. The recognition of sexual difference and desire is implicitly presented here as the basis for the subject's (Pin's) entrance into the cultural and historical order of the adult world, for it leads to a differential mode of perception and decoding of the real. However, this is not simply a recognition of the "natural," somatic, and biological differences between male and female or, for that matter, of the mechanics of sexuality. On the contrary, as the above passage from Calvino's text clearly states, sexual difference and its physical manifestations are well known to Pin; it is their meaning that escapes him. Pin's sense of isolation is caused by his position outside the symbolic order, which articulates the meaning of sexual difference into a cultural code.[39] The temporary return to a blissful—if imaginary—union with the (m)other in Pin's dream-fantasy underscores his liminal position. As we have seen, the Imaginary (in the form of Pin's "long-forgotten happiness" that is restored to him in his dream-fantasy) corresponds to the pre-oedipal period in which the child believes itself to be a part of the (m)other and perceives no separation between itself and the world. The access to the Symbolic, Lacan suggests, can occur only through the repression of the desire for an imaginary unity with the (m)other's body and the undifferentiated continuum of the natural world, and through subjection to the Law of the Father (which is the threat of castration). Difference—the first cultural manifestation of which is sexual difference—makes possible symbolic relations, the production of meaning, and the channeling of desire towards an object other than the imaginary Other, by breaking up the imaginary direction of the ego.

Thus Calvino inscribes into *The Path* one of the crucial and (potentially) revolutionary discoveries of psychoanalysis, which is that sexuality and difference are not given in nature but historically produced by a given culture. "If sexuality is always a symbolic production, then there is a place for a politics of the unconscious," writes Stephen Heath, "for, that is, a grasp of the unconscious not as closed but as historically open, taken up in the historical process of its realisations, existing in transformation." [40] The question of the politics of the unconscious, which always seeks to define the unconscious of a historical formation that cannot be isolated from the other manifestations of human history, is the very same question that Calvino dramatizes through the story of Pin's initiation into adult sexuality over the course of the partisan struggle in Italy.

In his private game on the path to the nest of spiders, as well as in his dream-fantasy behind the partition in his sister's bedroom, Pin appears as a rather unusual kind of voyeur, for he is someone who, in looking at a scene of sexual encounter, does not really see it. His gaze is always based on a constitutive blindness of vision concerning sexuality. Yet Pin's voyeurism nonetheless remains a constant theme in *The Path*. For instance, Pin observes the advances that Dritto and Giglia (Mancino's wife) make to each other in the partisan camp, and, later on, he secretly watches Giglia undress. On the day of the battle, Pin's desire to stay behind at the camp to spy on Dritto and Giglia—who have at last found an opportunity to be alone together—is stronger than his desire to join the men who have gone off to fight; although he witnesses what occurs between the two adults, he at the same time misses his chance to take part in a "historical" action. What is the meaning of this voyeurism, and how is it related for Calvino both to a "politics of the unconscious" and to the question of the production of sexual difference through insertion into the Symbolic?

According to Freud, voyeurism—the curiosity to see the genitals of others—is in the child always a spontaneous sexual manifestation, as well as one of the original components of the human libido.[41] There is, moreover, as he points out in his essay "The Uncanny," a fundamental symbolic relation between the eyes and the male sexual organ, which is often an explicit part of dreams, myths, and fantasies.[42] The most notorious instance of this is, of course, the blinding Oedipus inflicts on himself; this is—Freud contends—a symbolic substitute for castration and submission to the father's will. The experience of seeing the male and the female sexual organs is in fact, for Freud as well as for Lacan, the crucial experience of the oedipal phase in the development of human sexuality. For the masculine subject, to see the feminine "lack" of a penis and, consequently, her "difference" from the male means to see the female as "other." In this way the masculine subject experiences the threat of castration (or becomes aware of the possibility of castration), and therefore the imaginary identification with the (m)other comes to an end. From this original vision of the penis, the "phallus" emerges as the all-powerful signifier of difference; however, as Lacan argues, it is vitally important not to confuse the former and the latter. The phallus is not a part of the body but a signifier that functions as the inauguration of a series of differences within the cultural order. Yet the emergence of the phallus as a signifier that "opens up" the unconscious through the repression of incestuous love, allowing the subject to establish itself in the cultural order under the Law of the Father, is nevertheless dependent on that original vision. This constitutes a paradox, not only because it reduces the feminine to a "lack," "absence," or, in other words, to an essential negativity, but also because it takes psychoanalysis and the cultural production of sexuality in history back to a biological point of departure (i.e. to an essence in nature).[43]

Voyeurism is also linked to narcissistic autoeroticism, or self-love; "the scopophilic instinct is auto-erotic: it has indeed an object, but that object is the subject's own body."[44] Voyeurism, then, inevitably leads back to the level of the Imaginary; in a rigorously closed dialectic, the voyeuristic subject loves itself in the other and sees itself in the other. Voyeurism eludes castration, for it suspends the censoring gaze of the Father or (in Lacan's terms) of the Other. "What occurs in voyeurism?" asks Lacan. "What is the subject trying to see? . . . What the voyeur is looking for and finds is merely a shadow, a shadow behind the curtain. There he will fantasize any magic presence. . . . What he is looking for is not, as one says, the phallus—but precisely its absence."[45] The scene of Pin's dream-fantasy of a "forgotten happiness" behind the partition in his sister's room enacts exactly this scenario (although its full meaning eludes a strictly Lacanian interpretation). In modern western society, voyeurism is generally considered a deviant sexual activity, because it shuns the reproductive goal of human sexuality and its cultural regulation in the patriarchal order. However, as has often been noted, this is strictly a function of the repressive need to restrict and control the uses of the body and its pleasures. Once this notion of deviancy is itself questioned (for what is the "norm" from which it swerves away?), voyeurism may no longer appear as a perversion because there is nothing from which to "deviate." Voyeurism is a structure of desire in which, as Lacan notes, "the subject as such is not yet placed." Voyeurism "becomes" a perversion, that is, a transgression of the Law of the Father, only when the subject becomes aware of its own gaze as "separate" from the object. The gaze is precisely what the voyeur elides in the illusion of "seeing himself seeing himself," like Valéry's Young Parque.[46] When the gaze becomes visible to the subject, it is in the form of a violent threat to its imaginary unity (which is the threat that Pin senses in the scene of the game and the anxiety that he feels in looking into his sister's bedroom). The visibility of the gaze constitutes the menace of castration whereby the subject recognizes itself as a subject alienated from the (m)other by the division of the phallus (the Other).

Both the scene of the game on the path and the scene of Pin's dream-fantasy clearly connote an indistinct, ambiguous condition of pre-oedipal sexuality on his part. His imaginary world having been violated by the intrusion of the Symbolic, Pin is no longer either instinctively and blissfully at one with the natural order, on the one hand, or able to identify the female body as something radically "other," and thus as the object of a desire that both locates and defines the subject in the symbolic order, on the other hand. It is Pin's alienation from both the natural and the sociocultural orders that leads to his perception of the coupling of the spiders as something no less strange and repulsive than the coupling of humans. Pin is suspended on the path to the nest of spiders and on the threshold of his sister's bedroom; he is, in other words, suspended on the border between nature and culture, childhood and adulthood, myth and history. However, as even a perfunctory reading of *The Path* makes clear, Calvino is not interested in the psychopathology of pre-adolescent sexuality in and of itself, nor does his portrayal of Pin's character serve a primarily naturalistic function (the way such portrayals often do, for example, in Alberto Moravia's fiction). On the contrary, Pin's psyche is only a narrative device that Calvino uses in order to stage dramatically the problematic of the life and development of individual human beings in history. Calvino shows how individual "history" and the construction of sexuality in the history of the subject engage from the beginning the social relations of production, the patriarchal regimentation of power, and the historical structures of domination. What role, Calvino asks in *The Path*, does the cultural construction of sexuality play in channelling the subject's libido in a socially acceptable direction, or in directing the course of human action in conjunction with (or in opposition to) the dynamics of larger sociopolitical events, such as World War II and the collapse of the Fascist regime? Through Pin's story, Calvino aims to show his readers how individual history is shaped by the contradictory and heterogeneous articulation of psychosexual mechanisms of desire and domination with cultural and political forces which operate in a larger historical context.

Pin's alienation, as defined by his not belonging to any single stable order of representation, makes him a kind of wild card in the game of Calvino's narrative. The use of Pin as a focalizer allows the narrative to move back and forth across different levels of representation and point of view. The narrative of *The Path* is able to problematize the binary logic of the oppositions subject/object, self/other, Imaginary/Symbolic, nature/culture, normal/deviant, masculine/feminine, childhood/adulthood, fantasy/reality, and myth/history because it is framed through the unstable, shifting perspective of a naive focalizer who does not know the differences on which these cultural oppositions are based and through which individual and collective history are represented.[47] Thus Pin's threshold position allows Calvino to coordinate the question of the cultural definition of the body, of sexuality, and of the symbolic construction of difference with the equally pressing question of history and its most truthful and "realistic" mode of representation.

One of the key passages in which Calvino coordinates these two questions in *The Path* revolves around Pin's experience of the fear of castration, which is clearly *not* the direct consequence— as it would be in the Freudian scenario—of his original vision of the biological difference between the sexes. On the contrary, Pin's introduction to sexual difference coincides with his introduction to the discourse of domination and to the political representation of difference in the specific historical context of the Resistance. The central scene of symbolic castration in the novel is, not surprisingly, the encounter between Pin and the men in the tavern. An exchange of glances opens this scene: "Gli uomini smicciano Pin che entra, poi smicciano lo sconosciuto" ("As Pin comes in the men frown at him, then at the unknown man"; p. 7; 36). *Smicciare* is a very unusual word in Italian; "to frown" conveys only one of its many connotations. First of all, it is a colloquial expression that roughly means "to look secretively at someone" or "to glance rapidly at someone while trying to avoid eye contact." Literally, this same verb is the equivalent of the ex-

pression *levare la miccia*, or "to remove a slow match," suggesting that here Pin is confronted with a potentially "explosive"
situation whose danger resides in the power of the eye and the
look that it gives. Immediately, in fact, "Pin sees that the atmosphere is different." The men are unwilling to joke with him as
they did when Comitato was not there; they do not want to listen to Pin's tale of the prank he has played on his sister's German
lover. Under the gaze of Comitato, the men turn their own gaze
towards Pin, for the figure of Comitato is also that of a benevolent but forbidding father. They "deflect" towards Pin the power
of Comitato's gaze, in other words, which is the "paternal" gaze
of a man who has come to ask them to risk their lives by forming
a GAP (literally, "An Action Group of Patriots"). In the name of
the *pater*, Comitato has asked them to take up arms and become
defenders of the *patria* or fatherland. They in turn—out of a
sense of shame and guilt that Comitato ably exploits—take on
the symbolic function of the forbidding and punishing father towards the orphan Pin. The men's unfriendly gaze and harsh
words force Pin to define his relationship with his sister as a
transgressive one: "The men . . . turn slowly round, one by one.
Frenchy Michel first frowns at him as if he's never seen him before, then says slowly: 'You're a filthy little pimp'" (p. 8; 36).
This brutal definition marks Pin's position as a subject in the
Symbolic as well as in the political-historical order; the rest of his
story is, in a sense, a consequence of this definition. At the same
time, by dominating Pin, the men are able to define their own
political position in Comitato's eyes.

Before the crucial scene in the tavern, Pin (like his sister) does
not associate the German sailor with the idea of "the enemy."
From Pin's perspective, the sailor is a rather comic figure instead, who serves as the constant butt of Pin's obscene jokes and
childish pranks; the fact that he is just a man like any other, willing to buy the favors of another body in order to satisfy the
needs of his own, makes him appear ridiculous and vulnerable
to Pin. In Pin's eyes, the German's alien language, uniform, and
weapon—the visible signs of the Nazi occupation of Italy—carry
no obvious symbolic connotations. Consequently Pin does not
take these signs seriously; they simply strike him as a cause for

laughter and derision. He repeatedly mocks the sailor with the spontaneous laughter of someone who, like the child who sees only the nudity of the emperor in "The Emperor's New Clothes," has not yet been taught how to recognize the trappings of power: "It's easy for Pin to make fun of the German, who can't understand what he says and looks at him from a shapeless congealed-looking face, shaven to the temples. Then, when the sailor's back is turned, Pin can shout insults after him, certain he won't turn round. Seen from behind the sailor looks ridiculous, with those two black ribbons hanging down from his little cap over his short tunic to his bare-looking bottom; a fleshy bottom, like a woman's, with a big German pistol dangling over it" (p. 3; 31). Pin's perception of the German in this passage is both superficial and ambiguous. Not only does he never associate the sailor with the specific historical context of the war and of the German occupation; the text also suggests that while Pin sees the sailor quite clearly, he is unable to organize his perceptions of him into a whole. The sailor's face is seemingly shapeless; seen from the back, his body appears strangely similar to a female body to Pin (and therefore unthreatening). Finally, the P.38 pistol is equally unthreatening to Pin, for he does not associate it with the sailor's masculinity (which remains concealed), but can only see it as dangling incongruously on the man's bottom like a comic prop. Pin's fluctuating comic perspective and his way of seeing different parts of the sailor's body as separate objects resemble the playful, shifting visual logic of the Imaginary. At this early point in the narrative, Pin's perception is not yet organized along the axis of that differential system which makes up the order of the Symbolic and is essentially linguistic and social in nature.[48]

In the tavern scene, Pin becomes conscious for the first time that his relationship with his sister (on whom Pin depends for food and shelter) is a reason for shame. Rina's open promiscuity—to which Pin is an accomplice ("you're a filthy little pimp")—makes her a social outcast, if not an outlaw. In practicing her trade, she grants the privilege of sexual intercourse to anyone who has the money to pay for it and does not discriminate along political lines. Pin's sister is, in this perspective, the living embodiment of feminine sexuality as a drive that must—

like incest—be constantly repressed by the patriarchal order, because it threatens the social regimentation of sexuality on which culture itself is built. As a prostitute, she is universally despised in the *carrugio*—even by the same men (like the men in the tavern) who desire her—both because of the profession that she practices and because she makes no distinction between clients who belong to the enemy and those who do not, or, to paraphrase the title (*Uomini e no*) of Elio Vittorini's 1945 novel about the Resistance, between those who are not men and those who are. The name by which she is known, "la Nera" (or the "Dark Girl"), has rather obvious negative connotations. Only by cutting himself off from her and by submitting to the will of the men can Pin become a "man" himself; that is, only in this way may he assume a position of his own within the social order and take on a positive role as a historical subject in the context of the Resistance.

What the men say to Pin (and, through him, to his sister) at this point in the tavern scene contains an implicit castration threat: "The day everything changes—you know what I mean— the day everything changes we'll send your sister round town with her head as shaved and bare as a plucked chicken. . . . And for you . . . for you we'll think up something you haven't even dreamt of" (p. 8; 37). Immediately after making this threat, the men ask Pin to sneak into his sister's bedroom while she is making love with the German sailor and to steal his standard-issue pistol when no one is looking. Pin, if he wants to be accepted as a member of their GAP, must then give the pistol to the men in the tavern:

[The men] are now looking at Pin in silence. What can they want of him?
"Say," exclaims Michel, "have you seen what a pistol that sailor has?"
"Yes, a hell of a big pistol," replies Pin.
"Well," says Michel, "you must steal that pistol from him."
"How can I do that?" exclaims Pin.
"Try."
"But how? He always wears it clamped to his bottom. You go and steal it."
"Well, let's see . . . Doesn't he take his trousers off at a certain moment? Then he must take his pistol off too, surely. Go and steal it. Try."
"I will if I feel like it."

"Listen," says Giraffe, "we aren't joking here. If you want to be one of us you know what you must do. Otherwise . . ."
"Otherwise?"
"Otherwise . . . D'you know what a G.A.P. is?"
The unknown man gives Giraffe a nudge and shakes his head: he does not seem to like the way the others are behaving.
New words to Pin always have a halo of mystery, a hint of something dark and forbidden. A *Gap*? What could a *Gap* be?
"Yes, of course I know what it is," he says.
"What is it?" asks Giraffe.
"It's where you can go get f . . . , you and your whole family."
But the men aren't listening to him. The unknown man has signed to them to bring their heads close and is whispering to them and seems to be rebuking them for something, and they are making signs of agreement.
Pin is out of all this. He can creep away without saying a word; perhaps it's best, he thinks, not to mention that business of the pistol any more, it probably wasn't important, and they may have forgotten all about it.
But Pin has just reached the door when Michel raises his head and says: "Pin, then we're agreed about that."
Pin would like to begin acting the fool again, but suddenly he feels a child surrounded by grown-ups, and stands there with his hand on the jamb of the door. (pp. 9–11; 38–39)

Pin is portrayed here, as he is at many other points in *The Path*, as standing on a threshold. This time, however, he is no longer free to come and go as he wishes or to keep playing his childish games. The men's gaze, along with their menacing and yet revelatory words, now force him to assume a fixed position in relation to them. Pin is compelled to commit himself to an act that will definitively cut him off from his sister and initiate him into the mysterious world of adulthood and history represented by that obscure word, GAP. As is clear in the above passage, the pistol is—for Pin—the key to that world.

The German sailor's P.38 pistol is, granted, a "phallic symbol" of sorts in *The Path*. It is not, however, the kind of stereotypical phallic symbol so notoriously popular in vulgar Freudian literary analysis or Hollywood films of the 1940's. The P.38 is, rather, the equivalent of the Lacanian phallus in Calvino's novel, for "the phallus is not a question of form, or of an image, or of a fantasy, but rather of a signifier, the signifier of desire."[49] It is, more specifically, the fundamental signifier of "mature" psychic life and the privileged signifier of the Symbolic as the realm of the Law of the Father. According to Lacan, through the Oedipus complex the child—whether male or female—takes on the phallus as a signifier, which always entails a confrontation with the function of the father. The Oedipus complex and the crisis induced by the threat of castration (which supposedly "resolves" the complex) lead the child to identify with his or her own sex and to accede to a position homologous to that of the father. In *The Path*, the pistol-as-phallus is the signifier that articulates Pin's insertion into the differential order of the adult social world represented by the men in the tavern.

In *The Path* the agents of Pin's oedipal rite of passage are not his natural parents; this is a specific strategic move of Calvino's, for one aim of the novel is to foreground the strictly symbolic and culture-specific character of the Oedipus complex. As an orphan with only the vaguest memories of his parents, Pin is outside of the traditional oedipal triangle, which is (at least for Calvino) a structure through which the individual is defined as a social being who is subject to the dialectic of power relations and to the dominant ideological codes of a specific historical moment. The oedipal mechanism—castration, repression, subjugation to the Law—is not naturally inherent in the family, as *The Path* points out. The family structure (in the form of the "3 + 1" formula, namely the father-mother-child triangle plus the phallus) assumes an oedipal function only because it has become an instrument for the reproduction and perpetuation of the mechanisms of repression (of individual desires) in a given political and historical situation. In *The Path*, the Dark Girl functions as Pin's link to the image of the maternal body, while the men replace the father, who is possessor and figure of the phallus (and thus guarantor of the order of the Symbolic). The pistol-as-phallus represents Pin's access and subjection to the differential structures of sexuality, language, power relations, and history itself: it becomes the signifier through which all difference is articulated for Pin. Pin must steal the pistol-as-phallus from its usurper (the German sailor) and restore it to its rightful possessors (the men in the tavern). At a symbolic level, this act leads to Pin's recognition of the meaning of sexual difference, which had remained hidden to him in the scene of his dream-fantasy behind the partition of his sister's bedroom. The pistol-as-phallus is the missing element whose appearance will shatter the dual relationship that still binds Pin to the (m)other's body, for the forbidding of any further contact with his sister leads to the collapse of the specular dialectic of voyeurism. Thus the child, by breaking out of this closed dialectic, becomes "like" the father, thanks to the symbolic intervention of the castration threat and the symbolic acquisition of the phallus. However, the child still cannot take the father's place; the desire for the mother must be repressed by internalizing the Law of the symbolic Father. This primary repression of a desire that—according to Lacan—is in essence a desire for annihilation, leads the subject into a quest for a fulfillment that can never be attained. The fundamental experience of lack, in fact, which is brought about by the castration threat, is what sets the subject into motion in the first place. The men in the tavern ask Pin to choose between his bond with his sister and a pact with them, but what they propose is not really a choice, inasmuch as there is no freedom involved. Pin is, rather, faced with a double bind: either he must become like them, even if it means a violent break with the Imaginary (m)other, or else never (as they see it) become a man. His desire to cross over the threshold into the world of adults must be bound to the desire to be like the men. Pin's theft of the pistol is thus the "symbolic debt" that will bind him to them (as they in turn are bound to Comitato) and will make him a member of the GAP. He will arm himself to fight against the Germans when, after he has stolen the pistol and taken it back to the tavern, the men grant him the use of it. Ultimately, like them, he will see his sister as a traitor and her German client as an enemy.

However, the experience of castration is in itself constructed, or, to put it another way, culturally and historically produced. This, in *The Path*, the men in the tavern make Pin see his association with his sister as a punishable transgression on the basis of a paternal law which is in effect a partisan law. In fact, as it turns out, this is but a scene that they are staging under Comitato's gaze in order to persuade him that they actually intend to carry out his orders by forming a GAP and taking up arms against the Fascists and the Nazis. In exercising his authority, Comitato tries to dictate the behavior of the men in the tavern and to make them assume an active role within the system of the partisan organization; this is mirrored in turn by the men's exercise of their own "paternal" authority over Pin. But the men actually distrust Comitato, and they plan to keep for themselves any arms that they will be able to obtain. From Comitato's point of view, and that of the partisans whom he represents, everything must be subordinate to the cause of national liberation; however, the men do not see things in the same way. If armed, they could hope to break out of the cycle of poverty in which they are trapped (by breaking the laws of property, or robbing). Their desire is ultimately one and the same with Pin's and with Rina's (who is dispossessed of everything, including her own body).[50] This is the more radical and basic desire that is repressed and erased when the men tell Pin that what he really wants is to be one of them; Comitato's call to arms is in effect a call to abandon any such anti-institutional desires. As pointed out in Chapter 4, in fact, the CLN leadership exploited the nationalistic rhetoric of patriotism to preempt any potentially revolutionary thrust on the part of the partisan base. The military discipline of the partisan organization, with its commissars and commanders (in turn subordinate to the Central Committees), was designed to contain any attempt by the partisan bands to transform the Resistance into a full-scale social revolution.

The oedipal structure of repression is represented in the novel as a cultural mechanism that exceeds the boundaries of the family and traverses the entire sociopolitical field. But Calvino—and this is, in the last analysis, one of the historical and cultural limits of his anti-oedipal critique—has only a generalized notion of liberation to offer, one that simply includes all those whose history is one of "exclusion, expulsion, obliteration."[51] Gilles Deleuze and Félix Guattari have argued that the oedipal mechanism is a means of integration into a group and thus a means of segregation of individuals from other individuals outside of that group. The segregative function of the oedipal double bind generates a sense of "being one of us" that sublimates individual desire through the identification with the group as a collective ego ideal.[52] A powerful instrument in the hands of the dominant group (as is evident, for example, in Fascist politics), the segregative function of the oedipal mechanism also appears within subaltern groups, such as the men in the tavern. What is most troubling in *The Path*, in fact, is that Calvino shows this mechanism, usually associated with the forces of Fascism, at work within a group that is supposed to be fighting against Fascism. Furthermore, Calvino includes Comitato and the process of the partisan mobilization of the masses within this same dialectic. In this way he tries to suggest that the CLN itself placed the masses in Italy in a position similar to that in which the men place Pin. The leadership of the Resistance in Italy—in Calvino's view—placed the masses in a repressive double bind: either they could subscribe to the policy of the Resistance as a national (rather than social) liberation struggle and renounce all revolutionary aspirations in order to fight with the partisans, or they could remain prisoners to the dictates of the Fascist regime and the Nazi occupational forces. While the end (i.e. the Liberation) was intended to justify the means and to serve as a springboard to an authentically socialist and "mature" future, free of the irrational and "adolescent" discourse of Fascism, the repression of revolutionary desire nonetheless played a crucial role in the integration of the partisan forces. As in the case of Pin, the masses in Italy were not confronted with a true (if utopian) possibility of choice, because there was no authentic freedom involved. This is the point that the tavern scene is intended to drive home. Those who chose to fight Fascism in Italy contracted—as does Pin when he accepts the men's challenge to steal the P.38 pistol—a symbolic debt with the Resistance organization and its leaders in the CLN. The irony is, as Calvino tries to show in *The Path*, that the quest for freedom from Fascism was governed in Italy by a paternal(istic) discourse and a patriarchal organizational structure that reflected many of the very same values against which it aimed to struggle.

In his pioneering work on group psychology, which prophetically foresaw the rise and nature of Fascism as a mass movement, Freud suggests that the bond which integrates individuals into the masses is of a libidinal nature. The narcissistic identification with the leader as an ego ideal represents for Freud a regression to an early phase of the Oedipus complex. The leader, as an object of love, serves as a substitute for some unattained ego ideal of our own.[53] The group itself is constituted by a "number of individuals who have substituted one and the same object for their ego ideal and have subsequently identified themselves with one another in their ego."[54] While totalitarianism may prescribe values that are alien to the members of the group, a negative image or idea may function quite as well as a positive one in providing a focus for the group's self-identity; in fact, as Adorno points out, "The leader or the leading idea might also, so to speak, be negative; hatred against a particular person or institution might operate in just the same unifying way, and might call up the same kind of emotional ties as positive attachment."[55] In his essay "Freudian Theory and the Pattern of Fascist Propaganda," Adorno adds that the "unity trick" is a key strategy of Fascist agitators: "They emphasize their being different from the outsider but play down such differences within their own group and tend to level out distinctive qualities among themselves with the exception of the hierarchical one. 'We are all in the same boat.'"[56] In *The Path*, Calvino implicitly probes— along the lines suggested by Adorno's analysis—the difference between Fascist propaganda and the mobilization of the masses by the CLN. While the Resistance had no leader who could function as a collective ego ideal or superego (although the myth of Stalin certainly took on this role for many communist partisans), the CLN sought to mobilize the masses on the basis of a "negative ideal," namely a widespread hatred of Fascists and Nazis, and used the "unity trick" to close off the many conflicts within the anti-Fascist front and to repress the more radical desires of the masses.

Adorno asks: "Why is the applied group psychology discussed here peculiar to Fascism rather than to most other movements that seek mass support?" Freud, of course, was not interested in the political aims of the groups involved and made no difference between "good" and "bad" group libido. But the political differentiation introduced by Adorno does nothing to dispel the uncanny similarity in the strategies of persuasion associated with Fascist propaganda and those of the CLN. "Liberal" propaganda, according to Adorno, differs from Fascist propaganda because it addresses the rational rather than the irrational, and it sets rational goals that correspond to the objective needs of the population in a given historical moment. Fascist propaganda cannot, unlike liberal propaganda, rely on rational "discursive thinking," because the objective aims of Fascism are largely irrational (at least insofar as these aims contradict the material interests of a great many of those whom Fascism seeks to embrace). Fascism mobilizes the irrational in politics, or, to put it another way, it politically mobilizes the unconscious in its regressive form. "This task is facilitated by the frame of mind of all those strata of the population who suffer from senseless frustrations and therefore develop a stunted, irrational mentality. It may well be the secret of Fascist propaganda that it simply takes men for what they are: the true children of today's standardized mass culture, largely robbed of autonomy and spontaneity, instead of setting goals the realization of which would transcend the psychological *status quo* no less than the social one," Adorno notes ("Freudian Theory," p. 131). His association of Fascism with the rational mobilization of the irrational appears overly simplistic, however, for in effect the anti-Fascist leaders of the Resistance adopted a not-altogether dissimilar strategy, even to the extent of employing some of the same myths so skillfully used by the Fascist propaganda machine. This was, of course, a calculated risk on their part, but the intricate balance of power between (and within) the members of the partisan coalition, the monarchy, and the Allies seemed at the time to mandate the continued avoidance of debate on the need for far-reaching social and institutional reform in Italy, in order to preserve the precious unity of the anti-Fascist bloc. In *The Path* Calvino consistently dramatizes the contrast between the goals set by the Resistance leaders and the primary needs of the subaltern groups belonging to the "base" (i.e. the men in the tavern and Dritto's partisans). Resistance propaganda promises neither a change in the psychological status quo nor in the social one; it is for this reason that it is obliged to try to "mobilize the irrational" in opposition to Fascism. While this political tactic was an effective one (the Resistance would not have been a relatively unified movement without it), it also had some profoundly negative consequences. No systematic rational argument was ever put forward as the basis for distinguishing between Fascists and non-Fascists; the members of the younger generation who had grown up under Fascism were left more or less on their own in this regard. The propaganda of Mussolini's new Social Republic was, paradoxically, more oriented toward issues of social reform than Resistance propaganda.[57] The defection of Michel and Pelle to the Fascists serves in the novel to demonstrate how the Resistance leadership failed to set goals with which the masses could identify in the sense outlined by Adorno.

The deployment of a paternalistic mechanism of repression to contain the revolutionary demands of many partisans led in turn to a progressive disenchantment among left-wing militants after the war. For the leftist parties this meant the loss of the ascendency among the masses that they had gained during the Resistance. An anonymous communist activist during the Resistance once asked: "What are we fighting for if, once the Germans have been chased out, others want to impose a new kind of Fascism on us?"[58] This is indeed the fundamental question posed by *The Path* as well. The Resistance leaders did nothing— Calvino suggests—to prevent the restoration after the Liberation of a social order that was still largely defined by Fascist tendencies. They did nothing (and, quite obviously, perhaps there was nothing they could do) to alter the mechanisms of psychic repression that had constructed the Fascist man and woman. Fascism—writes Foucault—is "not only the historical Fascism, the Fascism of Hitler and Mussolini—which was able to mobilize and use the desire of the masses so effectively—but also the Fascism . . . in our heads, in our everyday behavior, the Fascism that causes us to love power, to desire the very thing that dominates and exploits us. . . . How does one keep from being a Fascist, even (especially) when one believes oneself to be a revolutionary militant? How do we rid our speech and our acts, our hearts and our pleasures, of Fascism? How do we ferret out the Fascism that is ingrained in our behavior?"[59] Neither political parties nor individuals can hope to generate constructive changes in the social order—Calvino suggests in a way similar to Foucault—as long as they remain the agents of a totalitarian regime of the body, of the psyche, or of language itself.

In the tavern scene, and in the sequence of the theft of the pistol that immediately follows it, Pin's eradication from the realm of the Imaginary is presented in a highly schematic fashion. But Calvino's portrayal of this psychosocial mechanism in such a schematic manner in *The Path* is a deliberately ironic one, for Pin's entrance into the Symbolic and the discourse of history clearly takes the form of a violation, rather than of a successful rite of passage, in the self's quest for a fully authentic adult consciousness. Once he has encountered the men in the tavern, a return to a state of imaginary plenitude (the "long-forgotten happiness" of his dream) is clearly no longer possible for him. Nor does Calvino posit such a return, in the form of a regression to the free play of the Imaginary, as the basis of a more legitimate mode of existence. The impossibility of such a regression is thematized in Calvino's later novel, *The Baron in the Trees* (1957), in which the similar idea of a return to a Rousseauistic state of nature is likewise shown to be an impossibly utopian fantasy. However, the register of the Imaginary—namely Pin's endless *fantasticare*—points in the direction of a different relation between the ego and reality, one which would no longer be under the sway of the Oedipus complex and the patriarchal reality principle of the Symbolic. Pin's *fantasticare* gestures broadly in the direction of a non-repressive relation, not "bound up with the father," but rather with the mother, yet it calls neither for an escape from the burden of history nor for the dissolution of the category of the subject itself.[60]

In *The Path*, the conquest of the Imaginary by the Symbolic is represented as an agonizing transition for the subject in question, and the relations of domination involved in the process are revealed in their essential brutality. Thus Calvino undermines the conventional celebration of the self's access to a "mature" psychic and social life—through the oedipal triangulation of desire—as a natural and positive development in the life of the subject and shows that it is instead a regimentation of the unconscious in the name of power itself. In the sequence that follows the tavern scene, the theft of the pistol acquires the ironic overtones of both a rite of passage and a fall from prelapsarian innocence:

Now Pin has to twist round to see where the German is putting down the belt with the pistol on it; there it is, hung on the back of a chair; Pin wishes he had an arm as narrow as the slit so that he could pass it through, reach the weapon and pull it towards him. . . . Now is the moment. Pin must enter the room with bare feet, on all fours, and pull the belt down from the chair without making any noise; all this is not just a game to laugh and joke about afterwards; no, it is connected with something secret and mysterious said by the men in the tavern with an opaque look in the whites of their eyes. (pp. 12–13; 42–43)

For Pin the theft of the pistol is an unsettling, even painful moment, rather than a "fortunate fall" from innocence. He is dramatically torn between his imaginary fantasies and the urge to do as the men have ordered him to do:

Yes, Pin would like always to be friends with grown-ups, for them always to joke with him and to take him into their confidence. Pin loves grown-ups. . . . He even loves the German. And now he is doing something irreparable; perhaps he'll never be able to joke with the German again, after this; and things will be different with the men in the tavern, too; they'll have a link with him beyond laughter and obscenities. . . . Pin would like to stretch himself out on his little bed and lie there fantasizing with his eyes open . . . lie there imagining himself being accepted by bands of boys as their leader because he knows so much more than they do, and them all going out against the grown-ups together and beating them up and doing such wonderful things that the grown-ups are forced to admire him too and ask him to be their leader, loving him and stroking his head at the same time. But now, instead of that, he has to move about at night with the grown-ups hating him, and steal a pistol from a German, things not done by other boys, who play with tin pistols and wooden swords. (p. 13; 43)

Pin's stream of consciousness (in the form of free indirect discourse) is characterized in the above passage by the intersection of conflicting desires and mimetic drives. The instability evident in the flow of his consciousness (Pin "loves grown-ups . . . he even loves the German" and immediately thereafter dreams of "beating them up") is that of a subject who must attempt to master the Imaginary and insert itself into the Symbolic. But the theft

of the pistol is, like that of the forbidden fruit of the tree of knowledge in the Garden of Eden, an irrevocable act that marks Pin's
fall into the language of the real and defines his position in it:

Pin is now crawling on all fours into his sister's room, bare-foot, with
his head already beyond the curtain, into that smell of male and female
which goes straight to the nostrils. . . . There; now that dialogue of
groans is beginning from the bed, and he can creep in on all fours,
taking care not to be heard. . . . Pin is now touching the belt, and it
turns out to be quite solid, not magical, and it slips down from the back
of the chair almost frighteningly easy, without even banging on the
floor. Now "it" has happened; the fear he had only imagined before has
become real fear. . . .
    Once out of the room he realizes that he can't now go back to his little
bed. (pp. 13–14; 44)

Once he possesses the pistol, a narcissistic fantasy of omnipotence immediately occurs in Pin's mind: "A real pistol. A real
pistol. Pin tries to excite himself with the thought. Someone
who has a real pistol can do anything, he's like a grown-up. He
can threaten to kill men and women and do whatever he likes
with them. Pin now thinks he will grasp the pistol and walk
round with it always pointed at people; no one will be able
to take it away from him and everyone will be afraid of him"
(pp. 14–15; 42). This is a fantasy of being an absolute subject, for
it expresses the desire to gain control over the symbolic Father at
the very point at which, paradoxically, Pin has become subject to
the Law of the Father through his theft of the pistol-as-phallus.
Pin's fantasy of omnipotence—in which the pistol-as-phallus still
functions as an imaginary signifier—is followed by a castration
fantasy that abolishes the phallus altogether as a symbolic signifier of difference, thus disavowing the "real fear" Pin has just
experienced in stealing the pistol: "But the pistol, wrapped in its
belt, is still under his vest, and he cannot make up his mind to
touch it; in a way he almost hopes that when he looks for it it
will have vanished, melted away from the heat of his body"
(p. 15; 42). Through his castration fantasy, Pin "withdraws"—if
only momentarily—from the reality of the Symbolic and from
the Law of the Father symbolized by the pistol. A withdrawal of
this sort does not entail an act of repression but rather a rejection of repression; it is "a primordial rejection of a fundamental

'signifier' . . . : the phallus insofar as it is a signifier of the castration complex." [61] Pin's retreat is similar to what Lacan calls the "foreclosure" of the signifier of the father, which is a phenomenon generally associated with schizophrenic or psychotic subjects. Maude Mannoni describes the phenomenon of foreclosure in one of her patients as follows:

> The Oedipal personages are all in their places, but in the play of permutations brought about, there is something like an empty place. . . . What appears as rejected is everything referring to the phallus and the father. . . . Each time Georges tries to take hold of himself as a desiring-person, he is driven back to a form of dissolution of identities. He is another, enthralled by a maternal image. . . . He remains trapped within an imaginary position in which he is captivated by the maternal imago; he situates himself within the Oedipal triangle in terms of this locale, which implies an impossible process of identification, involving forever after, in the mode of a purely imaginary dialectic, the destruction of one or the other of the partners. [62]

While Calvino's novel certainly does not celebrate psychosis or schizophrenia as a liberation from the psychosocial imposition of a regime of controls over the unconscious, [63] it posits Pin's *fantasticare* as a significant form of resistance to social as well as psychic repression. Pin's *fantasticare* is not simply the bad immediacy or the necessarily alienating specular dialectic of the Lacanian Imaginary. Rather, in *The Path* it represents Calvino's fictional attempt to disclose the possibility of a different kind of subjectivity, unbound by the oedipal mechanism that historically has come to constitute the subject in our civilization of discontents.

After the theft, Pin continues to pursue an imaginary relationship with the pistol, which is, the narrative tells us, "a mysterious, almost unreal thing" (p. 15; 46). Pin uses it to play a series of fantastic games in which he himself takes on the most disparate of roles; the pistol helps him "to tell marvellous tales" (p. 15; 46). There is, however, nothing directly related to the mother's body in the games that he plays. His fantasy does not express a desire for the mother per se, as the most reductive reading of the Oedipus myth would claim, but rather a desire to be free to be whatever he imagines. [64] But the last of Pin's fantasies, while playing with the stolen pistol, is a fantasy of self-destruction, for in it he tries to imagine what it would be like if the gun went off while held up against his face, and he has a sudden, hallucinatory memory of having seen another boy blinded by a gunshot. This frightening image of castration, which relates the pistol to the possibility of death (mortality is *the* reality that the Oedipus complex discloses to the subject, according to Lacan), takes Pin back to where everything began, namely the men in the tavern: "Pin has now played with a real pistol. He has played with it enough, and can give it to the men who asked for it, he is now longing to give it to them, in fact. When he has not got it any more it will be the same as if he'd never stolen it, and the German can be as furious as he likes and Pin can laugh at him behind his back again" (p. 16; 46). Pin's wish to dispose of the gun and to pretend that the theft had never taken place represents a desire not only to withdraw from the rule of the phallus but also to deny the fact of death disclosed by the phallus as the signifier of desire. The bond that binds Eros and desire to the death instinct is the innermost obstacle to any project for a non-repressive development: "The mere anticipation of the inevitable end," writes Marcuse, "introduces a repressive element into all libidinal relations. . . . This primary frustration in the instinctual structure of man becomes the inexhaustible source of all other frustrations—and of their social effectiveness. Man learns that 'it cannot last anyway.' . . . He is resigned before society forces him to practice resignation methodically. The flux of time is society's most natural ally in maintaining law and order, conformity, and the institutions that relegate freedom to a perpetual utopia."[65] In wishing to return to the time when he could tease and mock the German, Pin seeks to defer his subjection not only to the world of adults and the role that they have assigned to him but also to time and death. Yet the theft is an irreparable act; it introduces Pin to the fatal nature of time and history and to the inexorable limits this sets, not only to the subject who desires and acts but to collective praxis as well.

When he returns to the tavern to give the pistol to the men, Pin discovers that they have deceived him; they too really have no desire to play the part that "Committee" has assigned to them. The men in the tavern are ready neither to join the Resistance nor to act as paternal adjuvants in Pin's quest for an identity in the social and historical process. Although Pin does not understand the political implications of the men's resistance to the Resistance, he feels deeply betrayed by the adult world:

> Grown-ups are an untrustworthy treacherous lot, they don't take their games in the serious wholehearted way children do, and their own games are so complicated and involved that it's difficult to discover what the real one is. Before it seemed that they were playing a game with the unknown man against the German, now they are playing one of their own against the unknown man; what they say can never be trusted.
>
> "Well, sing us something, then, Pin," they say now, as if nothing had happened, as if there had never been that definite pact between them, a pact consecrated by that mysterious word: *Gap*. (pp. 17–18; 49)

It is at this point that Pin decides to go back to his secret place on the path to the nest of spiders and to hide the gun there.

The burial of the gun at the end of the first narrative sequence is a key moment in *The Path*, for it represents a deferral of Pin's entrance into adulthood and into history itself. In submitting to the men's injunction to steal the pistol, however, and in breaking with his sister as a consequence of the theft, Pin has *already* entered into the men's world. When he acts out his own death (by playing his game with the pistol) or discovers the men's duplicity (upon his return to the tavern), Pin experiences temporality and desire as loss. The act of burying the pistol therefore symbolizes—like the burial of Babeuf—the defeat of Pin's hopes. There is, however, another, more positive side to this defeat, just as Babeuf's burial leads in turn to a vision of liberation for Pin. In burying the pistol in the place where the spiders make their nests, Pin also hopes that he will be able one day to return there—once his quest for a friend has reached its end—and bring the pistol out once again into "the light of disconcealment." The return to the path will in fact disclose the secret of Pin's origin, for the friend Pin seeks is really a father figure, who alone will be able to grant Pin a positive, rather than alienated, sense of selfhood. This search for a non-oedipal father—one who will be a friend to Pin instead of an enemy—is also a search for another mode of experiencing temporality and desire, unencumbered by the oedipal "fate" that condemns man to live with the specter of death and (self-)deception always before him. Throughout the rest of the narrative, Pin will continue to search for someone with whom he will be able to return to the path and who will help him to surmount his fear of the gun: "Perhaps one day Pin will find a friend, a real friend, who understands him and whom he can understand, and then to him, and only to him, will he show the place where the spiders have their lairs" (p. 19; 51). In each of the subsequent narrative sequences, though, Pin's hope is once again deferred.

In its periodic reappearance as a locus of repetition and sameness, the image of the path to the nest of spiders undercuts or interrupts the forward movement of *The Path*'s plot. Each time this image appears, it subverts the sense of Pin's progress by denying that he could possibly be getting anywhere in his quest. Each time that it appears, the image brings Pin back to the beginning of his quest, leading him once again to the marginal space which originally was his. After his period of captivity in the Fascist prison and his adventure-filled escape in Red Wolf's company, Pin wonders "whether or not to tell Red Wolf about the spiders' nests" (p. 43; 79). Red Wolf deserts him, however, and Pin is left alone in the dark, "alone now, alone in the whole world" with no recourse but to retreat once more to "his" place. At the end of the prison sequence, before Pin arrives at the partisan camp and meets the members of Dritto's detachment, he runs into the partisan Cousin, a figure who immediately attracts him as a sort of benevolent (if warlike) giant: "The man comes nearer; he is large and tall, dressed in civilian clothes and armed with a tommy-gun" (p. 49; 85). Pin's hope that Cousin may prove to be "the great friend he has sought for so long, the friend who is interested in spiders' nests" (p. 143; 193) is, however, dashed when Cousin disappears to fight his battles alone. Cousin seems to be only a substitute for the eternally absent friend in the figural pattern of repetition which informs Pin's itinerary in the novel.

In the central narrative sequence of *The Path*, which takes place at the partisan encampment, Pin discovers that his rela-

tionship with the partisans is an exact duplicate of his relationship with the men in the tavern. He is, once again, relegated to
the margins of a group that is itself on the margins of the Resistance struggle. Although living with the partisans in the mountains, Pin still feels deeply detached from the adult world's rules
and rituals, which continue to fascinate and repel him (as, for
instance, in the men's desires for women and for violence, for
love and for death: "The urge to kill . . . is remote, vague, like
the urge to love; it has an exciting and unpleasant taste like cigarettes and wine; it is a strange urge, it's hard to understand why
all men feel it; it must give some mysterious and secret pleasure" (p. 68; 106).[66] Like the men in the tavern, the partisans
challenge Pin to prove that he is "one of them" through a test of
manhood: he must go down into the town to kill an officer. But,
like the men in the tavern, they are only toying with him; their
challenge is a false one, posed only "to make fun of him" (p. 68;
107). They refuse to let him have a weapon, and when Pin
boasts about his P.38 hidden in the place where the spiders make
their nests, they think that he is lying: "'A naval pistol; it must
be one of those water ones.' Pin chews his lips; one day he'll go
down and dig up the pistol, and do wonderful things with it that
will astonish them all" (p. 68; 107). Only Pelle, who is obsessed
with weapons of every sort, shows some interest in Pin's secret.
This leads Pin to believe for a moment that Pelle may be "the
great friend" for whom he is looking. Pelle, however, turns out
to be a Fascist collaborator, and his only interest in Pin is in tricking him into disclosing the location of the hidden gun before Pelle
defects to the Black Brigade. At this point in the narrative, Pin's
hope of finding "the great friend" seems to vanish altogether.

The novel's climax, in Chapter 7, combines the oedipal theme
with the allied themes of Eros and Thanatos. The conflict between individual desire and the needs of the group reemerges
once again as a central concern of the novel. This climactic scene
is a tragicomic peripeteia in which Pin's dreams literally seem to
"go up in smoke." One night, sitting around the fire in their
primitive shelter, the men listen to Pin sing "a wild song" that
he picked up in the streets, a song which was sung once by

storytellers at fairs. The song tells of a son who comes home to
his mother after the end of the war, only to kill her by cutting
her head off with his sword:

> Who is it knocking at my front door?
> 'Tis a Moorish captain with all his slaves.
> Tell me, woman, where is your son?
> My son has gone to war and can't return.
> May he be choked by the bread he eats.
> And may he be drowned by the water he drinks.
> May he be swallowed by the earth he treads.
> Woman, what are you saying? For I am your son.
> Forgive me, son, for speaking badly of you.
> He drew out his sword and cut off her head. (pp. 79–81; 120–21)

In the haunting atmosphere created by the song, Pin and the
other partisans watch almost spellbound as Dritto and Giglia,
hypnotized by their desire for each other, absentmindedly stoke
the fire until the flames get out of hand. In the ensuing blaze,
which destroys the encampment and most of their weaponry
and supplies, the group's fragile sense of cohesion is destroyed
as well. The detachment relocates to a new campsite, but Dritto
knows he will be punished by the brigade's command; he is a
"finished man," who, in accordance with the strict rules of partisan justice, will most likely face a firing squad. Dritto's execution is deferred only because a joint action by the partisan brigade, in which Dritto's unit will have to participate, is about to
take place. But Dritto withdraws at this point from his role as
leader of the group, saying only that "I am ill . . . I can't come"
(p. 111; 156). On the day of the battle, Dritto delegates his command to Cousin and remains at the camp with Giglia. Dritto's
withdrawal into the private sphere of Eros is thus linked to a failure of the will to act. His desire is doubly destructive, since it
leads to both the breakup of the unit and his own execution. The
(hi)story of Dritto and his men thus appears to be governed by
an oedipal plot, which Pin's song ironically underscores. This
song is in fact a variant of the story of Perseus and the Medusa
(which is itself a variant of the Oedipus myth). The Medusa's
head, the sight of which hypnotizes man and turns him into
stone, represents the obstacle that sexuality poses to the hero's

quest unless it is regulated by patriarchal law.[67] In the song, the son has been initiated into manhood by the trials of war; when he at last returns home, however, he finds himself faced with the threat of destruction from another quarter, for the mother (Godea) curses her son for having abandoned her. By beheading his own mother, the son takes on the role of the symbolic Father, while the mother's body becomes the site of castration for the son. Like Perseus, the son saves himself from the loss of his manhood and power to act. Dritto, on the contrary, falls under the Medusa's hypnotic spell; his desire for Giglia, who is Mancino's wife and the only woman at the encampment, is expressly forbidden by the partisan code of war.[68] Like Oedipus himself, Dritto is the source of catastrophe for those closest to him and for the community at large.

Pin also withdraws from combat at the last moment, just when his wish to carry a rifle has finally been granted. Instead of going off to fight with the men, Pin decides that he too will stay behind, for his own desire to watch Dritto and Giglia make love is more than he can resist. Once again, then, Pin moves backward to a liminal position on the margins of the adult world, where he appears as a spectator looking in from the outside; once again he finds himself in the position of a voyeur, as a prisoner of his fantasy and his fears. For Pin, Giglia is in fact another simulacrum of the maternal body, and his voyeurism duplicates the foreclosure of oedipal "normalization." Following the theft and burial of the pistol, however, Pin's vision of the maternal body is no longer associated with a "long-forgotten happiness" but rather with entrapment. The maternal womb represents— like the spiders' nest with which it is associated—both a longed-for place of shelter and a frightening place of confinement. The spider is the archetypal symbol of the malevolent mother who keeps the child imprisoned in her web, and, like the Medusa, paralyzes her victims.[69] The ambivalence of Pin's relation to the image of the maternal body is apparent in his first encounter with Giglia, whose misleading name means "lily"—usually associated with "purity," "whiteness," and "virginity"—and makes her a specular double of Rina (who is "la Nera"): "'And who are you, child?' says Giglia, passing a hand over his thatch of scruffy hair, though Pin draws his head away as he has never been able to stand women's caresses. . . . 'Your little son! Didn't you realize last night that you were giving birth to someone?'" (p. 57; 94). The spell that makes Pin an eternal voyeur is, like the Medusa's gaze, that of a malevolent mother.[70] No positive father figure has, however, yet materialized to free Pin from his captivity. Dritto's failure, and the news that the unit will be broken up, appear nonetheless to have a constructive effect on Pin, for at this point the boy realizes that he alone can be his own father and liberator. The secret of his origin and the key to his path were his from the moment that he stole the pistol-as-phallus, but he failed to recognize this truth. Pin's return to the path to the nest of spiders thus appears as the fulfillment of his quest for selfhood in which all ties to the Family Romance are finally severed: "Now he will leave these windswept unknown parts and go far away, back to his own kingdom in the river-bed, back to the magic spot where the spiders make their nests. Down there his pistol is buried. . . . With his pistol Pin will become a partisan all on his own, with no one to twist his arm till it nearly breaks, no one to send him off to bury dead hawks. . . . He will do wonderful things, will Pin, always on his own" (p. 136; 186).

When Pin actually returns to the path to the nest of spiders, however, as the narrative draws to a close, his quest appears to have come to a definitive dead end. Pin goes back down the mountainside to "his place," only to find that it has been violated by Pelle, who has guessed where the path to the nest of spiders is and has already stolen the gun. Pin has fallen victim to a double betrayal, for his magic space has been invaded, and, as a consequence, he no longer has the talisman which was to be the key to his happiness:

Pin starts walking up the path, his heart in his mouth. Yes, there are his nests. But the earth is disturbed, some hand seems to have passed over it all, tearing up the grass, moving the stones, destroying the nests and breaking open their little doors; Pelle! Pelle knew the place; he's been here . . . scooped the loose earth out with his hands, pushed sticks into the tunnels and killed all the spiders one by one. . . .

Pin puts his head in his hands and sobs. No one will ever give him his pistol back now. . . . The pistol was the last thing Pin had in all the world; what is he to do now? (p. 138; 188)

The pistol, this eternally elusive object and signifier of desire, is once again missing, stolen, lost. In a reversal of Pin's original wish, the gun (whose disconcealment was to be the key to Pin's path to self-liberation) has been unearthed by a traitor to the partisan cause. Desire itself—which rules human existence and history—is, finally, only the Hegelian and Lacanian desire to desire. Pin is faced with an insurmountable absence or lack which forces him to seek satisfaction elsewhere: "What is he to do now?" The discovery of the spiders' nests destroyed by Pelle and the theft of the pistol that gave Pin his illusory self-identity mark the moment of Pin's confrontation with the violent desire of the Other, who constantly robs us of what we long for most of all—an authentic sense of identity and, with it, access to freedom.[71]

An Uncanny Ending

Pin has, finally, no choice but to go back to his sister in town. In spite of everything, the Dark Girl is relieved to see Pin again and welcomes him back into her apartment. She gives Pin a piece of German chocolate to eat and tells him that he should stop being a "rebel." Instead, she points out, he could stay with her and work for the Fascists; that way they will be able to survive together as best they can. The narrative of *The Path* has come full circle, and Pin has returned to the same position from which he started; the partisan experience has apparently made no difference for him. However, Pin discovers at this point that the pistol he thought definitively lost is in his sister's possession; a Fascist client—whom Pin guesses to be none other than Pelle himself—has given it to her so that she can protect herself: "One never knows these days" (p. 140; 189). Ironically, the pistol too has made its return to the place from which Pin originally stole it. This reemergence of Pin's magical object, talisman, and fetish— as the quintessential signifier of desire in the novel—starts the narrative off on a new cycle that duplicates the first one, for it leads to another theft and another departure. Pin takes the pistol from his sister and runs away once again, back to the path to the nest of spiders. Here Calvino's text comments explicitly on its own pattern of repetition: "Pin takes the path to the river-bed. He feels as if he were back at that night when he stole the pistol. Now he has his pistol, but everything is just as it was; he is alone in all the world, and lonelier than ever. And Pin's heart is overflowing with a single question: 'What shall I do?'" (p. 141; 191). The spatial configuration of the novel—through the meta-phor of the path to the nest of spiders, with its intricate web of connotations—once again depicts Pin's formation and his experience of the Resistance as a blind series of repetitions of sameness-in-difference, rather than as a linear progress towards liberation. The above passage confirms that the pattern of repeti-tion established in *The Path* through the recurrence of the meta-phoric motifs of the path, the pistol, the theft, and the eternally absent Great Friend works to undermine the organic form of the narrative. These metaphoric motifs call the reader's attention to the way in which each episode in Pin's story repeats or mirrors another episode, instead of marking a transitional point in the progress of the narrative towards its conclusion.[72] In the dizzy-ing vortex of doublings and mirrorings that engulfs Pin's quest, the possibility of development dissolves and is replaced by the image of a vicious circle.

The novel does provide Pin with at least one way out of his dilemma in its fairy-tale ending, which seems to solve in one stroke (as if with the touch of a magic wand) all the conflicts present in the narrative. As Pin wanders along in the dark, after taking back "his" pistol from Rina, he quite suddenly finds Cousin, the "good" partisan, standing on the path in front of him. Cousin, it seems, has finally come to rescue Pin and to fulfill his fantasy: "These are enchanted places, where magical things always happen. The pistol is enchanted too, like a magic wand. And Cousin is also like a great magician, with his tommy-gun and his woollen cap, as he puts a hand on Pin's shoulder and asks: 'Well, Pin, what are you doing down here?'" (p. 141; 191). In the final scene of the novel, Pin's desire to find a great friend is apparently at last fulfilled. Cousin and Pin walk off to-gether hand in hand into the night, leaving the path to the nest of spiders behind them. The narrative implies that Cousin is the sought-after father figure who will take Pin under his wing and carry him to that faraway land to which Babeuf flew in Pin's fantasy. With the appearance of Cousin on the path, then, Pin's quest would seem to have reached its logical conclusion. Although this interpretation satisfies our sense of a conventional ending or closure to a fairy tale, several elements in the ending contradict it; it is only a part of the story, and there is more to the ending of *The Path* than this.

Critics have generally glossed over the interpretive difficulties inherent in the conclusion of *The Path*. If read in the key of a conventional fairy tale, as is usually done and as the novel itself encourages us to do, the end of *The Path* seems indeed to suggest that Pin and Cousin "lived happily ever after." As long as the novel's end is interpreted along these lines, the overall sense of the work may appear to share unproblematically in the idealism and populism characteristic of the Italian neorealist "school."[73] By reading *The Path* in this key, many critics have concluded that its ending is not only wholly "escapist" but also deviates from the neorealist commitment to portraying the far-from-idyllic reality of the end of the war in Italy, and thus is symptomatic of Calvino's ideological contradictions as a bourgeois intellectual. However, still another reading, one which interprets the same ending in a different key, may instead uncover in it implications that can only be described as "uncanny" rather than idyllic or escapist. The conclusion of *The Path* is actually double-edged, and the narrative language used by Calvino to describe the final encounter of Pin with Cousin raises the possibility that Pin's story does not come to a happy ending but rather to one which—true to the tone of the rest of the work—is deeply marred by betrayal and deception.[74]

Before turning to this crucial scene, however, we need to examine briefly the notion of the "uncanny" (or the *unheimlich*) in more detail. For Todorov, the theory of the uncanny as a literary genre bordering on the fantastic finds its basis in Freud's famous essay. Todorov, it will be recalled, defines the uncanny as a narrative in which "events are related which may be readily accounted for by the law of reason, but which are . . . shocking, singular, disturbing or unexpected."[75] In the nineteenth cen-tury—Todorov argues—the fantastic-uncanny genre employs supernatural elements in order to represent forbidden themes relating to the perversions of human sexuality. In the twentieth century, on the other hand, psychoanalysis deals openly with such themes by rationalizing them. Since the end of the nine-teenth century, Todorov contends, psychoanalysis has therefore "replaced (and thereby made useless) the literature of the fan-tastic" (*Fantastic,* p. 160). Psychoanalysis eliminates the undecid-ability of the fantastic-uncanny because it demonstrates—as Freud states in *The Psychopathology of Everyday Life*—that "in the psychic life, there is nothing arbitrary, nothing undetermined" (*Fantastic,* p. 161). Yet Freud himself, in his essay on the un-canny, differentiates between the uncanny as a psychoanalytic concept and the uncanny as a literary strategy and provides us with a counter-argument to Todorov's:

> It may be true that the uncanny [*unheimlich*] is something which is se-cretly familiar [*heimlich-heimisch*], which has undergone repression and then returned from it, and that everything that is uncanny fulfils this condition. But the selection of material on this basis does not enable us to solve the problem of the uncanny. . . . Are we after all justified in entirely ignoring intellectual uncertainty as a factor? We might say that these preliminary results have satisfied *psychoanalytic* interest in the problem of the uncanny, and that what remains probably calls for an aesthetic enquiry.[76]

In his essay, Freud points in the direction of a specific "un-canniness"—or, in other words, a residue of uncertainty—that is generated by literary texts and that defies or transgresses against psychoanalytic logic and "reason." It is this literary un-canniness which cannot be fully rationalized from a psycho-analytic perspective. Indeed, if the logic of psychoanalysis has helped certain forbidden themes to emerge from the under-world of nineteenth-century fantastic literature, the uncanny—as a literary strategy of estrangement—still has a major role to play in the twentieth century by generating "intellectual" (as Freud says) uncertainties regarding the validity of psychoanalysis itself as a rational science of human behavior that can make our psychic "darkness" visible and comprehensible.

Once the world of everyday reality is evoked as the referential frame of a given work of fiction, Freud points out, the writer of the work is able to produce "intellectual uncertainty" in the reader by "keeping us in the dark for a long time about the precise nature of the presuppositions on which the world he writes about is based" and by "cunningly and ingenuously avoiding any definite information on the point to the last. . . . [In this way] fiction presents more opportunities for creating uncanny feelings than are possible in real life." [77] Our desire to know contrasts with the writer's desire to leave something unsaid, thus toying with the demands of understanding and the need of the reader for enigma. Looking at *The Path*'s ending from this perspective, we see that its uncanny effect is produced precisely by the narrative's *reticentia*, its deliberate and manipulative strategy of withholding information from the reader, and the intellectual uncertainty that it generates in relation to psychoanalytic logic itself (i.e. the normalization of the Oedipus complex as the necessary path to "normal" adulthood). As the novel draws to a close, the reassuringly paternal figure of Cousin—the Great Friend—returns to the place where the spiders make their nests from a shadowy, uncanny scene whose precise nature the reader is forever unable to ascertain but whose meaning is, in essence, the conclusion of Pin's odyssey of psychic and social estrangement.

Before the story comes to its fairy-tale conclusion, there is a brief but crucial detour that must not be overlooked. Cousin tells Pin that he has not been with a woman in a long time and that before they go off together back into the mountains he would like to pay a visit to the Dark Girl of the Long Alley, if Pin will tell him where she lives. Pin is disappointed; Cousin is—Pin thinks—like all the others, with his absurd desire for women. He nonetheless tells Cousin how to get to his sister's apartment in the old city. Pin laughs when he sees that Cousin is taking his weapon with him: "God, Cousin, are you taking your tommygun with you?" (p. 143; 193). When Cousin replies that he is afraid to go unarmed, Pin observes that Cousin's tommy-gun is too conspicuous to go unnoticed in the city and proposes that they exchange weapons, since the P.38 can be hidden more easily. Pin then waits for Cousin's return to the path:

> Now Pin is alone in the darkness, by the spiders' nests, with the tommy-gun on the ground near him. But he is no longer in despair. He has found Cousin, and Cousin is the great friend he has sought for so long, the friend who is interested in spiders' nests. . . .
> Shots, down in the Old Town. Who can it be? Patrols, perhaps, on their rounds. Shots, at night like that, are always frightening. Cousin was really rather rash to go alone into that nest of Fascists, for a woman. . . .
> He needn't begin worrying, though, for some time, he must wait. Instead of which he now sees a shadow coming nearer, and there he is already. (pp. 143–44; 194)

Cousin explains to Pin that he felt ashamed of his own desire and therefore returned "without doing anything." Pin is, not surprisingly, delighted by this turn of events: "He really is the Great Friend, Cousin is" (p. 144; 194). Yet once again things are not nearly as simple and univocal as they appear to be to Pin, or to many of the novel's readers and critics.

The narrative does not openly state whether the shots that come from the old city are pistol shots fired by Cousin at Pin's sister. However, Calvino implies that Cousin has indeed "executed" the Dark Girl; this act of violence takes place, so to speak, in the interstices of the text, and it is left up to the reader to decide what the meaning of this *reticentia* may be. The unanswered question in the above passage—"who can it be?"—echoes the opening line of Pin's song ("Who is it knocking at my front door?") and suggests that Cousin has indeed gone to knock at Rina's door, whose location Pin has just revealed to him. The first answer that comes to Pin's mind ("patrols, perhaps, on their rounds"), while plausible, is called into question by the irony of the preceding statement that "Pin understands these things." If anything, the narrative seems to suggest, Pin regularly misreads Cousin's (and the other adults') real motives and understands little at all about "these things." The text of *The Path* places such emphasis on the exchange of weapons between Pin and Cousin that the reader is consequently led to wonder why Cousin should carry Pin's gun into town on a visit to his sister, and at the same time, what Pin could possibly understand about the hidden meaning of this exchange. The gun is, of course, the privileged signifier of difference and desire in Calvino's novel (it is the "phallus" in the Lacanian sense of the term). In killing the Dark Girl, Cousin takes on the role of the forbidding father who administers the punishment that was first threatened by the men in the tavern scene. Pin's song prefigures this "scene" hidden in the interstices of the text; the gun is like the sword used by the son to cut off his own mother's head, and it is with Pin's gun, upon his "return" from the war, that Cousin kills Rina, who has been the only maternal figure in Pin's life. The reappearance of Cousin is, then, the fulfillment not only of Pin's dreams but also of his nightmares; yet it is unclear how much of this still eludes Pin's understanding at the end of his quest.

As *The Path* draws to a close, Pin's oedipal trajectory is at last complete, and with its completion he comes to the end of his own path to psychic maturity. The execution of the Dark Girl (even if Pin is unaware of it) breaks the vicious circle of repetition in his own life and marks the moment of his accession to culture and to history. The Dark Girl plays the role of the scapegoat whose ritual sacrifice (according to René Girard's interpretation of the Oedipus legend) serves to reestablish difference, thus ending the vicious circle of violent reciprocity that periodically violates cultural order.[78] Rina is—like Pin—a victim of the undifferentiated violence of the war, yet by prostituting herself to Fascists and non-Fascists alike, she is also the living embodiment of the violent reciprocity of the war. She represents the transgression of the difference between Fascist and non-Fascist that gives a meaning to the war for its participants and justifies the use of violence against the "other" side. At another level, she also represents a transgression of the very law on which the patriarchal order—and the order of psychoanalytic discourse—are founded: namely the traditional structure of the family and the right of the father to exclusive possession of the woman's body. From this perspective, Rina embodies an essential disorder in Italian society; she is an obstacle in Pin's path to freedom, or, in terms of the fairy tale, a monster that must be slain by the hero. It is the Dark Girl's death, and his subsequent break with the disorder that she represents, that allows Pin to escape from a condition in which he is fatherless and vulnerable to the violence of Fascists and partisans alike and to recognize at last the difference between enemy and friend through his identification with Cousin, who upholds the patriarchal cultural order.

This "happy ending" of *The Path*, with Pin's emergence as a historical subject, is predicated on the suppression of the Dark Girl, that is, on her erasure as a subject. Calvino takes pains to thematize the bitter irony of this process in the novel. Pin's new vision is achieved through an act of blindness; in becoming a subject, Pin is in effect the unknowing victim of duplicity and deceit. Cousin manipulates Pin in a number of ways, yet in order to hide his act of violence and (presumably) to gain Pin's admiration, he pretends to feel ashamed of his own sexual drive by letting Pin think that he never went to the Dark Girl's apartment. Thus Cousin succeeds in exerting his will over the child in a paradigmatic "paternal" fashion; he reappropriates the phallic signifier Pin had stolen, he sanctions his exclusive right to possess and punish the transgressive female body of the Dark Girl in the name of male "historical justice," and he captures Pin's admiration through the persuasive power of his words, presenting himself to Pin as a virile figure and role model.

Cousin's pathological hatred of women, of which the reader is aware from the outset, nevertheless suggests that he is far from being either a true representative of the "adult world" or a benevolent father figure for Pin. The text of *The Path* goes to considerable lengths to place Cousin's views on women, and on sexuality in general, in a questionable light. "I'd cut my soul out rather than have a son" (p. 54; 91), he declares when Mancino— seeing them appear together at the partisan encampment—asks him if Pin is his son. Cousin's antisocial behavior and his participation in the Resistance are, it turns out, motivated by an all-too-familiar mythical tale about history and its causes: "Of course, behind all the stories with a bad ending there's always a woman," he tells Pin when they first run into each other, "make no mistake about that. You're young, just listen to what I tell you. War's all due to women" (p. 51; 87). This recourse to a myth of woman as the essence of negativity—as, in short, the original cause of all that is destructive—as an explanation for the war reveals the patriarchal "reality principle" as a mystification of which Cousin himself is a victim. His mythical version of the role of woman as an annihilating force that "always" threatens to destroy man (a myth which appears altogether fantastic in the context of *The Path*) is a reversal of the historical reality of the patriarchal order, where woman is the object and the victim of male violence rather than its source. The myth of woman as man's curse is also, of course, linked to the myth of Prometheus as the "culture-hero"; "in the world of Prometheus, Pandora, the female principle, sexuality and pleasure, appear as curse— disruptive, destructive. . . . Prometheus is the culture-hero of toil, productivity, and progress through repression."[79] Cousin is no less a victim of repression than Pin himself, and the necessity of this repression for the sake of human progress is ironically the only wisdom and the only "reality principle" that Cousin imparts to Pin.

This emergence of the historical subject and Promethean "culture-hero" through the repression of the feminine figure as "other" is the focal center in the final page of the novel. The turning point in Pin's existence is thematized by Calvino through a particular version of the "return of the repressed," for, unlike any fairy tale, *The Path* closes on a deeply uncanny note. The "uncanniness" of the closing lines of the work is chiefly constituted by the astonishing appearance, like a ghost from the past, of the image of Cousin's dead mother. The last lines of *The Path* are as follows:

They walk off into the country, with Pin holding Cousin's big soft calming hand.
    The darkness is punctured with tiny spots of light; numberless fireflies are flickering over the hedges.
    "Filthy creatures, women, Cousin . . ." says Pin.
    "All of them . . ." agrees Cousin. "But they weren't always; now my mother . . ."
    "Can you remember your mother, then?" asks Pin.
    "Yes, she died when I was fifteen," says Cousin.

"Was she nice?"

"Yes," says Cousin, "she was nice."

"Mine was nice too," says Pin.

"What a lot of fireflies," says Cousin.

"If you look at them really closely, the fireflies," says Pin, "they're filthy creatures too, reddish."

"Yes," says Cousin, "but looking at them from here they are beautiful."

And they walk on, the big man and the child, into the night, amid the fireflies, holding each other by the hand. (p. 145; 195)

This abrupt appearance of the image of the lost mother in *The Path* may be defined—following Schelling's definition of the uncanny, which was later adopted by Freud—as the disclosure of something which ought to have been kept concealed but which has nevertheless come to light.[80] Cousin's allusion to his mother, who died when he was fifteen and who is unlike any other woman because she was *brava* (nice), throws an altogether different light on the story's apparently "happy ending" by revealing or "disconcealing" something that ought to have remained hidden.

Cousin recalls the venerated image of his mother immediately after telling Pin about the sense of disgust which prevented him from going to the Dark Girl as a client. Cousin's association of the mother figure with the prostitute is only momentary, however, and he immediately diverts Pin's attention and his own from it by focusing on the image of the *lucciole* ("fireflies") instead. The term *lucciole*, it should be noted, is still commonly used in colloquial Italian to refer to prostitutes. There is, therefore, an effect of displacement and condensation in this image which serves as the linguistic signal of an act of repression. But the uncanny meaning of this association between mother and whore will not let itself be easily deflected, resurfacing immediately in Pin's comment (which also alludes to the theme of vision, or the gaze, that is characteristic of the uncanny): "If you look at them really closely . . . fireflies . . . are filthy creatures too."[81] Pin's uncanny insight draws the reader back to the meaning of the text's *reticentia* and to the question of what it is that is being distanced and repressed in this scene. The "happy ending" of *The Path*, which apparently abolishes all hesitation and conflict, is contingent on and contiguous to the erasure of the Dark Girl and her replacement with the luminous image of the mother. Yet, at the same time, the destruction of the Dark Girl is the "blind spot" that the text will not allow the reader to forget. The Dark Girl's home in the *carrugio*, from which Cousin has just returned, is the site of what is truly *unheimlich*—it is, in so many words, the home that can no longer be a home for Pin.

In Pin's dialogue with Cousin at the end of the novel, a single, sublimated maternal figure replaces the threatening Eros possessed by the Dark Girl. From the perspective of the paternal "reality principle," Rina's undifferentiated Eros, along with all impulses to reestablish a lost narcissistic/maternal unity, must be repressed because they are perceived to threaten the ego with annihilation. Returning from what is essentially a scene of symbolic castration (the "execution" of Rina), Cousin appears as the savior who will allow Pin finally to free himself from his maternal space and to see his mother's image in the proper (i.e. distancing) perspective. The scene of castration itself—with its real and symbolic violence—is what must be distanced in order for Cousin to assume his role as a father figure who upholds the Law. Calvino's use of the *lucciole* metaphor stresses the ambivalence of this conclusion. Cousin describes the *lucciole* as "beautiful" when seen from afar, and this same image is usually interpreted by critics as a sign of hope. Cousin's description of the fireflies corresponds to a totalizing historical perspective in which individual wartime atrocities committed for the cause of the common good appear fully justified and even necessary. Within the historical context of the Liberation and the partisan movement, the killing of the Dark Girl appears as a just punishment for her crimes. It is also, according to this same interpretive line, part of a coherent and aesthetically satisfying overall narrative design, coinciding with the course of human liberation and progress. Like the anonymous German soldier whose death is envisioned by Kim in the concluding section of his interior monologue in chapter 9, the Dark Girl too is destined to be relegated to oblivion; she is erased by Cousin from the book of history. The scene of her death is therefore not included in the novel; only its traces remain in order to signify Pin's access to the realm of history through the mediation of Cousin. When he gives Cousin his pistol in order to kill his sister, Pin contributes unknowingly to the progressive movement of history as well as to his own liberation. Through this final gesture of his, each step of his odyssey over the course of *The Path* becomes retrospectively endowed with historical significance. Yet what allows the *lucciole* to appear beautiful is their distance from the eye of the observer; when Pin looks at them more closely, they only look like repulsive, "filthy" insects to him.

Pin is blinded not by the deceptive beauty of the fireflies but rather by the deceptive power of Cousin's words. Cousin's evocation of his dead mother, which in turn recollects the image of his own dead mother for Pin, generates an effect of ironic pathos for the reader, for Pin is unable to see through the mystification of Cousin's words. Pin has escaped from the degradation of his life with his prostitute sister only to become the unknowing instrument through which Cousin—who is himself the prisoner of a deluded notion of historical justice—has expressed his pathological hatred of all women, those repulsive creatures who must be destroyed in order to preserve the illusory but luminous beauty of his mother's distant image in his memory. But it is Pin's blindness that allows for a different insight into the story's conclusion and overall meaning. The term *lucciole* also appears in a proverbial Italian expression concerning the deception created by the illusion of distance: *prendere lucciole per lanterne* ("to mistake fireflies for lanterns"). In light of this other meaning, which Pin has already brought to our attention in his own vision of the *lucciole*, Cousin's "enlightened" judgment appears as an attempt to make fireflies look like lanterns in the eyes of Pin. The execution of the Dark Girl, in other words, appears in the end as a brutal scapegoat killing—rather than a morally and ethically justifiable act—of whose true nature Pin himself is ironically unaware.

Like Verga's *vinti*, Rina and Pin are members of the group of the down-and-out whose lives are rendered invisible by the blindingly bright light of history and progress. The optical metaphor used by Verga in the preface to *I Malavoglia* conveys this perspective on the historical process of modernity in terms that are strikingly similar to those of Calvino's novel:

The fateful, incessant, often difficult and feverish course that human-kind travels to achieve the conquest of progress is grandiose in its re-sults when seen as a whole, from a distance. The glorious light accom-panying it obliterates the anxieties, the greed, the selfishness, all the passions, all the vices that are turned into virtues, all the weaknesses that aid the tremendous task, all the contradictions from whose friction the light of truth is generated. . . . Only the observer, he too swept along by the flood, has the right to be interested, as he looks around, in the weak who fall by the wayside . . . the doomed who raise their arms in despair.[82]

Like Verga's *osservatore*, in his novel Calvino provides us with a different perspective on the course of historical progress by showing how the partisan struggle—this new Risorgimento in Italian history—may appear as a grand achievement only retro-spectively, in the dazzling light of the final Liberation. Seen from up close, though, in the perspective of the people who lived through it, the Resistance appears as a tortuous and tor-turous path marked by the contradictory intersection of individ-ual desires, frustrations, fears, power struggles, and suffering. For this second perspective on the Resistance, the word "Libera-tion" itself loses all meaning and becomes only an empty ab-straction. In the end Pin would seem to be all but liberated from the condition of marginality and subalternation in which he found himself at the beginning of his quest. Through Cousin—his long-awaited Great Friend—Pin has become the prisoner of a network of deception and duplicity which ironically confirms his initial perception of the adult world (and of history itself) as "a tale of blood and naked bodies." Contrary to Verga, though, who writes in the name of a more enlightened "truth," Calvino excludes the possibility of transcending this discrepancy in per-spectives. As the narrative comes to its end, we are unable to interpret its closure as the necessary and "happy" outcome of Pin's progress toward liberation and "historical consciousness."

The critic Cesare Cases has pointed out the constitutive am-bivalence generated by the metaphor of the fireflies in Calvino's novel. Borrowing an expression of Nietzsche's, he defines this ambivalence as "the *pathos* of distance"; Cousin's and Pin's opposing perspectives represent "extreme situations" and "the mutilation of man." [83] But the conclusion that Cases draws from this observation fails to grasp the irony of Calvino's text. *The Path*, Cases claims, sets itself the task of healing this alienated vision of man, "something which can happen only in a fairy tale." He does not see, then, that the irony generated by Pin's "entrance" into history—hand-in-hand with the partisan Cousin at the end of the Resistance—is caused precisely by its being couched in the language of fairy tales. By projecting the end of Pin's estrangement into a fantasy world, in fact, the novel generates yet another in a long series of ambivalent meanings. The ending may indeed be interpreted as the positive vision of a historical future for Pin; compared to the nightmare of Fascism and the war, Pin's future looks like the fulfillment of a fantasy. But the ending may also be interpreted as implying that Pin's redemption is indeed *only* a utopian fantasy, in which case the pathos of distance remains.

The Path, like all of Calvino's self-reflexive narratives, implicitly foresees its own misreading by thematizing misreading itself. Pin is in fact a naive reader (almost archetypically so), since he lacks the codes and the frames of reference needed to understand the meaning of the words that he hears and the things that happen to him. Particularly at the end of the novel, Pin sees Cousin not for what he is but rather—in a crucial equivocation—as the fulfillment of his old dream of the "Great Friend." Pin makes the fundamental error of literalizing a figure of speech: "He is truly the Great Friend, Cousin" (p. 143; 193). [84] The narrative subverts this reading by supplying the information necessary to understand the way in which Pin is powerfully self-deluded. Yet many readers have been unwilling or—like Pin—unable to see beyond the literal meaning and have continually mistaken *lucciole per lanterne*. The two possible readings of the novel's ending are, in the last analysis, irreconcilable. The second, figural reading suggests that the perspective of Pin's redemption is an ironic trompe l'oeil, and that the devastation of the lives of the *vinti* will continue long after the Liberation has passed into the annals of history itself. The pattern of repetition which defines

Pin's deluded quest prevents any easy interpretation of *The Path* on the basis of the linear sequence of the story. As an emplotment of the history of the Resistance, unlike so many other works in the neorealist vein, Calvino's novel raises more questions than it answers. *The Path*—above and beyond its reference to the events of 1944–45 in northern Italy—insistently confronts the reader with the problem of the interpretive indeterminacy of human action. It interrogates the meaning of a collective historical "reason" which cannot account for the degradation and suffering of individuals. It posits the dilemma of a "trans-subjective subject"—that of the collective partisan movement—that perpetuates the very same structures of domination and the very same strategy of repression of individual desire which it condemns as inhuman in the enemy. Finally, *The Path* asks whether a political philosophy or ideology that remains blind to the reasons of the body, of sexuality, and of desire is indeed a legitimate basis for the transformation of history, even if it claims to speak in the name of those who stand to gain the most from such a transformation.

6 • Reading in the Book of the World: A Dialogue of Interpretive Models

Chapter 9 of *The Path*: The Politics of Myth

There can be little doubt that, in *The Path*, Calvino thinks and writes—like so many of his European contemporaries in the 1940's—*à partir de* Marx and Freud. Yet he also takes a definite critical distance from them both; the fictional arguments that are put forward in *The Path* are neither Marxist nor Freudian in any generally accepted sense (as is evident in the contemporary critical reception of the novel in Italy). Calvino seeks rather to *dialogize* Marxist and Freudian thought in his work of fiction, playing each off against the other in an effort to challenge dominant modes of neorealist representation in postwar Italian narrative and hegemonic cultural assumptions in Italian society. The purpose of his fiction writing is to provide readers with access—no matter how indirectly—to psychic and sociopolitical dimensions of existence that are expurgated, forgotten, or simply unavailable not only in the "master-text" of high culture but also within the codes that organize perception in everyday life. In particular, and whether this takes the form of reflection on the problem of alienation in social or in psychic life, *The Path* seeks to examine what is left unsaid in neorealist discourse and in its claims to represent and criticize the conditions of existence in Italy in the 1940's. This literary dialogization explores what is left unsaid not only in the aesthetics and politics of neorealism but also in Marxist and Freudian theory itself, especially in their respective modes of emplotment of human experience and history. Chapter 9 makes this its central concern and thus stands at the center of the novel's interpretive labyrinth.

Most of the critics who object to the ninth chapter of *The Path*, and they are many, argue that it either destroys the novel's organicity or fails to integrate the different levels and themes of the rest of the narrative into an organic whole of its own. The ninth chapter, these critics claim, represents an unsuccessful attempt on Calvino's part to provide an interpretation of the ideology of the Resistance and to remedy the political contradictions implicit in his own novel.[1] Carlo Annoni, for example, finds that chapter 9 tries to justify—in terms of an optimistic and overly simplistic vision of history as progress—its author's inability to think through the problem of the relationship between Italian intellectuals and workers, or partisans and Fascists. The lack of an organic political vision is reflected in turn—according to Annoni—in Calvino's failure to reconcile the fairy-tale motifs, the ideological-political themes, and the theme of sexuality in the novel.[2] Other critics, on the contrary, find that the same chapter recomposes and organizes the narrative into just such an organic, realistically mimetic whole. Giovanni Falaschi contends that chapter 9 resolves all the formal and thematic contradictions of *The Path* and provides a unified political interpretation of the narrated events, precisely because it offers an accurate understanding of the overall meaning of the partisan struggle. Its story is therefore integrated with history; it is through the laws of history—according to Falaschi—that the individual behavior of the partisans is rationally explained in this chapter; this is why *The Path* is essentially a work of realism, despite its imaginative deformation of the real. In this perspective, chapter 9 fully clarifies the sequential logic and the overall meaning of the narrated events of the work in terms of the logic of history.[3]

These paradigmatically opposed readings of *The Path* share, however, a fundamental presupposition: namely, a belief in "organicity" as the only valid form which historical, political, ideological, and artistic representation can take. By directing our attention to this notion of "realistic" organicity and what is at stake in it, both of these interpretations in turn help us to see that the very same notion of organicity itself figures as a central problem of chapter 9. "Organicity" is ultimately the equivalent of totalization, as Lukács's work shows, since it calls for all narrative elements—whether in a *grand récit* or a realist novel—to be grasped together by a single interpretive code. Although he affirms the value of such totalizations Calvino at the same time thwarts the reader's "mimetic" desire for organicity and a unified meaning in *The Path* by deferring the closure of signification. Calvino's resistance to neorealism emerges in chapter 9 not as a denial of the intrinsic narratability of the real (which is neorealism's fundamental assumption) but as a reminder that the real is susceptible to a multiplicity of narrative representations whose motivation (or emplotment) is rooted in the narrator's subjectivity, rather than—as Lukács claims—in the objective totality of the real itself.

•

The ninth chapter is divided into three principal segments. The first is set up as an encounter between the men of the partisan detachment to which Pin belongs and the two leaders of the larger partisan brigade: Ferriera, the commander, and Kim, the political commissar. By providing a link between Dritto's men and the brigade at large, Ferriera and Kim also function as mediators between the partisan detachment and the historical process of the Resistance. They come to the camp to announce and organize a joint action to be carried out the following day, together with other partisan brigades, against a German column advancing toward the mountains. For this "decisive battle"— Ferriera orders—everyone "must go into action, without any exception" (p. 99; 142). This will be the first battle to involve Pin directly, as well as the first actual scene of combat to figure in the narrative. The first segment of chapter 9, then, leads the reader quite naturally to expect that the following chapter will be both the climax of the story and a crucial point in Pin's itinerary from the margins of history (the mythic "place where the spiders make their nests") to its center. However, the battle itself is not climactic and is not even shown to the reader in the following chapter. Like the death of the Dark Girl in the final chapter of *The Path*, this event takes place offstage, and Pin does not witness it, for, defying Ferriera's orders, he stays behind in camp during the fighting. Chapter 9 thus comes at a crucial juncture in the story of Pin's search for a place in history and offers a key to understanding Pin's destiny and its implications for *The Path*. The rest of the chapter, on the other hand, serves as a critical/ philosophical interlude in the novel, one which asks the reader to pause and reflect on the meaning of the action that has been narrated thus far. This interlude is "staged" as a dialogical exchange of questions and answers, first in the form of a philosophical discussion between Ferriera and Kim in the second segment of the chapter, and then in the form of Kim's inner ruminations in the third and conclusive segment. Through the dialogically opposed voices of Ferriera and Kim, and the self-questioning of Kim himself, Calvino tries both to find a rational explanation for the plight of people like Pin and to analyze the gamut of possible causes of their involvement in the Resistance. In the course of the conversation between Kim and Ferriera, and later in Kim's interior monologue, a series of hypotheses is elaborated, each of which corresponds to an interpretive model or paradigm which could potentially lead to the discovery of these causes. Yet these explanations are all ultimately found by Calvino to be inherently unsatisfactory, for Kim's point of view on the meaning of history and on the role Pin plays in the historical process poses insurmountable obstacles to the legitimation of such ideological and narrative paradigms, and to their incorporation into the overall design of the novel. Thus Kim's function in the narrative is both that of explicitly thematizing the political and ideological concerns of Calvino's own form of (neo)realism and of exposing its limitations. Perhaps here, more than anywhere else, Calvino openly portrays the difference between critical interpretation and fiction as an illusory one.

Ferriera is a worker who has developed his class consciousness and his Marxist vision of history through his experiences in the factories of northern Italy. For him, partisan warfare is as exact and precise as the operation of a lathe or a press, and the strategies needed to drive history ahead are equally clear to him. "Ferriera knows why he fights, everything is perfectly clear to him" (p. 101; 144); significantly, Pin is not even mentioned in Ferriera's remarks except in an indirect manner. Ferriera disapproves of Kim's idea for a partisan unit such as Dritto's, made up of men who cannot be trusted: "If we'd divided them up among the good ones it might have kept them on the right lines. . . . Let's straighten them out the way I say" (pp. 99–100; 143–44). For Ferriera, with his foundational reason and strong class affiliation, the proletariat must assume a hegemonic position in the united struggle of the exploited against the exploiters. "Lumpenproletarians" such as Pin and the men in Dritto's band must be made aware of the need to fight for the communist cause alongside the workers. Ferriera, in fact, reproaches Kim for not attempting to politicize Dritto's band: "The political work you ought to be doing, it seems to me, is mixing them all up together and giving a class-consciousness to those who haven't got it, so as to achieve this blessed unity" (p. 100; 143–44). Ferriera's understanding of "unity" and his vision of the goals of the partisan movement are far more radical than the official policy of the PCI during the Resistance (see Chapter 4 of the present work). He is one of the many communist militants who think of the Resistance chiefly as a class struggle, but significantly enough, he is not the political commissar of the brigade, only the military commander. Kim, who has a much more orthodox notion of unity—a notion entirely consistent with CLN policy— is instead in charge of the political leadership of the brigade.

Kim's political commitment to the cause of the Communist party is based on a Marxist notion of history as "the great machine of class movements" (p. 96; 139). However, as a bourgeois intellectual, he believes himself to be—unlike Ferriera—on the margins of the historical conflict rather than at its center. This condition of marginality in point of fact places him in a privileged critical position, though; on the one hand he is, unlike Ferriera, able to perceive and empathize with the predicament of Pin and those like him, since Pin and Dritto's men are as mar-

ginal to the course of history as he is. Being a peripheral observer rather than a protagonist of the class struggle, he also
has—on the other hand—a more dispassionate and altogether
broader view of the historical process, and he is presumably capable of seeing it and describing it in a more complete and objective fashion. Kim is presented, throughout chapter 9, as a lucid
and intelligent observer of human reality in wartime; in his work
as a commissar he employs a "scientific" approach which allows
him to interpret specific situations and conflicts in terms of a rational theory of the overall Italian social and historical situation.
Thus the answer that he provides to the question of Pin's fighting is: "He doesn't know it's so that he should no longer be the
brother of a prostitute" (p. 105; 149). Kim has allowed each partisan unit to develop its own "spontaneous" identity, for the
purpose of analyzing their behavior closely; he wants to discover
what drives them to fight for the Liberation and thus to contribute consciously or unconsciously to the historical process as a
rational, progressive, and emancipatory movement. His chief
methodological premise is that all findings at the level of the
individual partisans themselves will eventually lead up in a
smooth and seamless way to the broadest, most inclusive gener-
alities, and that historical generalization will in turn mesh with
the empirical data gathered from individual test cases:

He has a great yearning for logic, for certainty about cause and effect. . . . He has an enormous interest in humanity; that is why he is a
medical student, for he knows that the explanation of everything is to
be found in the grinding moving cells of the human body, and not in
philosophic speculation. He will become a mental specialist, a psychiatrist. People do not like him very much because he looks them fixedly in
the eyes as if he were trying to discover the source of their thoughts;
and then he comes out suddenly with point-blank questions that have
nothing to do with the conversation, about the other's childhood or
love-life. For him also, behind human beings, there is the great machine
of class movements, the machine that is fed by little daily gestures and
in which other gestures burn away without leaving a trace; the machine
of history. (pp. 95–96; 138–39)

While Kim possesses a basically Marxist vision of history as the
history of class struggle, he is also interested—as a future psychiatrist—in a different kind of history, one that was consis-

tently neglected by Marx's interpreters of the period: the history of the psychic formation of personality from childhood on and the analysis of the innermost drives of the individual subject. His is, in other words, an attempt to reconcile the basic tenets of Marxism with those of Freudianism, and through this project of Kim's Calvino thematizes his own efforts at such a reconciliation in the fictional framework of *The Path*. Kim's quest to integrate the analysis of the psychobiological drives and desires of individual subjects with the inexorable logic of modern history makes him an alter ego or, better still, a persona of the novelist himself. The assonance of the names Pin/Kim is only one among a number of elements in the text which would suggest that the two characters represent in effect a fictional doubling (*dédoublement*) of the author's empirical self. If Pin represents Calvino's own sense of estrangement and bewilderment when faced with the war and the Resistance, Kim stands for Calvino's commitment, as a "progressive" and "engaged" intellectual, to understanding and analyzing those same historical experiences within the general guidelines of Italian left-wing critical culture.[4]

Kim is, like Calvino himself, aware of the fundamental contradictions in his search for a totalizing historical rationality. He recognizes that no single theory can account for the discrepancy between the patterns of individual existence and the collective logic of the historical process: "Everything must be logical, everything must be understood, both in history and in men's minds; but there is still a gap between one and the other, a dark area where collective reasons become individual reasons, forming monstrous deviations and unexpected combinations" (p. 96; 139). So, while Kim "studies the men, analyzes the position of each one, breaking every problem down into its component parts; 'a, b, c,'" (p. 96; 139), there nevertheless remain "ambiguous or dark areas" (p. 104; 148) which cannot be reconciled with the vision of history as a unified and rational totality so deeply ingrained, for instance, in Lukács's theory of realism. It is Kim who has decided to let Dritto's men have a band of their own but for reasons that do not entirely coincide with the CLN policy of patriotic "national unity." In the interest of a more comprehensive and scientific analysis, Kim places himself "experimentally" on the same level of observation and perception as Pin and his comrades in order to see their reality at first hand for himself. In so doing, however, Kim comes to the disturbing conclusion—at least in his own eyes—that the overall historical meaning of the Resistance struggle may indeed be something mythical, that is, arbitrary and provisional rather than logical and necessary. As Kim points out in his reply to Ferriera's objections to the isolation of Dritto's men from the more politicized partisan units, in fact, Ferriera's communist ideal is as meaningless for Dritto's men as is the ideal of a free *patria* (home and fatherland). They cannot be asked to fight for the freedom of the *patria* any more than they can be asked to fight for the hegemony of the working class, because they identify neither with the idea of a *patria* nor with the idea of a working class. They are literally homeless, workless, and classless—lacking in any authentic affiliation or group interest—and are therefore indifferent to any kind of political discourse that relies on these categories as a means of persuasion. They are subjects who survive on the edges and in the hidden folds of the social fabric, or slip through its fissures and tears and are lost forever to the world of "productive work." Kim's analysis in retrospect is suggestive of the thought of Althusser; Dritto's men are elusive political and historical subjects because they are on the margins of the discourse of the ideological state apparatus, one which defines the subject's position in the first place and makes it the "place" to which the representations of ideology are directed.[5] Unlike all the other participants in the Resistance struggle, Kim points out, Dritto's men lack an ideological framework which could motivate their actions toward specific goals and so are condemned to be swept back and forth by the powerful tides of history.

Kim uses the widely different meanings that the word *patria* possesses for the people who have joined the partisans (officially called "patriots" by the CLN) in order to show how each class and each group articulates its specific identity and its relation to the social and historical process on the basis of an "ideal," or, in other words, an ideology. It is this ideology—a more or less conscious and objective way (in Kim's perspective) of imagining both their relation to the real and the way this relation can be changed—that gives the different classes and groups a sociopolitical identity and impels them to action. For the peasants, for example, the defense of the *patria* means the defense of what they themselves own, which is also what they *are*: "The Germans burn their villages, take away their cattle. Theirs is a basic human war, one to defend their own country" (p. 101; 145). By identifying their property as their *patria*, though, the peasants may be easily manipulated by the conservative ideology of Fascism: "To keep all that they become spies, Fascists . . . there are whole villages which are our enemies" (p. 101; 145).

The industrial workers have, on the other hand, a quite different vision of what the *patria* is. Their identity as a class, which is bound up with their specific story of wages, strikes, and unions, has made them conscious of all that they are denied by the present political order and of the fact that they must fight in order to assert their claim to dignity and freedom. The ideology of the workers is the most objective one of all, according to Kim, for "there's no sentimentality in them. They understand reality and how to change it" (p. 101; 145). Their notion of the *patria* corresponds to the socialist society of the future. The intellectuals and students who fight in the Resistance tend, on the contrary, to have only "vague and twisted ideas," and Kim implicitly includes himself in this category. They are the victims of a mystified ideological vision: "Their 'country' consists of words, or at the most of some book" (p. 102; 145). However, Kim thinks (and he is obviously referring to himself as well) that their contact with the workers in the partisan struggle will help them to see through the inherent contradictions of their own way of thinking. Finally, among the partisans there are also many non-Italians, who have escaped from Nazi prison camps. They fight for yet another *patria*, a nation this time, which they imagine as the very thing that gives them an identity, precisely because they are exiled from it.

Kim comes to the conclusion that, while the partisan struggle is a legitimate fight for freedom and justice which will have genuine historical consequences, it is paradoxically based on a multiplicity of imaginary representations of the real. Each group involved in the Resistance imagines—in a different way—that the defeat of the Nazis and the Fascists will restore it to an ideal *patria*, a state of being "at home" in an organic social community, free from the threat of exile, exploitation, or dispossession. Each group fights the Nazis and Fascists because the latter stand for something negative that must be overcome and transcended, but this "something" is different for each group and represents in each instance the symbolic expression of a different kind of desire. Thus the notion of a "common goal" shared by all the partisans and the idea of the Resistance as a fundamentally unified national movement are both discovered by Kim to be a mythic synthesis of substantially heterogeneous ideologies and class interests. The single myth of the *patria* that must be rescued from the enemy, Kim realizes, masks over an infinity of divergent and reciprocally contradictory desires; the partisans are thus engaged in a deluded collective quest for liberation, since liberation itself signifies something different for each one of them. The Nazis and Fascists are not, in the last analysis, the actual enemy but rather a symbolic target of hatred, which permits all violence to be channelled in a single direction, while at the same time disguising the true nature of each individual subject's desire, Kim concludes: "Don't you see that this is a struggle made entirely of symbols? That in order to kill a German one must think not of that German but of something else, with a play of substitutions that is enough to turn one's brain, because everything and everybody have become part of a Chinese shadow-play, a myth?" (p. 102; 146). Ferriera finds this skeptical conclusion of Kim's—which effectively forecloses the possibility of political action, short of a general unleashing of violence in an infinity of conflicting directions—unacceptable, and even incomprehensible, from his point of view. Ferriera, with his "ice-cold eyes" that see "no ambiguous or dark areas" and with his belief that the partisan struggle is a finely tuned machine of which he knows the workings and the purpose, embodies an unshakable political faith (as his name, which means literally "ironworks," as well as "forge" and "foundry," suggests) in the strategic value of the Resistance as a Gramscian "war of maneuver." For him, the Resistance in Italy is indeed a significant step forward in the international war against capitalism and private property. When seen in this perspective that seamlessly blends together politics with a philosophy of history, the fact that the peasants are fighting in the Resistance in order to *defend* private property or that the foreign partisans are fighting to defend their national identity, does not appear contradictory to Ferriera. His disapproval of Kim's "experimental" segregation of the partisan units according to their common interests is consistent with his belief that the revolutionary goal of the Resistance transcends all individual contradictions, sacrifices, and losses, fully justifying the "straightening out" and (eventually) the elimination of those who do not belong to the working class. Ferriera's response suggests that Kim's insight into the mythic nature of the anti-Fascist unity is only an intellectual mystification and that Kim's political vision is blurred and out of focus, because he is not looking at the Resistance from a "correct" political perspective. Ferriera's bird's-eye view of the historical process, with its foundational axiom of inevitable revolution, however, makes him in turn blind to the specific realities that fill the field of Kim's vision. For the former, Kim's insight and judgment are distorted by his proximity to the individuals in the partisan units, which has made him lose sight of the ultimate strategic goal of the Resistance movement, yet all else is without importance in comparison to that goal. In the ninth chapter of *The Path*, then, Kim's insight is Ferriera's blindness, and vice versa.

Unexpectedly, however, as the conversation continues, Kim reverses himself and finally agrees with Ferriera, in a guilt-ridden effort to see things the way Ferriera and the workers do: " 'No, it's not like that,' Kim goes on, 'I know that too. It's not like that'" (p. 102; 146). At this point Kim provides an explanation of the meaning that Dritto's unit has for him and of his "invention" of Dritto's unit as a symbol of the essence of the Resistance. Since the men of Dritto's detachment have "nothing to defend and nothing to change" or, in other words, since they have no *patria* and yet fight nonetheless, Kim reasons, there must be an authentic common denominator which unites them to the others. Their participation in the Resistance proves that the struggle is motivated by something that precedes ideology and is not mythic, but rather expresses an elementary human desire for freedom:

> Because there's something else, common to all of them. Take Dritto's detachment; petty thieves, *carabinieri*, ex-soldiers, black marketeers, down-and-outs; men on the fringes of society, who got along somehow, with nothing to defend and nothing to lose. . . . No revolutionary idea can ever appear there, linked as they are to the millstones grinding them. Or if it does it will be born twisted, the child of rage and humiliation. . . . Why do they fight, then? They have no "country," either real or invented. And yet you know there's courage, there's fury in them too. It is the injury of their lives, the darkness of their streets, the filth of their homes, the obscenities they've known ever since childhood, the strain of having to be bad. (p. 102; 146)

Here Kim alludes to Pin's life as prototypical of the life of the insulted and the injured, whose *furore* ("fury" and "wrath") corresponds to an instinctive rebellion against the inhuman conditions in which they are forced to live and to a natural (if inarticulate) desire for freedom. The *furore* which motivates Dritto's men represents for Kim the genuine origin of the Resistance struggle; it offers a source of legitimacy for the latter which Ferriera's theory completely overlooks. According to Kim, only the discovery of this point of origin allows for a vision of the Resistance as an essentially motivated and meaningful action unfolding in history toward a specific end. The very fact of the existence of Pin and of Dritto's men discloses the hidden reality of the Resistance as a chapter in a single fundamental narrative, which is the history of all of humanity—not just one group or class—as a struggle for freedom from oppression.[6] The men in Dritto's band—like Pin himself, who is its most marginal member—feel the desire for freedom that propels this master narrative forward in its most instinctive form. This desire becomes fully conscious of itself and of its revolutionary value only in the industrial working class, however, which has (according to Kim) the clearest and most pragmatic vision of reality because it is most aware of its own alienation within the capitalist system. Kim's *punto d'arrivo*—the end point of his own desire for a totalizing historical rationality—is "to be able to think like Ferriera, to see no other reality but Ferriera's. Everything else doesn't count" (p. 104; 148).

The potentially endless play of symbolic displacements that open up the partisan struggle to a mythic dimension can therefore be closed off, subsumed and contained within the logic of a unified historical narrative. The story of each individual is a part of the same plot, Kim reasons, which is that of the history of the desire for liberty: "This is the real meaning of the struggle now, the real, absolute meaning, beyond the various official meanings. An elementary, anonymous urge for emancipation from all our humiliations; the worker from his exploitation, the peasant from his ignorance, the petty bourgeois from his inhibitions, the outcast from his debasement" (pp. 103–4; 147). However, the basis for Kim's rationalization of the Resistance movement turns out to be an unreliable one, for the desire for freedom that orients the actions of Dritto's men and leads them to fight— he soon realizes in his philosophical dialogue with himself— constantly threatens to turn into a mimetic desire for violence in which the difference between enemy and ally is ultimately effaced. Kim has to admit that the possibility of reversal is always present and that it threatens to dissolve the logic of his narrative totalization of the "real, absolute meaning" of the quest for freedom: "Any little thing, a false step, a momentary impulse, is enough to send them over to the other side, to the Black Brigade, like Pelle, there to shoot with the same fury, the same hatred, against either side, it doesn't matter which" (p. 103; 146). The desire of the outcast for a more authentic mode of existence turns into a desire to insult and injure others—or even, in Dritto's case, to self-destruct—through what René Girard has called "the reciprocity of violence."[7] When Kim concludes that every subject fights for something different, he acknowledges the arbitrary nature of the distinction between "good" and "bad" violence, a distinction upon which the unity of the partisans (and, for Girard, of any such group) is based. As the actions of Pelle and Dritto show, there is no limit to violence once this distinction is dissolved; the death instinct is but its ultimate and most disturbing manifestation (again according to Girard).[8]

In this light, then, Kim's distinction between the partisans and their enemies appears to be an impossibly contradictory one. Are not those on the other side driven by the same basic *ressentiment* as well? If this is so, then what is it that makes them the antagonists rather than the protagonists of the narrative of human history, or even requires them—like the Dark Girl—to be erased from its pages altogether? Ferriera, in fact, immediately points out the weakness in Kim's argument: "So you think the spirit of our men . . . and the Black Brigade's . . . the same thing?" (p. 103; 146). He reminds Kim that, contrary to what the latter would like to think, no difference between a "good" and "bad" use of violence can be established outside of the confines of ideology; violence may only be justified in terms of some ethical or political belief, not in terms of a supposedly neutral philosophical or psychoanalytical logic. Hence the need, in Ferriera's mind, to "straighten out" Dritto's men and to give a specific political direction to their spontaneous *furore*.[9] Partisan acts of violence do not correspond, from his own point of view, to an innate human need for freedom which could be said to precede all ideological representations of the real.

Faced with Ferriera's objection, Kim is forced to admit that his own vision of the Resistance as a chapter in the history of human liberation is—and his reply makes this clear—a mythic totalization in its own right. Any difference between "good" and "bad" violence can be drawn only by setting up a system of symbolic oppositions and endowing them with positive and negative values within the framework of a totalizing narrative logic. It is precisely the difficulty in determining—within the specific historical context of the Resistance—where this negativity should be located, and who the real antagonist is in the narrative's development towards its ultimate goal of freedom for all, that mars Kim's vision:

"The same thing, the same thing . . . but, if you see what I mean . . ." Kim has stopped, with a finger pointing as if he were keeping the place in a book, "The same thing but the other way round. Because here we're in the right, there they're in the wrong. Here we're achieving something, there they're just strengthening the rivets. The age-old burden of evil which weighs down on Dritto's men, on all of us, including you and me, and which finds expression in shooting and killing enemies, is the same that makes the Fascists shoot, that leads them to kill, with the same hope for purification, for emancipation. But then there is history. There is the fact that in history, we are on the side of emancipation, and they are on the other side. With us nothing is lost, not a gesture, not a shot, though each may be the same as theirs—do you see what I mean?—they will all serve if not to free us then to free our children, to create a humanity that is serene, without rage, a humanity in which no one has to be bad. The other side is the side of lost gestures, of useless fury, lost and useless even if they should win, because they do not make history, they do not liberate but only perpetuate the same fury and the same hatred, until in another twenty or a hundred or a thousand years it will begin all over again, the struggle between us and them; and we shall both be fighting with the same anonymous hatred in our eyes, though always, perhaps without knowing it, *we* shall be fighting to free ourselves from it, *they* to remain its slaves." (p. 103; 147–48)

At this point Kim's argument shifts its ground. Turning away from Ferriera's rigidly deterministic Marxist vision, he puts forward a theory which he hopes will integrate the particular and the universal, the daily gestures of Dritto's men and the whole history of humanity, with the notion of the fundamental purposefulness of human history in its totality. The history of the world, he now contends, is a narrative in which the smallest details, the most banal everyday acts, and the most disparate phenomena—in short, all things that appear mutually incongruous or inconsequential—are unified and organized in such a way as to become meaningful parts of a global design. The book Kim envisions has the form of a teleological narrative of universal dimensions, and his argument becomes a sort of prophetic gloss that allows him to resolve apparent contradictions through allegorization.

Although no theological overtones are present in Kim's discussion, the multi-levelled narrative of the Holy Scriptures, with their epic structure of unsurpassed range, consistency, completeness, and "seamy side of bits and pieces,"[10] serves as the model for the book in which he reads. Kim interprets the history of humanity as a conflict between good and evil that will lead to the redemption of man and to his restoration to the realm of freedom in a classless society. Within this salvational allegorical design, Pin's individual plight, the apparently senseless and endless series of betrayals, and the suffering which marks his existence are no longer devoid of all meaning. Pin may not know it, but his experience is, like the exile of the chosen people, a part of a vast struggle for the liberation of humanity from bondage.

The Holy Scriptures are certainly not the only example in world literature of a text in which myth and actual history are inseparable; however, they provide the single most influential Western model for a teleological interpretation of history as a universal narrative encompassing the destiny of mankind as a whole. On the basis of the Scriptural model, the particular story of the Resistance and the partisan struggle for the liberation of Italy can be rewritten and reinterpreted in global terms; it is this universal and teleological perspective that allows Kim to perceive the struggle's "real, absolute meaning, beyond the various official meanings." "When we do look into it"—writes Northrop Frye—"we find that the sense of unified continuity is what the Bible has as a work of fiction, as a definitive myth extending over time and space, over invisible and visible orders of reality, and with a parabolic dramatic structure of which the five acts are creation, fall, exile, redemption, and restoration."[11] The desire to transcend the present condition of "exile" from the true *patria* and the perspective of a future "restoration" to an original state of freedom are the chief elements of Kim's resolutely secular teleology; this interpretation—Calvino would seem to imply—underscores the oft-noted parallel between the Christian and Marxist approaches to the narration of history.[12] Yet as seductive as the Scriptural model of teleology may appear, both as an interpretive and as a narrative ideal, in *The Path* it still does not provide a satisfactory answer for either Kim or the reader. We have already seen how the narrative oscillates at the end and leaves the prospect of Pin's redemption a problematic one at best. Indeed, if the conclusion of *The Path* finally rejects even this last interpretive model, it is because there is no place in it for Pin. In Calvino's own fable of estrangement, Pin is neither on the side of the winners nor on the side of the losers, neither in the book of history nor excluded from it; he is by definition outside of any global narrative design of the kind that Kim seeks to define. His involvement in the struggle that (at least according to

Kim) will redeem him does not in point of fact ever take place in the novel, except in the highly ambiguous and arguably tragic form of his unknowing participation in his sister's execution by Cousin.

In chapter 9 itself, moreover, the feasibility of this Scriptural interpretive model is questioned first by Ferriera, who finds Kim's reasoning overly abstract and insufficiently dialectical, and then even by Kim himself, when he walks alone toward the next partisan camp as the chapter draws to a close. Mentally reviewing the implications of his argument, Kim is filled with doubt once again. At the heart of his search for a historical *telos* lies a fundamentally moral vision of the opposition between good and evil, between right and wrong, and between the damned and the saved, one whose absolute authority could alone permit the passage of his analysis from ethics to ontology, in which questions of "right" versus "wrong" also become questions of "true" versus "false." As a highly self-conscious intellectual, however, Kim must admit that he can appeal to no such authority. The absence of the kind of genuine theological—and not just teleological—dimension which informs Manzoni's *The Betrothed* renders the Scriptural narrative model ultimately unsuitable in *The Path*. The absence of a God who would guarantee the necessity and moral propriety—from the point of view of a universal providential design—of each sacrifice, each defeat, and each act of violence places Kim in the position of a modern-day prophet deprived of any real knowledge of, or power over, what is to come. Kim's attempt to explain and foresee an end to the misery and *furore* in the lives of people like Pin and Dritto resembles what Calvino himself would later call "the abstract fury of Silvestro in [Vittorini's] *Conversation in Sicily*, which is the fury of a man who feels the tragedy of history but can only move on its margins." [13] The teleological vision of history as the history of human emancipation gives way in Kim's mind to the intolerable thought that history may be a tragedy, the perpetual triumph of a blind fate or *ananke*—a fatal necessity without cause or *telos*—that sets inexorable limits to human praxis and malignantly reverses or nullifies the effects of even the best of intentions and the most constructive of desires. It is a thought, however intolerable, that Calvino himself wrestles with not only throughout *The Path* but also throughout his entire career as a writer.

After he and Ferriera have parted ways for the evening and he has headed off into the dark (like Binda in "Fear on the Footpath"), Kim's thoughts begin to take the form of strange and fragmentary fantasies, to the point that he feels "in preda a furibondi squilibri . . . all'isteria" (p. 149; "he has fallen prey to a wild mental unbalance . . . [and] to hysteria").[14] To calm himself, Kim tries to retrace in his mind the multiple threads of the individual lives of the partisans, each with its own story, its "secret wound," and its conflicting unconscious urges and desires. Even though he conceives of his political work as revolutionary and redemptive, Kim finds it difficult to look beyond the immediate problems of individuals such as Pin. No matter how persuasive Ferriera's and his own interpretive models may be, Kim realizes at the same time that they can never fully justify individual suffering and sacrifice because they can never convey the entire "truth" behind them, only their historical necessity. Thus he agonizes over the decision to execute "Dritto, that Barabbas" (p. 108; 152), even though Dritto has let his men go into combat while saving his own skin. Likewise, he is unable to see Pelle as simply another Judas, even though Pelle is the man from Dritto's brigade who has betrayed his comrades to the Fascists, causing four of them to be captured and shot. Seen as an individual, at least for Kim, Pelle is simply another pitiful *vinto*; he is a loser in life and a victim rather than a true enemy:

Perhaps, one day, thinks Kim, I won't understand these things any more. I'll be serene, and understand men in a completely different way, a juster way, perhaps. Why perhaps? Well, I shan't say "perhaps" any more then, there won't be any more "perhaps" in me. And I'll have Dritto shot. Now I am too linked to them and all their deformities. To Dritto too. I know that Dritto must suffer horribly, with that stubborn determination to behave like a bastard no matter what. . . . He knows we'll shoot him. He wants to be shot. That wish gets a hold of men sometimes. . . . And Pelle, what is Pelle doing at this moment? Kim walks through a larch wood and thinks of Pelle down in the town going round on curfew patrol with the death's head badge on his cap. (p. 106; 150–51)

While he engages in these speculations on the hearts and minds of the men he has been studying, Kim once again feels a sense of guilt for doing so, as if he were indulging in some childish fantasy: "Now, instead of escaping into fantasy as I did when I was a child, I should be making a mental study of the details of the attack, the disposition of weapons and squads. But I like thinking about those men, studying them, making discoveries about them. What will they do 'afterwards,' for instance? Will they recognize in postwar Italy something made by them?" (p. 107; 151). Gradually, as the night wears on, he lapses into a state of uncertainty similar to Pin's and feels more and more like a child lost in a world of symbols whose meaning continually eludes him:

Kim walks on alone. . . . The tree trunks in the dark take on strange human shapes. Man carries his childhood fears with him for his whole life long. . . .
    Kim is logical when he is analysing the situation with the detachment commissars, but when he is walking along alone and reasoning with himself things become mysterious and magical again, and life seems full of miracles. . . . Sometimes he feels he is walking amid a world of symbols, like his namesake, little Kim in the middle of India, in that book of Kipling's which he had so often re-read as a boy.
    "Kim . . . Kim . . . Who is Kim . . . ?" (p. 105; 148–49)

The language used here by Calvino echoes the description of Pin's wanderings alone along the path to the nest of spiders at the beginning and again at the end of the novel. Kim's and Pin's paths, Calvino would seem to suggest, coincide in this chapter of *The Path*; the intellectual Kim's efforts to determine the sense of the Resistance are in the end no less fragile than the boy Pin's own *bricolage* of fantastic tales.

Finally, though, as his dialogue with his conscience draws to a close, Kim comes to see that he can free himself from his paralyzing doubts and uncertainties and "find everything clear within himself" (p. 107; 152) only by returning to Ferriera's original position and abandoning altogether his defense of subjectivity. Although Kim knows of no ironclad logic that justifies this choice, he concludes that he must believe in belief itself if he is to carry on as a partisan leader; he must, in other words, blind himself to the problems of the individual members of the movement in order to be able to act in accordance with the "true" development of history itself (as Ferriera has defined it). Like Kipling's Little Kim in his journey with the Lama, he too must find a "river of purification" or cathartic faith in the redemptive historical value of his actions as a partisan leader. History can be seen only in the collective terms of Marx's quest-romance for a "paradise on earth"; if one can come to believe in the necessity of this narrative and to privilege it above all else, even if it has no basis in "scientific" logic, then the problems of the subject lose their importance, for the subject itself has no meaning apart from this narrative.

This turn to a mythic narrative of the "romance" of collective human history as a solution for Kim's sense of the tragic nature of individual existence is—Calvino suggests—charged with irony. Although Kim wants to imagine that the path of his own life, his choices, the pursuit of his individual desires, and even his own death may have a meaning that transcends the limits of his existence as an individual subject through integration into the collective meaning of human history, it is only by blocking out his disruptive insight into the psychic nature of Dritto's men that he can satisfy this need to envision an organic link between the individual and history. Kim's leap of faith is made in the name of political action in the here and now and in the hope of freeing himself from guilt and anxiety. Like so many other left-wing Italian intellectuals caught in the same vise, Kim ends up wishing away the incommensurability between the private and the public, the psychological and the social:

Kim thinks of the column of Germans and Fascists who are perhaps at that moment advancing up the valley, towards the dawn which will bring death pouring down on their heads from the crests of the mountains. It is a column of lost gestures. One of the soldiers is waking up in a jolt of the truck and thinking "I love you Kate." In six or seven hours he'll be dead, we'll have killed him; even if he hadn't thought "I love you Kate," it would have been the same; everything that he does or thinks is lost, cancelled from history.
    I on the other hand am walking through a larch wood and every step I take is history. I think "I love you Adriana" and that is history. . . . Perhaps I don't do any great things, but history is made up of little anonymous gestures; I may die to-morrow even before that German,

but everything I do before dying and my death too will be little parts of history, and all the thoughts I'm having now will influence my history to-morrow, to-morrow's history of the human race. (pp. 106–7; 151)

Written on the pages of the historical master-narrative, as Kim imagines it, we will find only the lives of the winners (such as the partisans), whose victories signify humanity's progress toward its final goal. Those who oppose this march of progress (such as the Nazis and the Fascists) are instead the losers and are, in the end, destined to disappear forever from the master-narrative; they are obstacles that serve only—like boulders strewn on a steep mountainside—to help define the direction of the path the winners must take to go around them and thus have strictly a negative function. Their traces will eventually be lost because they have no bearing on the final outcome of the tale; they will not, in other words, "figure" in the inevitable triumph of reason in history. The fictional argument (or plot) of *The Path* itself leaves no doubt but that this is to be read in an ironic light; it is—in narrative form—Calvino's critique of the constitutive blindness of a whole generation of "committed" intellectuals in Italy.

History—as Kim sees it—has the structure and nature of a mythic tale and a quest-romance (the "inevitable" triumph of a class), and this alone allows him to act in a pragmatic political way. If history is seen as a mythic teleological narrative whose protagonist is a social group rather than an individual, then the door is opened, as both Georges Sorel and Antonio Gramsci point out in different ways, to historical and political action in modern mass society. "The Sorelian myth"—Gramsci writes— "is a political ideology expressed neither in the form of a cold utopia nor as a learned theorizing, but rather by a creation of concrete fantasy which acts on a dispersed and shattered people to arouse and organize its collective will." [15] Myth works to a pragmatic end, in a way that neither "cold" utopias nor "learned" discourses ever can; it is a powerful rhetorical tool of persuasion that operates on the collective political imagination of the masses. As a kind of "person-idea" in Bakhtin's sense of the term, [16] Kim may be said to embody in *The Path* this maxim of Gramsci's: "Pessimism of the intelligence, optimism of the will." Each individual invests the partisan struggle with a radically different meaning, and the liberation each individual envisions for himself is based on a mythic but non-"concrete" fantasy; this, Kim concludes, can and must be exploited for political ends, since no other end can be as important. The notion of an Italian *patria*, in particular, represents for the Resistance a concrete mass myth capable of unifying the actions of individuals and of generating real historical change through struggle, for although this myth has no foundations in historical reality, and even though each individual discovers in it a different value, all partisans can be "aroused" and "organized" (in Gramsci's terms) by reference to it. It is the *filo rosso*, or connecting strand, that runs from one subject to the next and links them all together into a mass movement. Such fictions are simply a necessity in mass politics—although, of course, they will be done away with when reason has won out in its efforts to determine the destiny of mankind—even more so than in the inner life of the subject. The commissar, who "knows better" (in a rather paternalistic way) than the troops in his charge, must ably—and sometimes even cynically—manipulate the power of all such fictions and myths in the name of a "correct" political praxis that will help direct history toward its inevitably triumphant conclusion. Thus Kim believes that, with this instrumental vision of mass myth, he has found a way to transcend the "pessimism of the intelligence" generated by his study of the essential disorder and psychic chaos of the individuals who make up the partisan units, and to reassert an "optimism of the will" without discarding altogether the factor of individual desire.

Gramsci first used his famous maxim in the 1920's, when he helped to organize the factory councils in Turin and coedited the weekly *Ordine Nuovo*. Gramsci claimed that he had taken his maxim from Romain Rolland, the French poet, novelist, and dramatist who played an important part in the international campaign in 1933–34 for his release from prison. Rolland was also a lifelong friend and admirer of Freud, with whose work Gramsci was only summarily and indirectly acquainted, even though the "question" of psychoanalysis and of its political implications emerges several times in his notes and letters. The maxim "pessimism of the intelligence, optimism of the will" expresses, in epigrammatic form, the deep contradiction between the essentially pessimistic view of human destiny implicit in Freudian thought and the optimism of the Marxist quest-romance that leads to a future workers' state. Freud's political pessimism emerges particularly in *Civilization and Its Discontents*, a text Freud worked on in the very same years (the early 1930's) in which Gramsci composed his notes on the political function of myth. Although Freud himself relies on myth and romance to make sense of both individual stories and collective history, he remains to the end skeptical that the fulfillment of individual desire and individual happiness could ever coincide with collective desire and collective well-being.[17] Gramsci, on the other hand, places great emphasis on the control of individual desires and fantasies as a precondition for the affirmation of a collective will for political change:

Daydreams and fantasies . . . show lack of character and passivity. One imagines that something has happened to upset the mechanism of necessity. One's own initiative has become free. . . . One can do whatever one wants, and one wants a whole series of things which at present one lacks. It is basically the present turned on its head which is projected into the future. Everything repressed is unleashed. On the contrary, it is necessary to direct one's attention violently towards the present as it is, if one wishes to transform it. Pessimism of the intelligence, optimism of the will.[18]

Kim "resolves" or, better still, represses his own intellectual crisis by deciding that it is only by coming to terms with the limits that collective existence places on individual freedom and desire that the reality of history as necessity may be truly grasped and that liberation may be justified, even though the latter cannot be achieved without doing violence to the desire of the individual subject. Kim's self-censorship faithfully reproduces the political mechanism of repression that Gramsci describes, whose object is not so much the repression of individual desire as of pessimistic intelligence, corroded by its own self-awareness ("it is necessary to direct one's attention violently toward the present as it is, if one wishes to transform it"). The committed intellectual must consciously "forget" that individual desires are

constantly displaced and negated in the sociopolitical regimentation of the unconscious, or at best transmuted into a mass
myth of political action, if the present is to be transformed into a
new and brighter future for all.

Certain terms and expressions found in two letters Gramsci
wrote from prison are strikingly similar to the thoughts running
through Kim's mind in the ninth chapter of *The Path*. Writing to
his sister-in-law on February 15 and March 7, 1932, concerning
the psychoanalytic treatment his wife Giulia was planning to undergo in the Soviet Union to cure herself of a state of profound
anxiety and emotional unbalance, Gramsci suggests that psychoanalysis represents a fundamentally false way of dealing
with the problem of "the insulted and the injured." [19] Although
he refers directly to Dostoyevsky's novels in order to explain the
meaning of this expression, he also gives a more specific sociopolitical definition which closely resembles the way in which
Kim uses the terms *umiliazione* and *offesa* in his dialogue with
Ferriera. The "insulted" and "injured" for Gramsci are those
who become social misfits when social pressures, ethical codes,
the fabric of civil society, and the coercive structure of the state
itself appear in sharp contradiction with "natural law," that is,
the libidinal urges and desires of the individual. This, he argues,
is what causes "morbid outbursts of repressed feeling" in the
modern subject (*Letters*, p. 227). The lack of a cultural and political mediation between the law of organized society and "natural
law"—a mediation which is, in Gramsci's view, the specific
function of intellectuals in the West—augments the sense that
the mechanisms of both state and society are external to the individual or, in other words, incapable of integrating the individual into the social structure. (Dostoyevsky himself, unable to assume the politically mediating role of the intellectual, felt this
conflict to be an irreconcilable one and was consequently himself, according to Gramsci, one of the "insulted and injured.") In
such a situation, the individual who does not fall prey to psychic
illness finds refuge either in social hypocrisy (and abides by the
letter of the law) or, more simply, in "common skepticism"
(*Letters*, p. 227). While psychoanalysis, according to Gramsci,
shows us the damage that this produces in many minds, it can in

no way lead to an authentic resolution of the problem, for that can only be achieved through the acquisition of a political consciousness and will. Those who turn to psychoanalysis merely delegate to a figure of authority—the analyst—the responsibility of giving a political meaning and direction to one's own existence:

> Such persons, trapped in the iron-tight conflicts of modern life . . . are not able with their own means to find reasons for these conflicts and thus go beyond them toward a new serenity and moral tranquillity, balancing impulses of the will with goals that must be reached. . . . It strikes me that Giulia is suffering from . . . unreal "unsolvable problems" and struggling against phantasms created by her own feverish, disordered fantasy. . . . I believe . . . someone like Giulia, active in social life not only officially, that is, because a [Communist party] card in her wallet says that she is, must be and can be the sole and best psychoanalytic therapist for herself. (*Letters*, pp. 222–23) [20]

Gramsci's diagnosis closely corresponds to Kim's recognition that the only possible "cure" for the men in Dritto's detachment, as well as the solution to his own intellectual dilemma, ultimately lies in an unqualified commitment to a revolutionary political praxis, even one that must make recourse to myths, fictions, and representations. As commissar of the partisan brigade, Kim finds himself in a particularly dramatic situation, where "political praxis" is a matter of deciding not only to risk one's own life but also to dispose of the lives of others. Again, in Gramsci's letter, we find a description of the self-denial and the force of individual will required in such a situation (which was Gramsci's own, since he chose to sacrifice his own existence for a political cause): "In particular historical moments and *milieux*, when the environment is heated to a point of extreme tension and when gigantic collective forces, unleashed, press single individuals painfully to obtain the maximum creative response from their will, the situation becomes dramatic" (*Letters*, p. 222). The rational serenity Kim finally achieves with his decision to have Dritto shot as a traitor after the battle closely corresponds to the "serenity" described by Gramsci in the same letter: "It is possible to find serenity even in the face of the most absurd contradictions and under the pressure of the most implacable necessity, if one succeeds in thinking 'historically' and dialectically and in identifying one's own defined and limited task with intellectual sobriety" (*Letters*, p. 227).

•

Although Kim's political will to act follows Gramsci's own vision of dialectical materialism, in both his dialogue with Ferriera and (later on) in his interior monologue he often refers to the tenets of existentialism (as does Battaglia at the end of *Un uomo: un partigiano*). While Marxism served as the most vital mode of thought for understanding the "objective" and collective dimensions of history and politics in Italy after the fall of Fascism, existentialism offered—for Italian intellectuals of the period— one of the most compelling conceptual frameworks for dealing with the nature of subjective individual experience. In the short period between the collapse of the regime and the defeat of the Left in the April 1948 elections, existentialism in Italy was of considerable interest for many members of the intelligentsia— an interest motivated to a considerable extent by the debate over historical materialism and its relationship to the question of the subject. A series of articles by and about Sartre and Simone de Beauvoir, for instance, was published during this period in *Il Politecnico*, including a translation of Sartre's first editorial for *Les Temps modernes*.[21] However, partly because of the deeply sedimented presence of Croce's idealism in the Italian cultural milieu and partly because of the Zhdanovist turn in the postwar cultural policy of the PCI, existentialism was pushed to the margins of Italian culture, at least in the first decade following the Liberation. When, on occasion, it did emerge into the contemporary debate during that period, existentialism often became the object of bitter polemics. In an article published in 1947 by *Il Politecnico*, Fabrizio Onofri accuses Sartre's existentialism of being "against the spirit of socialism" and of being all the more dangerous because in its attempt to appropriate socialism it ends up depriving socialism of its true meaning. The "individualistic spirit" which transpires in Sartre's literary and philosophical work, Onofri goes on to argue, makes him not a revolutionary but rather a counterrevolutionary writer.[22] The seeming irreconcilability of Marxism and existentialism—which argues that the subject is inherently free and is not determined by the material conditions of production—is in fact one of the most important intellectual dilemmas of not only Italian postwar culture but also of European culture as a whole over the course of the 1940's and 1950's. The development of Sartre's own thought, from *Being and Nothingness* to *Search for a Method* to *The Critique of Dialectical Reason*, embodies the history of the postwar European search for a solution to this dilemma.[23] After the period of relative open-mindedness between 1945 and 1948, though, the increasingly powerful cultural hegemony of Marxism and the pressure exerted by the PCI leadership and intelligentsia effectively contributed to block the development of existentialist thought in Italy, even as its influence grew by leaps and bounds elsewhere in the West. As pointed out in Chapter 2 of the present study, these objections to existentialism in effect extended to the entire tradition of modernism (thanks in part to the increasing resonance in Italy of Georg Lukács's work) and to any kind of "crisis" art involving a critique of traditional narrative and mimetic realism.[24] Writers as diverse as Sartre, Kafka, Joyce, and Hemingway came under fire for precisely this reason; Vittorini, Moravia, Pavese, and Pratolini—who were all supporters or members of the PCI but were engaged at the same time in one way or another in an attempt to represent "realistically" contemporary subjective and collective experience—found themselves increasingly under attack by more "hard-line" Marxist critics such as Alicata, Salinari, Muscetta, and Trombatore, who accused them of such heresies as "irrationalism," "voluntarism," "subjectivism," and "decadentism."[25] In this context, then, it is germane to point out that the ninth chapter of *The Path*, where the issues of the power of desire and of the Marxist vision of history are openly set in a dialogical relationship through the words and thoughts of the person-idea named Kim and his comrade Ferriera, became itself an object of critical controversy in Italy after the novel's publication.

In *L'Existentialisme est un humanisme* (1946), Sartre illustrates his key notions of anxiety (*angoisse*), freedom, choice, and re-

sponsibility—and the role they play in shaping the subject's actions—with an example that is strikingly homologous to Kim's
existential situation in *The Path*. Anxiety, according to Sartre, derives from our awareness that although man is caught in a specific historical situation which is a network of material and "psychoanalytic" conditions, he is nevertheless not determined by
those conditions; man is, on the contrary, free to choose a position within this network and thus free to give his existence
a specific orientation.[26] But one's choice of action—the choice
for which one is fully responsible, since there is, according to
Sartre, no overdetermining cause or absolute moral imperative
outside the subject itself—is never purely subjective. This choice
of action engages humanity as a whole because every choice
emits an intersubjective message; it affirms a value, for it projects an "image" of man which is there for everyone to see and
to judge. The individual who does not hide from this responsibility is bound to feel its weight as an anxiety; he is bound, as
Sartre notes, to ask himself whether his behavior is such that
humanity should wish to behave in a similar way, in the absence of any universal moral authority or transcendental ethics.[27] Sartrean anxiety derives from the subject's conscious projection of the will into the future, that is, into the existence of
which he is the "legislator" and maker. It therefore stands in
marked opposition to the Freudian concept of anxiety, in which
the ego must struggle with both its "moral judge" (or, in other
words, the superego, which arises from the past, as defined by
the child's early relations with its parents) and the timeless and
amoral drives of the id as well.[28] Sartrean anxiety is unrelieved
by any sense of a common social, political, or moral goal for
which humanity as a whole ought to strive; the will to act is
therefore, at least at this stage of development in Sartre's thought,
profoundly different from the Marxist notion of political engagement as well. Existentialism—contrary to Marxism—admits neither continuity in human history nor narrative causality in the
dialectic of class struggle. Radically Cartesian in its positing of
the subject as the only human reality, Sartre's existentialism (at
least in 1946) conceives of political action in the Marxist sense
only as a possible individual project. This project is based on a

concrete relation established by the individual with his comrades in a political party or group, whose collective will he can
reasonably expect to harmonize with his own in the consensual realization of a common enterprise. However, the idea
that, after one's death, other comrades will take up the struggle
and the project that one has undertaken in life, thus furthering
the cause of socialism and bringing it eventually to fulfillment
is, Sartre notes, an illusion. Men are (in a radically existential
sense) free and may decide tomorrow either to establish a Fascist state or simply to let Fascism take over. Thus, Sartre writes,
since no one can know what is going to happen in the Soviet
Union, it is impossible to affirm that what is happening there
now (just after the end of the war) will lead to the fulfillment of
the ideal workers' state. When a military leader (like Kim) must
send soldiers to their deaths, he is singly responsible for that
choice; although he may have received orders from above, he
still has to interpret them and to make a decision that must come
exclusively from him. In this situation, such a leader cannot but
feel the anxiety of his responsibility, yet this does not keep him
from acting; indeed it is this very anxiety that makes him aware
of the value of his choice and of the possibilities that are open to
him. Anxiety is an integral part of his action, inasmuch as it engages him in a responsible relation with other men.[29]

From such an existentialist perspective, Kim's self-questioning—as he walks alone through the woods the night before the
battle—expresses an anxiety that is an integral part of his opposition to Fascism. That night Kim finds that he walks in a
world of symbols for which there is no given interpretive code;
he senses that he must construct his itinerary step-by-step and
that each of his steps is bound up with the lives and deaths of
the men under his command; and he broods over the decision to
have Dritto shot. All these thoughts and doubts are doubly
bound not only to the civil war raging in Italy but to the civil war
within Kim's divided self as well. From the same perspective, of
course, the serenity at which he finally arrives by justifying his
actions in light of the value that they will have for the history of
humanity as a whole represents an act of self-delusion or rather,
in Sartre's terms, an act of "bad faith." In *The Path*, the character

of Kim would appear to be modelled (at least in part) on Sartre's "engaged" intellectual, which had a pervasive (albeit often unacknowledged) influence on Italian neorealism and, in general, on "politicized" literature in Italy, prior to the general acceptance of the Gramscian model of the "organic" intellectual. The maverick Kim is attracted to the existentialist exploration of both the inner life of the subject and intersubjective relations as a possible way to resolve his own personal crisis. But Kim's Gramscian optimism of the will essentially differs from the *"dureté optimiste"* of existentialism because, as in the case of Gramsci himself, it is based on a teleological vision of history. For Kim, as for Gramsci, the individual may justify the value of his actions and the sacrifice of his own and others' lives on the basis of a belief in the historical change(s) which will someday be brought about by others, even after that individual has long since ceased to exist. Gramsci proposes an ethics of sacrifice, which in moments of historical crisis—such as war and revolution—may come to resemble an ethics of martyrdom.

Kim, at the end of his interior monologue, makes a pointed reference to such an ethics when he envisions his own future death for the partisan cause. His is the fearlessness in the face of death of the revolutionary who, as in Ernst Bloch's portrayal of the sixteenth-century radical Thomas Muenzer, "having passed to the level of collective solidarity, no longer really has an individual life to lose."[30] As Calvino remarks in his 1949 article on the literature of the Resistance, Gramsci's letters from prison are among the most astonishing of all modern testaments to revolutionary courage and self-abnegation.[31] Calvino notes in his article that "serenity" and "strength" are the qualities which make Gramsci representative of the revolutionary spirit of the Resistance itself, and, we may add, these are the same qualities that Kim exhibits at the end of the ninth chapter of *The Path*.[32] In Calvino's novel, though, Kim's serenity is constantly endangered by the sense of compassion that he feels for the existential plight of the partisans in Dritto's unit and of all those who suffer or die for the sake of a cause without understanding the reason why. Although, from Kim's perspective, their *furore* does take on a larger meaning (which is the universal human desire for freedom), the tragedy of their lives is that this "anagogical" meaning is simply not available to them, or not "chosen" by them, since they do not recognize themselves as parts of a universal human reality in the making. While Kim senses that his own death will be a "historical fact" of significance for future generations and for the eventual liberation of humanity, the tragic destiny of the dispossessed partisans in Dritto's detachment will instead be that of silently vanishing forever into the margins of history and the interstices of history books, like—in a bitterly ironic twist—those against whom they are fighting for their freedom.

The ending of Pin's story certainly raises retroactively the question—for Calvino's fictional argument in chapter 9—of the "necessity" of individual sacrifice for the benefit of future generations. Pin's own life acquires its true meaning—one which may finally redeem his alienated existence—only through the death of his sister and through his own decision to join the partisan ranks side-by-side with Cousin. Pin thus belongs to the category of "the winners," if we apply the terms of Kim's analysis to his situation, but this positive vision of the meaning of Pin's life may be sustained only through an allegorization of history. Consequently, we may hold to this vision solely through the projection of Pin's own existence, and the very history of the partisan struggle, onto an anagogical level of interpretation. A less abstract vision yields a different perspective: "For a long time it will be difficult to say if someone or something has won this war," Vittorini writes in his first editorial for *Il Politecnico*. "What is certain is that a lot has been lost, and we can see how it has been lost. The dead, if we count them, are more children than soldiers." [33] Indeed, Calvino's novel indicates in the end that this redemptive meaning of sacrifice in the name of an ideal is itself but a mystification and that people like Pin and his sister will continue to be dominated by others, even if their suffering may be historically "justified" in the name of the future liberation of all of humanity. [34]

In his editorial from *Les Temps Modernes* published by *Il Politecnico* in 1946, entitled in Italian "Una nuova cultura come 'Cultura Sintetica'" ("A New Culture as 'Synthetic Culture'"), Sartre provides an existentialist definition of liberation, a concept whose meaning is explicitly or implicitly explored in almost every article and essay published in *Il Politecnico* during its brief existence from September 1945 to December 1947. Seen from today's vantage point, Sartre's definition clearly gestures in the direction of a notion of liberation that would reconcile the existentialist notion of the free subject (a subject that has no preconstituted identity or human nature which could make it—as is the case in bourgeois ideology—the "equal" of every other human being) with both the fundamental discoveries of Marxism in the field of political economy, on the one hand, and those of Freudianism in the realm of libidinal economy, on the other hand: "The final goal we give to ourselves is a liberation. Since man is a totality, it is not enough, in reality, to grant him the right to vote without dealing with the other factors which constitute him; he must free himself totally, he must in other words make himself *other*, acting both on his biological constitution and his economic condition, both on his sexual complexes and on the political facts of his situation." [35] But it is Simone de Beauvoir, in an essay published in 1946 by *Il Politecnico* under the title "Idealismo morale e realismo politico" ("Moral Idealism and Political Realism"), who most lucidly connects the question of liberation through political action with the problem of individual freedom and the justification of "sacrifice." Contrary to what some Marxist "political realists" may believe, de Beauvoir contends, there is no objective reason for sacrifice or indeed for any kind of political act inherent in the logic of historical facts (or, in other words, what Gramsci calls the "mechanism of necessity"). No historical situation or dialectic "dictates" a specific course of action; on the contrary, ideological and political choices are always in the last analysis *moral* choices, essentially subjective and ultimately arbitrary. Indeed, the very vision of history that justifies the sacrifice of an individual for the presumed future benefit of humanity is grounded, de Beauvoir observes, not in objective reality but in subjective morality:

[To the realist] the sacrifice of some individuals to the whole of humanity appears natural; it is only a transitory moment leading to a fulfillment destined to last indefinitely; it is the provisional in the face of the eternal; the contingent in the face of the absolute. The individual does not exist except by going beyond himself towards others; and the present is only a step towards the future. . . . This is why one accepts without undue surprise that certain individuals may be sacrificed for the community, and that a living generation may be sacrificed for the benefit of men who have not yet been born. . . . I can have someone killed (and a million people are a small thing compared to the infinity of humanity) in order to bring about lasting peace in the world. The realist justifies himself in these terms. One can find this solution reassuring, but it is by no means such a sure thing. The collectivity is not made of a different substance from the individuals of which it is composed . . . and the future is nothing but a succession of instants which become present one after the other, and are therefore transitory. If the realist chooses the whole over the part, it is because he adopts a material and quantitative point of view. A thousand men are more than one man if one looks at man as a thing to which a number can be given. But quantity is not value. . . . If man has no other end than himself, for whom are a thousand men more than one man? Only one answer is possible: for himself. But this numeric superiority is not inscribed in the real; it is not an established fact; it depends on a human choice. If then man declares in certain cases that the sacrifice of a human being is more important in his eyes than the victory of ten thousand other men, he can refuse this sacrifice: he must choose and decide; the facts, in and of themselves, dictate nothing. . . . Man does not find in things . . . any ready-made answer. In each situation he must again interrogate himself on his goals, and he must choose them and justify them without help. . . . Morality is not a pre-constituted system of values and principles, it is the constitutive movement through which values and principles are posited; and the truly moral man must reenact this movement on his own. . . . To reconcile morality and politics is to reconcile man with himself; it is to affirm that in each instant he is totally responsible for himself. But this requires giving up the certainty that he hoped to reach by closing himself off in the transcendent subjectivity of traditional morality, or in the objectivity of realist politics. . . . Man must renounce serenity, and he must take on his freedom. (pp. 34–35)

Kim's own hard-won serenity is indeed, in de Beauvoir's terms, that of both traditional morality and pragmatic politics. But, like de Beauvoir, the text of *The Path* exposes this serenity as a mode of "bad faith" and blindness, for as Kim approaches both the solution to his intellectual crisis and the end of his path through the woods, he ceases to be the ironic focalizer of the narrative (by way of his questioning and self-questioning) and turns into the focalized object of the narrative's irony instead.

As the chapter ends, the reader realizes in fact that Kim's path has taken him only (like Pin's) full circle, back to his original point of departure:

> Everything is clear with him now. Dritto, Pin, the Calabrian bothers-in-law. He knows how to behave towards each of them, without fear or pity. Sometimes when he is walking at night the fog in the minds of others seems to condense around him like the fog in the air; but he is a man who analyzes; "a, b, c," he will say to the partisan commissar. He is a "Bolshevik," a man who dominates situations. I love you Adriana. . . . Tomorrow there will be a big battle. Kim is serene. "A, b, c," he will say. Again and again he thinks: I love you Adriana. That, and that alone, is history. (pp. 107; 152–53)

In the above passage, the term "serenity" and Kim's final vision of historical understanding and political praxis can only assume ironic connotations for the reader, when seen in the light of a previous passage at the beginning of Kim's interior monologue, in which his *lack* of serenity (and particularly his inability to reason like a true Bolshevik) are presented as a function of his analytical powers of understanding:

> His thoughts are logical, he can analyze everything with perfect clarity. But no, he's not serene. His forefathers were serene, the old bourgeois creators of wealth. The proletariat is serene for it knows what it wants, so are the peasants who are now doing sentry duty over their own villages. Serene are the Soviets who have made up their mind about everything and now fight the war methodically and with determination not because they like to do it but because it is necessary. The Bolsheviks! Perhaps the Soviet Union is already a serene country. Perhaps there isn't any human misery over there any more. Will Kim ever be serene? One day perhaps we will all get to be serene and we will no longer understand many things because we will have understood everything. (p. 105; 149) [36]

To gain this global and pragmatic perspective (with its "serenity") means—as this passage emphatically points out—to lose sight of everything that does not fit in one's plan for action and, above all, to blot out or defer the question of the subject with its fears and desires. In the above passage, Calvino shows us a character who clearly lacks the moral and political certainties which come from a class consciousness, a totalizing worldview, or a specific political ideology. While this lack is precisely what makes Kim want to identify with Ferriera and to come to share his pragmatic point of view, it is also what allows him to perceive the fundamental inadequacy of any strictly class-bound vision of history. Thus when at the end of chapter 9 Kim finally posits a totalizing allegorical vision of history as a means to overcome his doubts, we can hardly see this as anything other than a wish fulfillment in its own right (although he himself cannot see this); it is—at least in light of the emplotment of *The Path*—a utopian dream of a humanity partaking of a single narrative whose endpoint is a society without exploitation and class divisions. This is also the ultimate sense of Marx's own teleological vision of history, which represents a movement towards the "true realm of freedom."[37] When set in the perspective of the above passage, Kim's Gramscian vision, with its foundational serenity in the face of the violence of history, appears no less mystified than Pin's vision of the events taking place under his eyes as if in some enchanted play. Calvino's double-edged critique of both the policies of the PCI in the 1940's and the rationalization required of intellectuals by the Party's political pragmatism condemns the fact that although politics is always a rhetorical practice and not a philosophy, committed intellectuals (such as Kim) are obliged to rationalize short-term political goals in terms of a long-term historical "truth." Kim's sense of identification with Kipling's Little Kim resurfaces once again at the end of his interior monologue, reinforcing the irony of the chapter's conclusion, for it is precisely when he feels that reason has prevailed and that he no longer walks "in a world of symbols" that Kim comes to resemble Little Kim—and Pin—the most. Kim's serenity is indeed, as Calvino implies with his fictional irony, no less of a private fulfillment of a fantasy than Pin's belief that he has found the Great Friend at the end of his path.

The Path to Freedom and the Power of Writing

The contradictory views that critics have held, and continue to hold, with regard to *The Path*'s purported aesthetic unity or disunity are indicative of the deeply problematic nature of the work itself. Calvino's novel has even raised doubts in the minds of some critics about its status as a legitimate work of fiction.[38] As a narrative, *The Path* undeniably forms an organic totality of sorts, for there are no evidently gratuitous or unmotivated elements in its plot structure ("for if the presence or absence of a thing makes no visible difference, then it is not an integral part of the whole," *Poetics* 8.35, 1451a). However, the narrative of *The Path* does not allow for an organicist reading, in the sense that no final and all-embracing "dominant" perspective can be identified which retrospectively would allow the reader to grasp the meaning of the work as a narrated totality. There is, to put it another way, no single interpretive code available to the reader which could ultimately account for the meaning of the text as a whole (which explains why, in the present work, we have been obliged to approach *The Path* from a number of different critical angles). In *The Path* we find a text that holds its codes in a dialogical tension, rather than in a relation of correlation between mutually validating sign-functions. In this interplay, and even struggle, of codes within the text, each code is foregrounded, allowed to become dominant and to reabsorb within itself all the elements of the narrative, only to be estranged by the surfacing of another code. It is through this "internal" dialectic that *The Path* establishes a critical dialogue with its cultural context and the conflicting emplotments of the real that it projects. What makes *The Path* a legitimate novel—a "modern epic" in Calvino's sense of the term—is the breadth of its inquiry, through a single story about a specific individual in a specific moment in history, into a collective problematic involving the definition of both real and possible relationships between the individual, nature, and history. As Bakhtin has pointed out, the novel assimilates historical time in all its essential aspects, but it is by no means a concise exposition or a summation of the whole of historical time.[39] *The Path* is a *realistic* "novel of emergence," in the Bakhtinian sense of the term, insofar as it represents the emergence of an individual as a historical being at a real historical moment, with all the "problems of reality and man's potential, problems of freedom and necessity, and the problem of creative initiative" which this representation involves.[40]

Although a realistic novel in this sense, *The Path* is an ironic and hybrid text because it deploys a multiplicity of interpretive codes and because it incorporates a multiplicity of genres and modes of discourse but always "with reservations." That is to say, it always frames the use of other genres and modes in terms of a self-conscious lack of "indisputability, unconditionality, [and] unequivocality."[41] *The Path* is, and at the same time is not, a historical novel, a fable, a *Bildungsroman*, and a quest-romance. The literary genres and narrative paradigms incorporated into *The Path* imply different semantic directions and conflicting ways of seeing, mapping out, interpreting, and representing particular aspects of the world and thus cannot be synthesized into a single whole.[42] While these generic or modal definitions are ultimately only arbitrary categories which do not account for the text's specific individual design, they nevertheless provide us with a provisional analytic framework through which to conceptualize the way in which Calvino's work of fiction functions. The very essence of *The Path*'s narrativity is constituted through the interweaving of reciprocally irreducible interpretive codes, narrative paradigms, and literary genres and modes. Each of these performs a positive symbolic function in the narrative, for each affirms the value of embarking on a quest for meaning through the imaginary reconfiguration of time and experience into a narrative order. The integration of individual and collective history, the fulfillment of childhood fantasies, the reconciliation of self and other (or of nature and culture), the conquest of sexual maturity and political consciousness, the positive significance of collective political praxis: these are all "resolutions" which *The Path* allows us to glimpse, in one form or another, through its tireless textual interplay. Yet the ideological relations which legitimize each of these and the value-charged oppositions which inform them (individual-collective, self-other, nature-culture, etc.) are themselves constantly defamiliarized as the novel shifts its mode of narration. While each of them projects a totalization of meaning in its own right (in the form of a narrative resolution), this totalization also necessarily conflicts—to a greater or a lesser degree—with those of each of the other codes, modes, and genres that Calvino has embedded in the text. The ideological valorization of each changes radically as well, depending on the code that is foregrounded at any given juncture in the text. Thus the fairy-tale elements in *The Path* demystify the dominant (for the neorealists) logic of the "epic" narrative representation of the historical events of the Resistance. The fairy tale also stresses the liberating potential of individual fantasy and the value of the individual quest for happiness at the expense of the "reality principle" of the Freudian *Bildungsroman* and of the collective political-ethical imperatives of Kim's Marxist quest-romance for the "truth" of history and its *ratio*. When read as a psychoanalytic *Bildungsroman*, on the other hand, Pin's story appears as a tale of alienation which reduces individual fantasy to a mere delusion and political praxis to a sublimation of irreducible psychosocial conflicts. Finally, the existentialist perspective which emerges in chapter 9 calls into question any "resolution" based on the valorization of either an individual past or a collective future, for the narrative time of *The Path* is an absolute present (as it is for de Beauvoir in her "Moral Idealism and Political Realism": "The future is nothing but a succession of instants which become present one after the other, and are therefore transitory").

Each one of these narrative possibilities, however, configures in turn a possible itinerary of human liberation; indeed, there can be little doubt that the novel's most persistent narrative line—and its "absent center"—is ultimately found in the word "liberation" itself, with its constellation of possible meanings emerging from a meditation on the reality of the partisan struggle and its conclusion, *la Liberazione*. Significantly, this historical event is not represented in the novel; the story stops on the eve of the Liberation and thus forecloses the possibility of interpreting *la Liberazione* as a moment of genuine resolution. The "visionary" emplotment of the past, present, and future of humanity into a great collective quest-romance—or a universal master-narrative—is the ultimate form of narrative totalization that *The Path* projects and rejects through Kim's meditations. It is this ultimate master-narrative that promises to bring all of the other, heterogeneous narratives into harmony with each other and to integrate all the various meanings of the word "liberation." Through its representation of the person-idea of Kim, who is torn between the conflicting demands of truth and myth, *The Path* acknowledges the possible political value of a complex teleological vision of history as a totality, while simultaneously disclosing the idea of totality itself as a myth without foundation. While Kim's notion of history is utopian and fundamentally mystified, Calvino's is neither one nor the other; within *The Path*, Kim's is represented as only one among a multiplicity of narrative paradigms through which history can be grasped. Calvino's lucid awareness of the mythic nature of Kim's narrative, and his ironic treatment of it, does not in the last analysis invalidate it altogether; rather, it attempts to show that turn to myth for what it really is, namely the *symbolic* expression of a legitimate and ineradicable desire for a life beyond alienation and beyond the need for further fables of totality or, for that matter, of estrangement.

Reference Matter

Notes

Complete authors' names, titles, and publication data are given in the Works Cited, pp. 399–412.

Introduction

1. Biasin, "Le rare isole," pp. 179–80.
2. De Lauretis, "Narrative Discourse," p. 425.
3. Ragusa, pp. 195–201.
4. Barth, pp. 66, 70–71. For a reading of Calvino's later fiction in terms of postmodernism and metafiction, see Hume, *Fantasy and Mimesis*, pp. 49–50, and Waugh, *Metafiction*, pp. 22–47.
5. Spriano, *Le passioni*, pp. 11–32.
6. See Cannon, *Italo Calvino*; Olken, *With Pleated Eye and Garnet Wing*; and Carter, *Calvino*.
7. Calvino, *Path*, pp. viii; xxiii–xxiv (*Sentiero*, pp. 17; 22–23). All page references to the English version of the novel will from now on be included in the text in parentheses, followed by the page references for the Italian original.
8. Bazin, *What Is Cinema?*, 1: 20.
9. Calvino, "Domande," p. 12. All translations in the text are mine unless otherwise indicated.
10. Calvino, "Right and Wrong Political Uses of Literature," in his *Uses of Literature*, p. 99.
11. Calvino, "The Written and the Unwritten Word," p. 39.
12. Calvino, "Lo sguardo dell'archeologo" (1972), in his *Una pietra sopra*, p. 265.
13. Calvino, "Filosofia e letteratura" (1967) and "Due interviste su scienza e letteratura" (1968), in his *Una pietra sopra*, pp. 150–56; 184–91.
14. See for example de Lauretis's analysis of the ironic interplay of different codes and lexicons in *Cosmicomics* and *t zero* in "Narrative Discourse" and Biasin's analysis of Calvino's use of scientific codes in the same works in *Italian Literary Icons*, pp. 166–90. For an analysis of

phenomenological estrangement in *Mr. Palomar*, see Cannon, "Calvino's Latest Challenge." There can be no question that a text like *The Castle of Crossed Destinies* calls for or even prescribes a narratological-structuralist reading, such as that by Corti in *Il viaggio*, pp. 169–84, or that *If on a Winter's Night a Traveler* obviously lends itself best to a semiotic reader-response reading, such as that by Rankin, "The Role of the Reader."

Chapter 1

1. Jakobson, "On Realism in Art," pp. 38–46.
2. Auerbach, *Mimesis*, p. 463.
3. See also Gombrich's classic study, *Art and Illusion*. On the conventionality of realistic motivation in narrative, see Genette, "Vraisemblance et motivation," in his *Figures II*, pp. 71–99, and the discussion of "naturalization" and "cultural *vraisemblance*" in Culler, *Structuralist Poetics*, pp. 134–60.
4. The parallel between Jakobson's argument and Shklovsky's notion of *ostranenie* (estrangement or defamiliarization) is clear here. See Shklovsky, "Art as Technique" (1917), pp. 3–24.
5. Barthes, "The Reality Effect," pp. 11–17.
6. This relativity may account for the extraordinarily confused critical debate generated by the notion of literary realism in the twentieth century. For a useful and incisive bibliographical summary, see Lucente, *Narrative*, pp. 162–3.
7. The critical bibliography on neorealism is vast. Some of the more important and useful studies and anthologies of recent years concerning neorealist cinema are: Armes, *Patterns of Realism*; Marcus, *Italian Film*; Miccichè, ed., *Il neorealismo*; Canziani, *Gli anni*; Tinazzi and Zancan, eds., *Cinema e letteratura*. Concerning neorealist narrative, see Salinari, *Preludio*; Ferretti, *Introduzione*; Asor Rosa, "Il neorealismo"; Muscetta, *Realismo*; Falaschi, *Realtà e retorica*; Corti, "Neorealismo," in *Il viaggio*, pp. 25–110; Milanini, *Neorealismo*; Asor Rosa, "Lo stato democratico." For a critical bibliography see Vitizzai, *Il neorealismo*, pp. 67–87. Very few critical studies of neorealist narrative have been published in English. Some of the most recent and insightful ones are Lucente, "Ignazio Silone and Neorealism," in *Beautiful Fables*, pp. 177–95, and Procaccini, *Francesco Jovine* (in particular the chapter entitled "Neorealism," pp. 1–22) and "Neorealism: Description/Prescription."
8. See Miccichè, "Per una verifica del neorealismo," in his *Il neorealismo cinematografico italiano*, p. 16.
9. Cited in Asor Rosa, "Lo stato democratico," p. 571.
10. Carocci, *Storia*, p. 351.
11. On the derivation of the term *neorealismo* from the term *Neue Sachlichkeit*, see Brunetta, "Neo-realismo," pp. 129–36.

12. On the relationship between the *Neue Sachlichkeit* and Italian neorealism, see Bo, ed., *Inchiesta*, pp. 65–67. Bo suggests that the German novel of the 1920's may have influenced the precursors of Italian neorealism, namely Moravia and Bernari. However, Bonaventura Tecchi points out that Italian neorealist narrative, unlike the German Neoobjectivist narrative, tends for the most part towards the poetic transfiguration of the represented object.

13. See for example Milanini, *Neorealismo*, p. 7.

14. *Il Politecnico* published "Prussianesimo e nazismo attraverso la letteratura" (33–34, Sept.-Dec. 1946) and "La crisi della filosofia borghese e le filosofie della crisi" (39, Dec. 1946).

15. Asor Rosa, "Lo stato democratico," p. 604; *Saggi sul realismo* and *Il Marxismo e la critica letteraria* were respectively published in 1950 and 1953 by Einaudi.

16. Cited in Livingstone, *Aesthetics and Politics*, p. 19.

17. Bloch, "Discussing Expressionism," in Livingstone, pp. 22–23.

18. Lukács, "Realism in the Balance," in Livingstone, p. 33.

19. Aristotle, *Poetics*, 51a30–51b13 and 59a20–59a30.

20. See Brown's study of the relationship between various forms of "causal" realism and Hegelianism in "Logic of Realism."

21. Lukács, *Meaning*, p. 114.

22. Bakhtin, "Bildungsroman," in *Speech Genres*, p. 23.

23. Lukács, *Meaning*, p. 62.

24. Lukács, "Realism in the Balance," in Livingstone, p. 56.

25. See Miccichè, pp. 21–22.

26. See Brunetta, *Storia*, p. 51.

27. See Brunetta, *Storia*, p. 282.

28. Livingstone, pp. 66–67.

29. Livingstone, p. 62.

30. Brecht, "Remarks on an Essay," in Livingstone, pp. 77–78.

31. Adorno, "Commitment," in Livingstone, pp. 177–95.

32. See Jameson, *Marxism*, pp. 169–73.

33. Brooks, *Reading*, p. 7. On Calvino's notion of praxis, see de Lauretis, "Narrative Discourse."

34. Adorno, "Reconciliation Under Duress," in Livingstone, p. 170.

35. Adorno, "Reconciliation," in Livingstone, p. 168.

36. Sartre, *What Is Literature?*, pp. 68–70.

37. Livingstone, p. 143.

38. Pasolini, "In morte del realismo," *La religione del mio tempo*, p. 152.

39. See "Risposte ai lettori," *Il Politecnico* 27 (March 30, 1946) and Franco Fortini, "Che cosa," p. 45.

40. On the Italian anti-Fascist Resistance before the development of the *Resistenza armata*, see Delzell, *Mussolini's Enemies*, pp. 42–258, and Collotti, *L'antifascismo*.

41. Quazza, *Resistenza*, p. 128.

42. Nora, "Il ritorno dell'avvenimento," in Le Goff and Nora, eds., *Fare Storia*, p. 140. An earlier version of Nora's essay was published in *Communications* 18 (1972) under the title "L'Evénement monstre."

43. The latter was the case, for example, of Gherardo Nerucci, a professional lawyer from Tuscany who collected and published *Sessanta novelle popolari montalesi* in 1880. As Roberto Fedi writes in his introduction to the 1977 edition of the anthology, while the *novelle* were rewritten by the author, they testify to a conscious attempt to "identify with the folk narrators" and to "bracket" the author's own "bourgeois identity," thus opposing the dominant literary and ideological conventions of the times. Vittorio Imbriani, on the other hand, a Neapolitan student of Francesco De Sanctis and a gifted poet, novelist, art critic, and folklore scholar, published a "stenographic" transcription of Florentine tales, *La novellaja fiorentina*. Calvino translated (and rewrote) stories from both these collections for his own *Fiabe italiane* (*Italian Folktales*).

44. Verga, "Lettera a Salvatore Farina," in *Tutte le novelle*, 1:167–8; *The She-Wolf and Other Stories*, p. 86.

45. Corti, *Il viaggio*, p. 43.

46. See Corti, *Il viaggio*, p. 29 and Calvino, "La letteratura," pp. 40–46.

47. Bakhtin, "Forms of Time and of the Chronotope in the Novel," in *Dialogic Imagination*, p. 208. A nostalgic recuperation of the "folkloric chronotope" characterizes most neorealist narrative in what I have called neorealism's second, "Mannerist" phase. The so-called *letteratura meridionalista* and *plebeista* tend to oppose the myths of simple peasant life and the authenticity of social strata still linked to precapitalist modes of production and social relations to the new, alienating reality of consumer capitalism in Italy. Among the most significant examples of this tendency are Francesco Jovine, *Le terre del Sacramento* (1950), Rocco Scotellaro, *È fatto giorno* (1954), Elio Vittorini, *Le donne di Messina* (1949), Domenico Rea, *Gesù, fate luce* (1950), Alberto Moravia's *La romana* (1947) and *La Ciociara* (1957), and Pier Paolo Pasolini, *Ragazzi di vita* (1955). A similar phenomenon may be traced in neorealist cinema, particularly in the films of Federico Fellini, *La strada* (1954) and *Le notti di Cabiria* (1957), and Vittorio De Sica's *L'oro di Napoli* (1954) and *Il tetto* (1956). See Carlo Lizzani, "Il neorealismo: quando è finito, quello che resta," in Miccichè, pp. 98–105.

48. See the entry "Fascismo," written in 1932 by Mussolini with the collaboration of Giovanni Gentile, for the state-sponsored *Enciclopedia Italiana* (vol. XIV), cited in Romano and Vivanti, eds., *Storia d'Italia* 4.2: 1479–80: "For the Fascist, everything is in the State, and nothing human or spiritual exists, or has any value, outside of the State. . . . Fascism is against socialism because socialism rigidifies the movement of history, reducing it to class struggle . . . and Fascism is against democ-

racy, which equalizes the people. . . . Fascism affirms the beneficial and irreparable inequality of men."

49. See in particular Asor Rosa, *Scrittori*.

50. De Sica, "Perché *Ladri di biciclette*," in Milanini, *Neorealismo*, p. 59.

51. Benjamin, *Illuminations*, p. 84.

52. Montale, "Non chiederci la parola" ("Don't Ask for the Word"), in *Tutte le poesie*, p. 47.

53. Among the few examples of full-fledged novels written in the wake of World War I in Italy is the justly famous *Rubè* (1921) by Giuseppe Antonio Borgese, the dramatic portrait of the disintegration of the ideals and the illusions of a whole generation. *Rubè* is (like Svevo's *Una vita*) an anti-*Bildungsroman*, a novel of disintegration rather than of formation.

54. Jakobson, "Closing Statement," pp. 350–77.

55. Sartre's influence on neorealism has been either ignored or underestimated by critics. See Milanini, "Introduzione," in *Neorealismo*, p. 11.

56. Cassola, "Ideologia o poesia?," in Milanini, *Neorealismo*, p. 229.

57. Bo, p. 11.

58. Among the autobiographical novels about the war in the Gettoni series are *La banda di Doehren* by Pietro Sissa, *Diario di un soldato semplice* by Raul Lunardi, *Il Campo degli ufficiali* by Giampiero Carocci, and *Il Sergente della neve* by Mario Rigoni Stern. The latter is often regarded as a "true masterpiece"; see Asor Rosa, "Lo stato democratico," p. 608. *Il visconte dimezzato*, the first novel of Calvino's fantastic trilogy *I nostri antenati*, also appeared—rather incongruously—in this same series.

59. Pavese, "Intervista alla radio" (1950), *Saggi letterari*, pp. 263–67. See also Elio Vittorini's statement on neorealism in Bo, pp. 28 and 30: "Each time you say the word [neorealism] you must endow it with a specific meaning. In essence you have as many neorealisms as there are valid narrators. . . . I also have written books . . . which explicitly reveal my own brand of neorealism. Nor has *Conversazione in Sicilia* shown me in a light that could justify saying I was no longer interested in neorealism." According to Corti, however, Vittorini's novels cannot be considered neorealist novels, with the partial exception of *Uomini e no*. See also Pampaloni, "La nuova letteratura," p. 859: "The Masters of neorealism . . . were Vittorini and Pavese, who were not neorealists." The reluctance of Corti, Pampaloni, and others to classify works by Pavese, Vittorini, and Moravia as neorealist narratives, however, seems caused by their rather limited view of neorealism itself.

60. Sartre, *What Is Literature?*, p. 284: "There is nothing more deplorable than the literary practice which, I believe, is called poetic prose and which consists of using words for the obscure harmonics which resound about them and which are made up of vague meanings which are in contradiction with clear signification."

61. In an important 1955 article, Calvino offers a positive re-evaluation of Montale and hermetic poetry, not only in terms of the crucial influence they had on his generation but also in terms of the political significance of their oppositional *reticentia*. See Calvino, "Il midollo del leone," in *Una pietra sopra*, p. 4. See also "Tre correnti del romanzo italiano d'oggi" (1959), in *Una pietra sopra*, pp. 48–49: "The poet of our youth was Eugenio Montale. His closed, harsh, difficult poems, devoid of any appeal to a history, except for an individual, inner history, were our point of departure. His universe without illusions—stony, dry, frozen—was for us the only one in which we could find our roots. . . . The rigor of Montale and Ungaretti . . . the rigor of Giorgio Morandi's paintings . . . have taught us that the things we can be sure of are very few and must be painstakingly scrutinized within ourselves: a lesson in stoicism." Concerning Giorgio Morandi, it is worth recalling that both his work and that of other painters (such as Carlo Carrà and Giorgio de Chirico) was severely criticized by left-wing critics after the war for ignoring the movement and dynamism of (present) history through its focus on the still life and for its disintegration of the human figure, thus presenting an image of man as irremediably alienated. See Trombadori, "Serietà," pp. 156–58. Trombadori explicitly compares Morandi to Montale in his article. The favored practitioner of a new kind of (neo)realist painting was Renato Guttuso, whose stark drawings of human figures often appear reproduced in *Rinascita* after 1947. See the letter to *Rinascita* (signed by Guttuso and several other Italian painters) advocating a "struggle against contemporary formalism . . . and the ideologies of decomposition," Dec. 12, 1948, repr. in Milanini, *Neorealismo*, pp. 84–85.

62. Commenting on the dissolution of the subject (the flow of the subject-in-process) in Joyce and in the *nouveau roman*, Calvino calls it a "nightmare" which relinquishes any positive vision of the subject as a historical being and contrasts it with Sartre's representation of the subject. See Calvino, "Natura e storia nel romanzo" (1958), in *Una pietra sopra*, pp. 37–38: "Sartre evoked the image of this nightmare . . . when the protagonist of *Nausea*, looking at himself in the mirror, loses the consciousness of his own individuality. But in Sartre this was only a point of departure to postulate self-consciousness, choice, and freedom." See also "La sfida al labirinto" (1962), in *Una pietra sopra*, pp. 96–97, where the Sartrean notion of commitment can still be clearly detected: "today we are beginning to ask from literature something more than the knowledge of an epoch or the mimesis of either objects or man's inner life. . . . We want from literature a global image, at the level of the epistemic planes which history has brought into play. And to those who in turn would like us to renounce . . . our constant need for historical meaning and moral judgment, I will answer that even in what claims to be a

metahistoric value what counts for us is the impact it has on the history of men."

63. Moravia, *L'uomo come fine*, pp. 113–30.

64. Sartre, *What Is Literature?*, p. 257.

65. Visconti, "Cinema antropomorfico," in Milanini, *Neorealismo*, pp. 32–34.

66. Pavese, "Ritorno all'uomo," in *Saggi letterari*, pp. 197–200.

67. Bo, p. 20.

68. These soldiers were nicknamed "Badogliani" for their royalist inclinations (but Fenoglio himself professed to be "apolitical").

69. For Fenoglio and the genesis of *Il partigiano Johnny*, see Corti, *Il viaggio*, pp. 40–41.

70. Calvino, "La letteratura italiana," p. 40.

71. See Calvino, preface to *Il Sentiero*, p. 22.

72. Spriano, p. 15.

73. See, for example, Corti, *Il viaggio*, p. 36.

74. A social historian and militant intellectual, Emilio Sereni had spent five years in Fascist prisons prior to the armistice, when he narrowly escaped execution by the Germans. In 1945 he became one of the heads of the CLNAI—the Committee for National Liberation in Upper Italy. After the war, he became the most outspoken advocate of Zhdanov's theories on culture and literature as "instruments" of socialism, which he expounded in a series of carefully and cogently argued conferences and essays written between 1948 and 1949, and collected in the volume *Scienza, marxismo e cultura*. On the influence of Zhdanovism in Italy after 1948, see Asor Rosa, "Lo Stato democratico," pp. 590–4.

75. See Calvino, "Natura e storia nel romanzo," in *Una pietra sopra*, p. 26: "It's a fact that when with Flaubert realist literature reaches the maximum of its faithfulness to the data of experience, the sense one derives from it is that of the vacuousness of everything. After having accumulated minute details and constructed an image of perfect truth, Flaubert taps it once with his hand to show us that it is hollow underneath, that everything that happens means nothing. The dreadfulness of that great novel which is *L'Education sentimentale* consists in this: that for hundreds and hundreds of pages you see flowing before your eyes the private lives of the characters or the public life of France, only to find finally that everything has dissolved like ashes in your hands."

Chapter 2

1. *Patrioti* (a publication of the First *Giustizia e Libertà* Brigade, Esercito Partigiano, Bologna Division) 1, no. 22 (1944) as cited in Falaschi, *La Resistenza armata*, pp. 16–17. On the partisan press, see Rosengarten,

Italian Anti-Fascist Press and Tarizzo, *Come scriveva*. For a bibliography of the partisan press, see Conti, *La Resistenza*. Conti lists 2,357 partisan newspapers.

2. On the symbolic space of romance as opposed to the space of realist narrative, see Jameson, *Political Unconscious*, p. 112.

3. Corti, *Il viaggio*, p. 40.

4. Austin, *How to Do Things*, pp. 101–8.

5. *Il Partigiano*, 3rd "Chichero" Division, 2, no. 12 (Aug. 1944), as cited in Corti, *Il viaggio*, p. 43.

6. Calvino, "La letteratura italiana," p. 41.

7. See Del Boca, *Dentro*, and Venturi, *Gli anni*. The latter includes only a few of Venturi's partisan stories. Silvio Micheli's stories were never published in book form, but he did publish a novel, *Pane duro*, which is a typically neorealist story about the difficult return of a war veteran to "normal life" and about the economic deprivations and hardships of that period. On Del Boca, Venturi, and Micheli as authors of partisan short stories, see Falaschi, *La Resistenza armata*, pp. 59–80. Although the partisan chronicles and mini-narratives influenced mostly younger writers, some writers of the older generation were also attracted and inspired by them. Elio Vittorini's "Scelti per la fucilazione" provides a typical example of the symbiosis between high literary style and the *narrativa clandestina*. See Corti, *Il viaggio*, p. 48. "Scelti" was published first as a short story in *L'Unità* and then inserted into *Uomini e no* as one of the documentary episodes of the novel. See *Uomini e no*, pp. 184–9.

8. The best and most comprehensive discussion of the partisan short story genre is in Falaschi, *La Resistenza armata*, pp. 54–81.

9. They do not, in other words, share the concern for the conflict between form and plausibility that Northrop Frye sees as characteristic of the realist writer. See Frye, *Fables*, p. 36: "The realistic writer soon finds that the requirements of literary form and plausible content always fight against each other."

10. Falaschi argues this point, I believe mistakenly, in *La Resistenza armata*, p. 76.

11. Calvino, preface to *Path*, p. xviii.

12. Calvino, "La letteratura italiana," p. 41.

13. Venturi, "Estate che mai dimenticheremo," in *Gli anni*, p. 11.

14. Ranke, p. 137.

15. Venturi, "I nostri morti," in *L'Unità*, Milan ed. (May 5, 1946).

16. Parri, "L'Italia partigiana," (Dec. 1945), cited in Delzell, p. 544.

17. Delzell, p. 545.

18. On Venturi's "Ci siamo," see Falaschi, *La Resistenza armata*, p. 65.

19. Bakhtin, *Dialogic Imagination*, pp. 15–17.

20. Muscetta, "Un diario dell'ultima guerra" (*La fiera letteraria*, July 24, 1947) in *Realismo*, p. 293.

21. Bianco, *Venti mesi*, p. 27.
22. Bianco, p. 8.
23. See Calvino, "Tre correnti del romanzo italiano d'oggi," in *Una pietra sopra*, p. 49: "The younger generation absorbed the lesson of Croce the moralist, rather than that of his philosophy and aesthetic theory."
24. Delzell, p. 100.
25. Delzell, p. 90.
26. See, for example, the front-page article by the Catholic philosopher Felice Balbo, "Cultura antifascista," in *Il Politecnico* 39 (Dec. 1947), 211–15.
27. See Quazza, pp. 28–29.
28. Delzell, p. 559.
29. Corti, *Il viaggio*, p. 57.
30. Calvino, "La letteratura italiana," p. 41.
31. Chiodi, *Banditi*, p. 1.
32. Bolis, *Il mio granello di sabbia*, pp. 9–10.
33. Pavese, "Guerriglia nei Castelli Romani," (*La nuova Europa*, Feb. 10, 1946) in *Saggi Letterari*, pp. 241–44.
34. *Società* 1, no. 1–2; 3; 4 (1946). On *Il Politecnico, Società*, and *Rinascita* in the immediate postwar period, see Zancan, "Tra vero," pp. 54–69. By Zancan see also "*Il Politecnico* mensile."
35. Piazzesi, "Necessità," p. 8.
36. Croce, *History*, pp. 282–3.
37. Unsigned editorial, "Letteratura d'occasione," *Società* 1, no. 4 (1946), pp. 6–7. These ideas were not, of course, altogether new in the Italian cultural landscape. The word *occasione* immediately calls to mind the title of a famous collection of poems by Eugenio Montale, *Le occasioni*, written from the late 1920's to the late 1930's. The word *cronaca* evokes in turn one of Romano Bilenchi's novels, *Cronaca dell'Italia meschina*, and the short stories of *Anna e Bruno*, devoted to the minute occurrences and simple feelings of common people in the lyrical style of *prosa d'arte*. Vasco Pratolini's own narrative work of the early 1940's had been a kind of realistic-lyrical chronicle, and his novels of the neorealist period—most notably *Cronache di poveri amanti*—reflect a continuity of poetics, thematics, and style, rather than any radical postwar innovation.
38. Piazzesi, "Necessità," p. 8.
39. See De Sica, "Perchè ladri di biciclette," in Milanini, *Neorealismo*, p. 59: "My goal . . . is to trace the dramatic quality of situations from daily life, the marvelous in the minute—or rather, in the most minute—chronicle of everyday events, which most people think of as drab subject matter. . . . Realism cannot be, in my opinion, mere documentation." About De Sica's neorealist films and the aesthetics of neorealism, see the still-fundamental essays by Bazin in *What Is Cinema?*, particu-

larly "An Aesthetic of Reality: Cinematic Realism and the Italian School of the Liberation," 2: 16–40, "*Bicycle Thief*," 2: 57–60, "De Sica: Metteur en Scène," 2: 61–78, and "*Umberto D*: A Great Work," 2: 79–82. Bazin refers to the Italian neorealist films as "first and foremost reconstituted reportage" (2: 20).

40. Zavattini, "*Umberto D*," p. 10: "*Paisà*, *Roma città aperta*, *Sciuscià*, *Ladri di biciclette*, *La terra trema* all contain things of an absolute significancy which reflect the concept of a narratable whole, but are always in a certain sense metaphorical, *because they still have an invented narrative* and not a documentary spirit. In a film like *Umberto D.*, the analytic fact is rather more evident, *but still, however, within the traditional [narrative] order*. We have not yet attained a true neorealism." See also Zavattini, "A Thesis on Neo-Realism," in Overbey, pp. 67–78.

41. Pratolini, "Cronache fiorentine," p. 27.

42. Braudel, p. 3.

43. Pratolini, "Per un saggio," pp. 14–19.

44. On the "cinematic" strategies of *Cronache di poveri amanti*, see Asor Rosa, "Il neorealismo e il trionfo del narrativo," in Tinazzi and Zancan, pp. 94–102.

45. The poetics of the chronicle, the themes of the everyday life of the poor in urban environments, the use of the reality effect, and the incorporation of dialect and vernacular forms variously "filtered" and/or translated into colloquial and literary Italian all characterize a vast amount of the literature of neorealism between 1945 and 1948. Giuseppe Marotta's *L'oro di Napoli*, Carlo Bernari's *Napoli pace e guerra*, Alberto Moravia's *Racconti romani*, and Domenico Rea's *Spaccanapoli* are examples of this kind of narrative.

46. Unsigned editorial, *Il Politecnico* 29 (May 1946), p. 45.

47. "Coerenza degli scrittori," unsigned editorial, *Società* 2, no. 6 (1946), p. 309.

48. Vittorini, "Una nuova cultura," p. 1.

49. See "Rispondiamo ai nostri lettori," *Il Politecnico* 27 (March 30, 1946), p. 4.

50. Fortini, "Documenti," p. 3.

51. Vittorini, "Letteratura sovietica."

52. Vittorini, "Letteratura e fini sociali."

53. Calamandrei, p. 3.

54. Calamandrei, p. 3.

55. Brooks, p. xi.

56. Brooks, p. 238.

57. Fortini, "La poesia."

58. Fortini, "Capoversi," p. 18.

59. Togliatti, "Politica e cultura." See also Alicata, "La corrente 'Politecnico.'"

60. Vittorini, "Politica e cultura."

61. Onofri, "Politica," p. 2.
62. Onofri, "*Uomini e no.*"
63. See Spriano, p. 57.
64. Togliatti, "Vittorini," p. 393.
65. See Grassi, "Responsabilità."
66. Pintor, "L'ultima lettera," p. 120.
67. On Del Buono, see Corti, *Il viaggio*, pp. 105–10. On the theme of the Resistance in Italian novels, see Rosengarten, "Italian Resistance Novel." Rosengarten traces the theme of the Resistance in seven novels: Elio Vittorini's *Uomini e no*, Vasco Pratolini's *Cronache di poveri amanti*, Calvino's *Il sentiero dei nidi di ragno*, Renata Viganò's *L'Agnese va a morire*, Cesare Pavese's *La casa in collina*, Carlo Cassola's *Fausto e Anna* (1952), and Mario Tobino's *Il clandestino* (1962).
68. Gadda, interviewed in Bo, pp. 49–50.
69. Brena, p. 3.
70. According to Lodge, *Modes*, p. 25, literary realism is indeed characterized by "the representation of experience in a manner which approximates closely the description of similar experience in non-literary texts of the same culture."
71. *Rome Open City* is a melodrama, and one "literary" model for its central scene, where Manfredi—the partisan CLN leader—is tortured under the eyes of Don Pietro, may indeed be Puccini's *Tosca*. Rossellini's key statements about neorealism may be found in "A Few Words on Neo-Realism," in Overbey, pp. 89–91. On Rossellini, see Bazin, "An Aesthetic of Reality" and "In Defense of Rossellini" in *What Is Cinema?*, 2: 93–101.
72. See Calvino, "*I promessi sposi*: il romanzo dei rapporti di forza," in *Una pietra sopra*, pp. 267–78.
73. Rossellini, *War Trilogy*, pp. 315–16.
74. See Bazin's classic analysis of this episode, "An Aesthetic of Reality," in *What Is Cinema?*, 2: 34–37.
75. Rossellini, p. 348.
76. See Armes, p. 148.
77. See Holquist's "Glossary," appended to Bakhtin, *Dialogic Imagination*, p. 427: "A word, discourse, language or culture undergoes 'dialogization' when it becomes relativized, de-privileged, aware of competing definitions for the same things. Undialogized language is authoritative and absolute."
78. Ermarth, p. 39.
79. For Bersani, p. 63, realism may serve as a strategy for containing and repressing a society's "disorder" through the telling of "significant stories about itself."
80. The theme of the life of the lower classes under the regime is central to Pavese's *Il compagno* and Pratolini's *Cronache*. However, as Calvino observes in "La letteratura italiana," pp. 44–45, the former is "a

novel that is beautiful above all as a love story," while the latter "plays too much on popular themes, sentimentality, and folklore." Other neorealist narratives set during the Fascist era are Carlo Bernari's *Prologo alle tenebre* (1947), Guido Seborga's *L'uomo di Camporosso* (1948), and Angelo Del Boca's *L'anno del Giubileo* (1948). None of these novels, however, provides more than a moralistic and Manichaean representation of Fascism. There are of course several other novels which scrutinize Fascist society and mores more in depth, but they are not neorealist novels. Some of the most important ones are Ignazio Silone, *Fontamara* (published in Switzerland in 1933; it appeared in Italy only in 1949); Carlo Emilio Gadda, *Quer pasticciaccio brutto de via Merulana* (1957, but published in *La Fiera Letteraria* in 1946–47); and Vitaliano Brancati, *Il Bell'Antonio* (1949).

81. Calvino, "Tre correnti del romanzo italiano," in *Una pietra sopra*, p. 55. On Moravia's use of the discourse of psychoanalysis the most important critical contribution is still Dominique Fernandez, *Il romanzo*, pp. 19–113.

82. "I had an experience which intellectuals don't usually have; I lived with peasants, ate their food, slept with them, stayed with them all day." Cited in Armes, p. 65.

83. Gadda, "Psicanalisi e letteratura," in *I viaggi*, pp. 43–45. The resistance to the critical discourse of psychoanalysis in Italy is a persistent postwar phenomenon which began to subside only in the 1970's, through the work of philosophers and literary critics such as Carlo Sini, Aldo Gargani, Remo Bodei, Franco Rella, Giuseppe Sertoli, Francesco Orlando, Mario Lavagetto, Alessandro Serpieri, and Sergio Zatti. See Pagnini, "La recezione" and David, *La psicanalisi*.

84. See, for example, "Psicanalisi e poesia" (*La Fiera Letteraria*, August 8, 1946), in *Nuove*, 1: 258–9 and the preface to the pamphlet "Come il Marx fece passare il comunismo dall'utopia alla scienza" (1948), in *Nuove*, 1: 128–31.

85. Croce, *Nuove*, 1: 215–16 and 222.

86. See Brunetta, *Umberto Barbaro*.

87. Viganò, *L'Agnese*, p. 20.

88. See Siti, *Il neorealismo*, pp. 233–50. Viganò's novel is one of the most typical products of Italian neorealism. The historical reality of the war and the Resistance is signified through specific historical dates and brief references to real events, as well as the traditional topoi codified as signs of the real in all neorealist war narratives: a scene of deportation of innocent victims to Germany (pp. 34–38); the execution of a partisan whose corpse is publicly exposed with a placard (p. 29), the execution of a spy (pp. 86–87). As Siti observes (p. 235), these scenes do not fulfill any plot need. They are, in other words, "reality effects" as Barthes has described them.

89. Puccini, "C'è già un'arte della Resistenza," in *Vie nuove* 1, no. 6

(1946), cited in Brunetta, *Storia*, p. 141. The priest in this scene is played by Carlo Lizzani, a communist and the future director of the film adaptation of *Cronache di poveri amanti*. The heroic role assigned to a catholic priest played by a communist in a left-wing film, and the attention devoted to the scene in which the priest's heroism is most evident (as well as to the work of a catholic director like Rossellini) reflect the atmosphere of national solidarity of the first phase of the Reconstruction.

90. *Paesi tuoi*, however, was clearly influenced by Pavese's reading of Faulkner, whatever Pavese may claim.

91. Pavese, "Sherwood Anderson," *Saggi*, p. 42.

92. Pavese, "L'arte: l'ordine dov'è il caos" (1932 preface to his translation of Sherwood Anderson, *Dark Laughter*), in *Saggi*, pp. 44–47.

93. Pavese, "Sherwood Anderson," in *Saggi*, p. 43.

94. Pavese was a reader of Frazer, and the Girardian logic that is detectable in his novel may be attributed to Frazer's influence on Girard himself. See René Girard, *La violence*, p. 184: "Le monde moderne n'ignore plus, en particulier depuis Frazer, que certaines fêtes comportaient anciennement des sacrifices humains."

95. Paradoxically, though, one of the most powerful of Pavese's characters is a woman, Clelia ("Tra donne sole"), in *La bella estate*. Calvino believes Clelia is not only the finest of Pavese's characters but also the most autobiographical; see "Il midollo del leone," in *Una pietra sopra*, pp. 7–8.

96. Pavese, *Paesi*, p. 13.

97. Girard, *La violence*, pp. 56–59. For a different interpretation of the use of myth and the theme of ritual sacrifice in Pavese, see Procaccini, "Pavese." Procaccini argues that myth for Pavese does not disclose an essential, meta-historical truth, but is rather a specific historical function.

98. See Lucente's insightful reading of Verga's story in *Narrative*, pp. 54–94 and also his briefer analysis of myth and ritualized violence in *La luna e i falò* (pp. 134–44).

99. This insight is developed by Pavese himself in his story "Jettatura" (1936), *Racconti*, 1: 149–54.

100. Derrida, "Structure," p. 254.

101. Cantoni, pp. 34–38.

102. Ferrata, p. 3.

103. Debenedetti, p. 27.

104. Debenedetti traces an anxiety-of-influence romance in his essay, deploying a series of tropes and metaphors and a creative critical-literary style which are characteristic of all his work and are reminiscent of Harold Bloom's poetic criticism.

105. Croce, "Psicanalisi e poesia," in *Nuove*, 1: 258.

106. Croce, "Concetti critici inadatti," in *Nuove*, 1: 201.

107. Eco, *Theory*, pp. 3–31.

108. Foucault, *Order*, p. 373.
109. See Nowell-Smith, p. 16.
110. Visconti, "Cadaveri" (*Cinema* 119, June 1941), in Mida and Quaglietti, pp. 147–49.
111. See De Santis's statement in this regard, in Mida and Quaglietti, p. 114.
112. Puccini, "La questione dei soggetti" (*Si gira* March 2, 1942), in Mida and Quaglietti, p. 217.
113. Pietrangeli, "Analisi spettrale del film realistico" (*Cinema* 146, July 25, 1942), in Mida and Quaglietti, p. 228.
114. See Alicata, "Ambiente e società nel racconto cinematografico" (*Cinema* 135, Feb. 10, 1942), in Mida and Quaglietti, pp. 152–3.
115. Nowell-Smith, p. 20.
116. Pietrangeli, "Analisi," in Mida and Quaglietti, p. 226.
117. On the conventions of commercial film during the Fascist period, see Mida and Quaglietti and Landy, *Fascism*.
118. Alicata and De Santis, "Verità e poesia: Verga e il cinema italiano" (*Cinema* 127, Oct. 1941), in Mida and Quaglietti, p. 201. See also Alicata and De Santis, "Ancora di Verga e del cinema italiano (*Cinema* 130, Nov. 1941), in Mida and Quaglietti, pp. 209–12.
119. Alicata and De Santis, "Verità e poesia," in Mida and Quaglietti, p. 203.
120. Sartre, *What Is Literature?*, p. 228.
121. Calvino, "Tre correnti del romanzo italiano," in *Una pietra sopra*, pp. 47–48.
122. Calvino, "Tre correnti," in *Una pietra sopra*, p. 48. See also Calvino, "Hemingway e noi." On the influence of American literature on Italian narrative, see Heiney, *America*, and Fernandez, *Il mito*. Regarding Hemingway's influence on the style of *Il sentiero*, see De Mara, "Pathway."
123. Pavese, "Intervista alla radio," in *Saggi*, p. 264.
124. Pavese's stubborn and almost religious commitment to Communism, and his vision of the masses as the only potential redeemers of modern man's alienation, served him as a myth which increasingly took on the character of a ritual exorcism, in an effort to transcend the fatalistic pessimism of his literary work. Pavese's suicide in August 1950 greatly embarrassed the PCI and was widely interpreted as the symptom of a "crisis" of Italian Marxist intellectuals. See Spriano, pp. 33–47. Spriano cites two letters written by Calvino to Valentino Gerratana about a month after Pavese's suicide, in which Calvino says that Pavese's lack of doubts regarding PCI policies indicated that he had never really come to terms with Marxism. Calvino concludes that Pavese's suicide was a "private" tragedy that could only have a cathartic effect on other Italian Marxist intellectuals.
125. Contini, *Letteratura*, p. 241. Contini compares this narrative de-

vice in Verga's *I Malavoglia* to the use of the voice of Pinocchio as the narrator of his own story in Carlo Collodi's classic *Le avventure di Pinocchio* (*The Adventures of Pinocchio*, 1883). This analogy is not as unlikely as it might seem at first, for both Verga and Collodi were steeped in the folk art of storytelling. Collodi's tale, with its mix of the fantastic and the historical, serves as one of the literary models for Calvino's *The Path*. For Calvino, the works of both Collodi and Verga show how a folk tradition of storytelling, with its seemingly naive point of view on historical events, can be incorporated into more complex fictional narratives.

126. See Baldi, *L'artificio*.

127. Pietrangeli, "Analisi spettrale," in Mida and Quaglietti, p. 228.

128. Verga, *The She-Wolf*, p. 209.

129. Verga, preface, *House*, p. 210.

130. Alicata, "Ambiente," in Mida and Quaglietti, p. 153.

131. Alicata and De Santis, "Ancora di Verga," in Mida and Quaglietti, pp. 211–2.

132. Miccichè, "Per una verifica del neorealismo," in *Il neorealismo*, p. 18.

133. Calvino, in *The Uses of Literature*, p. 96; *Una pietra sopra*, p. 290.

134. For an analysis of *Giorni di Gloria*'s rhetoric, see Canziani, pp. 147–49.

135. Two important "essayistic" political novels published in Italy in 1945, Carlo Levi's *Cristo si è fermato ad Eboli* (*Christ Stopped at Eboli*) and Ignazio Silone's *Fontamara*—both best-sellers around the world—contributed greatly to bring the *questione meridionale* to the forefront during the early Reconstruction period. For an overview of the economic and political aspects of the *questione meridionale* during the Reconstruction, see P. A. Allum, "The South and National Politics, 1945–1950," in Woolf, ed., *Rebirth*, pp. 95–120.

136. See the first version of Visconti's scenario for *La terra trema* published in *Bianco e nero* 12, no. 2–3 (1951). See also the film's transcript, *La terra trema*.

137. Nowell-Smith, pp. 33–42. For a more balanced perspective, see Ishaghpour, *Visconti*, pp. 48–52.

138. See Berti, "La situazione," and Tarrow, *Peasant Communism*.

139. Allum, "The South and National Politics," in Woolf, pp. 115–8.

140. The use of the actors' own names is another convention of neorealist film; see Bazin, 1: 55; 65.

141. Cited in Armes, p. 97.

142. The Catholic Church continued these rather unorthodox maneuvers, which included the practice of allowing members of the clergy to accompany and "assist" incapacitated or illiterate people in the voting booth, well into the 1950's and 1960's. Calvino's satirical short novel *La giornata di uno scrutatore* recreates the grotesque atmosphere of an election poll in the famous Turin Catholic hospital for invalids and

incurables, "Il Cottolengo," during the 1953 national elections, as seen from the point of view of a Communist Party member assigned to work there as a poll-watcher.

143. Spriano, p. 18.

144. The most important of Calvino's contributions to the political debate of the early 1960's is the essay "L'antitesi operaia" (*Il Menabo 7*, 1964), in *Una pietra sopra*, pp. 100–113. In the introductory paragraph (written in 1980), Calvino defines this essay as his last attempt to provide a comprehensive analysis of disparate economic, social, and cultural phenomena.

145. Spriano, p. 17.

146. Calvino, in *Uses of Literature*, pp. 89–100.

147. De Man, *Allegories*, p. 19.

Chapter 3

1. "Liguria magra e ossuta," "Riviera di Ponente," "Sanremo città dell'oro." A bibliography of Calvino's early short stories, reviews, editorial notes, and articles (never republished) may be found in Falaschi, "Calvino," and in Ferretti, *Le capre*.

2. Introductory note, *Gli amori*, p. vi. Most of the biographical information available on the early phase of Calvino's career is contained in this note which, although unsigned, is surely by Calvino himself.

3. On Calvino's activity as an editor for Einaudi, see Eco, "On Calvino," p. 4: "As a consultant to the Einaudi publishing house, [Calvino] was a generous discoverer of new talents and worked on the texts of others as passionately as he worked on his own. . . . In 1959, when we met, he told me that he had read in a music journal an article of mine on the 'open work' (*opera aperta*). It interested him and he asked me to write a book on the subject. Then, as chance would have it, I wrote the book but for a different publisher [*L'opera aperta* (Milan: Bompiani, 1962)]. Without Calvino's encouragement, however, I would have never undertaken the task. . . . Beyond Calvino the great novelist, we should remember . . . Calvino the instigator of culture. He was an irreplaceable figure in the cultural history of recent decades."

4. *Gli amori*, p. vi.

5. Spriano, p. 17.

6. Spriano, p. 19.

7. Cited in Spriano, p. 29.

8. Spriano, p. 28.

9. Calvino's father was a professor of agriculture, his mother a professor of botany. Both spent many years in Mexico and the Caribbean (Calvino was born in Cuba) before moving back to Italy. They were both free thinkers and gave their children no religious education. See "By Way of an Autobiography," in *Uses of Literature*, pp. 339–40: "My par-

ents' knowledge was all concentrated on the vegetable kingdom, its marvels and virtues." Some of Calvino's early stories, such as "Uomo dei gerbidi" (1946), "I fratelli Bagnasco" (1946), "L'occhio del padrone" (1947), and "Pranzo con un pastore" (1948) are about the Ligurian peasants. These stories, collected in *Ultimo viene il corvo* along with a number of Calvino's stories about the Resistance, were later included in the section entitled "Le memorie difficili" in *I racconti*.

10. After *Ultimo viene il corvo*, Calvino eliminated these autobiographical stories from all subsequent editions and anthologies of his stories. A reprint of the original 1949 edition of *Ultimo viene il corvo* was, however, reissued in 1976. An end-note by Calvino explains that the author had no longer wished to republish the 1945 stories "because the experience of the Resistance is still rendered in the manner of an emotional re-evocation, in contrast to the style he developed later" (p. 247). For a reading of these stories, pointing to elements which re-emerge in *The Path*, see Falaschi, *La Resistenza armata*, pp. 108–26.

11. For a reading of the fairy tale as the dialogical antagonist of the epic, see Bloch, "Zerstörung, Rettung des Mythos durch Licht," in *Verfremdungen*, 1: 152–62. Concerning Bloch's notion of the fairy tale, see Jameson, *Marxism*, p. 131 and *Political Unconscious*, p. 86. The need for commitment in literature and the narrative mode of the fairy tale are explicitly linked by Calvino in "Il midollo del leone" (1955), in *Una pietra sopra*, pp. 12–15: "The novels we would like to write or to read are 'action' novels. . . . What interests us most are the trials and tests man must undergo and the way in which he overcomes them. The mould of the remotest fables (the child abandoned in the woods or the knight who must fight against wild beasts or magic spells) remains the fundamental scheme of all human stories."

12. Calvino, *"Rancore."*

13. In the prefatory note to *Gli amori*, p. vii, Calvino lists a series of film episodes, plays, songs, and artwork inspired by or based on a number of his stories.

14. Benjamin, *Illuminations*, p. 102.

15. Calvino, prefatory note, *Gli amori*, pp. x–xi.

16. See de Lauretis, "Narrative Discourse," p. 415: "The conceptual basis of structuralism and semiotics . . . intrigues and affects Calvino the writer, giving a new slant to motifs and concerns already apparent in his earlier works." On the notion of narrative *combinatoire*, see also Calvino's 1967 essay "Cibernetica e fantasmi (Appunti sulla narrativa come processo combinatorio)," in *Una pietra sopra*, pp. 164–81, trans. "Cybernetics and Ghosts," in *Uses of Literature*, pp. 3–27.

17. *Adam, One Afternoon*, p. 47. I have considerably altered the translation here and elsewhere to follow the original more closely.

18. See the 1964 preface to *The Path*, p. ix (*Il sentiero*, p. 10): "The daily scene of my whole life had become entirely extraordinary and ad-

venturous: a single story unwound from the dark arches of the Old City up to the woods. It was the pursuit and the concealment of armed men."

19. Benjamin, *Illuminations*, p. 102.

20. This strategy, particularly in *Il sentiero dei nidi di ragno*, has been called "cinematic" by Manacorda, p. 197.

21. Benjamin, *Illuminations*, p. 86. See also Calvino's introduction to *Fiabe italiane*, p. xlv: "The moral is always implicit in the folktale . . . rarely is it sententiously or didactically presented. No doubt the moral function of the tale, in the popular conception, is to be sought not in the subject matter but in the very nature of the tale, the mere fact of telling and listening."

22. See the interview with Corti, "Italo Calvino," p. 5: "Recently, re-reading the scene of the hunt in the 'Légende de Saint Julien l'Hospitalier,' I relived with precise intensity the moment in which that taste for the gothic and the animalistic, which surfaces in a story such as 'Ultimo viene il corvo' and in other stories of that period, formed in me." Carter, in *Calvino*, pp. 13–23, offers a detailed psychological reading of "Last Comes the Crow," without, however, referring to Flaubert's story.

23. Flaubert, *Three Tales*, p. 87; *Trois contes*, p. 97.

24. Appendix, Flaubert, *Trois contes*, p. 180.

25. Flaubert, *Trois contes*, p. 71.

26. Flaubert's story is therefore modeled on the archetype of what Bloch, in "Philosophische Ansicht des Detektivromans," in *Verfremdungen*, 1: 58, has called the "Oedipal metaphysic" of past-oriented religious cosmologies and heroic sagas, for which the origin of the world and of human existence itself is marked by transgression and violence. For a discussion of this idea of Bloch's, see Jameson, *Marxism*, pp. 130–31.

27. Jameson, *Political Unconscious*, p. 86.

28. Flaubert, *Three Tales*, p. 67.

29. For two different interpretations of this story, see Falaschi, *La resistenza armata*, pp. 137–42 and Carter, *Calvino*, ch. 1.

30. Calvino, preface, p. viii (pp. 9–10).

31. Brooks, p. 97. I am also indebted to the discussion of repetition in Miller, *Fiction*, pp. 1–21.

32. Croce, *History*, p. 19.

33. On historical narrative (and narrative in general) as a means to endow the past with a comprehensible form, see the fundamental essay by Mink, "Narrative Form." On the notion of narrative mimesis, specifically in historical narrative, see Ricoeur, *Time and Narrative*. Ricoeur, 1: 3–87, argues that narrative mimesis is based on a threefold process of figuration, involving the author's prefiguration (or mapping out) of the practical field of experience, textual configuration, and refiguration through the reception of the work.

34. Bakhtin, *Dialogic Imagination*, p. 15.

35. Bakhtin, *Dialogic Imagination,* p. 17: "Thanks to this epic distance, which excludes any possibility of activity and change, the epic achieves a radical degree of completedness not only in its content but in its meaning and its values as well. The epic world is constructed in the zone of an absolute distanced image, beyond the sphere of possible contact with the developing, incomplete and therefore re-thinking and re-evaluating present."

36. Lukács, *Historical Novel,* p. 416.

37. Lukács, *Historical Novel,* p. 36.

38. Lukács, *Historical Novel,* p. 42.

39. Lukács, *Historical Novel,* p. 52.

40. Lukács, *Historical Novel,* p. 50.

41. For a critique of the notion of historical progress, see Bloch, *Differenzierungen*; Gehlen, "Die Saekularisierung"; and Vattimo, *La fine,* pp. 98–120.

42. On focalization as a narrative device, see Genette, *Narrative Discourse,* pp. 189–94.

43. Calvino's fiction is filled with naive narrators and/or focalizers; Dickens's Pip (*Great Expectations*) and Robert Louis Stevenson's Jim Hawkins (*Treasure Island*) are among Calvino's recurring models. For a discussion of this device and of its ideological-political function in the *Trilogy* and in some of Calvino's short stories, see Woodhouse, *Calvino,* pp. 58–70. For a critique of both this device and the use of the fairy-tale paradigm as a form of "mere play," see Baudrillard, "Les Romans."

44. Pin does "instinctively" what Mr. Palomar does consciously through his attempts to see the objects around him by bracketing all cultural presuppositions through a kind of phenomenological reduction to pure perception (only to discover that perception itself is culturally constructed). See Cannon, "Calvino's Challenge," p. 192.

45. That is, a member of a GAP, or *Gruppo armato patrioti,* which was the smallest unit of the Italian partisan organization in urban areas.

46. Lévi-Strauss, *Savage Mind,* p. 17. Calvino did not, of course, know Lévi-Strauss's work (which first appeared in French in 1962), but he may have derived his interest in the notion of "game" and "play" as an epistemological/cultural activity from Huizinga's *Homo Ludens* (1939), which was published in Italy in 1946, as well as from his reading of Freud. The Freudian connotations of Pin's game in this and other scenes will be explored in detail in Chapter 5 of this study. On the function of play in Calvino's narrative, see Gatt-Rutter, "Calvino Ludens"; Iliano, "Per una definizione"; and Segre, "Se una notte."

47. Battaglia, *Un uomo,* pp. 236–38.

48. See Pavone, "Le idee della Resistenza," and Quazza, pp. 10–15.

49. Quazza, p. 12.

50. Battaglia, *Storia,* pp. 114–15, 251, 264, 280, 349.

51. White, "Value of Narrativity," p. 27.

52. These "motivations" include the desire to make the Resistance into a chapter in the continuing history of class-conflict while rationalizing the PCI's policies from 1943–45.

53. Longo, p. 196 and p. 204.

54. For a different reading, see Milanini, "Natura." Milanini argues that the absence of historical information and of data about the characters' background is because the past "is not worth remembering" (p. 532).

55. Barthes, *Writing Degree Zero*, p. 30.

56. See the mini-narrative by "Alpino" analyzed in Chapter 2.

57. On double-voicedness, see Bakhtin, *Dialogical Imagination*, p. 324.

58. On the stylistic refraction of speech in the novel, see Bakhtin, *Problems*, pp. 202–4.

59. Bahktin, *Problems*, p. 225.

60. *Il sentiero*, p. 17. This passage is missing from Colquhoun's English translation.

61. See Calvino, "Guide to *The Charterhouse of Parma* for the Use of New Readers" (originally published in *La Repubblica*, Sept. 8, 1982), in *Uses of Literature*, pp. 256–58: "No statistics will be able [to tell us] how many young readers will be overwhelmed from the very first pages [of Stendhal's novel], and will be suddenly convinced that the most wonderful novel in the world could only be this one, and recognize it as the novel they have always wanted to read and one that will be a touchstone for all the novels they read in the future. I am speaking chiefly of the first chapters. As one reads, one finds a different novel—in fact several novels, all different from one another, and this demands adjustments in the way we participate in events. However, the power of the opening continues to make itself felt. . . . The atmosphere of pure adventure that one enters with the sixteen-year-old Fabrice on the sopping battlefield of Waterloo . . . is the true novelistic [*romanzesco*] spirit of adventure, made up of a mixture of peril and safety with a strong dose of candor. What is more, the corpses, with their staring eyes and rigid arms, are the first real corpses the literature of war ever used to explain what war really is. . . . Is it the fact of belonging to a generation that lived through wars and political disasters in its youth that has made me a reader of *The Charterhouse* for life?"

62. Calvino, "Natura," in *Una pietra sopra*, p. 30.

63. Marx, *Contribution*, p. 217.

64. See Manzoni, *Betrothed*, pp. 319–20.

65. Manzoni, *Betrothed*, pp. 321–22.

66. Shklovsky, *Teoria*, pp. 5–72.

67. Shklovsky, "Art," p. 17.

68. Erlich, *Russian Formalism*, pp. 122–24.

69. Lemon and Reis translate the terms *fabula* and *sjuzet* as "story" and "plot" in their anthology. *Histoire* and *récit* are Genette's terms.

70. For the notions of anachrony, analepsis, and prolepsis in narrative time, see Genette, *Narrative Discourse*, pp. 35–79.

71. Benjamin, *Illuminations*, p. 102.

72. Said, *Beginnings*, p. 352.

73. Corti, "Calvino Interviewed," p. 5. Lucente outlines the folktale motifs of *The Path* in *Beautiful Fables*, pp. 267–76. Lucente's insightful study, which appeared after I had already completed Chapter 3 of this book, confirms that Calvino makes highly self-conscious use of folktale devices and themes in *The Path*, analyzable in terms of Propp's method. Lucente also points out that Calvino thematizes the act of storytelling itself in the novel through Red Wolf's "inserted tale" about the killing of Pelle in chapter 11.

74. For a Proppian analysis of *Pinocchio*, see Génot, *Analyse*. The fairy-tale structure described by Propp is most evident in Calvino's *Marcovaldo, ovvero le stagioni in città*, a series of twenty stories Calvino wrote between 1952 and 1962. The naive protagonist and focalizer of these stories, Marcovaldo, has many traits in common with Pin. He is a *proletario povero* from the country, and his discovery (and constant misreading) of the realities of the "big city" and of consumer society is designed to produce an ironic estrangement effect on the reader. Corti offers a Proppian-structuralist reading of the Marcovaldo stories in *Il viaggio*, pp. 185–200. She points out that in the later stories the linear fairy-tale structure is subverted through the interference of fantastic, surrealistic, symbolic, and allegorical motifs which prevent any narrative closure and render the texts polysemic. Corti attributes this "radical change" (p. 196) to Calvino's development of a subtler understanding of the relationship between ideology and literary discourse in the late 1950's and early 1960's. However, *The Path* already exhibits the same kind of structural and semantic complexity that Corti finds only in the later Marcovaldo stories.

75. Propp, *Morphology*, p. 21.

76. Some of the classic texts of structuralist narrative analysis inspired by Propp are Bremond, "La logique"; Greimas, *Sémantique*; and Todorov, *Grammaire*.

77. Propp, *Morphology*, p. 64.

78. See Propp, *Morphology*, p. 64.

79. Propp, *Morphology*, p. 112.

80. Jameson, *Prison-House*, pp. 79–81.

81. Shklovsky, "Art," p. 18.

82. See, for example, Jameson, *Prison-House*, p. 75 and Steiner, *Russian Formalism*, pp. 55–57.

83. Shklovsky, "The Resurrection of the Word" (1914), cited in Steiner, p. 49.

84. Shklovsky, *Materials and Style in Lev-Tolstoj's "War and Peace."* See Erlich, pp. 122–23.

85. Erlich, pp. 179–80.

86. Calvino, *Fiabe italiane*, p. xx.

87. At least according to the Aarne-Thompson Index of folktale types (which Calvino used), where fairy tales are classified under folktale types 300–749. See Dundes, introduction to Propp, *Morphology*, p. xiv.

88. Calvino, introduction, *Italian Folktales*, p. xxxi (*Fiabe*, p. xx). I have slightly altered the translation of the introduction (by Catherine Hull) here and elsewhere to be more faithful to the original (the introduction and Calvino's commentary to the tales have been condensed by the translators, chiefly at the expense of scholarly references).

89. Propp's book was translated into Italian and published by Einaudi in 1949.

90. Calvino, introduction, *Fiabe italiane*, p. xviii.

91. See the useful analysis by Beckwith, "Italo Calvino." Beckwith does not discuss Propp's influence on Calvino.

92. Calvino, introduction, *Fiabe italiane*, p. xli.

93. Calvino, introduction, *Italian Folktales*, p. xxx (*Fiabe*, p. xliv).

94. See de Lauretis's interpretation of Propp's reading of the Oedipus story in *Alice Doesn't*, pp. 113–16.

95. De Lauretis, *Alice Doesn't*, p. 115.

96. Calvino, introduction, *Italian Folktales*, p. xxi (*Fiabe*, p. xxvi).

97. Calvino, introduction, *Italian Folktales*, p. xxi (*Fiabe*, p. xxvi).

98. Calvino, introduction, *Italian Folktales*, p. xxii (*Fiabe*, p. xxviii). Calvino observes, for example, how much the specific historical milieu and the individual personality and imagination of Agatuzza Messia, the illiterate old Sicilian woman (a quilt maker) from whom Giuseppe Pitré takes most of his tales (Calvino retells ten of them in his own anthology) influenced the form and content of the tales themselves: "Messia, like a typical Sicilian storyteller, fills her narrative with color, nature, objects; she conjures up magic, but often grounding it in a realistic situation, a picture of the condition of the common people. . . . She is always ready to bring to life female characters who are active, enterprising, and courageous, in contrast with the traditional concept of the Sicilian woman as a passive and withdrawn creature. This strikes me as a personal, conscious choice" (p. xxii; xxx).

99. Calvino, introduction, *Fiabe*, p. xxii.

100. Calvino, introduction, *Italian Folktales*, p. xxxii (*Fiabe*, p. xlvi).

101. Calvino, *Italian Folktales*, p. 616. Another of Messia's tales, entitled "Sfortuna" ("Misfortune"), is, according to Calvino, "an odyssey about poor women's work and tribulations" (introduction, p. xxxii).

102. Calvino, introduction, *Italian Folktales*, p. xxxii (*Fiabe*, p. xlvi).

103. Calvino, introduction, *Italian Folktales*, p. xxxii (*Fiabe*, p. xlvi).

104. Calvino, introduction, *Fiabe*, p. lvii.

105. Calvino, "Cibernetica e fantasmi," in *Una pietra sopra*, pp. 164–65; "Cybernetics and Ghosts," in *Uses of Literature*, pp. 3–4.

106. Lotman, *Structure*, p. 59.

107. *Uses of Literature*, p. 4 (*Una pietra sopra*, pp. 164–65). On Calvino's use of a Lévi-Straussian dialectic of mythic versus scientific thought in *Le cosmicomiche* and *Ti con zero* see de Lauretis, "Calvino," pp. 57–74.

108. Lévi-Strauss, *Savage Mind*, p. 15.

109. Lévi-Strauss, *Savage Mind*, pp. 21–22.

110. Todorov, *Fantastic*, p. 168. Cf. Calvino's brief note on Todorov's book, "Definitions of Territories" (1967), in *The Uses of Literature*, pp. 71–73 (*Una pietra sopra*, pp. 211–14). See also Calvino's introduction to *Racconti fantastici dell'Ottocento*, 1: 5–14.

111. Not all histories are necessarily narratives, of course. On antinarrative and non-narrative historiography, see White, *Metahistory* and "Value of Narrativity."

112. De Sica's *Bicycle Thieves* and *Umberto D* both open this way. Vasco Pratolini's *Cronache di poveri amanti* also opens with a "cinematic" long shot of via del Corno, before focusing on its inhabitants. A similar opening is common in nineteenth-century realist narrative, for example Stendhal's *Le Rouge et le noir*.

113. See Genette, *Narrative Discourse*, pp. 113–16.

114. On the fantastic as a hybrid genre, and on the fantastic in the twentieth century, see Brooke-Rose, *Rhetoric*, pp. 64–67 and Jackson, *Fantasy*, pp. 13–42.

Chapter 4

1. Battaglia, *Un uomo*, p. 81.

2. Bocca, *Partigiani*, p. 59.

3. Levi Cavaglione, *Guerriglia*, pp. 96–97. Falaschi, *La Resistenza armata*, pp. 48–49, argues that Levi Cavaglione's book is the diary of a childlike "regression," which coincides with an "immature" understanding of the partisan struggle.

4. Battaglia, *Un uomo*, p. 231.

5. Battaglia, "La storiografia," p. 179.

6. Benjamin, *Illuminations*, p. 102.

7. Jameson, *Marxism*, p. 82. On the positive value of "nostalgic utopianism," see also Calvino's "On Fourier III" (1973; the last of three essays devoted to Fourier and the notion of utopia), in *Uses of Literature*, pp. 248–49 (*Una pietra sopra*, p. 250): "During the course of the centuries, criticism of the present moment has in the literary *topos* . . . expressed itself in terms of the return of the golden age, of the mythical past (or at the very least in terms of Arcadia), and then of the Noble Savage, and, more sporadically, of the homologous myth of the city of the future, where justice and happiness reign according to reason. This goes to show that in the face of what is unacceptable in the present, the tendency to regress is more common than the aspiration toward an *eschaton*. . . . Is this escapism? I have always reservations about the

negative meaning that the word 'escapism' has in the language of historical and literary criticism. For a prisoner, to escape has always been a good thing, and an individual escape can be a first necessary step toward a collective escape. This must also be true on the level of the words and images of fantasy. To escape from the prison of representations of the world that remind you of your slavery with every phrase they contain means to suggest another code, another syntax, another vocabulary, by means of which to give shape to the world of your desires. Certainly anyone who thinks that by doing this he has found freedom, and who is content with it, is the victim of a cruel misunderstanding, but no more than someone who is satisfied with a verbal and symbolic freedom, even if the language he uses exposes its flank less to the accusation of 'escapism.'" Calvino's interest in utopia as a literary-political strategy has been summarily outlined by Pautasso in "Favola."

8. Quazza, *Resistenza*, p. 360.

9. Quazza, *Resistenza*, p. 244.

10. Quazza, *Resistenza*, pp. 340–41. See also, along the same lines, Ragghianti, *Disegno*, pp. 254–55. For a different view, see Salvadori, *Storia*, pp. 183–84. According to Salvadori, the conflict between "democrats" and communists was such that it could only leave the way open for a resurgence of interests and political forces sympathetic to Fascism.

11. For a different reading of the politics of fantasy in *The Path*, see Gatt-Rutter, "Calvino," pp. 319–20. In 1962, six years after having left the PCI and ceased any form of political militancy, Calvino wrote in response to an inquiry by the editors of the journal *Paradosso* (who had asked a variety of Italian intellectuals what impact the war had on their formation): "After so many years . . . I must say that the spirit of the Resistance which allowed the partisans to do the marvelous things they did remains still today an invaluable and unmatched model for how to cope with the conflictual reality of the world" (Albertoni, *La generazione*, p. 78). Calvino's reply to *Paradosso*'s inquiry first appeared in the issue 23–24 (Sept.–Dec. 1960) of the journal, but it was completely rewritten when the results of the inquest were republished in volume form.

12. See Quazza's bibliographical references and his summary of the achievement of Resistance historiography between 1955 and 1975, *Resistenza*, pp. 15–19. For a critical assessment of Quazza's approach to Resistance history and historiography, see Pavone, "Guido Quazza." Pavone finds in Quazza's book a persuasive critique of Renzo De Felice's thesis on Fascism as an autonomous revolutionary movement, but he also finds that Quazza's "continuity" thesis is not entirely substantiated by the historian.

13. Quazza acknowledges the influence of the Annales school and of Braudel on his historiographical approach in *Resistenza*, pp. 24 and 337.

14. See Pietro Secchia's editorial published in *La nostra lotta* 11 (May

1944), cited in Quazza, *Resistenza*, p. 278: "The Committee for National Liberation, which has so far been only a coalition of political parties, must widen its unitary base, gathering in a united front all Italians who are ready to fight against the oppressor. It must connect with all mass organizations and become the representative of all the national forces organized and active in the struggle against the Germans and the Fascists." See also Catalano, *Storia*, pp. 117–19.

15. Amendola, *Lettere*, pp. 116–17.

16. *Il sentiero*, p. 48, my translation; this entire dialogue has been omitted from Colquhoun's translation.

17. Braudel, *On History*, pp. 3–4; 28–29. On this question, see also Kracauer, "The Structure of the Historical Universe," in *History*, pp. 104–38.

18. On the "Jacobin leadership" of the CLN, see Quazza, *Resistenza*, pp. 287; 363.

19. Togliatti came back to Italy from Moscow in March 1944 and announced that the communists were ready to join the government without the prior abdication of the King, thus beginning—with a sudden turn in the communists' position—a new policy of compromise with the liberal and moderate parties as well as with the Allies. Togliatti's step led to the formation on April 24 of a cabinet of all six anti-Fascist parties headed by Badoglio. In December 1944, the CLNAI (Committee of National Liberation for Upper Italy) signed an agreement with the Allies in Rome whereby the partisan forces were to consider themselves under Allied command; the CLNAI itself was to act only as temporary "delegate" in the occupied territory of both the Allied command and the Italian government. Although it included representatives from the CLN, the new government formed on December 7 was a conservative one. After much negotiation with the Allies, the CLN gave up any claim to a more direct role in the appointment of the new government and accepted the nomination of the conservative Bonomi to head the cabinet made by the King's son, Umberto II (Vittorio Emmanuele had "delegated" the throne to him after the Liberation of Rome). The policy of the Allies was intended to normalize the situation in Italy and to arrest the momentum gained by the Resistance so that no radical changes in the country's institutions would be likely after the end of the war. The CLNAI agreed, among other things, to order the partisans to surrender all weapons to the Allies immediately after the Liberation. On the 1944 *Svolta di Salerno* and its aftermath, see Delzell, *Mussolini's Enemies*, pp. 336–39 and Urban, *Moscow*, pp. 190–215.

20. See the text of Togliatti's directives sent to all the Party's sections and to the CLN sections in June 1945, cited in Quazza, *Resistenza*, p. 254: "You must remember that the goal of the insurrection we want is not the imposition of social and political transformations in a socialist or communist direction, but rather national liberation and the destruction

of Fascism. All other problems will be solved by the people, tomorrow—after the entire country will have been freed—through a free democratic election and the appointment of a Constituent Assembly."

21. See G. Warner, "Italy and the Powers, 1943–1949," in Woolf, pp. 30–56.

22. See Quazza, *Resistenza*, p. 257.

23. Cited in Quazza, *Resistenza*, p. 170.

24. See S. J. Woolf, "The Rebirth of Italy 1943–50," in Woolf, pp. 212–43.

25. P. Vercellone, "The Italian Constitution of 1947–48," in Woolf, pp. 121–34.

26. Togliatti, "La politica di Corbino," *Rinascita* 3, no. 8 (Aug. 1946), p. 177.

27. Woolf, "The Rebirth of Italy," in Woolf, p. 227.

28. Gramsci, *Selections*, p. 54.

29. Gramsci, *Selections*, p. 237.

30. Calvino in an interview, *Il Paradosso* 23–24 (Sept.–Dec. 1960), cited in Spriano, p. 14. (See note 11 above.)

31. Spriano, p. 14.

32. Anderson, "Antinomies," p. 28.

33. Calvino, *Watcher*, p. 11 (*La giornata*, p. 19).

34. Calvino, *Watcher*, p. 13 (*La giornata*, p. 21).

35. See P. A. Allum, "The South and National Politics," in Woolf, pp. 107–15.

36. Longo, p. 17.

37. Compare Longo, p. 209. Longo denies there were ever any desertions to the black brigades from the partisan ranks.

38. Lucente, "Interview," pp. 246–47.

39. Adorno, "Commitment," in Livingstone, pp. 179, 190.

40. Adorno, "Commitment," p. 194. For a critique of Adorno's position, see Vattimo, *La fine*, pp. 59–70.

41. Quazza, *Resistenza*, p. 124.

Chapter 5

1. Ricoeur, 1: 66.

2. Aristotle, 50a1.

3. The English translator of *The Path*, Archibald Colquhoun, has added a specific reference to the winter of 1944 in the opening paragraph of the novel (p. 1).

4. See Chapter 4, note 19.

5. Battaglia, *Storia*, chapters 11 and 12.

6. See Delzell, pp. 448–55, and G. Warner, "Italy and the Powers, 1943–49," in Woolf, pp. 42–46.

7. Salvadori, p. 169.

8. Salvadori, p. 175.

9. For the notion of the reader's "horizon of expectations," see Jauss, *Toward an Aesthetic of Reception*, p. 23.

10. See, for example, Varese's review; Asor Rosa, *Scrittori*, pp. 244–45; Calligaris, *Calvino*, pp. 12–18; Annoni, "Calvino," p. 969. A notable exception is Cesare Pavese, who in his 1947 review of *The Path* (*Saggi*, pp. 245–47) praised the novel's subtle literary style, its effective use of fairy-tale images, and its Ariostesque flavor of epic romance.

11. See, for instance, Luperini, *Il Novecento*, 2: 761–62. But the most striking example of an "idyllic" reading of *The Path* is the review by Caprara, which may be considered the "official" PCI reading of Calvino's novel. For Caprara, the novel is the "heroic and dramatic story of a partisan brigade in the mountains." Totally ignoring the ninth chapter, Caprara goes on to say that no one in the novel has "problems to solve (I mean the *ubi consistam*, or the 'anxiety' and existential doubts we find in other novels)" (the latter may be a reference to *Uomini e no*). Finally, Caprara claims that in treating the delicate subject of the sexual awakening of a boy, Calvino—unlike Moravia in *Agostino*—presents the image of an utterly "unproblematic and non-Freudian childhood."

12. See Ragusa, p. 197, and Falaschi, "Calvino," p. 540.

13. Calligaris, pp. 13–17.

14. See Cannon, *Calvino*, p. 19, and Carter, p. 13.

15. A similar tension can be found in Visconti's *Ossessione*.

16. There is a description of a similar sadistic game played by a preadolescent boy (little Marcello) in Alberto Moravia's *Il conformista* (1951). In Moravia's novel, like in *The Path*, a scene in which the boy comes to possess a revolver through the mediation of an adult comes to symbolize the boy's rite of passage into adulthood. Moravia's treatment of this theme is, however, rather mechanical and predictable. Moravia fails, as even Fernandez has pointed out in *Il romanzo*, to integrate the theme of sexuality with his satire of the Fascist regime, a satire which remains "external or cold" (p. 93).

17. Vico, *New Science*, pp. 85–86; 97–98.

18. Vico, p. 96: "The world of civil society has certainly been made by men. . . . Its principles are therefore to be found within the modifications of our own human mind. Whoever reflects on this cannot but marvel that the philosophers should have bent all their energies to the study of the world of nature, which, since God made it, He alone knows; and that they should have neglected the study of the world of nations, or civil world, which, since men had made it, men could come to know." Cf. Jameson, *Marxism*, p. 181.

19. Sartre, *Being and Nothingness*, p. 347.

20. Lacan, *Four Fundamental Concepts*, p. 84.

21. Calvino attended Lacan's famous seminars in the 1960's when he lived in Paris. For a rather superficial reading of the Lacanian frame-

work of *Invisible Cities*, see Pedullà. A far more enlightening reading of *Invisible Cities* may be found in de Lauretis, "Semiotic Models." More recently, de Lauretis has explored the paradigmatic implications of one of Calvino's "cities," "Zobeide," for feminist critical theory, outlining both the insights and limits of Calvino's text in *Alice Doesn't*, pp. 12–14.

22. Jameson, "Imaginary and Symbolic," p. 356.

23. See Lacan, "Le Stade du miroir comme formateur de la fonction du Je, telle qu'elle nous est révélée dans l'expérience psychanalytique" (1949) in *Ecrits*, pp. 93–110. See also "The Function of Language in Psychoanalysis," in his *Speech*, p. 11: "Does the subject not become engaged in an ever-growing dispossession of that being of his, concerning which . . . he ends up recognizing that this being has never been anything more than his construct in the Imaginary and that this construct disappoints all his certitudes? For in this labor which he undertakes to reconstruct this construct *for another*, he finds again the fundamental alienation which made him construct it *like another one*, and which has always destined it to be stripped from him *by another*."

24. Lacan, *Speech*, p. 100.

25. Lacan, *Four Fundamental Concepts*, p. 210. Calvino focuses on the theme of alienation in its various manifestations in many of his subsequent works; *Il visconte dimezzato* is in effect an allegorical tale about alienation, and the other two novels of the trilogy, *Il cavaliere inesistente* and *Il barone rampante* are informed by a similar problematic. See Calvino's own comments in his 1960 introduction to *I nostri antenati*, p. xii: "Divided, mutilated, incomplete, an enemy to himself is modern man; Marx called him 'alienated,' Freud, 'repressed'; a state of ancient harmony is lost, and we long for a new kind of completeness. This is the ideological-moral motivation of my story" [*The Cloven Viscount*]. See also p. xix, concerning the trilogy as a whole: "I intended to make it a trilogy of experience, about how to realize oneself as a human being: in *The Nonexistent Knight* the conquest of being; in *The Cloven Viscount* the aspiration toward wholeness beyond the mutilations imposed by society; in *The Baron in the Trees* a way to a non-individualistic wholeness, to be achieved through individual self-determination; three degrees of an approach to freedom."

26. Edmond Ortigues, *Le Discours et le symbole*, cited in Jameson, "Imaginary," p. 378.

27. For an interpretation of Freud along these lines, see, among others, Marcuse, *Eros*, and Jameson, *Political Unconscious*.

28. Lacan, *Speech*, p. 83: "*Fort! Da!* It is precisely in his solitude that the desire of the little child has already become the desire of another, of an *alter ego* who dominates him and whose object of desire is henceforth his own affliction."

29. There was a revival of Hegelian studies in Italy after the war. See, for example, the 1945 essay by Massolo, "L'essere."

30. Hyppolite, *Genèse et structure de la 'Phénoménologie de l'Esprit,'* as cited in Lacan, *Speech*, p. 285.

31. In Lacan, *Speech*, p. 94.

32. Lacan, *Four Fundamental Concepts*, p. 210.

33. Freud, "On Narcissism," *Standard Edition*, 18: 90.

34. See Freud, *Civilization, Standard Edition*, 21: 66–68: "An infant at the breast does not as yet distinguish his ego from the external world. . . . Originally the ego includes everything, later it separates off an external world from itself. Our present ego-feeling is, therefore, only a shrunken residue of a much more inclusive, all-embracing feeling, which corresponds to a more intimate bond between the ego and the world about it."

35. Marcuse, pp. 210–11.

36. See Lacan, "Propos sur la causalité psychique" (1947), as cited in Lacan, *Speech*, p. 126: "I have often taken a stand against the risky way in which Freud interpreted sociologically the capital discovery for the human mind that we owe to him [the discovery of the Oedipus complex]. I do not think that the Oedipus complex appeared with the origin of man (if indeed it is not completely senseless to try to write the history of that moment), but rather at the dawn of history, of 'historical' history, at the limit of 'ethnographic' cultures. Obviously the Oedipus complex can appear only in the patriarchal form of the institution of the family—but it has a no less contestable value as a threshold, and I am convinced that in those cultures which exclude it, its function must have been fulfilled by initiation experiences, as ethnology in any case still permits us to see this fact today, and the value of the Oedipus complex as the closing-off of a psychic cycle results from the fact that it represents the family situation, insofar as by its institution this situation marks the intersection, in the cultural sphere, of the biological and the social."

37. Lacan, Seminar of March–April 1957 ("La Relation d'objet et les structures freudiennes"), as cited in *Speech*, p. 271.

38. Mitchell, p. 187.

39. See Lacan, *Four Fundamental Concepts*, p. 204: "In the psyche, there is nothing by which the subject may situate itself as a male or female being. . . . The ways of what one must do as a man or as a woman are entirely abandoned to the drama, to the scenario, which is placed in the field of the Other—which, strictly speaking, is the Oedipus complex. . . . Sexuality is represented in the psyche by the relation of the subject that is deduced from something other than sexuality itself. Sexuality is established in the field of the subject by a way that is that of lack."

40. Heath, p. 74.

41. Freud, "Infantile Sexuality," *Standard Edition*, 7: 192.

42. Freud, "The Uncanny," *Standard Edition*, 17: 231–32.

43. Heath, p. 66.
44. Freud, "Instincts and Their Vicissitudes," cited in Heath, p. 66.
45. Lacan, *Four Fundamental Concepts*, p. 182.
46. Lacan, *Four Fundamental Concepts*, p. 74. Voyeurism, and the notion of seeing oneself seeing oneself, play a central role in *Mr. Palomar*, where voyeurism is explicitly linked to the foreclosure not of castration but of death itself. The greatest of Calvino's stories about voyeurism, however, which is also a parable about alienation and desire as lack or absence is "L'avventura di un fotografo" ("The Adventure of a Photographer"), a 1957 short story in *Gli amori*.
47. Calvino uses a similar strategy of destabilizing focalization in *Mr. Palomar* to problematize the subject/object opposition and even the very categories of sensorial perception. Biasin, in "Le rare," p. 181, hints at a possible parallel between Pin and Mr. Palomar. Calvino stated in the 1972 essay "Lo sguardo dell'archeologo," (*Una pietra sopra*, pp. 263–66)—an essay whose problematic is prefigured in *The Path*—that the "male-female" opposition must be questioned and criticized as a cultural-historical formation no less than the opposition "rational-mythic," and even the most elementary topologies of human perception: "the high and the low, the living and the thing" (p. 263). Such a critique is geared toward the anticipation of a possible change in the status of the human subject as a historical construct.
48. In Ortigues's excellent formulation (cited in Jameson, "Imaginary," p. 377): "The same object may be considered imaginary if taken absolutely, and symbolic if taken as a differential value correlative of other terms which limit it reciprocally."
49. Lacan, Seminar of April–June 1958, cited in *Speech*, p. 188.
50. See Mackinnon, "Feminism," p. 515: "Sexuality is to feminism what work is to Marxism: that which is most one's own, and most taken away."
51. Calvino, "Lo sguardo dell'archeologo," in *Una pietra sopra*, p. 263.
52. Deleuze and Guattari, *Anti-Oedipus*, p. 103.
53. See Adorno, p. 125.
54. Adorno, p. 126.
55. Adorno, p. 130.
56. Adorno, p. 131.
57. Delzell, pp. 267–69.
58. Cited in Quazza, *Resistenza*, p. 179.
59. Foucault, preface to Deleuze and Guattari, *Anti-Oedipus*, p. xiii. The role of psychoanalysis in the history and understanding of the "deployment" of sexuality has been discussed by Foucault in *Sexuality*, 1: 115–31. According to Foucault, psychoanalysis represented a fundamental development for the understanding of how sexuality is tied to general mechanisms of political and ideological domination. However, the historico-political critique of sexual repression developed by

Wilhelm Reich, Erich Fromm, and others between the two world wars (Foucault's argument could be extended to Marcuse as well) was essentially flawed and rendered politically inadequate by its inability to transcend the very conceptualization of sexuality whose repression it sought to dismantle: "The fact that so many things were able to change in sexual behavior in Western societies without any of the promises or political conditions predicted by Reich being realized is sufficient proof that this whole sexual 'revolution,' this whole 'antirepressive' struggle represented nothing more, but nothing else—and its importance is undeniable—than a tactical shift and reversal in the great deployment of sexuality" (p. 131).

60. No valorization of the Imaginary—or what Julia Kristeva, in *La Révolution du langage poétique*, has called the semiotic *chora* (from the Greek word for "enclosed space," or "womb")—as the register of a heterogeneous "subject-in-process" is implicit in Calvino's metaphor of the path to the nest of spiders, however. See Calvino, "La sfida al labirinto," in *Una pietra sopra*, p. 89: "Expressionism, Céline, Artaud, some of Joyce's work, interior monologue, the dampest kind of surrealism, and Henry Miller all have in common a certain visceral/existential/religious thrust which is still to be found today. I do not wish either to underestimate or to condemn this current of the avant-garde, for it is a current that continues to count, and constitutes the key to some present expressive possibilities that matter for me as well. . . . It is not that I do not believe in existential or interior revolutions: but the great event of the century . . . was the revolt against the father, carried out in the territories of the paternal empire of Franz Josef by a psychiatrist and a young visionary, Freud and Kafka. . . . I do not consider either Freud or Kafka to be visceral in nature: they are masters because they are both—each in his own way—hard, dry and tough as nails."

61. Laplanche and Pontalis, pp. 163–164.

62. Cited in Deleuze and Guattari, p. 90.

63. Such a celebration is to be found, on the other hand, in *Anti-Oedipus* and in Kristeva's *La Révolution du langage poétique*.

64. Cf. Deleuze and Guatarri, pp. 46–47. See also Marcuse's comment (p. 186) about Freud's notion of happiness: "The reactivation of prehistoric and childhood wishes and attitudes is not necessarily regression; it may well be the opposite—proximity to a happiness that has always been the repressed promise of a better future. In one of his most advanced formulations, Freud once defined happiness as the 'subsequent fulfillment of a prehistoric wish. That is why wealth brings so little happiness: money was not a wish of childhood.'"

65. Marcuse, pp. 211–12.

66. Colquhoun's translation of this sentence stops at the word "wine."

67. See Freud's reading of the Medusa myth, "Medusa's Head,"

Standard Edition, 18: 273–74. Freud links the sight of Medusa explicitly to voyeurism and the fear of castration.

68. As Lupo Rosso points out, women are considered "off limits" for the partisans: "I don't even look at women at the moment. . . . There'll be time after the rising" (p. 33; 66).

69. See Durand, p. 104. Cf. Milanini, "Natura," p. 543, for a different reading of the function of this symbol in *The Path*.

70. The fusion of the figures of the two women into the single image of the "bad" mother is explicitly thematized in chapter 10, when Pin remains alone with Dritto and Giglia at the camp: " 'Pin! D'you want some chestnuts?' [Giglia] calls with that false motherly air of hers as if she were trying to keep him sweet. Pin hates women putting on maternal airs; he knows it's all a trick and that they, like his sister, really hate him" (p. 114; 159).

71. The importance of the Hegelian notions of the Other and of desire for literary fiction has been argued by Girard in *Mensonge*. There is no doubt that these notions are fundamental for Calvino's work, although their presence in *The Path* has not been recognized thus far. Calvino's short stories of the series called "Gli amori difficili" ("Difficult Loves"), written between 1949 and 1967 and collected in the volume *Gli amori difficili* (along with the novellas "La formica argentina" and "La nuvola di smog"), are perhaps the most unassuming and yet among the most powerful of Calvino's fictions dealing with the politics of desire. About these stories Gatt-Rutter, p. 324, writes: "The taboo against Eros—like all taboos—is ultimately political—an atavistic social prohibition, internalized by each individual as unconscious repressions or conventions, but reinforced by the churches and the police. These stories of Calvino's show 13 different ways in which this repressed Eros seeks fulfillment (a meeting of human beings as *persons*) but never meets with more than a fraction of success. . . . These unpretentious stories . . . are . . . to my mind among the best products of political literature—or of *any* literature—written in Italy since the war."

72. For the notion of narrative repetition as mirroring and as subversion of organic form, see Miller's analysis of Conrad's *Lord Jim*, in *Fiction*, pp. 34–35: "*Lord Jim* is a chain of repetitions, each event referring back to others which it both explains and is explained by, while at the same time it prefigures those which will occur in the future. . . . The narration in many ways, not least by calling attention to the way one episode repeats another rather than being clearly a temporal advance on it, breaks down the chronological sequence and invites the reader to think of it as a simultaneous set of echoing episodes spread out spatially like villages or mountain peaks on a map." The repetitive/disruptive structure I have traced in Calvino's novel may indeed reflect the influence of Conrad's *Lord Jim* on Calvino (Calvino wrote his thesis on Conrad at the same time as he was writing *The Path*). It is Conrad's *The*

Shadow Line, however, with its simpler story line about a young man's rite of passage and its abundance of fairy-tale motifs, that seems to have influenced *The Path* the most. Calvino's dedication of the novel to his partisan comrades "A Kim, e a tutti gli altri" ("To Kim, and all the others") is a synopsis of Conrad's dedication "To Borys and all others who, like himself, have crossed in early youth the shadow line of their generation with love." Calvino's own partisan experience was, as the dedication suggests, the crossing of a "shadow line." Concerning Conrad, Calvino wrote in 1958 ("Natura e storia nel romanzo," in *Una pietra sopra*, pp. 28–29): "Man is, for Conrad, suspended between two images of chaos; that of nature, or the cosmos, a dark and meaningless universe; and that of the murky depths of man and his unconscious. . . . His heroes succeed, in spite of either of these, in saving the ship. The moral ideal of Conrad is to be up to the situation, on the deck of the ship as on the page itself. The hero of *The Shadow Line* succeeds, and refuses to draw back in the face of fear . . . [by] taking and passing the test of his manhood. Lord Jim . . . [instead] gives in once to this sense of insecurity, and will always give in [thereafter]. . . . I spoke of nature. And history? [Conrad's fiction] would seem to take place in a purely atemporal and symbolic world. And yet all of his narrative has its origin in an acute sense of history. His fundamental theme is the transformation of the merchant fleet from the age of sail to the age of steam. . . . In the world of colonial commerce, the civilization of the old British mercantile bourgeoisie (or even the romanticism of the first businessmen/adventurers) is replaced by a flood of crooked agents and corrupt bureaucrats. But this atmosphere of *cupio dissolvi* that is often found in Conrad's works never extinguishes his faith in the powers of man, in his moral order and his courage."

73. See for example Luperini, 2: 762; Falaschi, *La Resistenza*, pp. 119–21; and Rosengarten, "Italian Resistance Novel," p. 225.

74. Not all readers of *The Path* have "missed" the double-meaning of the ending, however. See Eversmann, pp. 59–61, and Milanini, "Natura," p. 544.

75. Todorov, p. 46.

76. Freud, "The Uncanny," *Standard Edition*, 17: 245–47.

77. Freud, "The Uncanny," *Standard Edition*, 17: 251.

78. Girard, *La Violence*, pp. 105–32.

79. Marcuse, p. 146. See also de Lauretis, *Alice Doesn't*, pp. 109–10.

80. Freud, "The Uncanny," *Standard Edition*, 17: 225.

81. The translator, A. Colquhoun, spells out the meaning of this implicit association when he adds, in the preceding paragraph describing Pin's reaction to Cousin's "disgust," the phrase "Cousin . . . understands everything; even how filthy women are." The Italian text reads simply, "Cousin is really the Great Friend."

82. Verga, preface, *The House of the Medlar Tree*, p. 4.

83. Cases, pp. 33–35.
84. Translation slightly altered to reflect the original.

Chapter 6

1. See Asor Rosa, *Scrittori*, p. 245; Gatt-Rutter, p. 320; Pescio Bottino, p. 275; and Bonura, p. 49.
2. Annoni, p. 969.
3. Falaschi, *La Resistenza*, p. 159.
4. About Pin as a projection of the author's self, see the preface to *The Path* (p. xx; 19–21): "The relationship between the character of the boy Pin and the partisan war corresponded symbolically to the relationship with that war that I myself had come to have. Pin's inferiority as a child in the face of the grownups' incomprehensible world, corresponds to my own, in the same situation as a bourgeois."
5. See Althusser, *For Marx*, pp. 231–36, and "Ideological State Apparatuses," in *Lenin*, pp. 170–77.
6. Or, in other words, the opposite of the Crocean notion of history. See *History*, p. 59: "Hegel's famous statement that history is the history of liberty was repeated without being altogether understood. . . . Jubilant announcements, resigned admissions or desperate lamentations that liberty has now deserted the world are frequently heard nowadays; the ideal of liberty is said to have set on the horizon of history, in a sunset without promise of sunrise. Those who talk or write or print this deserve the pardon pronounced by Jesus, for they know not what they say. If they knew or reflected they would be aware that to assert that liberty is dead is the same as saying that life is dead."
7. Girard, *La Violence*, pp. 173–78.
8. Girard, *La Violence*, p. 178. Cf. Kim's comment about Dritto's desire to die: "[Dritto] wants to be shot. That longing gets hold of men sometimes" (p. 106; 150).
9. The need to control the "spontaneous" rebellion of subaltern groups through the leadership of the proletariat is in fact one of the principal tenets of Lenin's *What Is to Be Done?*. See Gramsci's reflections in this regard in *Selections*, pp. 196 and 198–99: "'Spontaneity' . . . is characteristic of the 'history of subaltern classes,' and indeed of their most marginal and peripheral elements; these have not achieved any consciousness of the class 'for itself,' and consequently it never occurs to them that their history might have some possible importance. . . . The unity between 'spontaneity' and 'conscious leadership' or 'discipline' is precisely the real political action of the subaltern classes. . . . Between the two there is a 'quantitative' difference of degree, not one of quality. . . . Neglecting, or worse still despising, so-called 'spontaneous' movements, i.e. failing to give them a conscious leadership or to raise them to a higher plane, may often have extremely serious consequences."

10. Frye, *Anatomy,* p. 325.
11. Frye, *Anatomy,* p. 325. Kim's Biblical vision of history parallels Vittorini's in *Conversazione* and *Uomini e no,* and serves at the same time to problematize it. See *Uomini e no,* p. 221: "Noi non pensiamo che agli offesi. . . . Appena vi sia l'offesa, subito noi siamo con chi è offeso, e diciamo che è l'uomo. . . . E chi ha offeso che cos'è? . . . Diciamo oggi: è il fascismo." ("We think only of the offended. . . . No sooner is there offense than we side with the offended, and we say the offended are mankind. . . . And he who offends—what is he? . . . Today we say: it is Fascism.")
12. See Jameson, *Political Unconscious,* pp. 28–33.
13. Calvino, "Il midollo del leone," in *Una pietra sopra,* p. 5. The term *furore* in *The Path* does in fact evoke the *astratti furori* of Silvestro, the anti-Fascist protagonist of Vittorini's *Conversazione,* dismayed by what appears to be irremediable injustice against humanity, "il genere umano perduto" (p. 6). Silvestro's *furori* are abstract, rather than "heroic" (as in the famous work by Giordano Bruno, *Gli eroici furori*), precisely because he feels that there is nothing that can be done about this injustice. The novel is, however, a fable of initiation that leads away from the immediacy of present history into a timeless and more humane history—the folkloric chronotope of the homeland, Sicily (a motherland, rather than a fatherland), to which the protagonist returns to retrace his origins. For a reading of *Conversazione* as a fable of initiation, based on Propp's narrative morphology, see Bianconi Bernardi.
14. This passage is not included in Colquhoun's translation of *The Path.*
15. Gramsci, *Selections,* p. 126.
16. For the notion of the novelistic character as a "man of the idea," see Bakhtin, *Problems,* pp. 78–100. In discussing Dostoyevsky's *dialogical* use of this narrative device, Bakhtin points out that the idea concretized through a specific character or hero is never just the author's ideology placed in the character's mouth (as it is in monologic narratives), but it is offered, rather, as a question; there is always, writes Bakhtin, a "distance between the author's position and the hero's position" (p. 84). Kim's monologue performs in this sense the same function Bakhtin attributes to the monologues of Dostoyevsky's idea-characters: "The idea wants to be heard, understood, and 'answered' by other voices from other positions. . . . [It] is by nature dialogic, and monologue is merely the conventional compositional form of its expression" (p. 88).
17. See Freud, *Civilization, Standard Edition,* 21: 96: "A good part of the struggles of mankind centre round the single task of finding an expedient accommodation—one, that is, that will bring happiness—between this claim of the individual and the cultural claims of the group; and one of the problems that touches the fate of humanity is whether such an accommodation can be reached by means of some particular form of civilization or whether this conflict is irreconcilable."

18. Gramsci, *Selections*, p. 175.

19. Gramsci, *Letters*, pp. 221–23 and 226–28. An edition of Gramsci's letters was published by Einaudi in 1946, and several extracts of Gramsci's writings appeared in various Italian journals and newspapers, beginning in 1944.

20. Cf. one of Togliatti's notorious editorials of the period, in *I corsivi*, p. 198: "A writer who starts from Freud will inevitably go astray, and find himself either in a whorehouse or in a madhouse, but never closer to Karl Marx and our difficult socialist struggle."

21. The journal *Primato* opened the debate on existentialism in 1943 with an issue entitled "L'esistenzialismo in Italia." Nicola Abbagnano, one of the foremost interpreters of existentialism in postwar Italy, published his *Esistenzialismo positivo* in 1948.

22. Onofri, "Politica," p. 32. See also Massolo, "Esistenzialismo." Norberto Bobbio's sweeping *La filosofia del decadentismo*, with an attack on existentialism as an example of "decadent" thought, came out in 1944. On the Marxist resistance to existentialism in Italy after the war, see Pineri, "Philosophes-professeurs," pp. 10–11: "L'existentialisme et le marxisme sont les deux régimes théoriques que parcourt l'intellectuel italien de l'après-guerre, en essayant des passages et des travaux de greffe d'une région à l'autre . . . [mais] le 'mariage de coeur' entre existentialisme et marxisme ne pouvait être accepté, surtout après 1945, par l'appel à la raison jdanovienne."

23. See Jameson, *Marxism*, p. 22. On the problem of reconciling existentialism, Freudianism, and Marxism, see Calvino, "La sfida al labirinto" (*Una pietra sopra*, p. 93): "Historical materialism [concentrates] on the 'public' and [avoids] the 'private,' in a kind of centrifugal thrust. . . . A vacant area remains, in which existentialism, phenomenology and psychoanalysis attempt to globally integrate themselves into an organic discourse. But this organic discourse has not yet found its bearings. It is lacking in a 'social supplement' . . . [while] militant ideology has left the place of the individual subject empty."

24. Gramsci significantly identified an illustrious triad of modernist writers as targets: "Proust-Svevo-Joyce." See *Quaderni*, 1: 26.

25. See Asor Rosa, "Lo stato democratico," pp. 594–95. The most striking document of this attitude is the sharply negative assessment of postwar Italian narrative (inspired by Lukács's recently published *Saggi sul realismo*) in Niccolò Gallo, "La narrativa italiana del dopoguerra" (*Società* 6, no. 2, 1950), in Milanini, *Neorealismo*, pp. 99–120.

26. Sartre, *L'Existentialisme*, p. 137.

27. Sartre, *L'Existentialisme*, pp. 22–28.

28. Freud, *New Introductory Lectures on Psycho-analysis*, Lecture 31, *Standard Edition*, 22: 78: "The ego, driven by the id, confined by the super-ego, repulsed by reality, struggles to master its economic task of bringing about harmony among the forces and influences working

upon it. . . . If the ego is obliged to admit its weaknesses, it breaks
out in anxiety—realistic anxiety regarding the external world, moral
anxiety regarding the super-ego and neurotic anxiety regarding the
strength of the passions in the id."

29. Sartre, *L'Existentialisme*, pp. 28–33.

30. Jameson, *Marxism*, p. 135.

31. Calvino, "La letteratura italiana," p. 46.

32. Calvino, "La letteratura italiana," p. 47: "This is the greatest
book of the Resistance. And the greatest example of the new man born
from this Resistance is surely the serene and immensely strong Sar-
dinian revolutionary."

33. Vittorini, "Una nuova cultura," p. 1.

34. On the question of sacrifice in relation to the Marxist vision of
liberation based on non-alienated labor (as opposed to Fourier's "libidinal utopia"), see Calvino, "On Fourier, II: The Controller of Desires,"
in *Uses of Literature*, 228–29 ("Per Fourier II: l'ordinatore dei desideri,"
in *Una pietra sopra*, pp. 233–34): "Marx, who was less keen than his
friend [Engels] to exalt Fourier's work *in toto*, also read it with amused
familiarity, but points out its basic incompatibilities. In the *Grundrisse*,
while quarreling with Adam Smith, who looked upon labor as sacrifice
and nothing but, Marx at the other extreme taxes Fourier with in-
genuousness and frivolity for having believed that labor could ever become a pleasure and a diversion. For Marx, emancipated labor—free
creativity or participation in the socially productive process—will no
longer be a sacrifice because man will fulfill himself as the *subject* of productivity, though this will involve no less effort. Today we may realize
that this raises the most dramatic question of our time. If socialism realistically accepts that suffering is still a necessary element in the process
of production, what distinguishes exploited labor from emancipated labor will in the end boil down to a sublimation of the toil and suffering
on the part of the workers. The conviction that one is realizing socialism
as a philosophical model absolutely must precede any perceptible satisfaction. But for how long? And who can guarantee that this conviction
is not also the result of some ideological manipulation, and that the true
revolution that will lead to freedom will not always be yet to come?
When we come to think about it, the utopian imagination, with a model
that was immediately perceptible to the senses, also had a certain 'realism' of its own; or better, its own possibility of a swift comparison with
reality. One could see at once whether the attempt to put it into practice
corresponded to the model: if *le bonheur* was not an immediate result,
then the experiment was a failure. And this did not mean that the
model itself could not go on exerting its irreducible force of opposition
against the present reality. In opposition to eighteenth- and nineteenth-
century thought, which looked to reason as a basis for morality, Fourier
thought that the only solid ground on which to base a moral position

was the pleasure principle. In this sense the modern commentators who tend to consider him a precursor of Freud have every right to do so, as long as they bear in mind that Freud did not think that any kind of human civilization was possible without repression and sublimation. What I mean is that the relationship between Fourier and Freud emerges as something not unlike his relationship with Marx. Fourier aims to construct a cognitive and practical system without sublimating anything or anyone, let alone repressing them."

35. Sartre, "Una nuova cultura come 'cultura sintetica,'" p. 1.

36. The entire passage about the Bolsheviks has been omitted from Colquhoun's translation of *The Path*.

37. Marx, *Capital*, 3: 820.

38. See Milanini, "Natura," pp. 533–34.

39. Bakhtin, "The *Bildungsroman* and Its Significance in the History of Realism," in *Speech Genres*, pp. 45–46.

40. Bakhtin, "*Bildungsroman*," in *Speech Genres*, p. 24.

41. Bakhtin, "From Notes Made in 1970–71," in *Speech Genres*, pp. 132–33.

42. Cf. Jameson's comments on Manzoni's novel in *Political Unconscious*, pp. 144–45. Calvino's dialectics of totalization and its undermining through the interplay of codes and conflicting narrative modes is most evident (and self-conscious) in *Il castello dei destini incrociati* and *Se una notte d'inverno un viaggiatore*. On the former, see de Lauretis, "Calvino," pp. 57–74, and Schneider, "Calvino."

Works Cited

Adler, Sara Maria. *Calvino: The Writer as Fablemaker*. Madrid: Porrua Turanzas, 1979.

Adorno, Theodor. "Freudian Theory and the Pattern of Fascist Propaganda." In *The Essential Frankfurt School Reader*, ed. Andrew Arato and Eike Gebhardt. New York: Continuum, 1982: 118–137.

Albertoni, Ettore A., Ezlo Antonini, and Renato Palmieri, eds. *La generazione degli anni difficili*. Bari: Laterza, 1962.

Alicata, Mario. "La corrente 'Politecnico.'" *Rinascita* 3, no. 5–6 (1946): 116.

Althusser, Louis. *For Marx*. Trans. Ben Brewster, 1969. London: Verso, 1979.

———. *Lenin and Philosophy*. Trans. Ben Brewster. New York: Monthly Review, 1971.

Amendola, Giorgio. *Lettere a Milano. Ricordi e documenti 1939–1945*. Rome: Editori Riuniti, 1974.

Anderson, Perry. "The Antinomies of Antonio Gramsci." *New Left Review* 100 (1976–77): 5–78.

Annoni, Carlo. "Italo Calvino: La Resistenza tra realtà e favola." *Vita e pensiero* 51, no. 12 (Dec. 1968): 968–75.

Aristotle. *Poetics*. Trans. Gerald F. Else. Ann Arbor: Univ. of Michigan Press, 1967.

Armes, Roy. *Patterns of Realism: A Study of Italian Neorealist Cinema*. New York: Garland, 1986. Orig. pub. 1971.

Asor Rosa, Alberto. "Il neorealismo." In *Storia d'Italia*, ed. Ruggiero Romano and Corrado Vivanti. 4 vols. Turin: Einaudi, 1975. 4.2: 1604–14.

———. *Scrittori e popolo*. Rome: Samonà e Savelli, 1965.

———. "Lo stato democratico e i partiti politici." In *Letteratura italiana*. 9 vols. Turin: Einaudi, 1982. 1: 549–614.

Auerbach, Erich. *Mimesis: The Representation of Reality in Western Literature*. Trans. Willard R. Trask. Princeton: Princeton Univ. Press, 1968.

Austin, J. L. *How to Do Things with Words*. Ed. Georg G. Iggers and Konrad Moltke. Indianapolis: Bobbs-Merrill, 1973.

Bakhtin, M. M. *The Dialogic Imagination: Four Essays*. Ed. Michael Holquist. Trans. Caryl Emerson and Michael Holquist. Austin: Univ. of Texas Press, 1981.

——. *Problems of Dostoevsky's Poetics*. Ed. and trans. Caryl Emerson. Minneapolis: Univ. of Minnesota Press, 1984.

——. *Speech Genres and Other Late Essays*. Ed. Caryl Emerson and Michael Holquist. Trans. Vern W. McGee. Austin: Univ. of Texas Press, 1986.

Balbo, Felice. "Cultura antifascista." *Il Politecnico* 39 (Dec. 1947): 1–2.

Baldi, Guido. *L'artificio della regressione. Tecnica narrativa e ideologica nel Verga verista*. Naples: Liguori, 1980.

Barth, John. "The Literature of Replenishment: Postmodernist Fiction." *The Atlantic* 245 (1980): 65–71.

Barthes, Roland. "The Reality Effect." In *French Literary Theory Today: A Reader*, ed. Tzvetan Todorov, trans. R. Carter. Cambridge: Cambridge Univ. Press; Paris: Editions de la maison des sciences de l'homme, 1982: 11–17.

——. *Writing Degree Zero*. Trans. Annette Lavers and Colin Smith. New York: Hill and Wang, 1968.

Battaglia, Roberto. *Storia della Resistenza italiana*. Turin: Einaudi, 1964. Orig. pub. 1953.

——. "La storiografia della Resistenza." In *Risorgimento e Resistenza*, ed. Ernesto Ragionieri. Rome: Editori Riuniti, 1964.

——. *Un uomo: un partigiano*. Rome: Edizioni U, 1945.

Baudrillard, Jean. "Les Romans d'Italo Calvino." *Les Temps Modernes* 192 (1962): 1728–34.

Bazin, André. *What Is Cinema?* Ed. and trans. Hugh Gray. 2 vols. Berkeley: Univ. of California Press, 1971.

Beckwith, Marc. "Italo Calvino and the Nature of Italian Folktales." *Italica* 64, no. 2 (1987): 244–62.

Benjamin, Walter. *Illuminations*. Ed. Hannah Arendt. Trans. Harry Zahn. New York: Schocken, 1969.

Bernari, Carlo. *Napoli guerra e pace*. Rome: Cronache, 1946.

——. *Prologo alle tenebre*. Milan: Mondadori, 1947.

——. *Tre operai*. Milan: Rizzoli, 1951. Orig. pub. 1934.

Bersani, Leo. *A Future for Astyanax*. Boston: Little, Brown, 1976.

Berti, Giuseppe. "La situazione in Sicilia e i compiti nostri." *Rinascita* 5, no. 8 (1948): 381–88.

Bianco, Dante Livio. *Venti mesi di guerra partigiana nel cuneese*. Turin: Panfilo, 1946.

Bianconi Bernardi, Franca. "Parola e mito in *Conversazione in Sicilia*." *Lingua e stile* 1, no. 2 (1966): 161–90.

Biasin, Gian-Paolo. *Italian Literary Icons*. Princeton: Princeton Univ. Press, 1985.

———. "Le rare isole del razionale." *Intersezioni* 7, no. 1 (1987): 179–86.

Bloch, Ernst. *Differenzierungen im Begriff Fortschritt*. Berlin: Akademie Verlag, 1956.

———. *Verfremdungen*. 2 vols. Frankfurt: Suhrkamp, 1963.

Bo, Carlo, ed. *Inchiesta sul neorealismo*. Rome: Edizioni Radio Italiana, 1951.

Bocca, Giorgio. *Partigiani della montagna*. Borgo San Dalmazzo: Bertello, 1945.

Bolis, Luciano. *Il mio granello di sabbia*. Turin: Einaudi, 1946.

Bonura, Giuseppe. *Invito alla lettura di Italo Calvino*. Milan: Mursia, 1972.

Brancati, Vitaliano. *Il bell'Antonio*. Milan: Bompiani, 1949.

Braudel, Fernand. *On History*. Trans. Sarah Mathews. Chicago: Univ. of Chicago Press, 1980.

Bremond, Claude. "La logique des possibles narratifs." *Communications* 8 (1966): 60–76.

Brena, Stefano. *Bandengebiet*. Turin: Baravalle e Falconieri, 1946.

Brooke-Rose, Christine. *A Rhetoric of the Unreal: Studies in Narrative and Structure, Especially of the Fantastic*. Cambridge: Cambridge Univ. Press, 1981.

Brooks, Peter. *Reading for the Plot: Design and Intention in Narrative*. New York: Knopf, 1984.

Brown, Marshall. "The Logic of Realism: A Hegelian Approach." *PMLA* 96 (1981): 224–41.

Brunetta, Gian Piero. "Neo-realismo: alle fonti di un mito." In *Intellettuali, cinema e propaganda tra le due guerre*. Bologna: Patron, 1972: 129–36.

———. *Storia del cinema italiano dal 1945 agli anni ottanta*. Rome: Editori Riuniti, 1982.

———. *Umberto Barbaro e l'idea di neorealismo (1930–1943)*. Padua: Liviana, 1969.

Calamandrei, Franco. "Narrativa vince cronaca." *Il Politecnico* 26 (Mar. 23, 1946): 3.

Calligaris, Contardo. *Italo Calvino*. Milan: Mursia, 1972.

Calvino, Italo. *Adam, One Afternoon, and Other Stories*. Trans. Archibald Colquhoun and Peggy Wright. London: Pan Books, 1984. Orig. pub. 1957.

———. "Andato al comando." *Il Politecnico* 17 (Jan. 1946): 4.

———. *The Baron in the Trees*. Trans. Archibald Colquhoun. New York: Random House, 1959. (*Il barone rampante*. Turin: Einaudi, 1957.)

———. *The Castle of Crossed Destinies*. Trans. William Weaver. New York: Harcourt Brace Jovanovich, 1977. (*Il castello dei destini incrociati*. Turin: Einaudi, 1973.)

———. *The Cloven Viscount*. Trans. Archibald Colquhoun. In *The Non-existent Knight and The Cloven Viscount* (San Diego: Harcourt Brace Jovanovich, 1962), pp. 145–246. (*Il visconte dimezzato*. Turin: Einaudi, 1952.)

———. *Cosmicomics*. Trans. William Weaver. San Diego: Harcourt Brace Jovanovich, 1968. (*Le cosmicomiche*. Turin: Einaudi, 1965.)

———. *Difficult Loves*. Trans. William Weaver, Archibald Colquhoun, and Peggy Wright. San Diego: Harcourt Brace Jovanovich, 1984. (*Gli amori difficili*. Turin: Einaudi, 1970.)

———. "Domande sul romanzo." *Nuovi argomenti* 38–39 (1959): 12.

———. *La giornata di uno scrutatore*. Turin: Einaudi, 1963.

———. "Hemingway e noi." *Il contemporaneo* 13 (Nov. 1954): 3.

———. *If on a Winter's Night a Traveler*. Trans. William Weaver. New York: Harcourt Brace Jovanovich, 1983. (*Se una notte d'inverno un viaggiatore*. Turin: Einaudi, 1979.)

———. "Ingegneri e demolitori." *Rinascita* 5, no. 11 (1948): 400.

———. *Invisible Cities*. Trans. William Weaver. New York: Harcourt Brace Jovanovich, 1974. (*Le città invisibili*. Turin: Einaudi, 1972.)

———. *Italian Folktales Selected and Retold by Italo Calvino*. Trans. George Martin. New York: Harcourt Brace Jovanovich, 1980. (*Fiabe italiane raccolte dalla tradizione popolare durante gli ultimi cento anni e trascritte in lingua dai vari dialetti*. Turin: Einaudi, 1956.)

———. "La letteratura italiana sulla Resistenza." *Il movimento di Liberazione in Italia* 1 (1949): 40–46.

———. "Liguria magra e ossuta." *Il Politecnico* 10 (Dec. 1945): 2.

———. *Marcovaldo: or, The Seasons in the City*. Trans. William Weaver. San Diego: Harcourt Brace Jovanovich, 1983. (*Marcovaldo, ovvero le stagioni in città*. Turin: Einaudi, 1966.)

———. *Mr. Palomar*. Trans. William Weaver. San Diego: Harcourt Brace Jovanovich, 1985. (*Palomar*. Turin: Einaudi, 1983.)

———. *The Nonexistent Knight*. Trans. Archibald Colquhoun. In *The Nonexistent Knight and The Cloven Viscount* (San Diego: Harcourt Brace Jovanovich, 1962), pp. 3–141. (*Il cavaliere inesistente*. Turin: Einaudi, 1959.)

———. *Our Ancestors*. London: Secker and Warburg, 1980. (*I nostri antenati*. Turin: Einaudi, 1960.)

———. *The Path to the Nest of Spiders*. Trans. Archibald Colquhoun, 1957. New York: Ecco Press, 1976. (*Il sentiero dei nidi di ragno*. Turin: Einaudi, 1982. Orig. pub. 1947.)

———. *Una pietra sopra: Discorsi di letteratura e società*. Turin: Einaudi, 1980.

———. *I racconti*. Turin: Einaudi, 1958.

———. "*Rancore* di Stefano Terra." *L'Unità*, Turin ed., June 30, 1946.

———. "Riviera di Ponente." *Il Politecnico* 21 (Feb. 1946): 2.

———. "Sanremo città dell'oro." *Il Politecnico* 21 (Feb. 1946): 2.

———. "Saremo come Omero." *Rinascita* 5, no. 12 (1948): 448.

———. *t zero*. Trans. William Weaver. San Diego: Harcourt Brace Jovanovich, 1969. (*Ti con zero*. Turin: Einaudi, 1967.)

———. *Ultimo viene il corvo*. Turin: Einaudi, 1949.

———. *The Uses of Literature: Essays*. Trans. Patrick Creagh. San Diego: Harcourt Brace Jovanovich, 1986.

———. *The Watcher and Other Stories*. Trans. William Weaver. New York: Harcourt Brace Jovanovich, 1971.

———. "The Written and the Unwritten Word." *The New York Review of Books*, May 12, 1983: 38–39.

———, ed. *Racconti fantastici dell'Ottocento*. 2 vols. Milan: Mondadori, 1983.

Cannon, JoAnn. "Calvino's Latest Challenge to the Labyrinth: A Reading of *Palomar*." *Italica* 62, no. 3 (1985): 189–200.

———. *Italo Calvino: Writer and Critic*. Ravenna: Longo, 1981.

Cantoni, Remo. "Dostoyevsky come esistenzialista." *Il Politecnico* 35 (Jan.–Mar. 1947): 34–38.

Canziani, Alfonso. *Gli anni del neorealismo*. Florence: La Nuova Italia, 1977.

Caprara, Massimo. "Italo Calvino: *Il sentiero dei nidi di ragno*." *Rinascita* 5, no. 2 (1948): 86.

Carocci, Giampiero. *Storia d'Italia dall'Unità a oggi*. Milan: Feltrinelli, 1975.

Carter, Albert Howard, III. *Italo Calvino: Metamorphoses of Fantasy*. Ann Arbor: UMI Research Press, 1987.

Cases, Cesare. "Calvino e il 'pathos della distanza.'" *Città aperta* 7–8 (1958): 33–35.

Catalano, Franco. *Storia del C.L.N.A.I.* Bari: Laterza, 1956.

Chiodi, Pietro. *Banditi*. Alba: ANPI, 1946.

Collodi, Carlo. *Le avventure di Pinocchio. Storia di un burattino*. Turin: Einaudi, 1968. Orig. pub. 1883.

Collotti, Enrica Pischel. *L'antifascismo in Italia e in Europa 1922–1939*. Turin: Loescher, 1975.

Conrad, Joseph. *The Shadow Line*. New York: Doubleday, 1917.

Conti, Laura. *La Resistenza in Italia. 25 luglio 1943–25 aprile 1945. Saggio bibliografico*. Milan: Feltrinelli, 1961.

Contini, Gianfranco. *Letteratura dell'Italia unita (1861–1968)*. Florence: Sansoni, 1968.

Corti, Maria. "Italo Calvino Interviewed." *Normal: A Quarterly of Arts and Ideas* 3 (1986): 5–9.

———. *Il viaggio testuale*. Turin: Einaudi, 1978.

Croce, Benedetto. *History as the Story of Liberty*. Trans. Sylvia Sprigge. London: Allen and Unwin, 1941.

———. *Nuove pagine sparse*. 2 vols. Naples: Ricciardi, 1948.

Culler, Jonathan. *Structuralist Poetics*. Ithaca: Cornell Univ. Press, 1975.

David, Michel. *La psicanalisi nella cultura italiana*. Turin: Boringhieri, 1966.
De Beauvoir, Simone. "Idealismo morale e realismo politico." *Il Politecnico* 31–32 (July–Aug. 1946): 32–35.
Debenedetti, Giacomo. "Probabile autobiografia di una generazione. (Prefazione 1949)." *Saggi critici*. Milan: Mondadori, 1969.
De Lauretis, Teresa. *Alice Doesn't: Feminism, Semiotics, Cinema*. Bloomington: Indiana Univ. Press, 1984.
———. "Calvino e la dialettica dei massimi sistemi." *Italica* 53, no. 1 (1976): 57–74.
———. "Narrative Discourse in Calvino: Praxis or Poiesis?" *PMLA* 90 (1975): 414–25.
———. "Semiotic Models: *Invisible Cities.*" *Yale Italian Studies* 2 (1978): 13–37.
Del Boca, Angelo. *L'anno del Giubileo*. Turin: Einaudi, 1948.
———. *Dentro mi è nato l'uomo*. Turin: Einaudi, 1948.
Deleuze, Gilles, and Félix Guattari. *Anti-Oedipus: Capitalism and Schizophrenia*. Trans. Robert Hurley, Mark Seem, and Helen R. Lane. Minneapolis: Univ. of Minnesota Press, 1982. Rpt. of 1977 ed.
Delzell, Charles F. *Mussolini's Enemies: The Italian Anti-Fascist Resistance*. New York: Fertig, 1974. Orig. pub. 1961.
De Man, Paul. *Allegories of Reading: Figural Language in Rousseau, Nietzsche, Rilke, and Proust*. New Haven: Yale Univ. Press, 1979.
De Mara, Nicholas. "Pathway to Calvino: Fantasy and Reality in *Il sentiero dei nidi di ragno.*" *Italian Quarterly* 14, no. 55 (1971): 25–49.
Derrida, Jacques. "Structure, Sign and Play in the Discourse of the Human Sciences." In *The Structuralist Controversy: The Languages of Criticism and the Sciences of Man*, ed. Richard Macksey and Eugenio Donato (Baltimore: Johns Hopkins Univ. Press, 1972), pp. 247–64.
Durand, Gilbert. *Les Structures anthropologiques de l'imaginaire. Introduction à l'archétypologie générale*. Grenoble: Allier, 1960.
Eco, Umberto. "On Calvino." *Normal: A Quarterly of Arts and Ideas* 3 (1986): 4.
———. *A Theory of Semiotics*. Bloomington: Indiana Univ. Press, 1976.
Erlich, Victor. *Russian Formalism: History-Doctrine*. New Haven: Yale Univ. Press, 1981. Orig. pub. 1965.
Ermarth, Elizabeth. *Realism and Consensus in the English Novel*. Princeton: Princeton Univ. Press, 1983.
Eversmann, Susanne. *Poetik und Erzählstruktur in den Romanen Italo Calvinos*. Munich: Wilhelm Fink, 1979.
Falaschi, Giovanni. "Italo Calvino." *Belfagor* 27, no. 5 (1972): 531–58.
———. *Realtà e retorica. La letteratura del neorealismo italiano*. Messina: D'Anna, 1977.
———. *La Resistenza armata nella narrativa italiana*. Turin: Einaudi, 1976.
Fenoglio, Beppe. *Il partigiano Johnny*. Turin: Einaudi, 1968.

Fernandez, Dominique. *Il mito dell'America negli intellettuali italiani*. Caltanissetta: Sciascia, 1969.

———. *Il romanzo italiano e la crisi della coscienza moderna*. Milan: Lerici, 1960.

Ferrata, Giansiro. "Le scorciatoie di un poeta." *Il Politecnico* 27 (Mar. 30, 1946): 3.

Ferretti, Gian Carlo. *Le capre di Bikini: Calvino giornalista e saggista 1945–1985*. Rome: Editori Riuniti, 1989.

———. *Introduzione al neorealismo*. *I Narratori*. Rome: Editori Riuniti, 1974.

Flaubert, Gustave. *Three Tales*. Trans. Robert Baldick. Harmondsworth: Penguin, 1961.

Fortini, Franco. "Capoversi su Kafka." *Il Politecnico* 37 (Oct. 1947): 14–19.

———. "Che cosa è stato *Il Politecnico*." In *Dieci inverni*. Milan: Feltrinelli, 1957.

———. "Documenti e racconti." *Il Politecnico* 28 (Apr. 1946): 3.

———. "La poesia è libertà." *Il Politecnico* 8 (Nov. 7, 1945): 2; 9 (Nov. 24, 1945): 2.

Foucault, Michel. *The History of Sexuality*. Trans. Robert Hurley. Vol. I: *An Introduction*. New York: Vintage, 1980.

———. *The Order of Things: An Archaeology of the Human Sciences*. New York: Vintage, 1973. Orig. pub. 1970.

Freud, Sigmund. *The Standard Edition of the Complete Psychological Works of Sigmund Freud*. Ed. James Strachey. 24 vols. London: Hogarth Press, 1966–74.

Frye, Northrop. *Anatomy of Criticism*. Princeton: Princeton Univ. Press, 1971.

———. *Fables of Identity: Studies in Poetic Mythology*. New York: Harcourt, Brace, and World, 1963.

Gadda, Carlo Emilio. *Quer pasticciaccio brutto de via Merulana*. Milan: Garzanti, 1957. Orig. pub. 1946–47.

———. *I viaggi e la morte*. Milan: Garzanti, 1958.

Gatt-Rutter, John. "Calvino Ludens: Literary Play and Its Political Implications." *Journal of European Studies* 5 (1975): 319–40.

Gehlen, Arnold. *Einblicke*. Ed. K. S. Rehberg. Frankfurt: Klostermann, 1978.

Genette, Gérard. *Figures II*. Paris: Seuil, 1969.

———. *Narrative Discourse: An Essay in Method*. Ithaca: Cornell Univ. Press, 1980.

Génot, Gérard. *Analyse structurelle de "Pinocchio."* Florence: Quaderni della Fondazione Carlo Collodi, 1970.

Girard, René. *Mensonge romantique et vérité romanesque*. Paris: Grasset, 1961.

———. *La Violence et le sacré*. Paris: Grasset, 1972.

Gombrich, E. H. *Art and Illusion: A Study in the Psychology of Pictorial Representation*. Bollingen Series 25, no. 5. Princeton: Princeton Univ. Press, 1960, 1969.

Gramsci, Antonio. *Letters from Prison*. Ed. and trans. Lynne Lawner. New York: Harper and Row, 1975.

———. *Quaderni dal carcere*. Ed. Valentino Gerratana. 4 vols. Turin: Einaudi, 1975.

———. *Selections from the Prison Notebooks*. Ed. and trans. Quintin Hoare and Geoffrey Nowell-Smith. New York: International Publishers, 1971.

Grassi, A. "Responsabilità dello scrittore." *Rinascita* 1, no. 3 (1944): 23–25.

Greimas, A. J. *Sémantique structurale*. Paris: Larousse, 1966.

Heath, Stephen. "Difference." *Screen* 19, no. 3 (1978): 51–112.

Heiney, Donald. *America in Modern Italian Literature*. New Brunswick: Rutgers Univ. Press, 1964.

Hume, Kathryn. *Fantasy and Mimesis: Responses to Reality in Western Literature*. New York: Methuen, 1984.

Iliano, Antonio. "Per una definizione della vena cosmogonica di Calvino: appunti su *Le cosmicomiche* e *Ti con zero*." *Italica* 49, no. 3 (1972): 291–301.

Imbriani, Vittorio. *La novellaja fiorentina. Fiabe e novelline stenografate in Firenze dal dettato popolare*. Leghorn: Vigo, 1877.

Ishaghpour, Youssef. *Visconti. Le sens et l'image*. Paris: Editions de la Différence, 1984.

Jackson, Rosemary. *Fantasy: The Literature of Subversion*. London: Methuen, 1981.

Jakobson, Roman. "Closing Statement: Linguistics and Poetics." In *Style in Language*, ed. Thomas Sebeok (Cambridge, Mass.: MIT Press, 1960), pp. 350–77.

———. "On Realism in Art." In *Readings in Russian Poetics: Formalist and Structuralist Views*, ed. Ladislav Matejka and Krystina Pomorska (Ann Arbor: Michigan Slavic Publications, 1978), pp. 38–46.

Jameson, Fredric. "Imaginary and Symbolic in Lacan: Marxism, Psychoanalytic Criticism, and the Problem of the Subject." *Yale French Studies* 55–56 (1980): 338–95.

———. *Marxism and Form: Twentieth-Century Dialectical Theories of Literature*. Princeton: Princeton Univ. Press, 1971.

———. *The Political Unconscious: Narrative as a Socially Symbolic Act*. Ithaca: Cornell Univ. Press, 1981.

———. *The Prison-House of Language: A Critical Account of Structuralism and Russian Formalism*. Princeton: Princeton Univ. Press, 1972.

Jauss, Hans Robert. *Toward an Aesthetic of Reception*. Trans. Timothy Bahti. Minneapolis: Univ. of Minnesota Press, 1982.

Kracauer, Sigfried. *History: The Last Things Before the Last*. New York: Oxford Univ. Press, 1969.

Kristeva, Julia. *La Révolution du langage poétique*. Paris: Seuil, 1974.

Lacan, Jacques. *Ecrits*. Paris: Seuil, 1966.

————. *The Four Fundamental Concepts of Psychoanalysis*. Ed. Jacques-Alain Miller, trans. Alan Sheridan. New York: Norton, 1981. Orig. pub. 1978.

————. *Speech and Language in Psychoanalysis*. Trans. and ed. Anthony Wilden. Baltimore: Johns Hopkins Univ. Press, 1981. Orig. pub. 1968.

Landy, Marcia. *Fascism in Film: The Italian Commercial Cinema 1931–1943*. Princeton: Princeton Univ. Press, 1986.

Laplanche, Jean, and J.-B. Pontalis. *Vocabulaire de la Psychanalyse*. Paris: Presses Universitaires de France, 1967.

Le Goff, Jacques, and Pierre Nora, eds. *Fare Storia. Temi e metodi della nuova storiografia*. Turin: Einaudi, 1981.

Levi, Carlo. *Cristo si è fermato ad Eboli*. Turin: Einaudi, 1945.

Levi Cavaglione, Pino. *Guerriglia nei Castelli Romani*. Rome: Giulio Einaudi, 1945.

Lévi-Strauss, Claude. *The Savage Mind*. Chicago: Univ. of Chicago Press, 1966.

Livingstone, Rodney, Perry Anderson, and Francis Mulhern, eds. *Aesthetics and Politics: Debates Between Bloch, Lukács, Brecht, Benjamin, Adorno*. London: Verso, 1980. Orig. pub. 1977.

Lodge, David. *The Modes of Modern Writing*. Ithaca: Cornell Univ. Press, 1977.

Longo, Luigi. *Un popolo alla macchia*. Milan: Mondadori, 1947.

Lotman, Jurij. *The Structure of the Artistic Text*. Trans. Gail Lenhoff and Ronald Vroon. Ann Arbor: Michigan Slavic Contributions, 1977.

Lucente, Gregory. *Beautiful Fables: Self-Consciousness in Italian Narrative from Manzoni to Calvino*. Baltimore: Johns Hopkins Univ. Press, 1986.

————. "An Interview with Italo Calvino." *Contemporary Literature* 26, no. 3 (1985): 244–53.

————. *The Narrative of Realism and Myth: Verga, Lawrence, Faulkner, Pavese*. Baltimore: Johns Hopkins Univ. Press, 1981.

Lukács, Georg. *The Historical Novel*. Trans. Hannah and Stanley Mitchell. Harmondsworth: Penguin, 1981. Orig. pub. 1962.

————. *Realism in Our Time: Literature and Class Struggle*. Trans. John and Necke Mander. New York: Harper and Row, 1964.

————. *The Theory of the Novel*. Trans. A. Bostock. Cambridge, Mass.: MIT Press, 1971.

Luperini, Romano. *Il Novecento. Apparati ideologici, ceto intellettuale, sistemi formali nella letteratura italiana contemporanea*. 2 vols. Turin: Loescher, 1981.

MacKinnon, Catharine A. "Feminism, Marxism, Method, and the State: An Agenda for Theory." *Signs* 7, no. 3 (Spring 1982): 515–44.

Manacorda, Gastone. "Nota su Calvino." *Belfagor* 2 (1957): 197–200.
Manzoni, Alessandro. *The Betrothed.* Trans. Bruce Penman. Harmondsworth: Penguin, 1972.
Marcus, Millicent. *Italian Film in the Light of Neorealism.* Princeton: Princeton Univ. Press, 1986.
Marcuse, Herbert. *Eros and Civilization: A Philosophical Inquiry into Freud.* New York: Vintage, 1962. Orig. pub. 1955.
Marx, Karl. *Capital.* 3 vols. New York: International Publishers, 1977.
———. *A Contribution to the Critique of Political Economy.* Ed. Maurice Dobb. New York: International Publishers, 1970.
Massolo, Arturo. "Esistenzialismo e borghesismo." *Società* 1, no. 3 (1945): 115–18.
———. "L'essere e la qualità in Hegel." *Società* 1, no. 1–2 (1945): 101–13.
Miccichè, Lino, ed. *Il neorealismo cinematografico italiano.* Venice: Marsilio, 1975.
Micheli, Silvio. *Pane duro.* Turin: Einaudi, 1946.
Mida, Massimo, and Lorenzo Quaglietti, eds. *Dai telefoni bianchi al neorealismo.* Rome: Laterza, 1980.
Milanini, Claudio. "Natura e storia nel *Sentiero* di Italo Calvino." *Belfagor* 40, no. 5 (1985): 529–46.
———. *Neorealismo. Poetiche e polemiche.* Milan: Il Saggiatore, 1980.
Miller, J. Hillis. *Fiction and Repetition: Seven English Novels.* Cambridge, Mass.: Harvard Univ. Press, 1982.
Mink, Louis O. "Narrative Form as a Cognitive Instrument." In *The Writing of History: Literary Form and Historical Understanding,* ed. Robert H. Canary and Henry Kozicki (Madison: Univ. of Wisconsin Press, 1978), pp. 129–49.
Mitchell, Juliet. *Psychoanalysis and Feminism.* London: Allen Lane, 1974.
Montale, Eugenio. *Tutte le poesie.* Milan: Mondadori, 1977.
Moravia, Alberto. *Agostino.* Milan: Bompiani, 1956. Orig. pub. 1944.
———. *La ciociara.* Milan: Bompiani, 1957.
———. *Il conformista.* Milan: Bompiani, 1951.
———. *Gli indifferenti.* Milan: Garzanti, 1974. Orig. pub. 1929.
———. *Racconti romani.* Milan: Bompiani, 1954.
———. *La romana.* Milan: Bompiani, 1947.
———. "L'uomo come fine." In *L'uomo come fine e altri saggi.* Milan: Bompiani, 1964. Pp. 193–248.
Muscetta, Carlo. *Realismo, neorealismo e controrealismo.* Milan: Garzanti, 1976.
Nerucci, Gherardo. *Sessanta novelle popolari montalesi.* Ed. Roberto Fedi. Milan: Rizzoli, 1977. Orig. pub. 1880.
Nowell-Smith, Geoffrey. *Visconti.* London: Secker and Warburg, 1973.
Olken, I. T. *With Pleated Eye and Garnet Wing: Symmetries in Italo Calvino.* Ann Arbor: Univ. of Michigan Press, 1984.
Onofri, Fabrizio. "Politica è cultura." *Il Politecnico* 36 (Sept. 1946): 2; 32.

———. "*Uomini e no*." *L'Unità*. Milan ed., Sept. 12, 1945.

Overbey, David, ed. *Springtime in Italy: A Reader on Neo-Realism*. Hamden: Shoe String Press, 1978.

Pacifici, Sergio, ed. *From Verismo to Experimentalism: Essays on the Modern Italian Novel*. Bloomington: Indiana Univ. Press, 1969.

Pagnini, Alessandro. "La recezione della psicanalisi nella cultura filosofica del secondo dopoguerra." *Intersezioni* 7, no. 1 (1987): 107–37.

Pampaloni, Geno. "La nuova letteratura." In *Storia della letteratura italiana*, ed. Emilio Cecchi and Natalino Sapegno (Milan: Garzanti, 1969), 9: 751–879.

Pasolini, Pier Paolo. *La religione del mio tempo*. Milan: Garzanti, 1961.

Patuzzi, Claudia. "Italo Calvino: un intellettuale tra poesia e impegno." *Nuova Antologia* 527 (1976): 140–47.

Pautasso, Sergio. "Favola, allegoria, utopia nell'opera di Italo Calvino." *Nuovi Argomenti* 35–36 (1973): 67–94.

Pavese, Cesare. *La casa in collina*. In *Prima che il gallo canti*. Turin: Einaudi, 1968. Orig. pub. 1948.

———. *Il compagno*. Turin: Einaudi, 1968. Orig. pub. 1947.

———. *La luna e i falò*. Turin: Einaudi, 1968. Orig. pub. 1950.

———. *Paesi tuoi*. Turin: Einaudi, 1968. Orig. pub. 1941.

———. *Racconti*. 2 vols. Turin: Einaudi, 1968.

———. *Saggi letterari*. Turin: Einaudi, 1968.

Pavone, Claudio. "Guido Quazza, *Resistenza e storia d'Italia*." *Belfagor* 32, no. 2 (1977): 233–42.

———. "Le idee della Resistenza. Antifascisti e fascisti di fronte alla tradizione del Risorgimento." *Passato e Presente* 7 (1959): 850–918.

Pedullà, Walter. "Calvino alla corte di Lacan." *Il caffè* 5–6 (1972): 77–85.

Pescio Bottino, Germana. *Calvino*. Florence: La Nuova Italia, 1967.

Piazzesi, Gianfranco. "Necessità di una cronaca." *Società* 1, no. 3 (1946): 8.

Pineri, Riccardo. "Les Philosophes-professeurs: La philosophie italienne 1940–1960." *Critique* 452–53 (1985): 7–17.

Pintor, Giaime. "Ultima lettera." *Rinascita* 3, no. 5–6 (1946): 393.

Il Politecnico. Anastatic reprint. Turin: Einaudi, 1975.

Pratolini, Vasco. *Cronache di poveri amanti*. Florence: Vallecchi, 1947.

———. "Cronache fiorentine del 20₀ Secolo." *Il Politecnico* 39 (Dec. 1947): 27–30.

———. "Per un saggio sui rapporti fra letteratura e cinema." *Bianco e nero* 9, no. 4 (1948): 14–19.

Procaccini, Alfonso. *Francesco Jovine: The Quest for Realism*. New York: Peter Lang, 1986.

———. "Neorealism: Description/Prescription." *Yale Italian Studies* 2 (1978): 39–57.

———. "Pavese: On the Failure of Under-standing." *Italica* 62, no. 3 (1985): 214–29.

Propp, Vladimir. *Morphology of the Folktale.* 2d. edition, rev. and ed. Louis A. Wagner. Austin: Univ. of Texas Press, 1968.

———. *Le radici storiche dei racconti di fate.* Trans. Clara Coisson. Turin: Boringhieri, 1972. Orig. pub. 1949.

Quazza, Guido. *Resistenza e storia d'Italia: Problemi e ipotesi di ricerca.* Milan: Feltrinelli, 1975.

Ragghianti, Carlo Ludovico. *Disegno della liberazione italiana.* Pisa: Nistri Lischi, 1962.

Ragusa, Olga. "Italo Calvino: The Repeated Conquest of Contemporaneity." *World Literature Today* 57, no. 2 (Spring 1983): 195–201.

Ranke, Leopold von. *The Theory and Practice of History.* Ed. Georg G. Iggers and Konrad Moltke. Indianapolis: Bobbs-Merrill, 1973.

Rankin, Ian. "The Role of the Reader in Italo Calvino's *If on a Winter's Night a Traveller.*" *Review of Contemporary Fiction* 6, no. 2 (1986): 124–29.

Rea, Domenico. *Spaccanapoli.* Milan: Mondadori, 1950.

Ricci, Franco. "Introversion and Effacement in *I racconti* of Italo Calvino." *Italica* 63, no. 4 (Winter 1986): 331–45.

Ricoeur, Paul. *Time and Narrative.* Trans. Kathleen MacLaughlin and David Pellauer. 2 vols. Chicago: Univ. of Chicago Press, 1984.

Rigoni Stern, Mario. *Il sergente della neve.* Turin: Einaudi, 1953.

Romano, Ruggiero, and Corrado Vivanti, eds. *Storia d'Italia.* 4 vols. Turin: Einaudi, 1975.

Rosengarten, Frank. *The Italian Anti-Fascist Press (1919–1945).* Cleveland: Case Western Reserve Univ. Press, 1968.

———. "The Italian Resistance Novel (1945–1962)." In *From "Verismo" to Experimentalism: Essays on the Modern Italian Novel,* ed. Sergio Pacifici (Bloomington: Indiana Univ. Press, 1969), pp. 212–38.

Rossellini, Roberto. *The War Trilogy: Open City, Paisan, Germany—Year Zero.* Ed. Stefano Roncoroni, trans. Judith Green. New York: Grossman, 1973.

Said, Edward W. *Beginnings: Intention and Method.* Baltimore: Johns Hopkins Univ. Press, 1975.

Salinari, Carlo. *Preludio e fine del realismo in Italia.* Naples: Morano, 1967.

Salvadori, Massimo. *Storia della Resistenza italiana.* Venice: Neri Pozza, 1955.

Sartre, Jean-Paul. *Being and Nothingness: An Essay on Phenomenological Ontology.* Trans. Hazel E. Barnes. New York: Washington Square, 1966.

———. *Existentialism and Humanism.* Trans. Philip Mairet. London: Methuen, 1963. (*L'Existentialisme est un humanisme.* Paris: Nagel, 1968.)

———. "Una nuova cultura come 'cultura sintetica.'" *Il Politecnico* 16 (1946): 1.

———. *What Is Literature?* Trans. Bernard Frechtman. New York: Philosophical Library, 1949.

Schneider, Marilyn. "Calvino at a Crossroads: *Il castello dei destini incrociati*." *PMLA* 95 (1980): 73–90.

Seborga, Guido. *L'uomo di Camporosso*. Milan: Mondadori, 1948.

Segre, Cesare. "Se una notte d'inverno uno scrittore sognasse un Aleph di dieci colori." *Strumenti Critici* 13, no. 39–40 (1979): 177–214.

Sereni, Emilio. *Scienza, marxismo e cultura*. Milan: Edizioni sociali, 1949.

Shklovsky, Victor. "Art as Technique." In *Russian Formalist Criticism: Four Essays*, trans. Lee T. Lemon and Marion J. Reis (Lincoln: Univ. of Nebraska Press, 1965), pp. 3–24.

———. *Teoria della prosa*. (*O teorii prozy*.) Trans. Cesare G. de Michelis and Renzo Oliva. Turin: Einaudi, 1976.

Silone, Ignazio. *Fontamara*. Milan: Mondadori, 1949. Orig. pub. 1933.

Siti, Walter. *Il neorealismo nella poesia italiana 1941–1956*. Turin: Einaudi, 1980.

Spriano, Paolo. *Le passioni di un decennio (1946–1956)*. Milan: Garzanti, 1986.

Steiner, Peter. *Russian Formalism: A Metapoetics*. Ithaca: Cornell Univ. Press, 1984.

Tarizzo, Domenico. *Come scriveva la Resistenza. Filologia della stampa clandestina 1943–45*. Florence: La Nuova Italia, 1969.

Tarrow, S. G. *Peasant Communism in Southern Italy*. New Haven: Yale Univ. Press, 1967.

Terra, Stefano. *Rancore*. Turin: Einaudi, 1946.

Tinazzi, Giorgio, and Marina Zancan, eds. *Cinema e letteratura del neorealismo*. Venice: Marsilio, 1983.

Todorov, Tzvetan. *The Fantastic: A Structural Approach to a Literary Genre*. Trans. Richard Howard. Ithaca: Cornell Univ. Press, 1975. Orig. pub. 1973.

———. *Grammaire du Décameron*. The Hague: Mouton, 1969.

Togliatti, Palmiro. *I corsivi di Roderigo. Interventi politico-culturali dal 1944 al 1964*. Ed. Ottavio Cecchi, Giovanni Leone, and Giuseppe Vacca. Bari: De Donato, 1976.

———. "La politica di Corbino." *Rinascita* 3, no. 8 (1946): 177–81.

———. "Politica e cultura" (Letter to Vittorini). *Il Politecnico* 33–34 (Sept.–Dec. 1946): 3–4.

———. "Vittorini se n'è ghiuto e soli ci ha lasciato." *Rinascita* 8, no. 8–9 (1951): 393.

Trombadori, Antonello. "Serietà e limiti di Morandi." *Rinascita* 2, no. 5–6 (1945): 156–58.

Urban, Joan Barth. *Moscow and the Italian Communist Party*. Ithaca: Cornell Univ. Press, 1986.

Varese, Claudio. Review of Italo Calvino, *Il sentiero dei nidi di ragno*. *Nuova Antologia* 443 (1948): 102–4.

Vattimo, Gianni. *La fine della modernità*. Milan: Garzanti, 1985.

Venturi, Franco. *Gli anni e gli inganni*. Milan: Feltrinelli, 1965.

———. "Ci siamo svegliati adulti." *L'Unità*, Milan ed., Oct. 27, 1946.

———. "I nostri morti." *L'Unità*, Milan ed., May 5, 1946.

Verga, Giovanni. *The House by the Medlar Tree*. Trans. Raymond Rosenthal. Berkeley: Univ. of California Press, 1983. Orig. pub. 1964. (*I Malavoglia*. Milan: Mondadori, 1983. Orig. pub. 1881.)

———. *The She-Wolf and Other Stories*. Ed. and trans. Giovanni Cecchetti. Berkeley: Univ. of California Press, 1973. Orig. pub. 1958.

———. *Tutte le novelle*. 2 vols. Milan: Mondadori, 1962.

Vico, Giambattista. *The New Science*. Rev. and trans. Thomas Goddard Bergin and Max Harold Fisch. Ithaca: Cornell Univ. Press, 1970. Orig. pub. 1948.

Viganò, Renata. *L'Agnese va a morire*. Turin: Einaudi, 1967. Orig. pub. 1949.

Visconti, Luchino. *Ossessione*. Ed. Enzo Ungari and G. B. Cavallaro. Bologna: Cappelli, 1977.

———. *La terra trema*. Ed. Enzo Ungari, Claudio Battistini, and G. B. Cavallaro. Bologna: Cappelli, 1977.

Vitizzai, Chicco E. *Il neorealismo. Antifascismo e popolo nella letteratura dagli anni trenta agli anni cinquanta*. Turin: Paravia, 1977.

Vittorini, Elio. *Conversazione in Sicilia*. Turin: Einaudi, 1975. Orig. pub. 1941.

———. *Le donne di Messina*. Milan: Bompiani, 1964. Orig. pub. 1949.

———. "Letteratura e fini sociali." *Il Bargello* 4, no. 41 (1932).

———. "Letteratura sovietica." *Il Bargello* 3, no. 27 (1931).

———. "Una nuova cultura." *Il Politecnico* 1 (Sept. 29, 1945): 1.

———. "Politica e cultura." *Il Politecnico* 35 (Jan.–Mar. 1947): 2–4.

———. "Scelti per la fucilazione." *L'Unità*, Milan ed., May 13, 1945.

———. *Uomini e no*. Milan: Bompiani, 1945.

Waugh, Patricia. *Metafiction: Theory and Practice of Self-Conscious Fiction*. London: Methuen, 1984.

White, Hayden. *Metahistory: The Historical Imagination in Nineteenth-Century Europe*. Baltimore: Johns Hopkins Univ. Press, 1973.

———. "The Value of Narrativity in the Representation of Reality." *Critical Inquiry* 7 (1980): 5–27.

Woodhouse, J. R. *Italo Calvino: A Reappraisal and an Appreciation of the Trilogy*. Willerby: Univ. of Hull Publications, 1968.

Woolf, S. J., ed. *The Rebirth of Italy 1943–1950*. London: Longman, 1972.

Zancan, Marina. "*Il Politecnico* mensile." *Rassegna della letteratura italiana* 3 (1975): 517–44.

———. "Tra vero e bello, documento e arte." In *Cinema e letteratura del neorealismo*, ed. Giorgio Tinazzi and Marina Zancan (Venice: Marsilio Editori, 1983), pp. 39–78.

Zavattini, Cesare. "*Umberto D*. Dal soggetto alla sceneggiatura. Precedono alcune idee sul Cinema." *Rivista del cinema italiano* 2 (1952).

Index

In this index an "f" after a number indicates a separate reference on the next page, and an "ff" indicates separate references on the next two pages. A continuous discussion over two or more pages is indicated by a span of page numbers, e.g., "pp. 57–58." *Passim* is used for a cluster of references in close but not consecutive sequence.

Library of Congress Cataloging-in-Publication Data

Re, Lucia.
    Calvino and the age of Neorealism : fables of estrangement/ Lucia Re.
        p.   cm.
    Includes bibliographical references.
    ISBN 0-8047-1650-1 (alk. paper) :
    1. Calvino, Italo—Technique.   2. Calvino, Italo—Sentiero dei nidi di ragno.
3. Realism in literature.   I. Title.
PQ4809.A45Z85   1990   89-49547
853'.914—dc20   CIP

   ⊗   This book is printed on acid-free paper